General Equilibrium, Capital and Macroeconomics

NEW DIRECTIONS IN MODERN ECONOMICS
Series Editor: Malcolm C. Sawyer,
Professor of Economics, University of Leeds, UK

New Directions in Modern Economics presents a challenge to orthodox
economic thinking. It focuses on new ideas emanating from radical
traditions including post-Keynesian, Kaleckian, neo-Ricardian and
Marxian. The books in the series do not adhere rigidly to any single
school of thought but attempt to present a positive alternative to the
conventional wisdom.

A list of published titles in this series is printed at the end of this
volume.

General Equilibrium, Capital and Macroeconomics

A Key to Recent Controversies
in Equilibrium Theory

Fabio Petri
Professor of Economics, University of Siena, Italy

NEW DIRECTIONS IN MODERN ECONOMICS

Edward Elgar
Cheltenham, UK • Northampton, MA, USA

Published by
Edward Elgar Publishing Limited
Glensanda House
Montpellier Parade
Cheltenham
Glos GL50 1UA
UK

Edward Elgar Publishing, Inc.
136 West Street
Suite 202
Northampton
Massachusetts 01060
USA

A catalogue record for this book
is available from the British Library

Library of Congress Cataloguing in Publication Data

Petri, Fabio, 1949-
  General equilibrium, capital and macroeconomics : a key to recent controversies in equilibrium theory / Fabio Petri
    p. cm. — (New directions in modern economics)
  Includes bibliographical references.
    1. Equilibrium (Economics) 2. Capital. 3. Macroeconomics. I. Title. II. Series.

HB145.P482 2004
339.5—dc22
                                                                    2004053287
ISBN 1 84376 829 1

Printed and bound in Great Britain by MPG Books Ltd, Bodmin, Cornwall

Contents

Figures

Preface

This book argues that a fundamental key to the roots of the current dissatisfaction with general equilibrium theory, as well as to many recent debates on the state of the theory of value and of macroeconomic theory, lies in the distinction between the traditional *long-period* method in the study of value and distribution – a method common to the old classical economists and to the first generations of marginalist (or neoclassical) economists – and the *very-short-period* method characteristic of contemporary general equilibrium theory. This distinction had nearly been forgotten when Pierangelo Garegnani brought it back into focus in 1976, and used it to argue that marginalist equilibrium theory has undergone a very important but little noticed shift from long-period to very-short-period (neo-Walrasian) versions. It argues that the nature of this shift, its very important analytical implications for the marginalist approach, even the fact itself that a shift has occurred, are still very imperfectly perceived by a large part of the economics profession; and that, as a consequence, there is much confusion as to whether a number of marginalist/neoclassical analyses, originating from the versions of marginalist theory internal to the long-period method, can still be defended on the basis of the modern versions of general equilibrium theory. Once the distinction and its analytical implications are fully grasped, considerable clarification can be achieved on many central issues in the theories of value, distribution, capital, investment, growth, and even money. Clarity on the questions discussed in this book would appear essential for useful debate in these theoretical areas, where nowadays there is little agreement and, often, little mutual understanding between different schools of thought.

This book shows that many of the problems of contemporary general equilibrium theory have arisen precisely with the shift which the supply-and-demand approach has undergone, from its original basis in models attempting the determination of long-period equilibria, to the contemporary basis in models that aim at determining very-short-period equilibria. The question then arises, why was such a shift undertaken? This question leads to the heart of the present debates in the theory of value, distribution and capital. A side effect is to show that the findings in capital theory which were at the centre of the 'Cambridge controversy' of the 1960s are much more important than it might seem from the very little (if any) space now allotted to them in undergraduate and graduate studies in most universities. This book introduces those results (in Chapter 6) in a way that presumes no prior acquaintance with that controversy (however no attempt has been made to provide a detailed description of how the controversy evolved), and then it shows their relevance for macroeconomic theory. (A final Appendix discusses the legitimacy of the use of aggregate production functions.)

Some of the points argued in fuller detail here have been advanced in concise form in some of my other recent publications (cf. Petri, 1998a, 1999, 2003b). In this book those points are presented in ways that make them as accessible as possible to readers who encounter them for the first time, or who come to them with erroneous preconceptions; and the argument is enriched and completed by many new and, I think, important points: for instance the examples illustrating the long-period method in Chapter 1, the considerations on stationary equilibria in Chapter 4, the critique of investment theories in Chapter 7 and of the labour demand curve in Chapter 8; and all the arguments in the Appendices.

I hope that this book will encourage a better dialogue between neoclassically trained economists, and those economists – like myself – who argue for a return to the classical, or surplus, approach to value and distribution. The latter economists argue for a conscious return to the long-period method; many misunderstandings of what they argue have their origin in an imperfect grasp of that method, and especially in the confusion of long-period positions with steady-growth positions – a confusion which this book dedicates considerable space to dispelling.

Since my first article (Petri, 1978) I have been trying to overcome the communication difficulties that dog the debates on these issues. Much of what I have written since is a continuation of that effort at clarification. Several working papers on these issues were collected in 1988 in a provisional monograph, entitled *The long period and the short in economic theory. An essay in clarification* (University of Siena, 1988), which I consciously limited to a semi-private circulation because I considered it to be in need of revision. Since then, with interruptions due to other tasks, I have been trying to improve the substance and the presentation of that monograph, and the result is the present book (which is entirely re-written and contains much new material).

I have tried to make the argument understandable to first-year graduate students (and even to last-year thoughtful undergraduates) with some familiarity with the notions of intertemporal and temporary general equilibrium but with little acquaintance with older authors. My teaching experience (for several years now I have presented the basic ideas of this book to fourth-year undergraduates and first-year Ph.D. students in the

University of Siena) induces me to optimism in this regard. A previous acquaintance with long-period models and analyses is not required; the mathematics is elementary. (Only in those Appendices that deal with debates among specialists has a level of acquaintance with the literature been assumed such as is not normally found among students.)

As so frequently happens, while I was in the process of re-writing, other authors published on the same problems; for example Donzelli (1986), Zaghini (1990, 1993), Currie and Steedman (1989, 1990), Garegnani (1990a, 2000), Kompas (1992), Ahmad (1991), Schefold (1997, 2000), Walker (1996, 1997), Ciccone (1999), Mainwaring and Steedman (2000), Mongiovi (2000), Gehrke (2003). Their arguments are taken into account where necessary, and the task of so doing explains in part the length of time the re-writing has taken.

The chapters that follow are divided into sections, and these into paragraphs: Section 3.2 means Section 2 of Chapter 3; §3.2.1 means paragraph 1 of Section 2 in Chapter 3. Appendix 5A1 is Appendix 1 to Chapter 5; §5A1.2.3 means paragraph 3 of Section 2 of Appendix 5A1; §2A.2.3 means paragraph 3 of Section 2 in the unique Appendix to Chapter 2.

The bodies of research included in this book have been supported over the years by grants and research funds from the following Italian institutions, for which I am certainly grateful: Banca d'Italia, Ministero della Pubblica Istruzione, Ministero dell'Università e della Ricerca Scientifica e Tecnologica (now MIUR), Consiglio Nazionale delle Ricerche. In particular, in the final phase of completion of the research, and draft of the manuscript, I have benefited from support from MIUR as a member of the Siena Unit of the Research Group 'La ripresa dell'impostazione "classica": fondamenti critici, sviluppi teorici e studi applicati in tema di distribuzione del reddito e crescita economica'. I thank the editors of *Australian Economic Papers*, and of *Review of Political Economy*, for permission to utilize some material contained in articles published in those journals (Petri, 1978, 1991).

I have been lucky to receive useful comments on earlier drafts of different parts of this book from G. Abraham-Frois, K. Arrow, C. Bidard, S. Bowles, S. Cesaratto, R. Ciccone, M.A. De Francesco, M. Di Matteo, J. Felipe, P. Flaschel, D. Foley, C. Gnesutta, G. Harcourt, B. Jossa, J. Kregel, M. Krüger, H.D. Kurz, S. Marglin, M. Morishima, E. Nell, U. Pagano, C. Panico, S. Parrinello, M. Pivetti, L. Punzo, F. Ravagnani, A. Roncaglia, N. Salvadori, B. Schefold, F. Serrano, I. Steedman, A. Stirati, F. Vianello; I am particularly grateful to Pierangelo Garegnani for the extremely useful conversations over the years on the problems discussed in this book, problems whose importance I learned from his writings. I also collectively thank all those who attended the various seminars (at the Universities of Bielefeld, Bremen, Cambridge, Catania, Frankfurt, Harvard, Massachusetts-

Amherst, Napoli-Federico II, New School for Social Research, Paris X-Nanterre, Siena, and at several Trieste International Summer Schools), where from 1983 onwards I have presented earlier drafts of various parts of this book.

But – as Dennis Robertson once put it – the path of true knowledge is not always plainly marked; and for my strayings into the fields of error I must accept full blame.

Siena, November 2003
Fabio Petri

1. The Long-Period Method

1.1. INTRODUCTION: ON SOME CRACKS IN THE NEOCLASSICAL EDIFICE

1.1.1. The theory of value and distribution is at present in a state of uncertainty. Beginners are seldom aware of this fact because, with great assurance, most textbooks introduce them to only one theory: that prices, both of products and of 'factors of production', are determined by the tendency toward an equilibrium between supply and demand. But in more advanced courses students discover that there are cracks and fissures in this assurance. For example, they may discover that a respected specialist in general equilibrium theory has written:

> ... we are at a turning point in economic theory. Much of the elegant theoretical structure that has been constructed over the last one hundred years in economics will be seen over the next decade to have provided a wrong focus and a misleading and ephemeral idea of what constitutes an equilibrium (Kirman, 1999, p. 8).

The textbooks that present the rigorous versions of supply-and-demand theory – the advanced theory of general equilibrium in its various forms – are seldom so negative; but even they cannot hide that this theory encounters a number of serious difficulties. One in particular is sure to raise some perplexities in the more attentive student: namely, the admission – accompanied by no indication of clearly better solutions – that the study of the stability of equilibrium through the auctioneer-guided tâtonnement is hardly satisfactory, given its unrealistic assumption of no transactions and no production until equilibrium is reached. The question inevitably arises: what is the relevance of conclusions reached on the basis of so patently unrealistic an adjustment process?

The ensuing perplexities are usually repressed, or after a while, forgotten. But the attentive student will find it less easy to forget them if she comes across statements such as the following:

> I have always regarded Competitive General Equilibrium analysis as akin to the mock-up an aircraft engineer might build ... theorists all over the world have

1

become aware that anything based on this mock-up is unlikely to fly, since it
neglects some crucial aspects of the world, the recognition of which will force
some drastic re-designing. Moreover, at no stage was the mock-up complete; in
particular, it provided no account of the actual working of the invisible hand
(Hahn, 1981b, p. 1036).

> ... it is a fair question whether it can ever be useful to have an equilibrium notion
> which does not describe the termination of actual processes (Hahn, 1984, p. 48).

The student who happens to read these statements by Frank Hahn may find
herself asking: but isn't the notion that the equilibrium is what the economy
tends toward, the basis of most economic theory? What have they taught us,
if, to the contrary, the truth is that the notion of equilibrium 'does not
describe the termination of actual processes'? What, then, is the use of such a
notion of equilibrium? Indeed, how can one be sure that the equilibrium *is* an
equilibrium, if there is still no acceptable account of the working of the
forces which are supposed to come to rest in equilibrium?

Our student may at this point remember having read, in her first-year
graduate microeconomics course, in a footnote of a textbook she most
probably consulted: 'For an extensive analysis of market adjustment
procedures in real time, see Fisher (1983)' (Mas-Colell et al., 1995, p. 625,
fn. 69). The wording of this sentence did not suggest that startling novelties
could be learned from that book, and since the workload of graduate students
is usually enormous, our student had not at the time gone on to read Fisher;
but now, after reading those disconcerting sentences by Hahn, she may feel
she wants better to understand what is going on in the foundations of the
economic theory she has been learning. At this point she may decide to
consult Fisher's book, where she will discover the following sentence:

> In a real economy, however, trading, as well as production and consumption, goes
> on out of equilibrium. It follows that, in the course of convergence to equilibrium
> (assuming that occurs), endowments change. In turn this changes the set of
> equilibria. Put more succinctly, the set of equilibria is path dependent ... [This path
> dependence] makes the calculation of equilibria corresponding to the initial state
> of the system essentially irrelevant. What matters is the equilibrium that the
> economy will reach from given initial endowments, not the equilibrium that it
> would have been in, given initial endowments, had prices happened to be just right
> (Fisher, 1983, p. 14).

In all likelihood, our student at this point will find it hard to avoid
succumbing to a feeling of dizziness. Not only is it unclear how the 'invisible
hand' actually works; what is clear is that, even if the 'invisible hand' takes
the economy to some equilibrium, it is *not* the equilibrium 'corresponding to

the initial state of the system', that is, corresponding to the initial endowments. But then what of comparative statics? What is the use for example of the theory of taxation, which studies how the equilibrium corresponding to given data is altered by the introduction of a tax, if after the introduction of the tax the economy will *not* tend to the altered equilibrium? And how can one hope to determine the equilibrium to which, if at all, the economy will finally arrive, if – according to Frank Hahn, one of the maximum authorities on the stability of general equilibrium – we still have 'no account of the actual working of the invisible hand'? Indeed, how can one be sure that the economy will reach an equilibrium at all?

But then – our student might ask – what sort of foundation is the edifice of applied economics built upon? In her studies, she has naturally formed the impression that among economists there is a whole series of firm beliefs about the tendencies of market economies, for example the tendency of the price of a good to decrease if its supply increases, the tendency of the demand for labour to increase if the real wage decreases, and so on and so forth. Now she cannot help asking: where have all these beliefs come from? Are they all purely gratuitous? Do these statements on equilibrium theory by Hahn and by Fisher imply that economic theory can at present make no predictions and that we should start again from scratch?

1.1.2. These are the questions dealt with in this book. It does not centrally aim at presenting new results on the issues of non-uniqueness or instability of general equilibria; rather, it concentrates on a *logically prior* issue: the widely admitted difficulty with using general equilibrium theory (in its modern versions) for explanatory and predictive purposes, given that the theory is unable to discuss where disequilibria, if realistically conceived, will take the economy. In other words, the theory is unable to exclude that disequilibrium adjustments may relevantly alter the data of equilibrium much before equilibrium is sufficiently approached. Indeed the theory cannot even *attempt* to prove that the direction of disequilibrium adjustments is toward an equilibrium, because, for reasons to be explained (in Chapter 2), it simply does not know what happens if disequilibrium adjustments involve the implementation of disequilibrium production decisions and disequilibrium exchanges. As a result, it is impossible to claim general equilibrium theory as the justification for the applications of the supply-and-demand approach to macroeconomic theory, growth theory, international trade, welfare economics, and so on.

These difficulties, it will be argued, provide an extremely useful key to an understanding of the present state of the supply-and-demand approach to value and distribution.

In a nutshell, the thread of the argument to be developed at length in this book is the following.

The marginalist, or neoclassical, approach came to dominate economics in versions which did not suffer from the difficulties just mentioned. It is doubtful that otherwise this approach would have come to dominate the economics profession. And even now, the applications of this approach to practical problems, such as to macroeconomic problems or to international trade issues, rely on those older versions (which will be called *traditional* in this book). These traditional versions aimed at determining *long-period* equilibria (and as such, they shared with the previous classical tradition of Adam Smith and David Ricardo the aim of determining long-period *positions*[1]). These long-period equilibria were endowed with sufficient persistence, and with data sufficiently unaffected by disequilibrium actions, as to make them compatible with the implementation of trial-and-error disequilibrium actions, and with comparative static exercises. But, given the logic of the theory, what made it possible to determine this type of equilibria was the conception of capital as a single factor of production capable of changing 'form' without changing in 'quantity'; this made it possible to leave the equilibrium composition (the 'form') of the capital endowment to be determined endogenously by the equilibrium conditions: a *given* composition of the capital endowment, being subject to rapid change, would on the contrary have deprived the equilibrium of persistence. Although this conception of capital was initially accepted, it gradually became evident that this conception presented a problem: the endowment of capital so conceived could only be specified as an amount of value; but values cannot be data of a general equilibrium which must determine values. Consequently, between the 1930s and the 1960s a shift gradually took place in the pure theory of value, from long-period versions to the now-dominant *very-short-period* versions, which will be called *neo-Walrasian* in this book. The latter versions determine equilibria that lack persistence and are relevantly affected by the implementation of disequilibrium actions, precisely because their data include a given endowment of *each* type of capital good. The shift was accelerated by the Cambridge controversies in capital theory of the 1950s and 1960s, which strengthened the doubts on the legitimacy of conceiving capital as a single factor. But the implications of the shift were and are very imperfectly understood. It seems not to be generally realized that, if the conception of capital goods as ultimately embodying a single factor 'capital' is really abandoned, then general equilibrium theory is no guide to the

---

1. Since the classics did not determine long-period prices and quantities as reflecting an equilibrium between supply and demand for factors, a term more general than long-period equilibria is necessary to encompass both approaches.

behaviour of market economies for reasons logically prior to the well-known difficulties with uniqueness and with stability of tâtonnement-like adjustments. Moreover, the two fundamental pillars of the applications of the neoclassical approach to real-world economies – the negative elasticity of aggregate investment vis-à-vis the rate of interest, and the negative elasticity of the demand for labour vis-à-vis the real wage – lose their foundation.

This book also asks, what are the reasons for the persistence of a very imperfect grasp of these consequences? The answer advanced is that the long-period method is no longer fully understood; the existence of a marginalist tradition of long-period equilibria is almost forgotten; and the analytical role of the conception of capital as a single factor of variable 'form' in that tradition is no longer clearly perceived. Striking examples of some of the resultant confusions will be presented in the Appendices to Chapters 5 and 6.

The implication of the argument is that contemporary neoclassical economics cannot have it both ways: it cannot reason *as if* capital could be treated like a single factor when it comes to applied analyses, only to deny any implicit reliance on that admittedly indefensible conception when it comes to 'rigorous' theory. The true consequence of the admission that capital goods cannot be conceived as the embodiment of a single factor 'capital' would appear to be that the entire neoclassical approach to value and distribution is deprived of foundations. Luckily, there are promising alternatives already in existence. In particular, there would appear to be little obstacle to a full rehabilitation of the long-period method, which has been abandoned in the pure theory of value not because of *intrinsic* deficiencies, but rather, due to the fact that the *neoclassical* approach to distribution was incompatible with it. No such incompatibility exists between that method, and other, non-neoclassical approaches to distribution, employment and growth. A short summary of some of the existing alternatives to the neoclassical approach on these issues is presented in the last chapter, in order to counter an attitude that, although not often made explicit, would appear to be quite widespread: that there exists nowadays no developed alternative to the supply-and-demand, or neoclassical, approach to value and distribution, and that therefore it is simply impossible to abandon the latter approach in teaching and applications.

1.1.3. One effect of the argument of this book is that it makes sense of the Cambridge controversy in capital theory of the 1950s and 1960s. Both the bitterness and the inconclusiveness of this controversy can be understood as the fruits of misunderstandings that stemmed from lack of clarity on the shift neoclassical equilibrium theory had undergone. Lack of clarity was present on both sides of the debate, and the resulting confusions (some of them caused by the critics, for example by Joan Robinson's concentration on a false target: aggregate production functions) were largely responsible for the prevailing conclusion that general equilibrium theory was left unscathed by the criticism of the notion of aggregate capital. One of the aims of this book is to help dispel these misunderstandings[2] and to help re-establish communication between the opposing sides. Younger readers not already acquainted with that important controversy will find here an introduction to its main aspects (although not a detailed examination of its evolution).

Actually, once one understands the shift undergone by the theory of general equilibrium from long-period to very-short-period versions, one gains clarification in a surprising number of fields beyond the Cambridge controversies in capital theory: from the reason why general equilibrium theory finds it difficult to abandon the fairy tale of the auctioneer, to why constant returns to scale cause problems in modern general equilibrium theory that were absent in its long-period versions; from monetary theory, to the theory of aggregate investment; from the reasons for Hicks's change of mind on the fruitfulness of the temporary equilibrium method, to the evolution of Walras' theory; from the nature of Keynes's equilibrium, to the stability of the momentary equilibrium of Solow's growth model; from the difference between long-period and steady-growth analyses, to the meaning of the non-substitution theorem, to the reasons to reject aggregate production functions.

It may appear surprising that such varied topics should all be discussed in a single book; but they all revolve around one issue, the shift in the notion of equilibrium and its consequences. I believe that by showing these consequences in a number of different fields, this book helps one fully to grasp the relevance of that shift.

1.2.   CHANGE IN THEORY WITHOUT CHANGE IN METHOD

1.2.1. The remainder of this chapter is dedicated to an initial description of the *long-period method* – a description which will acquire more and more flesh and colour as the book proceeds. This method remained fundamentally unaltered across the change in *theory*, undergone by the analyses of value and distribution during the second half of the nineteenth century when they

2.   Thus continuing and expanding upon previous efforts in the same direction, by myself (Petri, 1978, 1991, 1998a, 1999, 2003b; Panico and Petri, 1987) and by numerous others, among whom I would single out Garegnani (1970, 1976, 1990a, 2000), Schefold (1985, 1997), Kurz (1987), Eatwell (1979, 1982), Milgate (1979, 1982), Gehrke (2003).

shifted from a classical[3] to a neoclassical or marginalist or supply-and-demand approach to value and distribution. Only subsequently, while the basic theory remained the same, was there a gradual shift in *method*, that is, to a method based on sequences of very-short-period equilibria.[4] We start precisely by illustrating how the change in theory was not initially accompanied by any questioning of the long-period method. We take the opportunity briefly to illustrate the classical approach to income distribution, a topic not always taught nowadays, but important in order to understand that the supply-and-demand, or marginalist, approach is not the sole conceivable one. The section ends with an illustration of the implication of the long-period method for the treatment of the composition of capital.

1.2.2. If one compares the theories of value and distribution of, on one hand, classical authors such as Adam Smith or Ricardo and, on the other, marginalist authors such as Wicksell, J.B. Clark, Wicksteed or Marshall, one finds that the deep difference concerning the forces determining the distribution of the net product between wages and profits (or interest) does not entail an analogous deep difference concerning the forces determining long-run, or long-period, relative product prices.

Ricardo, largely implicitly, and Adam Smith very explicitly, considered conflict and power relations between classes as central features of capitalism.

3. 'Classical' is used in this book in its original meaning, as recalled by Keynes in these terms: ' "The classical economists" was a name invented by Marx to cover Ricardo and James Mill and their *predecessors*, that is to say the founders of the theory which culminated in the Ricardian economics'. Keynes continued: 'I have been accustomed, perhaps perpetrating a solecism, to include in "the classical school" the *followers* of Ricardo, those, that is to say, who adopted and perfected the theory of the Ricardian economics, including (for example) J.S. Mill, Marshall, Edgeworth and Prof. Pigou' (*KCW*, vol. VII, p. 3, n. 1, italics in original). Keynes's usage has dominated macroeconomics; it is behind, for example, the term 'New Classical Macroeconomics'. But Keynes's use of the term 'classical' is misleading, because it confuses two approaches which are in fact radically different: Marshall, Edgeworth and Pigou did *not* adopt and perfect Ricardian economics; they replaced it with the marginalist approach which was, if anything, anti-Ricardian. In the term 'neoclassical' the meaning of 'classical' is Keynes's, and the term is therefore just as misleading; but it is nowadays so widespread that it has been occasionally used in this book.
4. This distinction between a change in *theory* and the subsequent shift in *method* is due to Garegnani (1976). This terminology, 'theory' vs. 'method', is perhaps not totally felicitous, but it is not easy to find a better one. The 'method' of a science, that is how the hypotheses and results of theoretical analysis are connected with the explanation and prediction of empirical observations, is itself based on theoretical beliefs (for example the 'method' of long-period positions rests on the belief that there is a gravitation toward long-period positions), and therefore the reference to a change in *theory* without an abandonment of the traditional *method* must be understood to mean in fact a change only in a subset of the theoretical beliefs: in the present case, not in those beliefs justifying the reference to long-period positions as centres of gravitation.

They explained profits[5] as the appropriation of the surplus remaining on no-rent land after the payment of wages kept at a 'subsistence' level by the lower bargaining power of the labouring classes. The greater bargaining power of the capitalists was ascribed to their collective monopoly of the access to work, a monopoly protected by the state. It will suffice here to recall the famous passage from the *Wealth of Nations* where Adam Smith writes:

> The workmen desire to get as much, the masters to give as little as possible. The former are disposed to combine in order to raise, the latter in order to lower the wages of labour.
>
> It is not, however, difficult to foresee which of the two parties must, upon all ordinary occasions, have the advantage in the dispute, and force the other into a compliance with their terms. The masters, being fewer in number, can combine much more easily ... can hold out much longer ...
>
> ... Masters are always and everywhere in a sort of tacit, but constant and uniform combination, not to raise the wages of labour above their actual rate. To violate this combination is everywhere a most unpopular action, and a sort of reproach to a master among his neighbours and equals. We seldom, indeed hear of this combination, because it is the usual, and one may say, the natural state of things, which nobody ever hears of ... Such combinations, however, are frequently resisted by a contrary defensive combination of the workmen; who sometimes too, without any provocation of this kind, combine of their own accord to raise the price of their labour ... But whether their combinations be offensive or defensive, they are always abundantly heard of. In order to bring the point to a speedy decision, they have always recourse to the loudest clamour, and sometimes to the most shocking violence and outrage. They are desperate, and act with the folly and extravagance of desperate men, who must either starve, or frighten their masters into an immediate compliance with their demands. The masters upon these occasions are just as clamorous upon the other side, and never cease to call aloud for the assistance of the civil magistrate, and the rigorous execution of those laws which have been enacted with so much severity against the combinations of servants, labourers, and journeymen. The workmen, accordingly, very seldom derive any advantage from the violence of those tumultuous combinations, which, partly from the interposition of the civil magistrate, partly from the superior steadiness of the masters, partly from the necessity which the greater part of the workmen are under of submitting for the sake of present subsistence, generally

5. In the classical terminology, also used by Sraffa (1960), profits are defined as gross of interest payments and of the reward for the 'risk and trouble' of entrepreneurship; these are on the contrary included in the costs to be subtracted from revenue in order to arrive at the *marginalist* definition of profits. So it is profits in the marginalist sense that tend to zero in the long period. Unless specified otherwise, in this book 'profits' is used in the classical sense, and the marginalist definition will be conveyed with terms such as 'extra-profits' or 'pure profits'.

end in nothing but the punishment or ruin of the ringleaders (Smith, 1975, pp. 58–60).

Smith adds that the superior strength of the 'masters' does not, however, reduce the wages below a level, which Smith describes as 'the lowest consistent with common humanity' (ibid., p. 63), and which, although Smith tends to associate it with the minimum required for the reproduction of labour supply, is not to be intended as biologically determined: the 'subsistence' of labourers is admitted by all classical authors to include an element of habit, custom and convention. Thus Ricardo speaks of 'comforts which custom renders absolute necessaries' (Ricardo, 1951, p. 94), and explicitly admits that 'the natural price of labour ... essentially depends on the habits and customs of the people' (ibid., pp. 96–7).

But how do these habits and customs form, and how do they operate? The long passage from Smith quoted above suggests the importance of tacit rules of behaviour, which individuals adhere to in order not to lose the solidarity of the people socially close to them, a solidarity that is essential in the bargaining between groups with opposing interests. Therefore it appears legitimate to say that in the classical approach, real wages result from a continuous, open or latent conflict, and oscillate around a 'natural', or customary, real wage, which labourers expect to earn (and consider therefore a 'fair'[6] wage) because it reflects the average balance of bargaining power between capitalists and wage labourers over the recent past. This customary 'subsistence' wage, which guarantees a standard of living that through habit has come to be regarded as indispensable to decent living, is the starting point of further bargaining. The latter, if conditioned by a changed balance of bargaining power, may result in a lasting divergence of wages from their customary level, with a resulting slow change of the customary or 'natural' or 'fair' real wage itself. Any considerable divergence of the standard of

---

6. Historical and recent evidence confirms the importance of notions of 'a fair day's wage for a fair day's labour' to the concrete behaviour of workers (cf. for example Solow, 1990; Bewley, 1998, 1999). Viewing the real wage level as reflecting, in every period, an explicit or implicit armistice or truce sheds light on the reasons for the importance of the notion of fair wages, as well as on its meaning. An armistice is a pact that saves losses and suffering to both parties to a conflict by suspending active fighting; pacts must be honoured; honouring a pact is 'fair', that is, correct, behaviour; a fair wage is then simply the wage that workers must get if they work correctly, according to the truce signed by both parties. Paying less would mean reneging on the armistice, and then workers too would not be bound to respect their side of the pact. So 'fair' wages are not fair in the sense of reflecting some social justice of the resulting income distribution, but only in the sense that they correspond to the current truce, and must be paid if capitalists do not want a resumption of active conflict.

living of a social class from its customary level[7] can be expected to cause social unrest and turmoil: strikes (also by capitalists), protests, sabotage, even revolts or military coups. One may then consider the periods of social tranquillity as truces, regulated by an armistice, that will last as long as no party to it feels strong enough to question or violate its terms. When the armistice is questioned, then a period of unrest and bargaining ensues. If this results in a persistent change in the standard of living of a class, then after a while this change becomes incorporated in custom and expectations; it becomes an implicit component of the new armistice. But the changes are usually small and slow, because the improvements in the position of one class are at the expense of the position of other classes, and the social resistance of large groups to abrupt losses of income (or even only of their respective relative positions) is usually very great.

It is not surprising that from such a perspective the real wage should have been considered an input as indispensable to production as raw materials or as food for cattle: hence the conception that incomes other than wages arise as a *surplus* over the necessities of reproduction, and the treatment of the real wage as a *given* or independently varying parameter when attempting the determination of relative product prices and of the rate of profits (Garegnani, 1984a, 1987, 1990b). Note however that the given wage is not conceived as exogenous with respect to economic analysis, but only as determined by forces whose working can be studied separately from the forces determining relative prices and the rate of profit once the real wage, or wages,[8] is/are determined. Once the real wage or its changes are determined by these forces, then one can go on to determine the rate of profit.

1.2.3. The marginalist approach abandons the treatment of the real wage as determined before the rate of profit. Instead there is a simultaneous determination of wages and other incomes. This radical change is brought about by a generalization of the Ricardian analysis of differential rent, such that it is applied, not only as in Ricardo to the division of the product between rents on one side, and the sum of profits and wages on the other, but also to the division between profits and wages of what is left of the net product after paying rents. This latter problem is one that the classical authors had tackled in the entirely different way briefly referred to above.

7. In more modern times, in the industrialized countries, after decades of increases in the standard of living, a regular positive *rate of increase* of living standards may itself be part of what is customary, or indeed part of the social armistice; and its disappearance may accordingly cause social unrest.

8. *Relative* wages were analogously seen as depending on social and political forces and conventions, and hence best studied separately; they were thus taken as given when determining relative prices and the rate of profit.

The root of this generalization is the realization that Ricardo's theory of intensive differential land implies a symmetry between land, and capital-cum-labour (capital and labour are treated by Ricardo as one, because he includes the given real wages in the capital advanced, and indeed often reasons as if capital only consisted of advanced wages), such that both can be seen as receiving their marginal product.[9] It is then thought that the reasoning must be extensible to any source of income deriving from contributions to production: and therefore also to labour alone, and to capital alone.

Therefore the analysis is thought to apply symmetrically to the 'factors of production' labour, land, and capital; and it is re-interpreted as evidence of two factor substitution mechanisms: the first based on technical choices and the second on consumption choices; these substitution mechanisms are in turn seen as implying supply-and-demand equilibrating processes, acting symmetrically on labour, on land, and on capital; distribution is therefore seen as determined, in freely competitive conditions, by the tendency toward an equilibrium between supply of and demand for the various factors of production. The equilibrium is a situation of full employment of resources, and gives to each unit of each factor its full-employment marginal product, that is its contribution to production; this approach accordingly denies both the inefficiencies, and the exploitation of labour, which Marx had seen as inherent in capitalism.

The next paragraph will briefly bring to mind the operation of these equilibrating factor-substitution mechanisms as traditionally envisaged by marginalist economists. The topic is elementary, and it was once considered first-year economics, but its presentation here will illustrate why no need was traditionally felt for the fiction of the 'auctioneer' in order to argue that equilibrium is what the economy tends toward – a point not often made clear in the modern teaching of equilibrium theory.

1.2.4. The first mechanism, of 'direct' or technological factor substitution, operates in relation to cost-minimizing firms that tend to adopt production methods that utilize a higher proportion of the factor whose relative 'price'

9. The point cannot be developed here in the detail it would deserve. In Ricardo's theory of intensive differential rent, under the simplifying assumptions he makes (corn produced by capital advances consisting of corn combined with labour in fixed proportion), the unit reward of capital-cum-labour equals the increase in production obtainable from the utilization, on the given land, of one more unit of capital-cum-labour; and the rent of land is analogously equal to the increase in production obtainable if the given amount of capital-cum-labour is employed on a land surface larger by one unit. The theory of *extensive* differential rent was in turn probably the basis of the notion of decreasing marginal utility (utility was initially conceived as additive, and then the successive doses of a consumption good produced less and less additional utility just as the successive doses of corn applied on land of less and less fertility produced less and less additional product).

(that is rental) decreases. In order to see the operation of the mechanism with the utmost clarity, it is convenient to assume that the composition of the economy's output is given. Then it is as if only one good were produced. Due to free entry, industries behave as if there were constant returns to scale.[10] Consequently what is relevant is the 'factor intensity' (that is factor proportions) of the production process producing one unit of the composite good. Variations of relative factor rentals cause shifts along the unit isoquant. Thus if one assumes, for simplicity, that only one product, food (which is also the numeraire), is produced by labour and land, a decrease of the real wage will mean a decrease of the wage–rent ratio,[11] causing a shift along the unit isoquant, in the direction of the use of more labour and less land per unit of food.

The change in the optimal labour–land ratio, as relative factor prices change, is then used as the basis for the argument that the economy tends toward a full-employment equilibrium. To see why, let us initially assume that land is in rigid supply and fully employed; then the higher labour–land ratio brought about by a lower real wage rate entails a desire by firms to employ more labour. The decreasing labour 'employment curve' thus derived coincides with the curve of the economy-wide marginal product of labour. If it turns out that the assumption of full employment of land is justified, this

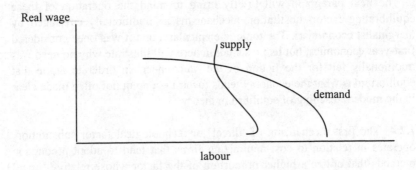

Figure 1.1 Supply and demand for labour in the labour-land economy

10. Cf. Appendix 5A3 on the illegitimacy of excluding free entry.
11. Due to competition, factor payments will exhaust the product, so if the real wage rate in terms of food decreases, the real rent rate in terms of food increases. This is obvious with fixed coefficients. With a differentiable production function, let $Y = F(L,T)$ with Y product, L labour, T land; let F_L and F_T indicate the marginal products of labour and land, respectively equal to the real wage rate and the real rent rate; then $dF = F_L dL + F_T dT$; constant returns to scale imply the adding-up theorem, $F(L,T) = F_L L + F_T T$, and by differentiation of both sides one obtains $dF = dF_L dL + F_L dL + dF_T dT + F_T dT$; hence $dF_L dL + dF_T dT = 0$, so dF_L and dF_T are of opposite sign.

labour 'employment curve' can be interpreted as a *demand* curve indicating the actual demand for labour as a function of the real wage; its decreasing shape gives plausibility to the thesis that in most circumstances the equilibrium on the labour market will be unique and stable: as is well known, the labour supply curve may be itself at least in part downward-sloping ('backward-bending'), but if the labour demand curve is not only downward-sloping but also fairly elastic, then in all likelihood the equilibrium will be unique and stable.

All that is needed then for the thesis of convergence to a full-employment equilibrium is a justification of the assumption that the supply of land is fully utilized. Actually, it is not easy to find such an explicit justification in   ?
marginalist authors. But the implicit justification would appear to have been the following. A reasoning, strictly symmetrical to the one applied to labour, also applies to land, if one assumes the supply of *labour* to be fully employed; and in fact the reasoning does not require that, in deriving the 'employment curve' for a factor, the other factor be *fully* employed; it only requires that the second factor's employment be given. However, since, at whichever level the second factor's employment is given, a tendency toward the full employment of the first factor will be at work, and since this holds true for either factor, it can be argued that the economy will be able to reach the full employment of both factors. Then the assumption that the second factor is fully employed comes out to be the correct one, when one wants to determine the rental of the first factor which competition will tend to establish; the marginal product curve of a factor, derived under the assumption of full employment of the other factor, can then be seen as its *demand curve*.

Let us note how in this example the tendency toward equilibrium does not need an auctioneer-guided tâtonnement preventing the implementation of decisions until equilibrium is reached. The data determining the equilibrium are unaffected by disequilibrium productions, so the equilibrium can be conceived as reached, or as realized on average, through a repetition of disequilibrium transactions and productions, permitting a correction or compensation of mistakes. In accordance with such a conception of the tendency toward equilibrium, the effects of a disequilibrium income distribution are described in such a way that they can be given a concrete interpretation as something actually observable: for example, too high levels of the real wage determine a level of employment below full employment, and the economy remains in that situation as long as the real wage does not change, because there is equilibrium on all other markets.

This last observation may perhaps be found surprising in view of Walras' law, but it derives from the implicit assumption that the purchasing power of factors derives from the incomes they actually earn; for example, when deriving the labour demand curve, the implicit assumption is that at each point of the demand curve for labour only the employed workers have incomes with which to demand output; so there is equilibrium both on the land market, and on the output market (assuming no savings). This is a much more realistic assumption than what is assumed in the tâtonnement with 'tickets' of the later Walras and of modern analyses. In these analyses the auctioneer collects *promises* of demands and supplies, only to be implemented if it turns out that a full-employment equilibrium has actually been reached. Therefore it is legitimate for factor owners to demand consumption goods on the basis of the income corresponding to the value of their *intended* factor supplies, because if it turns out that their factor supplies do not find purchasers, the equilibrium will not have been reached, and thus all promises will be cancelled; an excess supply on only one factor market then shows up in an excess demand in the output market. To the contrary, in real economies the potential purchasing power from the excess supply of unemployed factors cannot be translated into actual, effective demand for goods; thus, within the supply-and-demand approach, the effects of a wage that is fixed (for example by trade union power) above its equilibrium level can only be grasped through this 'non-Walrasian' analysis, which is therefore superior in realism and usefulness.

We get here an inkling of the possibility to discuss the tendency toward equilibrium in more realistic terms than through the tâtonnement with Walras' 'tickets' (*bons*). Early marginalist discussions of stability did not assume the tâtonnement with 'tickets'; our discussion of the stability of the labour market has closely followed Wicksell (1934, pp. 110–33); Walras himself had no 'tickets' in the first three editions of his *Eléments d'économie politique pure.* (Cf. Chapter 5, p. 141. Why then did he introduce them in the fourth edition? And why has this unrealistic assumption come to dominate the enquiries into the stability of equilibrium in more recent analyses? This is another question that will be answered in this essay.)

The same change in the aggregate labour–land ratio can also be brought about by a second factor substitution mechanism. This operates through changes in the relative dimensions of industries, as changes in relative factor prices alter the composition of the demand for consumption goods owing to changes in relative product prices. This second, indirect substitution mechanism can act alone if the first mechanism cannot operate owing to lack of technical substitutability, or it can render the factor demand curves more elastic by adding its operation to that of the direct, technological substitution.

The indirect substitution mechanism requires that there be more than one consumption good in existence, and it operates through the fact that the consumption goods, which use relatively more of the factor whose rental decreases, become relatively cheaper and are then – it is argued – generally in greater demand by consumers. In order to see this mechanism at work as clearly as possible, let us now assume the absence of technical substitution: each of the several consumption goods is produced by a fixed-coefficients-, Leontief-type technology. For instance, let us assume that there are two consumption goods, food f and cloth c, produced by labour L and land T, the respective technical coefficients being L_f, T_f, L_c, T_c. Relative prices p_f and p_c will be determined by the following equations, where w is the wage rate and r the land rent rate:

$$p_f = wL_f + rT_f,$$

$$p_c = wL_c + rT_c.$$

It is mathematically trivial to show that p_f / p_c will decrease or increase, as w/r decreases, depending on whether food production is characterized by a labour–land ratio greater or smaller than in cloth production. Let us assume that food production is relatively 'labour-intensive' that is that $L_f / T_f > L_c / T_c$. Then as the real wage decreases and hence w/r decreases,[12] food becomes cheaper relative to cloth. The argument is then that generally this will entail a shift in the average composition of demand, in favour of food.[13] Assuming again land to be rigidly supplied and fully employed, the adaptation of the composition of supply to the composition of demand will require that some units of land be transferred from the production of cloth to

12. It is trivial to show that, if w/p_f decreases, also w/p_c and w/r decrease.
13. It is well known nowadays that this result is not guaranteed, if one of the two consumption goods is an inferior good, or if factor ownership is unequally distributed among consumers, and the demand for food comes mainly from wage income. But except for the case of Giffen goods, no explicit discussion of this problem can be found among the early marginalist economists. For example Wicksell only admitted in passing the possibility of multiple equilibria in the economy with production (cf. Wicksell, 1934, p. 204), without any discussion of its causes nor of the possibility that this might raise problems for the plausibility of the theory; Walras did not mention at all the possibility of multiple equilibria for the economy with production. Later authors (for example Hicks, 1946, p. 104; Johnson, 1973, p. 61) have discussed these problems more explicitly but have argued (although not very convincingly) that their likelihood is low enough as to render them negligible in a general analysis. It appears therefore legitimate to say that the indirect factor substitution mechanism was historically seen as reinforcing the supply-and-demand approach to distribution rather than weakening it. This view can be criticized; but our concerns now are on a different set of issues, so we leave this question aside. Another problem of the theory is that the downward-sloping shape of the labour employment curve rests on an assumed vertical or upward-sloping land supply curve: if the supply of land is assumed fully utilized but the land supply curve is 'backward-bending', then as the real wage decreases and the rent rate increases, the increase in the L/T ratio might not be enough to offset the decrease of T, and thus it is no longer guaranteed that L will increase; but here we leave aside this question too.

the production of food; but in the production of food, a unit of land is combined with a greater amount of labour than in the production of cloth, so the total employment of labour will increase. So even when there is no technical substitutability, the existence of substitutability among consumption goods can be argued to give rise to decreasing demand curves for factors, analogous to the demand curves derivable from technical substitution, because the substitution among consumption goods implies an indirect substitution among the factors employed in their production. (*This* appears to be the main reason why so much attention is given to the abstract, general properties of consumer choice in the neoclassical approach.)

Obviously – the reasoning then continues – in general, both kinds of substitution will be simultaneously at work and the result will be a greater elasticity of the demand curve for a factor, than if only one of the two mechanisms were operative. The likelihood, caused by decreasing factor supply curves, of the possibility of multiple equilibria on factor markets, of which some are unstable, is accordingly diminished.

1.2.5. The difference between the classical and the marginalist approach as to income distribution could hardly be greater: according to one theory, income from the property of capital goods is analogous, in its origin, to the revenue of feudal landlords, it is the appropriation of a surplus, due not to any productive contribution of the owners of capital but simply to superior bargaining power. According to the other theory, each unit of each factor receives a rental which reflects its contribution to production, and which can therefore be seen as an appropriate reward for the sacrifice which the supply of that unit reflects.

But this difference is on the forces determining *distribution*,[14] not on relative long-period product prices once the rate of profits (or the real wage) is determined, nor on the role attributed to these prices in the explanation of economic phenomena. In both the classical or surplus approach, and in the traditional versions of the marginalist approach, it was accepted that, over sufficiently long time periods, product prices would gravitate toward the minimum 'costs of production' reachable on the basis of the given rates of wages, rents, and profits or interest. The term 'cost of production' is somewhat inappropriate for the classical authors, who did not conceive the

14. Actually the basic analytical difference between the two approaches – the absence in the classical approach of any notion of decreasing demand curves for factors of production – also entails vast differences in the analysis of employment and growth: in the classical approach there is no automatic mechanism ensuring a tendency to the full employment of labour, and the acceptance of Say's Law in Ricardo appears devoid of solid analytical justifications: other classical economists, such as Marx, found it easy to reject it. Cf. Garegnani (1978).

rate of profits or of interest as a cost on a par with wages and rents, and in fact included interest within profits (something that in recent times has been a cause of misunderstandings). However, it does convey to modern readers the idea, common to both classical and traditional marginalist authors, that long-period prices are the prices that cover the costs of inputs, including labour, and also guarantee the normal rate of return on capital, in a 'tranquil' state, in which relative prices change slowly enough that their change over time can be neglected.[15] These were the prices that analysis had to determine in order to be able to explain and predict the trend of the average day-by-day market price of a product.

Thus marginalist authors like Wicksell or J.B. Clark took it for granted – just as Smith, Ricardo or Marx did – that it is not only uninteresting but also impossible to describe fully the forces determining the details of each single transaction or production decision, and that therefore little can be known of, or predicted about, the accidental, continuous changes of actually observed day-by-day prices (Smith's 'market prices') or quantities. However, they shared with the classical authors the belief that it was possible to explain and predict *the average* of each price or quantity, because the actual path of a price or of a quantity, although unpredictable in its details, would tend to gravitate around and towards definite values or 'centres of gravitation', independent of the details of the gravitational process itself. The existence of this gravitation made the prediction of each single transaction unnecessary (and uninteresting). Changes of this 'centre of gravitation', caused by changes in the data determining it, could then be used to explain and predict the *trend* of the actual path of the variable under consideration, a trend determined by the tendency to gravitate toward the new (or the shifting) centre of gravitation. The difference in the theories determining these centres of gravitation meant that, in the marginalist approach, the determination of the centres of gravitation of quantities and relative prices had to be simultaneous with the determination of the centres of gravitation of the distributive variables, something that is not the case in classical authors; but the distinction between market and normal magnitudes, the latter being the centres of gravitation of the former, is found in both groups of theories.

1.2.6. Thus, just like Adam Smith who had written

> There is in every society ... an ordinary or average rate of both wages and profits ... When the price of any commodity is neither more nor less than what is sufficient to pay ... the wages of the labour, and the profits of the stock employed

---

15. The strict constancy of relative prices over time is *not* part of the definition of long-period prices, cf. Chapter 4.

..., according to their natural rates, the commodity is then sold for what may be called its natural price...

The natural price ... is, as it were, the central price, to which the prices of all commodities are continually gravitating. Different accidents may sometimes keep them suspended a good deal above it, and sometimes force them down even somewhat below it. But whatever may be the obstacles which hinder them from settling in this center of repose and continuance, they are constantly tending towards it (Smith, 1776 [1975], I, vii, p. 48, 51).

or Ricardo where we read

Having fully acknowledged the temporary effects which, in particular employments of capital, may be produced on the prices of commodities, as well as on the wages of labour, and profits of stock, by accidental causes, without influencing the general price of commodities, wages or profits, since these effects are equally operative in all stages of society, we will leave them entirely out of consideration, whilst we are treating of the laws which regulate natural prices, natural wages, and natural profits ... (1951, ch. 4, pp. 91–2)

we find Marshall writing:

The actual value at any time, the market value as it is often called, is often more influenced by passing events, and by causes whose action is fitful and short lived, than by those which work persistently. But in long periods these fitful and irregular causes in large measure efface one another's influence so that in the long run persistent causes dominate value completely (1920 [1970], V. 3.7, p. 291).

and Walras likening the equilibrium to the normal level of a lake:

It never happens in the real world that the selling price of any given product is absolutely equal to the cost of the productive services that enter into that product, or that the effective demand and supply of services or products are absolutely equal. Yet equilibrium is the normal state, in the sense that it is the state towards which things spontaneously tend under a régime of free competition in exchange and in production (Walras, 1954, pp. 224–5).

And Wicksell:

in the long run the prices of the various commodities will be stationary at, or oscillate about, the point of equilibrium between production and consumption ... (1923 [1934], p. 53).

1.2.7. In recent decades neoclassical textbooks have been very hesitant on the connection between the determination of equilibria and the explanation of real economic phenomena, and have been dominated by descriptions of the tendency to equilibrium in terms of instantaneous tâtonnements. So it is opportune to insist that the role traditionally assigned to equilibria by marginalist authors was the very concrete and relevant one of determining the average or trend of the observed prices and quantities of economies *admitted to be continually in disequilibrium*.

Let us provide some examples of applications of the traditional method – in a marginalist/neoclassical framework, the one with which the reader is certainly familiar.

We may start by considering an imaginary exchange economy where the big market fair is repeated once a week, always with the same data: week after week, the same agents arrive at the market with the same endowments of goods (for example hunting game, agricultural products, handicrafts) and the same tastes, and there are no intertemporal deals of lending and borrowing. When this economy is in equilibrium, then, week after week, the exchanges are repeated in unchanged fashion. If now the equilibrium (assumed, for the sake of argument, to be unique) were one day changed by, say, a once-and-for-all change in tastes (for example it is discovered that a certain meat is bad for health), it would be unrealistic to expect that the new equilibrium will be reached in the first market fair after the change; it will be necessary for the agents to discover the new equilibrium prices by trial and error, so the new equilibrium can only be approached over a number of fairs, in each of which there will be disequilibrium transactions and price changes.[16] *However, during this sequence of weeks the new equilibrium remains unchanged*, and, assuming the agents succeed in gradually correcting the disequilibrium mistakes as successive fairs unfold, the equilibrium can be viewed as a centre of gravitation attracting toward itself the actual behaviour of the economy. If we now introduce a bit more realism, then owing to a variety of accidental and transitory causes (for example irregular results of hunting or crops; or accidental fires destroying the accumulated handicrafts of some producers) the economy may be unable actually to reach the equilibrium before its data change (for example owing to deaths, births, changes of tastes). But, if the gravitation toward equilibrium exists, and if the data do not change too often or too quickly, then the equilibrium will still give a good indication of the average behaviour of the economy; and its changes can be used to explain and predict the changes in the actual averages of the observed, disequilibrium magnitudes.

I reproduce from a previous paper of mine (Petri, 1978) a further example, still internal to the marginalist approach, but now allowing for produced

16. 'Walras' system of prices [for an exchange economy] will be reached, either if contracts are made provisionally or (a more important case) if people come on to the market on successive "days" with the same dispositions to trade, and there is no carry-over of stocks (or a constant carry-over) from one day to the next' (Hicks, 1934, p. 91).

goods (but no capital goods). Let us imagine an economy with only two factors, both in fixed supply: one type of labour and one type of land; these are hired by entrepreneurs to produce a variety of consumption goods. Let us imagine that the (let's assume unique) competitive equilibrium of this economy is one day disturbed by immigration: the supply of labour undergoes a once-and-for-all increase. Traditional marginalist authors would have agreed that, given time, competition would push down the wage rate until a new full employment equilibrium were reached. They would have agreed that the process would be a gradual one, taking time and gradually extending to the whole economy from the town where the immigrants first arrive: the lower wage caused by excess labour supply in this town would take time to spread throughout the economy, in the meantime causing disequilibrium, non-zero 'extra-profits',[17] gradual alterations of rents, and internal migrations of labour. Product prices and quantities would also be changing, and time would be required for them to tend toward the new equilibrium. As in the exchange economy example, the (theoretically defined) new equilibrium is not affected by the trial-and-error processes of adaptation of supply and demand: it is the 'centre of gravitation' to which the economy approaches ever more closely. Thus, the comparison of the old and the new equilibrium allows an understanding of a process of change in real time.[18]

The usefulness of the equilibrium in these examples lies then in its indicating the 'centre of gravitation' of actual prices and quantities, and thus in giving a good indication (assuming the theory were sound) of the average values of the actual prices and quantities, and – through its shifts – of the trends of these average values.

1.2.8. In the above examples, in order for the equilibrium to have the explanatory role assigned to it (as well as in order to discuss its stability), there is no need to assume that the adjustment to equilibrium is carried out while economic activity is suspended (that is with no production and no actual exchanges taking place until equilibrium is reached). There is room for real time, mistakes, disequilibrium productions and disequilibrium exchanges. The reason for this is that the data which determine the equilibrium in these examples are independent of the details of the time-consuming disequilibrium processes which are supposed to push the economy toward equilibrium. In fact, a logical necessity of a method that tries to explain

17. Cf. fn. 5.
18. Cf. Petri (1978, p. 249) for a demonstration that only an implicit acceptance of fundamentally the same 'gravitation' hypothesis appears to justify the assumption, common to all price theories, that all the units of the same commodity or service sell at the same price.

actual observed magnitudes as oscillating around 'centres of gravitation' is that these 'centres' must not be affected by the day-by-day disequilibrium production and consumption activities of the economic agents.

Of course the persistence of the data in the sense specified does not require that the data do not change at all: marginalist economists adhering to this traditional method obviously did not deny that tastes, population and technical knowledge do change, but rather, estimated that their changes were generally either slow enough to be negligible relative to the presumable speed of adaptation of demand and supply for factors and products, or were once-and-for-all changes, whose effects could be dealt with through comparative statics, that is by assuming a tendency to the corresponding new equilibrium.

1.2.9. That this is the kind of equilibrium that it is sensible for a marginalist theorist to attempt to determine should be clear once it is accepted that, as John Hicks wrote in *Value and Capital*: 'the adjustments needed to bring about equilibrium take time' (Hicks, 1946, p. 116). Quotations to the same effect from other marginalist, or neoclassical, authors could easily be given; I cite only one, from a recent paper by Frank H. Hahn (1999, p. 189): 'adjustments take time and do not occur instantaneously as postulated in Chicago and Minnesota'.[19]

It seems impossible to disagree with Hicks or Hahn on this point. In most markets, agents take time to decide that they should alter the price they ask for what they offer, or the price they offer for what they ask. In some trades where customers are not very numerous, for example houses, or antiques, this time may be very long, even several months; but even in trades with a constant flow of customers, such as most retail trades, it takes time for a seller to make sure that an unusually low turnout of customers is not due to the normal stochastic element in the turnout of demanders and is on the contrary indicative of a lower average demand, requiring a lower price or a diminished flow of supplies, or both. The variation in demand, induced by a variation of price, may also take a considerable time to manifest itself: investment decisions, for example, often take a long time, requiring the gathering and assessing of information. And while prices change, production flows change too, such that the adjustment of demand to supply must start anew. In markets such as local fish markets, where every day a variable supply of perishable goods must be disposed of, the assumption that a 'temporary equilibrium price' is rapidly established every day for each kind

19. As a criticism of the monetarist and of the so-called New Classical schools of macroeconomic theory, it is not evident that Hahn's statement really hits the mark; but here we can leave this issue aside, the important thing for our purposes is Hahn's agreement that adjustments take time.

of fish is legitimate only as long as supply and demand conditions are within the consolidated experience of traders. If there were to be an important change in one of the constituent elements of the market, for example the disappearance of some kinds of fish owing to pollution, or an important change in tastes owing to new information about health effects of certain kinds of fish, it would take several repetitions of markets for traders to learn again which prices will clear the market on different days of the week and for different supplies.

1.2.10. An important implication, central to this book, is the following. If one wants to extend the method of the previous examples – the determination of a 'centre of gravitation' of time-consuming adjustment processes – to an economy with produced means of production (capital goods), then the need to conceive the processes establishing the convergence to equilibrium as real processes happening in real time, that is as processes taking time and involving mistakes, imperfect information, the implementation of out-of-equilibrium decisions, and so on, *makes it impossible to include the endowment of each type of capital goods among the data determining the 'centre of gravitation'.*[20] The amounts in existence of most capital goods are liable to change drastically in a very short time, if firms so decide. Let us in fact remember that, if one took a snapshot of an economy at a certain moment, the vector of endowments of capital goods would include given amounts of bolts, of nails, of intermediate products in the oil refining process, of component parts of goods-yet-to-be-assembled, and so on: in other words goods, the existing amounts of which might vary drastically even in a few hours, if for any reason firms were to decide to stop producing them, or to increase their production in order to increase the production of the final products for which they are needed.

   As a consequence, the positions qualifying as 'centres of gravitation' in a general equilibrium analysis must be such that the relative amounts of the several capital goods in existence have themselves reached an equilibrium. The need for an endogenous determination of the equilibrium endowments of the several capital goods is indeed admitted by traditional marginalist authors, as will be made clear by several citations below.

1.2.11. On the force, that would tend to adjust the stocks of capital goods to the demands for them, one again finds a total accord between classical and marginalist authors. This force was that same mobility of capitals in the search for the highest rate of return on investment, which was seen as

---

20. The *very* durable produced means of production (for example dams), once built, are more appropriately seen as analogous to natural resources.

responsible for the tendency of relative prices toward long-period prices; in other words, for the tendency of rates of return on supply price to tend toward uniformity. The argument is well known, and can be equivalently explained by assuming that the relevant rates of return are those to be earned on each capital good, or on the capital of firms. If for instance one assumes that consumers save by purchasing capital goods that are then hired by firms, then as entrepreneurs move about, entering and leaving industries in their search for positive extra-profits, this process will alter the rentals of the capital goods, and hence the rates of return to be earned by buying these capital goods and lending them to entrepreneurs. The prices of the capital goods yielding rates of return higher than the rate of interest (increased to make an opportune allowance for risk) will go up, owing to the high demand for them; this in turn will stimulate increases in their supplies (if the required flow of supply is greater than existing normal capacity, existing enterprises will build new plants or new enterprises will be set up). But their endowments having thus increased, their rentals will go down, and, with them, the rates of return obtainable by their purchase. These adjustments will go on until the rates of return on their purchase costs (supply prices) become equalized, and become equal to the rate of interest plus an allowance for risk (extra-profits, net of risk allowances, disappear). Only then will relative prices stop changing. Therefore the prices which qualify as 'centres of gravitation' of time-consuming adjustment processes must be associated with a Uniform Rate of Return (equal, when net of risk, to the rate of interest) over the Supply Prices of the capital goods: URRSP in the sequel.

Thus, corresponding to John Stuart Mill who wrote:

> The cost of production, together with the ordinary profit, may, therefore be called the *necessary* price or value, of all things made by labour and capital. Nobody willingly produces in the prospect of a loss. Whoever does so, does it under a miscalculation, which he corrects as fast as he is able ... Whenever a new line of business presents itself, offering a hope of unusual profits, and whenever any established trade or manufacture is believed to be yielding a greater profit than customary, there is sure to be in a short time so large a production or importation of the commodity, as not only destroys the extra profit, but generally goes beyond the mark, and sinks the value as much too low as it had before been raised too high; until the over-supply is corrected by a total or partial suspension of further production (Mill, 1904, bk. III, ch. III, §1, p. 274).

one finds for example Walras writing:

> Capital goods proper are artificial capital goods; they are products and their prices are subject to the law of cost of production. If their selling price is greater than their cost of production, the quantity produced will increase and their selling price

will fall; if their selling price is lower than their cost of production the quantity produced will diminish and their selling price will rise. In equilibrium their selling price and their cost of production are equal (Walras, 1954, p. 271).

(These lines indicate why Walras is a special case among traditional marginalist authors. In his general equilibrium equations, Walras assumes the equality between cost of production and 'selling price' (demand price), that is the uniformity of the rate of return on supply price, for all capital goods. This is the distinctive mark of long-period analysis. The above quotation furthermore argues that it is changes in the relative endowments of the several capital goods that bring about this equality: the reason why an increase in 'the quantity produced' brings about a lower 'selling price' for a capital good can only be the decreased scarcity of that capital good, brought about by the increase in its endowment caused by the increased production. Thus Walras admits here, no less than Wicksell or J.B. Clark, that the condition of a uniform rate of return on supply price implies that the endowments of the several capital goods should be treated as variables. But Walras, alone among the founders of the marginalist approach, includes the endowment of each capital good among the data of the equilibrium. This contradiction will require a discussion of the correctness of the reference to Walras as the founder of modern general equilibrium theory, in Chapter 5.)

1.2.12. The same idea of a gravitation towards uniform-rate-of-return prices, due to free entry and to alterations of the relative amounts in existence of the several capital goods, is found in Smith and Ricardo. In their terminology, this is expressed as a gravitation toward a uniform rate of profits, because they defined the profits of the firm as what is left of revenue, after subtraction of costs *except* interest and risk allowance: the rate of profits is then simply the rate of return (gross of the risk allowance) on the firm's capital; and they preferred to describe firms as purchasing the capital goods to be used, rather than hiring them from consumers. But of course the final result of the process is the same. Except for total flukes (differences in the rates of return on the several capital goods, which exactly compensate one another at the firm level), if and only if the rate of profits net of risk[21] is the same for all firms, will the rate of return (net of risk) also be the same on each different capital good's supply price.

---

21. It was admitted by classical economists that the rates of profits gross of the reward for risk might persistently differ in different industries owing to various causes, for example the different likelihood of unforeseen variations in demand, or the different irregularity in the results of productive activity (for example droughts in agriculture). For the sake of simplicity this is left out of the analysis in the usual theory of prices of production as formulated for example by Sraffa (1960).

We have touched here a point of great importance for a correct appreciation of the differences between the classical and the marginalist approaches. Both approaches argue that relative product prices gravitate toward those values that yield a uniform rate of profit (net of risk), or, equivalently, a uniform rate of interest on the supply price of capital goods. This accord between the two approaches is made less easy to grasp by the differences in terminology (especially the different meaning of profit), but the above discussion should have clarified the possible confusions. When a classical author like Ricardo (or Marx) argues that product prices tend toward natural prices or prices of production, that is prices which yield a uniform rate of profits (equal, apart from risk, to the rate of interest), he argues exactly the same thing as a marginalist author like Wicksell or Walras who argue that profits tend everywhere toward zero and the rate of return (net of risk) on the supply price of capital goods tends to be equalized and equal to the rate of interest.

1.2.13. A further element common to both classical and traditional marginalist authors is the persuasion that the changes that long-period relative prices may be undergoing over time, can be generally assumed to be either so slow as to be negligible, or to be once-and-for-all changes to be analysed through the method of comparative statics, that is by assuming a tendency to the new long-period position[22] defined by assuming the new data will again be constant. Therefore in both groups of authors one finds that in the equations defining long-period prices a product that is also used as an input (that is, a capital good) has the same price as an input and as an output: that is the changes that relative prices may be undergoing even in a situation of URRSP are neglected as normally of secondary importance.

It cannot then cause surprise that in Wicksell or in Walras, as will be shown in Chapter 3, the sub-group of the equations of general equilibrium, which determines the relative prices of produced commodities once the rate of interest (or the real wage) is given, is equivalent (if the same assumptions are made as to the type of technology, for example point-input-point-output) to the equations one finds in Piero Sraffa's *Production of commodities by means of commodities*, the 1960 book which is universally admitted to have finally satisfactorily formulated the theory of 'natural prices', or 'prices of production', that Ricardo was groping towards.[23]

22. Among classical authors, the absence of the supply-and-demand forces of marginalist theory renders the term 'equilibrium' inappropriate for the positions their long-period analyses tried to determine.
23. Sraffa (1960). For concise introductions to Sraffa's contribution and to its place in economic theory cf. Garegnani (1987), Kurz (1985), Schefold (1989, pp. 1–38).

Thus, it is not here that the difference between the two approaches lies; once the data necessary to determine relative product prices (technical coefficients, and either the real wage rate or the rate of profits, and also, if there are scarce natural resources, the quantities produced) are given, both approaches determine the same normal, or long-period, prices.

The fundamental difference between classical and marginalist approaches is rather to be found in the forces that, in the two approaches, determine the rate of profits (or of return, or of interest), and thus also the rate of wages in terms of the chosen numeraire (since, as will be shown, the system of equations determining long-period relative prices, the rate of profits, and the real wage, has only one degree of freedom, then whatever determines the rate of profits also determines the real wage, and vice versa).

One finds therefore, in the history of economic thought, an extremely strong consensus on two theses: first, that the prices around and toward which day-by-day prices can be taken to gravitate in competitive economies must be the prices which cover the costs of the means of production and of labour and, besides, guarantee a uniform rate of return, or of interest – or, in classical terminology, of profits – on the supply prices of the capital goods. Second, that the process which causes day-by-day prices to gravitate toward those prices is the process of adaptation of the productive capacities of the various industries to the respective normal demands. The same process was thought to cause the relative quantities produced to gravitate around and toward the quantities demanded at these long-period normal prices.

The method of explanation adopted was therefore the following: first, determine the long-period position of the economy; on that basis, use comparative statics to determine changes brought about by changes in the persistent forces acting on the economy; on that same basis, introduce rigidities, imperfect adjustments, short-lived phenomena in order to try and derive definite conclusions, where possible, on short-period deviations from long-period positions.[24] The spread of Marshallian terminology suggests 'method of long-period positions' as one possible name for this method.[25]

24. Cf. Ciccone (1999) for a detailed analysis of the differences in this respect between classical authors and Marshall.
25. For other descriptions of the method of long-period positions one may consult Garegnani (1976, where the term was first introduced), Eatwell (1979), Milgate (1982). For the sake of simplicity, the process of convergence to a long-period position has been described here as a process to a situation of constant prices. In fact the strict constancy of relative prices through time is not a necessary element of a long-period position, which therefore – contrary to a widespread opinion – need not be a stationary or steady-growth state; cf. Chapter 4. But when the composition of capital has adapted to the composition of demand, the endogenous changes in relative prices (for example brought about, in a marginalist framework, by a speed of accumulation of capital different from the speed of growth of labour supply) will

1.3. CAPITAL AS A HOMOGENEOUS FACTOR AND ITS ROLES

1.3.1. In relation to the marginalist tradition, we have now an initial basis to understand the reason for the generalized presence of capital conceived in some way or other as a single factor, embodying itself in the several physically different capital goods, and capable of changing 'form' without changing 'quantity'.[26]

The determination of an equilibrium between supply of and demand for factors rests, among other things, on the possibility of treating three groups of data as given, those on which the functioning and the results of the mechanisms of factor substitution rest, namely:

1. the endowments of factors of production (and their distribution among consumers),
2. the alternative production methods for the several products,
3. the tastes of consumers.

It is the data of the first group which interest us here. If among the factors there are capital goods, then a problem arises as to the specification of their endowments.

As already noticed, if one wants to couple the method of long-period positions with the marginalist attempt to determine the 'centre of gravitation' of prices and quantities as resulting from an equilibrium between supply of and demand for given factor endowments, then the several capital goods cannot appear among these factors. This is because their relative total endowments cannot be taken as given, since they are subject to quick alteration unless they are in those proportions that guarantee a uniform rate of return on supply price. But then how can supply and demand determine their prices and rates of remuneration?

1.3.2. The traditional marginalist solution consisted of conceiving the several capital goods as embodying different amounts of 'capital', a single factor capable of changing 'form' (that is composition) without changing its total 'quantity' (a quantity measurable in terms of a single unit). The best analogy I have been able to find is with a total quantity of carbon dioxide congealed into pieces of 'dry ice' of certain shapes and weights, which gradually

generally be so slow that traditional authors appear to have been correct in implicitly assuming that they can be disregarded.
26. The argument to be presented develops the analyses of Garegnani (1960, 1976, 1990a), Petri (1978), Eatwell (1979, 1982), Milgate (1982).

evaporate, but are replaced by other pieces created by the gradual congealing of gas equal in amount to that which has evaporated; the newly congealed gas might go to form pieces of different weights and shapes. In this analogy the quantity is measured by weight; as we shall better see later, the quantity of 'capital' was seen, and had to be seen, as a quantity of value: the change in the 'form' of this single factor was seen to be brought about by the employment of the resources, which might have been used to produce the no-longer produced capital goods, in the production of different capital goods – which, since produced by the same resources, would have the same total cost of production and hence the same total value as the no-longer produced capital goods.

This conception made it possible to treat the endowment of this homogeneous 'capital' as given, while at the same time allowing the endowments of the several capital goods to be determined endogenously by the equilibrium. The endowment of 'capital' was treated as given on a par with the endowments of the non-produced factors, when determining the (long-period) equilibrium.

The presence in J.B. Clark of this conception of capital as a single factor which can be taken as given in quantity although variable in 'form' is widely acknowledged. What is nowadays perhaps less widely perceived is that such a conception was nearly universal among marginalist authors until the 1930s (the sole relevant exception among the founders of marginalism, and an only partial one at that, being Walras – who will need special attention later), and remained generally accepted even after that date.

Jevons, the first author to formulate a marginal-productivity approach to the explanation of the return to capital, was the inventor of the notion that a greater quantity of capital ('amount of investment of capital' in Jevons's terminology) permits a lengthening of – in later terminology – the 'degree of roundaboutness' or 'average period' of production (that is the average interval between the application of original factors and the sale of the final result of the production process): a lengthening that, ceteris paribus, permits an increased production (this conception, usually associated with the Austrian school, is examined more analytically in Appendix 3A). The conception implies that, in order to combine the same capital with a different quantity of labour, the degree of roundaboutness of production must change, which entails different production techniques, hence different intermediate goods present in the economy, hence a different composition of the physical capital of the economy. Thus Jevons implicitly lets the physical composition of capital change when he changes the proportion between the quantity of capital and labour.[27]

27. Cf. Steedman (1972) for a careful examination of Jevons' theory of capital.

Jevons' conception of the quantity of capital as made up of the product of a quantity of advanced wage goods times an average period of production was later taken up and made more precise by Böhm-Bawerk, and then inserted into a formalized general-equilibrium analysis by Wicksell (1893). In the 'Austrian' school too, therefore, one finds a very explicit conception of capital as a single quantity, of variable 'form'.

In J.B. Clark, Marshall, and the Marshallian school, capital is more directly conceived as a quantity of exchange value (although references to the degree of roundaboutness of production methods also appear); the variability of its 'form' is explicity stressed in these authors. Thus one finds statements by J.B. Clark such as:

> Where there is a capital of five hundred dollars for each worker, that fund is in one set of forms; and where there is a capital of a thousand dollars per man, it is in a different set ... That the relative *amounts* of labor and capital should change, means that the *forms* of both should change (Clark, 1925, p. 159, 160);

> As we take away laborers, we leave the capital everywhere unchanged in amount; but we change the forms of it in every one of the industries, so as to make it accurately fit the needs of the slightly reduced working force ... The abandoned pick and shovel become, by miracle of transmutation, an improvement in the quality of horse and cart. There are fewer men digging; but they have as much capital as ever, and they have it in a form in which, with their reduced numbers, they can use it (ibid., p. 170).

These lines express the same conception as does Robertson when, in *Wage Grumbles*, he argues that when ten workers dig with ten spades, in order to determine the marginal product of an eleventh worker one must allow the ten spades to become eleven smaller spades, or perhaps ten smaller spades and a bucket, with which the eleventh worker brings refreshment to the other ten (Robertson, 1931, p. 227). The same conception again emerges clearly in Hicks when in *The Theory of Wages* he argues that the definition of a meaningful marginal product of labour requires that the 'form' of capital change together with the change in the capital–labour proportion, in a passage which deserves quoting at length:

> ... There can be no full equilibrium unless the wages of labour equal its marginal product ...
> It does not follow, however, that because the marginal product of labour has changed, therefore the level of wages will change in the same direction at once ... a rise in the marginal productivity of labour with constant wages (or a fall in the wage with constant marginal productivity) does not necessarily lead employers to expand their demand for labour at once ...

The principal reason for this 'lag' is to be found in the fact that one of the co-operating factors – capital – is, at any particular moment, largely incorporated in goods of a certain degree of durability ... if the capital is at present invested in durable goods, the change in conduct which follows from the change in relative profitability cannot immediately be realised. At the moment, only a small portion of the total supply of capital is 'free' – available for investment in new forms – and although this portion will be reinvested in ways more appropriate to the new situation, that in itself may make very little difference to the demand for labour ... In the short period, therefore, it is reasonable to expect that the demand for labour will be very inelastic, since the possibility of adjusting the organization of industry to a changed level of wages is relatively small ...

Since the whole conception of marginal productivity depends upon the variability of industrial methods, little advantage seems to be gained from the attempt which is sometimes made to define a 'short period marginal product' – the additional production due to a small increase in the quantity of labour, when not only the quantity, but also the form, of the co-operating capital is supposed unchanged. It is very doubtful if this conception can be given any precise meaning which is capable of useful application (Hicks, 1932, pp. 18–21).

This passage is interesting also because it exhibits one important aspect of the traditional marginalist conception of capital as a factor of variable 'form'. The variability of the 'form' was obviously not conceived as instantaneous: at each moment of time the 'capital' of an economy would be, so to speak, 'crystallized' in specific capital goods, and could take the 'form' best adapted to changed demand, price or technical-progress conditions only gradually, as the existing capital goods were consumed and the 'capital' embodied in them became 'free' to be reinvested in different capital goods (through the employment of the resources, which might have reproduced the scrapped capital goods, to produce different capital goods). This meant that the 'marginal product of capital' could only concretely manifest itself, and be adapted to the rate of interest, in the investments in new plants,[28] where the flow of 'free' 'capital' would meet the flow of labour 'freed' by the gradual closure of plants reaching the end of their economic life,[29] and where therefore the 'capital'–labour ratio could be chosen as the one dictated by the

28. Thus one finds for example Knight (writing in 1946): 'Under conditions of perfect competition, or in an economic system in the position of the theoretical equilibrium (stationary or moving), all sources would yield a uniform rate of return on their cost of production, which would be equal both to their cost of reproduction and their market value ... Under real conditions, this rate "tends" to be approximated at the margin of new investment (or disinvestment), with allowance for the uncertainties and errors of prediction' (Knight, 1946, p. 396).
29. The existing plants would normally keep employing most of the supply of labour, since, once in existence, it would be convenient to go on operating them as long as they yielded non-negative residual quasi-rents. Cf. Garegnani (1978).

current income distribution and demand conditions. Thus the notion of 'free' capital, which appears in one form or another in nearly all the traditional marginalist authors,[30] is only one more manifestation of the underlying conception of capital as ultimately a single factor of variable 'form'.

Further evidence of the general acceptance of that conception of capital even in subsequent years is provided by Kaldor, who very clearly treats capital as a single factor in his 1937 survey of the debates of those years on the theory of capital.

1.3.3. The reason for the general acceptance of that conception of capital was that it had fundamental analytical roles within the marginalist approach to value and distribution. A good grasp of these roles, such as is not often found nowadays, is fundamental to an understanding of the present situation of the neoclassical approach. A large part of the remainder of this book will be dedicated to clarifying these roles, after briefly indicating them now. We can distinguish a supply-side from a demand-side role.

The *supply-side role* has already been indicated: that conception made it possible to arrive at a determinate equilibrium, while leaving the endowments of the several capital goods to be endogenously determined by the tendency toward a uniform rate of return on supply price; thus the endowments of the several capital goods were *not* data of the equilibrium, what would have deprived the equilibrium of the persistence required to conceive it as the centre of gravitation of day-by-day magnitudes; it was the endowment of 'capital' (the single factor) which was taken as a datum. This gave the equilibrium the same persistence as when the factors were labour and land, and thus it allowed the use of the method illustrated in the examples of §1.2.4 and §1.2.7, based on time-consuming disequilibria. (This role is lost with the shift to the modern versions of general equilibrium: Chapter 2 will discuss the consequences.) Chapter 3, by illustrating the analytical structure of the (long-period) equilibria based on that conception

30. Cf. for example Marshall, 1920 [1970], VI, ii, §4 (p. 443): '... the income derived from capital already invested in particular things, such as factories or ships, is properly a quasi-rent and can be regarded as interest only on the assumption that the capital value of the investment has remained unaltered ... the phrase "the general rate of interest" applies in strictness only to the anticipated net earnings from new investments of free capital'; and cf. also ibid., VI, vi, §6 (p. 492), where he adds that, since replacement investment is the larger part of gross investment: 'It is therefore not unreasonable to assume for the present that the owners of capital in general have been able in the main to adapt its forms to the normal conditions of the time, so as to derive as good a *net* income from their investments in one way as another. It is only on this supposition that we are at liberty to speak of capital in general as being accumulated under the expectation of a certain net interest which is the same for all its forms'. For Wicksell's analogous notion of 'free' capital cf. for example Wicksell (1935, p. 192).

of capital, will make it possible to surmount the widespread misunderstanding which identifies the conception of 'capital' as a single factor with the use of aggregate production functions. It will be shown that the traditional equilibria were fully disaggregated general equilibria and nonetheless needed the conception of capital as a single factor of variable 'form', because they left the composition of capital to be determined endogenously by the equilibrium. But it will also be argued that this supply-side role is undermined by the impossibility of specifying the endowment of 'capital' so conceived independently of what the equilibrium should determine.

The *demand-side role* of that conception was that it justified the treatment of 'capital' as analogous to that of any other factor of production in the direct and indirect factor substitution mechanisms, thus permitting the conclusion that the demand for 'capital' was a decreasing function of its price, that is of the rate of interest. One may distinguish two aspects of this demand-side role. The first one was that the postulate that 'capital' could be treated as any physical factor made it possible to assume that the substitution mechanisms worked in the 'right' direction; the rate of interest could then be seen as the price bringing into equality the supply of and the demand for 'capital', and therefore also the supply of, and the demand for, savings or loanable funds.[31] Thus the decreasing demand curve for 'capital' was the basis for the acceptance of 'Say's Law', which for the purposes of this book will be taken to mean the tendency of investment to adapt to savings rather than vice versa.[32] The second aspect was that the variable 'form' of 'capital' made it possible to assume a *sufficient* substitutability between 'capital', and labour or land; such a sufficient substitutability was impossible to conceive for the single capital goods, as openly admitted for example by Hicks (cf. the quotation in §1.3.2, and Chapter 2). The Cambridge results on reswitching and reverse capital deepening undermine this second role, as will be explained in Chapter 6, with radical consequences for the mainstream approach to aggregate investment, and to the demand for labour, as will be explained in Chapters 7 and 8.

31. The traditional marginalist connection between demand for capital and demand for savings will be discussed in detail in Section 4.3.
32. It may be opportune to note that in the classical authors who, like Ricardo, accepted Say's Law (that is accepted that all savings would translate into investment so that the possibility of 'general gluts' could be excluded), the reason was *not* an equilibrating role attributed to the rate of interest on the basis of a decreasing demand curve for capital or for loanable funds (Garegnani, 1964 [1978]; Caminati, 1981; Petri, 1983). The absence of the notion of decreasing demand curves for factors in these authors also shows up in the fact that Say's Law was not meant to imply a tendency toward the full employment of labour.

1.4. NEO-WALRASIAN EQUILIBRIA

1.4.1. These analytical clarifications should make it easier to understand why the long-period method, although still largely used in much applied economics, has been increasingly abandoned in recent decades in the (maistream) pure theory of value.

The reason is that the general equilibria used as the foundation of this theory have been more and more formulated as including, among their data, the endowment of *each* of the several capital goods. The equilibria thus determined – equilibria that will be called *neo-Walrasian* in this book – are *very-short-period* equilibria, corresponding, but at the economy-wide level, to Marshall's momentary equilibrium on a fish market. Capital goods are produced inputs, whose endowments in most instances can be altered very quickly by a difference between the rate of production and the rate of destruction through use; so the endowment of a capital good cannot generally be taken as given for more than a *very* short time interval. This fact is sometimes partially obscured by a tendency to identify capital with *durable* capital goods only; but this tendency is clearly a mistake. If one considers an economy at a certain instant, then the quantities of intermediate capital goods existing at that instant, even if destined to be transformed into something else a few seconds later, nonetheless are constraints on the production possibilities of the economy just as much as the available quantities of durable capital goods.[33]

This treatment of the capital endowment as a given *vector* of endowments is the key to many other aspects of modern general equilibrium theory.

1.4.2. A first aspect which depends on the given vector of capital endowments is the need to take the subsequent presumable evolution of relative prices into account, in determining the decisions of agents. The reason is that the initial relative endowments of capital goods, being arbitrary, will often undergo very rapid alteration in order to be adjusted to the demand for them, with a consequent rapid change in their prices. Thus relative prices may easily be far from approximately constant; and then it is no longer legitimate to neglect relative price changes. Thus the equal convenience of investment in all kinds of income-producing assets cannot be determined while neglecting the subsequent changes in the relative rentals of

---

33. Thus for example Hicks has written that within the single 'week' of a temporary equilibrium: 'The actual outputs of products, and probably also the actual input of labour, would be largely predetermined' by the impossibility to change half-way a production process started before the 'week' commenced (Hicks, 1980–81, p. 55). Furthermore, even if the existing stock of a durable capital good cannot quickly *decrease*, it can often be very quickly *increased* if the productive resources of the economy are addressed to such an end.

the several capital goods, what was on the contrary legitimate in long-period equilibria owing to the slowness, if not absence, of those changes.

In this respect two approaches have been explored: on one hand, in the particular period under consideration, the existence of complete futures markets has been assumed such that it is possible to stipulate contracts for future (possibly contingent) delivery, in which case the subsequent prices of goods are actually quoted in the initial period and the equilibrium is simultaneously established for subsequent periods too (one has then an *intertemporal equilibrium*); or, on the other hand, it has been assumed that agents act on the basis of subjective, and possibly mistaken, expectations of subsequent developments (one has then a *temporary equilibrium*).

Modern neoclassical introductions to value theory propose the interpretation of the equilibrium in terms of dated commodities and discounted prices from the very beginning, that is already when discussing the pure-exchange case. The dating of commodities identifies the equilibrium with a specific instant, the instant from which the equilibrium commences; the arbitrary endowments include endowments of different dates, and nothing prevents them from being very different from one period to the next; this means that the temporal path of equilibrium prices and quantities may well show relevant changes of relative prices over time. This deprives the equilibrium of any possibility of being conceived as a persistent position that, so to speak, 'stays there' while the economy tries to approach it in real time. Thus the original role of equilibrium as the persistent situation which the economy approaches through time-consuming trial and error never appears in the modern neoclassical introductions to equilibrium theory. Modern students therefore remain ignorant of the original conception of equilibrium, the one on whose basis the entire edifice of marginalist/neoclassical economics was conceived, built and accepted. Furthermore, since in most applications they find the notion of equilibrium still used in the traditional way, modern students are induced to believe that the neo-Walrasian notions of equilibrium can support those applications – a mistake which much of this book aims to expose.

1.4.3. A second aspect in which modern general equilibrium models differ from traditional treatments, is the possible presence of inventories of pure consumption goods among the initial endowments even in production economies. This is because the equilibrium must have among its data the existing amounts of goods at a precise moment, and then inventories must also be included among these data. A long-period equilibrium, on the contrary, since it aimed at determining the normal flows of products once the composition of capital had adjusted, could neglect inventories (or determine them endogenously if need be), and took only the endowments of factors of production as given.

1.4.4. A third aspect is the need to study the stability of equilibrium through processes that do not entail production: otherwise production would change the endowments of capital goods and thus the data of the equilibrium. This is the reason why the tâtonnement with provisional 'tickets' has become central to stability studies. The main role of the mythical 'auctioneer' is that of preventing the endowments of the several capital goods from changing during the disequilibrium trial-and-error search for equilibrium.[34] But since such suspension of economic activity until an equilibrium is reached is never to be found in real economies, the auctioneer's story implies that one is simply assuming *instantaneous* equilibration.

This poses the problem of the extent to which the results of an assumption of instantaneous equilibration are misleading relative to a reality where disequilibrium transactions and productions do happen. In order to understand whether this extent is considerable or negligible, one would require an analysis of economies *not* all the time in equilibrium.[35]

At present there are two types of analyses of this kind. One is the study of non-tâtonnement adjustment processes in disaggregated economies, a study which is confined to pure-exchange economies except for Fisher (1983): the latter book is discussed in Chapter 2, and found unhelpful because it reaches very indeterminate results. The other is macroeconomic theory; but, it will be argued in Chapters 7 and 8, macroeconomic theory is only able to reach conclusions favourable to the neoclassical approach in so far as it relies upon an implicit or explicit adherence to the traditional conception of capital as a single factor. The importance of the Cambridge criticisms of that conception of capital will then be evident.

1.5. LONG-PERIOD DOES NOT MEAN LONG-RUN

1.5.1. Before entering more detailed analyses, it is opportune to eliminate some possible misunderstandings on the meaning of the term 'long-period equilibria'. In recent writings, *'long-run* analysis' usually refers to an analysis of growth, that is, of the effects of capital accumulation and labour supply growth; this is contrasted with *'short-run* analysis' by which is meant

---

34. Cf. Chapter 5 for a confirmation of this role on the basis of the evolution of Walras's analysis.
35. 'If disequilibrium effects are in fact unimportant we need to prove that they are. If such effects are important, then the way in which we tend to think about the theory of value needs to be revised' (Fisher, 1983, p. 217).

an analysis in which accumulation does not have the time to change significantly the overall productive capacity of the economy. But the term '*short-run* analysis' is also often intended in a more restricted sense, to mean that the vector of endowments of capital goods is given; thus the term 'short-run *equilibrium*' often means some kind of neo-Walrasian equilibrium where the endowments of the several capital goods are all given. By contrast, what is nowadays meant by 'long-run *equilibrium*' is generally a (full-employment) steady-state, or a secularly stationary equilibrium where the capital–labour ratio has itself reached an equilibrium (all these notions will be more precisely defined in subsequent chapters).

This is *not* the meaning of 'long-period' in this book. Here, the meaning of long-period analyses is the traditional, Marshallian one. Long-period analyses here are those where one abstracts from the effects of growth on the overall productive capacity of the economy, while the composition of capital is endogenously determined. This composition is assumed to adapt itself to the composition of production so as to yield a uniform rate of return on supply price for all capital goods (an assumption which does *not* entail steady growth nor a secular stationary state, as clarified later, in Chapter 4). Thus, in a long-period equilibrium, which is the form taken in traditional marginalist theory by the notion of long-period position, what is taken as given is the total *amount* of 'capital', treated as a homogeneous factor, but its *composition* is endogenously determined. The force assumed to determine the composition of capital is the tendency, during the time-consuming disequilibrium adjustments, to produce more of the capital goods yielding a higher rate of return on their costs of production, and to produce less of the other capital goods.

We touch here upon a very important point, to which we will return several times. Traditional marginalist authors esteemed that the effects of the just-mentioned tendency on the composition of capital and on value could be studied while at the same time neglecting the 'long-run' effects of accumulation on the 'total quantity' of capital. Nowadays there is little consciousness of this fundamental aspect of traditional analyses;[36] and yet, the reason justifying the traditional approach is not difficult to grasp: the potential speed of changes in the composition of capital is of a higher order of magnitude than the speed of capital accumulation; for example in a year the average productive capacity of an economy can seldom be increased by more than 15 per cent, while in the same time the productive capacity of a single industry could in most cases easily double, and often even increase

36. In classical analyses there was no given 'quantity of capital', but there was an analogous separation of the determination of long-period positions (and of comparative statics applied to a given long-period position, for example effects of changes of the real wage) from the study of the effects of accumulation. Cf. Garegnani (1990b, 1990c).

tenfold. For example, in a year it would be easy to double, or to multiply by ten, the number of steel-producing plants, of oil refineries, even of nuclear plants in a nation, if gross investment were mainly directed to such an end. Thus, in common with other scientific disciplines, traditional marginalist authors adopted the procedure of treating as fixed the variables (total capital stock conceived as a single magnitude capable of changing 'form'; labour endowment) whose velocity of variation was much lower than the velocity of change of the composition of capital, when their aim was to determine the composition of the latter and the corresponding normal prices.

By 'short-*period*' analyses, on the other hand, the Marshallian tradition did not mean temporary equilibria: it meant analyses where the composition of capital had not reached a *complete* equilibrium, but some adaptation had had the time to come into being at least for the more short-lived capital goods; consequently, only the amounts of the more durable capital goods were taken as given. Furthermore, while the neo-Walrasian short-run equilibria are viewed as autonomous theoretical notions by neo-Walrasian theorists, the previous tradition saw short-period analyses as concerned with *deviations from* long-period positions, the latter being the logically prior notion.

In this book the traditional terminology is of necessity adopted: accordingly, in a marginalist *long-period* equilibrium the composition of the capital endowment is endogenously determined while the 'quantity' of 'capital' is given;[37] '*short-period* analyses' are analyses that take the composition of capital as partly fixed (as in Keynes); a *very-short-period* or neo-Walrasian general equilibrium treats the composition of the capital endowment as entirely fixed (as in Arrow–Debreu or in temporary equilibria: not even the initial endowments of the most short-lived intermediate goods are endogenously determined). Lastly, a *very-long-period* or *secular* (steady-growth or stationary) equilibrium is one where the forces, tending to alter the relative amounts of capital and labour, have themselves come to a state of rest, that is it is what would be nowadays called a long-run or steady-growth equilibrium; it is the notion corresponding, within the marginalist approach, to Ricardo's secular stationary state, and it is of very little use for explaining distribution in a given historical situation, which may be very far from steady growth. (Also see Panico and Petri, 1987.)

The current usage of the long-run/short-run opposition suggests, on the contrary, that there are only two possible assumptions as to the capital

37. A different usage, common in introductory textbooks, but not adopted here, of the terms 'long-period equilibrium' and 'short-period equilibrium' distinguishes them according to whether there are or are not fixed factors *for the single firm*: but it is difficult to see why an equilibrium should be other than long-period according to this textbook usage, since a firm can always sell its 'fixed' factors to other firms (cf. §5A3.3.2).

endowment in equilibrium analysis: either the whole vector of capital endowments is taken as given (a very-short-period analysis), or both the composition *and the overall quantity* of capital are assumed to be endogenously determined (a very-long-period, or secular analysis). In this way no room is left for precisely the treatment of the capital endowment which was central to the rise of the marginalist approach; and one thereby loses sight of the historical evolution of the marginalist approach. Indeed, no room is left for the notion which was central to the theory of value from its first systematic elaboration by Adam Smith until recently – the notion of long-period positions – because the idea is obscured that the treatment of the composition of capital as endogenously determined need not imply a secular analysis, that is it need not imply a steady-state assumption.

2. The Problematic Relationship Between Neo-Walrasian Equilibrium Analyses and Real Economies

2.1. THE IMPERMANENCE PROBLEM, THE SUBSTITUTABILITY PROBLEM, THE INDEFINITENESS PROBLEM

2.1.1. The previous chapter started by noticing some problems with the modern notions of general equilibrium, and then it illustrated with examples the method associated with long-period equilibria. Many readers will have recognized in those examples the type of analysis they themselves would tend to apply to real-world issues; they will also have noticed that in those examples the problems associated with the modern, neo-Walrasian notions of general equilibrium did not seem to arise. This chapter examines in greater detail these issues, and it concludes that the abandonment of the long-period method does indeed create extremely serious problems to the use of neo-Walrasian equilibria for explanatory and predictive purposes; mainstream economic theory emerges as somewhat schizophrenic, since its applications to real-world problems ultimately rely on an approach to value and distribution whose rigorous formulations – general equilibrium theory in its modern variants – cannot support them. The question thereby arises: why was the fruitful long-period method abandoned if the result is this sterility of modern general equilibrium theory? The search for an answer motivates the subsequent chapters and Appendices of this book.

I start by more clearly identifying the difficulties with neo-Walrasian equilibria, hinted at in the opening pages and also in other points of Chapter 1. (I acknowledge here the influence of Garegnani, 1976, 1990a.)

The *impermanence problem* can be restated as follows. Some of the data of a neo-Walrasian equilibrium lack sufficient persistence: they may quickly change during any time-consuming process of adjustment, such that, before the economy has the time to approach equilibrium through trial and error, the data of the equilibrium may significantly change. In intertemporal equilibria with complete futures markets, the data in question are the initial endowments of produced goods: the endowments of the several capital goods, essentially; but also the inventories of consumption goods.[1] In addition, in temporary equilibria, the data in question include the shapes of expectation functions (cf. §2.1.4).

We have seen that, according to Franklin Fisher, this problem 'makes the calculation of equilibria corresponding to the initial state of the system essentially irrelevant' (Fisher, 1983, p. 14). Let us make sure we are clear as to why.

Unless in the periods preceding the one from which the analysis starts, the economy has already reached a long-period equilibrium, with prices and quantities remaining constant through time or changing in a slow and predictable fashion, and unless no novelties have arisen, one cannot presume that the equilibrium prices and quantities[2] will rule from the first moment; if there is no auctioneer, the quantities to be produced must be discovered through trial and error, and the correction of disequilibria may require numerous repetitions of transactions and productions. For example, let us remember that, when the employment of a factor increases, the marginal products of other factors change, so their previous rentals no longer reflect marginal products and must be changed; and the changes in costs alter product prices, hence demands, hence productions. Moreover it is not only the *composition* of production which cannot be presumed to be the equilibrium one from the very start: the *aggregate level* of resource utilization itself might be initially considerably different from the equilibrium one. Nor is it necessary for this to have recourse to Keynes. Even before Keynes, marginalist trade cycle theorists freely admitted that oscillations in the optimism of investors, or initially inappropriate levels of the rates of interest or of real wages, might cause unemployment. But, before the economy has had time to correct or compensate the initial disequilibria, production and utilization will have changed most of the capital goods' endowments, possibly significantly. Let us also remember that in real economies decisions are taken on the basis of expectations, and that these expectations will also be changing during the disequilibrium adjustments. Indeed, very few economists would deny that actual economies are very far from having complete futures markets, and that perfect foresight is

1. The data of a neo-Walrasian equilibrium include the inventories of goods existing at the moment when the equilibrium should be established, both of capital goods, and of consumption goods. The impermanence of these data is clear. The inventories of consumption goods, however, are part of the data only because of the decision to take the endowments of the several capital goods as given, thereby turning the general equilibrium into a very-short-period equilibrium. The fundamental choice therefore concerns the treatment of the capital endowment.
2. In order to concentrate on the different problem central here, I assume for the sake of argument that an equilibrium exists and is unique.

impossible;[3] the implication would appear to be that the sole neo-Walrasian notion of equilibrium that may be appropriate to real economies is that of temporary equilibrium, in which expectation functions are part of the data; then the shapes of expectation functions, which may be altered by learning processes during the disequilibrium adjustments, constitute a further group of data which lack persistence.

Therefore the equilibrium itself may significantly change before the repetitions of transactions and of productions have had the time to bring about prices and quantities sufficiently close to those of the original equilibrium. The relevance of the original equilibrium for explanatory and predictive purposes is therefore unclear, because *initial* prices and quantities cannot be assumed to be sufficiently close to those of the equilibrium, and their *subsequent evolution* cannot be presumed to be governed by a gravitation toward or around the original equilibrium, since the latter is altered by the disequilibrium actions.

This problem has been admitted by, among others,[4] Christopher Bliss, with reference to temporary equilibria: 'Does it not take time to establish equilibrium? By the time equilibrium would be established will we not have moved on to another 'week' with new conditions, new expectations, etc.?' (Bliss, 1975a, p. 210).[5]

2.1.2. It should now be clear why modern general equilibrium theory has great difficulty with abandoning the study of the stability of equilibrium on the basis of the unrealistic hypothesis, introduced by Walras in the fourth edition of his *Eléments*, of a tâtonnement based on provisional 'tickets' or 'pledges'[6] while economic activity is suspended. Up to that edition, as will be shown in detail in Chapter 5, Walras had not realized that, since he was including among the data of equilibrium given endowments of the several capital goods, he had been contradicting himself in allowing production to go on during the disequilibrium adjustments. The moment he realized it, he had to find some way to prevent the adjustment processes from altering the capital endowments,[7] and to that end he invented the 'tickets'. The same need

3. It will suffice here to remember the impossibility of predicting future advances of knowledge: this makes it also impossible to imagine complete markets in contingent commodities because it is impossible to list all possible future states of the world, since these states of the world should also be distinguished according to differences in the state of knowledge.
4. Also cf. Zaghini (1990), Walker (1997), Duménil and Lévy (1985).
5. A 'week' is the name given by John Hicks to the length of the period of his temporary equilibria in *Value and Capital*.
6. 'Pledges' is the (better) translation of Walras' *bons*, proposed by Walker (1996).
7. In fact, consumption activities must be prevented too, if some capital goods are also consumption goods (for example sugar) and therefore consumption activities might alter

to avoid disequilibrium productions arises in modern general equilibrium theory.

But it seems to have escaped general recognition that not even the tâtonnement story is capable of preventing a change in some data of the equilibrium during disequilibrium adjustments, the moment one admits that the assumption of complete futures markets overstretches credibility,[8] and one turns to temporary equilibria. The reason is that the data of temporary equilibria include expectation functions, and *the shape of expectation functions* cannot be assumed to remain unchanged during the tâtonnement, because the way prices change during the tâtonnement provides further information, which may be utilized to modify one's way of formulating predictions.

Let us in fact consider an economy trying to reach a temporary equilibrium via a tâtonnement. In the period preceding the current one, agents held expectations relative to the current period's equilibrium prices. It may well happen that during the tâtonnement the auctioneer calls the exact prices which an agent, in the preceding period, expected to be the equilibrium prices of the current period, and that these prices turn out not to be equilibrium prices. The agent thereby discovers that her way of formulating predictions was not correct. It may well ensue that she alters the shape of her expectation function. The alteration might be of minor importance; but it might also be very drastic, for example when it results from the switch to a different *theory*, that is to a different model of the functioning of the economy. Be that as it may, the accumulation of observations on non-equilibrium prices during the tâtonnement will result in changes in the way future prices are inferred from present equilibrium prices. Hence even the unrealistic tâtonnement with 'tickets' does not authorize one to consider the shape of expectation functions as unchanging during disequilibrium. Therefore we have here one more reason why the temporary equilibrium, associated with the capital endowments and expectation functions existing at a certain instant, cannot be presumed to come about:

their endowments, or more generally if among the data of equilibrium there are stocks of all goods, including inventories of consumption goods, as it seems necessary to assume in very-short-period neo-Walrasian equilibria. In the rest of the book, the initial endowments of 'capital goods' will be intended to include also the initial inventories of consumption goods, and by suspension of production it will also be meant suspension of sales (and consumption) from these inventories. As to expectations, Walras did not explicitly discuss them.

8. Let us remember, for example, that complete futures markets for a number of periods extending over, say, twenty years require the assumption that consumers yet to be born are already present in the initial period with their demands and supplies. The interpretability of intertemporal equilibria as sequential equilibria without complete future markets but with perfect foresight is discussed in Appendix 5A3.

even the unrealistic disequilibria adjustments governed by the mythical auctioneer would be unable to make it come about.

(Still, it is opportune to notice that, relative to the traditional marginalist notion of long-period equilibrium, it is the givenness of the several capital endowments which is at the origin of this problem of insufficient persistence of expectation functions in temporary equilibria. This is due to the fact that if data other than expectation functions were sufficiently persistent, then one would be justified in assuming, as was traditionally done, that erroneous expectations are modified by experience and that their convergence to the correct ones is part of the process itself of convergence to equilibrium – if such a convergence can be assumed. Thus the equilibrium would endogenously determine expectations as correct expectations, and the need for expectation functions as exogenous data would disappear: and in fact one does not find them as exogenous data in the traditional long-period marginalist equilibria.[9])

2.1.3. Actually, with the inclusion of expectation functions among the determinants of equilibrium, a serious problem arises in the determination of the initial temporary equilibrium itself, that is even *before* introducing the problem that the expectation functions will change during disequilibrium adjustments even if the latter adjustments are conceived as auctioneer-guided tâtonnements.

The problem may be called the *indefiniteness problem*: expectations, being subjective, and essentially unobservable, pose the problem that the assumptions about their initial state cannot but be arbitrary and unverifiable to a considerable extent, so that little more can be achieved than a taxonomy of possible equilibrium states of the economy depending on the assumptions about the state of expectations.[10] It suffices to think of the possible influence of the state of expectations on investment decisions to realize the great variability of equilibrium depending on the assumptions regarding expectations. This problem is by itself so serious – in its potential implication of indefiniteness of results of the analysis and hence sterility of the approach – as to suggest strongly that a different approach, which does not rely on unobservable subjective elements as data, should be sought. (Long-period

9. This is true for Walras as well, and its importance for a correct intepretation of Walras will be stressed later. It may be opportune to add that the assumption of convergence of *expectations* to the correct ones, given time, does not imply the convergence of *expectation functions* to the correct ones, that is it does not imply that agents would be able to have correct expectations even outside the long-period equilibrium, nor that agents would immediately know how the long-period equilibrium would change if some of its data were to change; so it is not equivalent to an assumption of rational expectations.

10. This is admitted by Hicks (1936, p. 87; 1946, p. 205).

equilibria avoided this problem by concentrating on the determination of 'tranquil' positions reflecting an adjustment of expectations to realized events, so that expectations fell out of the data determining those positions.[11])

2.1.4. That the initial deviations from the theoretical equilibrium magnitudes may be significant, and that the equilibrium may be considerably altered by disequilibrium actions, is confirmed by consideration of another problem of the neo-Walrasian notions of equilibrium: namely, a problem of *insufficient substitutability* (Garegnani, 1990a, pp. 57–8).

When what is taken as given is no longer an amount of 'capital' capable of adapting its 'form' to demand, but instead, the given is the vector of endowments of each distinct capital good, then there will not generally be enough substitutability to obtain plausible prices because most capital goods are specific to a product and to a method of production, and the proportions in which the capital goods in an industry must be combined according to a certain production method are very often fixed.[12] Thus if the endowments are arbitrary, the probability is extremely high that a very high proportion of the endowments of capital goods will not be fully employed, implying an implausibly high number of zero equilibrium rentals. For similar reasons the elasticity of the very-short-run demand for labour might easily be very low, with a considerable risk of a zero, or in any case an implausibly low, full-employment marginal product of labour, entailing an analogously implausible equilibrium real wage. Confronted with the low degree of correspondence between these theoretical outcomes and observed prices, the neo-Walrasian theorist appears to have little choice but to admit that prices (including wages) do not adjust very quickly;[13] but this means that prices may deviate from those of the equilibrium for a considerable time.

11. Cf. Garegnani (1976, p. 39).
12. For example, the parts to be assembled to form a finished car or a computer are capital goods, and their proportions are fixed.
13. The admission by Hicks of a very low short-period elasticity of the demand for labour (cf. the quotation in §1.3.2) implies that, as I have written elsewhere: 'if the composition (the "form") of the capital stock of the economy were taken as given, then the demand for labour would be too inelastic to determine plausible equilibrium values of the real wage. The probability would be high that an excess supply of labour (assuming the supply of labour to be rigid) would not be eliminated even if the real wage went down to zero, or that an excess demand for labour would push the wage up to absorbing the entire net product of the economy. Such results would deprive the theory of plausibility ... The important implication for the marginalist approach of this line of argument is that short-period analyses, and even more neo-Walrasian analyses, cannot aim at autonomously determining the real wage as an equilibrium real wage. In order to avoid implausible results (such as a high probability of a zero or near-zero wage, or enormous changes of the real wage from one 'week' to the next), the marginalist theorist must admit that the real wages are not so flexible as to try and bring into equality supply and *short-period* demand for labour; the short-period excess demand for

Furthermore, because of the little or zero substitutability, small changes in the relative capital endowments may easily change excess supplies into excess demands or vice versa, resulting in enormous changes in many equilibrium prices, possibly including the equilibrium wage; this confirms that the changes in the endowments of the several capital goods going on in disequilibrium will in all likelihood modify the equilibrium to a considerable extent.

2.1.5. The possibility of considerable initial deviations of prices and quantities from the path traced by the intertemporal equilibrium or by the sequence of temporary equilibria is only one aspect of the impermanence problem. A further aspect of the problem is the possibility of *cumulative* deviations of the actual path from the theoretical equilibrium path as time goes on.

In order to discuss this issue let us leave aside, for the sake of argument, the difficulties arising from the non-uniqueness, in general, of equilibrium and from the consequent indeterminacy, which might be considerable,[14] of the equilibrium path itself. Without in the least intending to deny the importance of these difficulties,[15] the problem which I want to highlight here is a different, or additional, one. Let us therefore assume, for the sake of argument, that the equilibrium path is always unique for each given set of initial data. The trouble is that neo-Walrasian theory gives us no right to presume that the deviations from the path in one period will be corrected or compensated in subsequent periods. Once the data's evolution has gone off

labour can only be admitted to govern the direction of a gradual movement of wages from an initial level, at the beginning of Hicks's 'week', which must be taken as exogenously given. Only long-period analysis, based on the conception of capital as a single factor capable of changing "form", can plausibly try to explain the (trend or average) level of the real wage in terms of [equilibrium between] supply and demand, because only the demand for labour derived from the schedule of the *long-period* marginal product of labour (determined by allowing the given 'capital' to take the "form" best appropriate to the various levels of labour employment) can be argued not to be so inelastic as to yield implausible results' (Petri, 1991, pp. 271–72).

14. When there are multiple equilibria they are all full-employment equilibria, but they may differ considerably for example as to the level of employment or as to income distribution or as to the level of aggregate savings, owing, for instance, to backward-bending factor supply curves.

15. One may add that, if one admits the absence of complete futures markets and the absence of perfect foresight and one turns therefore to temporary equilibria, then the possibility that the equilibrium may not exist is much less remote than for 'atemporal' equilibria, because of the complications introduced by expectations (Grandmont, 1987) and bankruptcies (Arrow and Hahn, 1971, pp. 151, 361). That this book concentrates on other, less well understood difficulties of the marginalist/neoclassical approach is not meant to imply that these, or those connected with non-uniqueness, are of minor importance.

the equilibrium path, the forces of supply and demand can only try to reach an equilibrium on the basis of the new actual data: there is no force bringing the economy back to the original path.[16]

Thus, for example, let us imagine an economy for which the Arrow–Debreu equilibrium path would imply a continuous growth of all capital stocks; let us suppose that the disequilibrium decisions actually taken in the first period cause less of all capital goods to be produced (that is less investment to be undertaken) than the intertemporal equilibrium would have entailed; and let us make the extreme assumption that, because of this, capital stocks remain exactly unaltered from the first to the second period. If we assume the possible changes in the wealth and debt situations of individual agents to be of secondary importance, and thus we leave them aside, then in the second period the economy finds itself with the same data as in the first period. Then the Arrow–Debreu equilibrium starting from the second period will be the same as in the first period, only moved forward by one period. Even if in this second period, and in all subsequent periods, equilibrium were actually established, the economy would always remain, so to speak, one period behind, relative to the original equilibrium path: the lost production of capital goods would be lost once and for all.[17]

Since the deviations from the original equilibrium path cannot be presumed to be self-correcting, that path might be claimed to give a tolerable approximation to the actual behaviour of the economy only if it could be argued that the initial deviation from equilibrium will be very small, and furthermore that there will be no further significant increase in subsequent periods of the divergence, from the equilibrium path, of the actual path followed by the economy. However, the modern theory of general equilibrium gives no basis for any such argument, because it is simply silent on what happens when adjustments are not instantaneous. For example, it has no way of excluding the possibility that an incomplete adjustment of wages

16. Duménil and Lévy (1985, p. 341) notice this problem of neo-Walrasian equilibria, but their criticism on this score runs the risk of being ineffectual, for the reasons pointed out in Petri (1999, p. 63, fn. 49).
17. The convergence, under certain assumptions, of intertemporal equilibria to steady growth (see for example Bewley, 1982; Yano, 1984a and 1984b; Epstein, 1987; Schefold, 1997, ch. 18) means that, if this convergence held for our example, the difference between the original equilibrium path and the new equilibrium path would decrease through time. However, this would not occur because the new path *goes back* to the old one in the sense that some mechanism causes the lower accumulation in the first period to be compensated by a higher accumulation in some later period; the situation reached by the old equilibrium path at *t* remains equal to the situation reached by the new equilibrium path at *t* + 1: the one-period lag never disappears. Thus the convergence, if it exists, is only a *secular* one, that is it is inappropriate to explain the problems for which long-period analysis was devised.

may cause an under-equilibrium level of labour employment,[18] with less aggregate production than in equilibrium, less savings, hence a lower marginal product of labour in the next period, hence a lower supply of labour, hence less savings, and an increasing deficiency of production in subsequent periods relative to the original equilibrium path. Nor (owing to the little substitutability illustrated earlier) can it exclude that the *full-employment* real wage may remain for many periods lower than that of the equilibrium, owing to 'mistakes' in the composition of the production of new capital goods. Again, this might have significant effects on savings (the moment income distribution is admitted to influence the average propensity to save) and hence it might cause cumulative divergences of the evolution of the capital stock from the equilibrium one, even if the full employment of a given labour supply were actually reached. Thus: 'the danger arises of a cumulation of errors due to the uncompensated deviations from equilibrium in preceding periods' (Garegnani, 1976, p. 140, fn. 30).

If one rejects intertemporal equilibria with complete futures markets and one considers sequences of temporary equilibria where expectation functions differ among agents and can be altered by realized events, the difficulty is compounded by the dependence of the equilibrium sequence not only on the capital goods endowments but also on the evolution of expectation functions.

In making assumptions about this evolution, the indefiniteness problem reappears: the assumptions not only about the initial state of expectations, but also about their subsequent evolution, can hardly avoid a considerable arbitrariness.

But even assuming that initial expectations could be ascertained, and that some not overly arbitrary theory could be advanced about how expectations evolve depending on realized events so that a theoretical sequence of temporary equilibria could be determined, the non-realization of equilibrium in the first period would presumably imply a different evolution of expectations from the one predicted by the equilibrium sequence. Then again neo-Walrasian equilibrium theory would give us no reason why expectation functions should re-approach those along the original equilibrium sequence.

The conclusion we have reached can be stated thus: the non-instantaneity of adjustments and the scarce substitutability among factors make it very difficult to believe that neo-Walrasian equilibria indicate, with sufficient approximation, the prices and quantities ruling in the very short period. If one turns to longer time horizons, then even assuming – and it is an

---

18. For the sake of argument I am assuming in this paragraph the correctness of basic marginalist notions, for example the existence in each period of a downward-sloping labour demand function, which ensures both the existence of a full-employment positive real wage and the possibility of reaching it if sufficient time were given to the forces of supply and demand. In subsequent chapters these notions will be shown to be highly questionable.

extremely strong assumption – that an equilibrium sequence can be uniquely determined in spite of the indefiniteness problem (and in spite of the general non-uniqueness of equilibria), the danger arises of a cumulation of 'errors' and therefore no reason is given why this sequence should represent, with a tolerable approximation, the actual behaviour of the economy – the moment the assumption is dropped that the economy is *always* in equilibrium.

(As an aside, it may be added here that these problems also arise in the so-called 'disequilibrium' quantity-rationed fixprice equilibria (Barro and Grossman, Drèze, Bénassy, Malinvaud, Grandmont and so on) and their sequences: 'The theory of "disequilibria" had been presented at the beginning as the theory of imperfectly co-ordinated systems, but the models ... are all founded on tâtonnement processes, which ensure a perfect co-ordination through quantities ... [the] critical remarks concerning the assumption of the instantaneous adaptation of prices apply, pari passu, to the case of instantaneous adaptation of quantities' (Fitoussi, 1983a, p. 15).)

2.2.   THE IMPORTANCE OF PERSISTENT TENDENCIES

2.2.1. The above conclusion is confirmed by the results reached by Franklin M. Fisher (1983),[19] the sole neo-Walrasian theorist so far to have tried

19. As the quotations earlier in the chapter show, the impermanence problem has been frequently admitted by general equilibrium theorists; but, before Franklin Fisher, Hicks appears to have been the only one to appreciate its importance, to the point of recanting on his earlier advocacy of the temporary equilibrium method, as demonstrated in Petri (1991) (in the same article I show that Hicks admits the indefiniteness problem and the substitutability problem too). The other economists who have acknowledged the impermanence problem appear to have made no attempt to find ways to overcome it. Bliss seems to have simply set it aside, since he has continued working on the theory of temporary equilibrium without trying to find ways to overcome the impermanence problem at all; as to Hahn, who seems less aware of the impermanence problem as such than of the need for more realistic theories of adjustment mechanisms, he has not so far produced any proposal for a more realistic insertion into value and employment theory of 'the actual working of the invisible hand'. Elsewhere all mention of the problem is accurately avoided. A good example is the highly esteemed textbook by Mas-Colell and others (Mas-Colell et al., 1995), which nowhere mentions the impermanence problem, and of a 'Marshallian' quantity tâtonnement (based on given factor endowments) it even says that 'we can interpret the dynamics as happening in real time' (ibid., p. 625), forgetting that in intertemporal equilibria with heterogeneous capital goods the disequilibrium productions would cause the actual path of the economy to diverge from the equilibrium path. In this book the sole reference to Franklin Fisher's study of disequilibrium adjustments (1983) is in a footnote which, as already remembered in Chapter 1, reads simply: 'For an extensive analysis of market adjustment procedures in real time, see Fisher (1983)' (ibid., p. 625, fn. 69). Given the book's generally careful coverage of the literature on other topics, and given the absence of all discussion of the possibility that time-consuming adjustments may drastically alter the

squarely to deal with the impermanence problem in models with capital goods. Having openly admitted that the equilibrium corresponding to the initial data is 'irrelevant', he tries to study the end results of disequilibrium processes actually taking time and involving production and consumption, while maintaining the analysis as close as possible to neo-Walrasian stability studies. His book aims at providing a more solid foundation to stability studies, within a perspective still broadly speaking neo-Walrasian; however, it ends up by having the opposite result. Fisher is able to prove that the economy will converge to some rest point only on the basis of extremely bold assumption, including an assumption of No Favourable Surprise (stipulating that during the disequilibrium process things never turn out to be better for any household or firm, than she/he/it had expected) which comes extremely close to an assumption of perfect foresight. The rest points to which the economy may converge remain anyway largely unspecified in their character; they need not be Arrow–Debreu equilibria, nor full-employment equilibria. This indeterminacy of results, it should be noticed, obtains in spite of the very restrictive assumption of No Favourable Surprise. The inevitable conclusion is that if the implausible assumption of No Favourable Surprise is dropped, then nothing definite can be said about the behaviour of the economy depicted by Fisher, since there appears to be space within it for nearly all theories of employment, distribution and cycles. (Some more detailed considerations on Fisher's book have been confined to Appendix 2A2.)

Fisher's results confirm that neo-Walrasian theory simply does not know what happens when there is no auctioneer (or analogous instantaneous adjustment process). Neo-Walrasian theorists must assume that the economy is *all the time* in equilibrium in order to be able to say anything about its behaviour.[20] This means, as Frank Hahn admits, to beg the question of how the economy actually behaves: 'imposing the axiom that the economy is at

analysis, this short sentence cannot but induce students to think that Fisher's book does *not* contain startling novelties. Therefore graduate students trained on this book most probably do *not* make the effort to go and read Fisher, and thus remain ignorant of the fact that the interpretation advanced by Mas-Colell et al. on p. 579 of the 'Walrasian equilibrium' as a 'positive prediction' of the behaviour of market economies is undermined by Fisher's admission that the equilibrium based on the initial data is irrelevant.

20. Nor can the problem be circumvented by assuming rational expectations: the assumption that individuals use all their information in the best possible way cannot be identified with the assumption that the equilibrium is established instantaneously; after each unexpected change in the shape of one of the 'structural relations' (for example unexpected technical innovations, or changes in tastes), expectations must be given time to converge, if at all, to the new rational expectations: 'Rational expectations are, if anything, a long run rather than a short run phenomenon' (Bray, 1982, p. 330); besides, as discussed in Appendix 5A3, the assumption of perfect foresight encounters serious problems in the presence of production with free entry and/or constant returns to scale.

every instant in competitive equilibrium simply removes the actual operation of the invisible hand from the analysis' (Hahn, 1984, p. 4). (Notice how here Hahn admits that 'the actual operation of the invisible hand' must include the implementation of disequilibrium actions.)

This shows that so far we have granted too much to the neo-Walrasian approach. In Section 2.1 we have mostly reasoned as if the forces of demand and supply were gradually eliminating the disequilibria on the various markets, and only the impermanence of some of the data prevented this tendency from ascribing, to the neo-Walrasian equilibrium (or sequence of equilibria) corresponding to the initial data, the role of indicator of the actual behaviour of the economy. But the presumption that the forces of supply and demand will, at any given time, be pushing toward the elimination of disequilibria on the various markets, becomes itself arbitrary once one grasps the full implications of the absence, in neo-Walrasian theory, of any indication of how 'the actual operation of the invisible hand' functions.

This conclusion derives here, not from the well-known negative results on the stability of general equilibrium under a tâtonnement process,[21] but rather, from a *logically prior* reason: that the stability or instability of the adjustment processes, compatible with the fixity of the data of neo-Walrasian equilibria, appears *devoid of implications for actual economies.*[22] Those adjustment processes must leave out of consideration the important elements of real adjustments, which are logically tied to the implementation of disequilibrium decisions. One example is the inability to buy if one has been unable to sell; another example is bankruptcies causing further bankruptcies of creditors; yet another example is the postponement of the purchase of a good, when one observes that the price of the good is decreasing, because one prefers to buy it when the price will be even lower, with a resulting decrease in the demand for the good in spite of the decrease in price; and so forth.

The result of all these possible disequilibrium phenomena is of course an amazing variety of possible outcomes of disequilibrium in individual markets as well as in the aggregate; as a consequence, economic analysis appears condemned to impotence, unless it can argue that there are persistent forces, capable of making themselves felt through the accidents and vagaries of disequilibrium, and pushing the economy toward sufficiently persistent

21. Apart from F. Fisher, non-tâtonnement processes have only been studied for exchange economies.
22. A similar conclusion is reached by Donald A. Walker in his discussion of the well-known work on the stability of general equilibrium by Arrow and Hurwicz. Walker argues that there is no plausible way to interpret the adjustment equations formulated by those authors as describing adjustment processes going on in real time, and concludes: 'Nowhere do the authors provide any reason for thinking that their model throws light upon the behaviour of the real economy, and, indeed, none exists' (Walker, 1997, p. 116).

positions. In fact, this is precisely what economic theory has argued since Adam Smith's distinction between market price and natural price. But the argument crucially rested on the determination of positions unaffected by the details of disequilibrium.

2.2.2. One should now be better able to appreciate the role of the conception of capital as a single factor of variable 'form' in the birth and success of the marginalist approach. That conception made it possible for traditional marginalist authors to base their analyses on long-period equilibria where what was taken as given was the *total quantity* of capital, a quantity which could be taken as unchanging during disequilibrium adjustments, which would only affect its 'form'. The variable 'form' meant that the insufficient substitutability problem did not arise. There was no need to include given expectations or expectation functions among the data of equilibrium, because equilibrium relative prices were constant or only very gradually changing (and in a predictable direction), and therefore expectations could be assumed to have become correct in equilibrium; therefore the indefiniteness problem did not arise. There was no need to take the inventories of consumption goods as given, since one could treat inventories as adapting to production levels, just like the endowments of the several capital goods; hence the data of long-period equilibria could be argued not to suffer from insufficient persistence.

Therefore the stability of that notion of equilibrium, in terms of time-consuming adjustment processes, could be discussed with the same legitimacy (having granted the conception of capital as a single factor) as for equilibria with only non-producible factors. No impediment arose from the side of the data, to arguing that the tendency toward equilibrium was implemented by the repetition of out-of-equilibrium transactions and productions, which would result in profits and losses that indicated mistakes that could be gradually corrected by experience.

On this basis, persistent forces *could* be indicated, and it is useful to distinguish them in forces determining the *composition* of production, and forces determining the aggregate *level* of production (and of employment of resources).

The discussion of the stability of equilibrium started from a premise, inherited from classical analyses and, I would argue, confirmed by observation: the general tendency of the *composition* of production to adapt to the composition of demand, owing to the tendency, in each industry, of production to increase or decrease according to whether the price is above or below average cost. The sole remaining problem was therefore the determination of the aggregate *level* of production: this determination was achieved by the tendency toward equilibrium on factor markets. Here the persistent forces indicated by the theory were the direct and indirect factor substitution mechanisms remembered in Chapter 1. The tendency of the composition of production to adapt to the composition of demand made it possible to derive long-period relative factor demands from relative factor prices and from the composition of the demand for products. No assumption of instantaneous adjustment was needed. What was relevant was the thesis that, over sufficiently long periods, on average, firms' technical choices and production choices would be sufficiently close to those determined by the theory. Then disequilibria on factor markets could be argued to bring about a tendency to diminution of the relative rentals of factors in excess supply, which would set in motion the factor substitution mechanisms.[23]

In this last step, as is well known, stability analysis encountered problems deriving from income effects. But, however relevant these problems, our focus now is not on them: what is relevant for the present argument is that the independence of the data of equilibrium from the accidents of disequilibrium made it possible to discuss 'the actual operation of the invisible hand' in meaningful terms.

2.2.3. Why all this insistence on the traditional versions of the marginalist approach and on a conception of capital that nowadays very few theorists would defend? The answer is, because the key to understanding the present-day situation of neoclassical economic theory lies here.

We have seen – and many general equilibrium specialists would concur – that it is highly problematic to derive any conclusion from contemporary general equilibrium theory as to the actual behaviour of market economies; and yet general equilibrium theory, and nothing else, is declared to be the rigorous foundation of the supply-and-demand approach to value, distribution and employment. But very few economists draw what ought to be the unavoidable conclusion, namely, that the applications of this approach to explanation and prediction of the behaviour of market economies are devoid of foundations. Mainstream macroeconomics, growth theory, international trade theory and so on remain solidly neoclassical. The resulting situation might well be called schizophrenic.

The reader who has found the argument up to here convincing will want to understand the causes of such a situation, and, even more, will want to understand how this schizophrenia might be surmounted. The claim of this

23. We are still waiting for a careful reconstruction of the evolution of marginalist stability analyses: such a reconstruction can now take advantage of the distinction between versions internal to the method of long-period positions, and neo-Walrasian versions. It is not impossible that such a reconstruction may find weaknesses in the traditional (pre-Samuelson) marginalist arguments in support of stability, so far only dimly perceived.

book is that pursuit of these goals requires an understanding of the evolution of the supply-and-demand approach.

First, it will be necessary to understand that the supply-and-demand (or marginalist, or neoclassical) approach was born and became dominant, on the basis of the belief in the existence of the persistent forces remembered in §2.2.2. The result of the operation of those forces was conceived as a *long-period* equilibrium; both in the formalization of the long-period equilibrium, and in the description of the forces pushing toward it, the conception of capital as a single factor of variable 'form' played a fundamental role; Walras was only a very partial exception.

Second, it will be necessary to realize that the subsequent shift to neo-Walrasian notions of equilibrium was not accompanied by clarity as to its causes and implications. The reason for the shift was the difficulties of the traditional conception of capital as a single factor; but the way the shift occurred obscured the fact that, if that conception of capital was questionable, the entire approach was thereby deprived of solid foundations.

In fact the confusions were such that many economists apparently did not even realize that a shift had occurred. Thus a misconception was able to spread, and to survive to the present day: namely, that the foundation for traditional marginalist beliefs in the forces at work in market economies can be found in neo-Walrasian general equilibrium theory.

The argument therefore will proceed by illustrating, first, the logic of long-period equilibria, including Walras' peculiarity; then the reasons for the shift to the neo-Walrasian versions; then the further weaknesses of the conception of capital as a single factor, brought to light by the results of the Cambridge controversies. This will be followed by an examination of the implications of those results for the theory of aggregate investment and for the labour demand curve; the conclusion will be that no justification can be found for the belief that sequences of neo-Walrasian equilibria approximate the behaviour of market economies. Finally, a sketch will be provided of one promising alternative to the marginalist or supply-and-demand approach to distribution and employment.

APPENDIX 2A1. WAS KEYNES'S EQUILIBRIUM A TEMPORARY EQUILIBRIUM?

2A1.1. Was Keynes a Temporary Equilibrium Theorist?

This Appendix tries to dispel the mistaken belief that 'Keynes was concerned with what we have called temporary equilibrium' (Arrow and Hahn, 1971, p. 347).[24] In all probability the acceptance and diffusion of neo-Walrasian notions of equilibrium have received some impetus from the widespread belief that Keynes's own notion of equilibrium was of the same type. It will be argued below that, to the contrary, there is a deep difference between Keynes's notion of equilibrium and a neo-Walrasian temporary equilibrium – a difference that entails that Keynes's equilibrium, differently from neo-Walrasian equilibria, is capable of being conceived as the centre of gravitation of time-consuming disequilibrium adjustments. The implication is that the fruitfulness of Keynes's analysis cannot be adduced as proof of the legitimacy and usefulness of the notion of Temporary General Equilibrium (referred to as TGE in the rest of this Appendix).

The need to distinguish Keynes's equilibrium from a TGE has been admitted, for example, by John Hicks. In 1939 Hicks had not been explicit as to whether Keynes's equilibrium, or his own IS–LM interpretation of Keynes, were to be interpreted as temporary equilibria of the type advocated in *Value and Capital*.[25] But when asked, over 40 years later, to reconsider the IS–LM model, Hicks rejects that interpretation, both of the IS–LM model and of Keynes's own analysis:

> Keynes's (he said) was a 'short-period', a term with connotations derived from Marshall; we shall not go far wrong if we think of it as a year. Mine was an 'ultra-short period'; I called it a week. Much more can happen in a year than in a week; Keynes has to allow for quite a lot of things to happen. I wanted to avoid so much happening, so that my (flexprice) markets could reflect propensities (and expectations) as they are at a moment... a very artificial device, not (I would think now) much to be recommended' (Hicks, 1980–81, p. 51).

Hicks goes on to argue that in a temporary equilibrium 'The actual outputs of products, and probably also the actual input of labour, would be largely

24. Malinvaud speaks of 'Keynes's theory of the short-term temporary equilibrium' in Krueger (2003, p. 190).
25. On p. 237 of Hicks (1946) there appears the expression 'temporary equilibrium theory of the Keynesian type' but it is not made clear whether this theory is also a fair rendition of Keynes's own notion of short-period equilibrium.

predetermined' (1980–81, p. 55[26]), while in the IS–LM model (as well as in Keynes) the equilibrium output and employment are endogenously determined.

But it seems possible to make more precise the distinction between a temporary equilibrium and Keynes's notion of equilibrium, and to highlight its importance, by focusing on the difference in the *data* of the two notions of equilibrium. It will be shown that precisely where a TGE differs from the traditional notion of long-period equilibrium (in taking as given the initial capital endowments, and expectations), Keynes's analysis – although not a long-period analysis – differs from a TGE and, in essence, still belongs to the traditional method, the one based on 'normal positions' having sufficient persistence so as to bear the traditional role of centres of gravitation of market prices and quantities. This may help one understand why, when it came out, Keynes's analysis was *not* perceived as a fundamental break with tradition, at the level of method. The subsequent tendency to identify Keynes's short-period equilibrium with Hicks's temporary equilibrium may then have contributed to obscuring the break with tradition implicit in the latter notion.

The data of a TGE include two groups of data: first, the initial endowments of each different type of capital goods, and second, the agents' expectations or expectation functions. These data are not to be found among the data of the traditional marginalist long-period equilibrium, and share the characteristic that it seems impossible generally to assume that they remain unchanged for any length of time, if they are arbitrarily given. Expectations or expectation functions are, further, unobservable, and, unavoidably, the assumptions about them and their evolution over time appear to be largely arbitrary. These two problems of the notion of equilibrium implicit in TGE models were named the *impermanence problem* and the *indefiniteness problem*. They are particularly relevant here, because it can be argued that they do not arise, or at least not to the same extent, in Keynes's own analysis: the reason being that Keynes's analysis aimed at determining positions which may function as (short-period) centres of gravitation of the economic system. In this analysis he divides both capital goods and expectations into two categories, more persistent and less persistent, and takes as given only the more persistent ones, while endogenously determining the less persistent

---

26. Note how Hicks admits again, 50 years later, what he had admitted in 1932, that is the little elasticity of output in the very short period, implying a highly inelastic demand for labour, with a high risk of implausible very-short-period equilibrium levels of the real wage (cf. §1.3.2).

ones; as a result, Keynes's equilibrium *is* compatible with the role of centre of gravitation.[27]

2A1.2. Keynes on Expectations

Let us first discuss Keynes's treatment of expectations. To that end, it is useful to start by distinguishing the point of intersection of the aggregate demand and the aggregate supply curves, i.e. what Keynes calls the 'effective demand', from Keynes's short-period equilibrium. When he writes: '... to-day's employment can be correctly described as being governed by to-day's expectations taken in conjunction with to-day's capital equipment' (*GT*, p. 50),[28] he is not defining the *equilibrium* level of employment, but simply the level of employment which, at any given moment, entrepreneurs will decide to offer. Each entrepreneur could be said to be in 'equilibrium' today only in the sense in which an agent is sometimes, and misleadingly, said to be in 'equilibrium' when she is acting according to her optimal choice (thus, in many textbooks, one finds for example the term 'equilibrium of the con-sumer' to mean the consumer's optimal choice): but in this case 'equilibrium' would be simply synonymous with 'rational behaviour'. An extension of this usage to the whole economy would mean that any situation where all agents are behaving rationally could be called an equilibrium: an economy without irrational agents would then necessarily always be in equilibrium. This would mean emptying the concept of equilibrium of its traditional content, and confusing the issues; and Keynes does not use 'equilibrium' in this sense (see below). Thus, I disagree, for example, with Casarosa (1981, p. 190) when he characterizes as 'daily *equilibrium*' (my italics) the point of 'effective demand' (although I agree with Casarosa's reconstruction of Keynes's functions of aggregate supply and aggregate demand).[29]

---

27. The fact that Keynes's analysis is largely immune to the impermanence and indefiniteness problems is not to say that it is acceptable in all its elements: cf., for example Chapter 7 for a criticism of his approach to investment.

28. All quotations from Keynes are from his *Collected Writings* (Keynes 1973–79); these will be referred to, for brevity, as *KCW* followed by the volume number in Roman numerals, except for the *General Theory* (vol. VII of *KCW*) referred to as *GT*.

29. I find Casarosa's reconstruction of Keynes's aggregate supply and aggregate demand curves (Casarosa, 1981) the most persuasive one, requiring the least amount of infidelity to Marshall on Keynes's part, and raising the fewest interpretative puzzles. On this interpretation, the aggregate demand curve D is derived by assuming *given* expected prices and assuming the individual firms' outputs to vary with the level of aggregate employment in the same way as when constructing the aggregate supply curve Z. The point of intersection of the Z and D curves (the point of effective demand, according to Keynes's definition) is therefore only the momentary outcome of the entrepreneurs' maximizations. It is *not* a point of equilibrium, unless price expectations are correct: if they are not, realized results will cause a revision of price expectations, which will cause the point of effective

What is relevant to the present discussion, though, is simply that – as seems to be accepted in almost all recent writings on the subject – although occasionally inconsistent with his own definitions, Keynes distinguishes between the 'daily' level of employment and the *short-period equilibrium* level of employment.

The famous two functions of aggregate supply, *Z*, and of aggregate demand, *D*, are both defined by Keynes in terms of *expected* proceeds: the value of *D* where *D* = *Z* is therefore the value of the proceeds entrepreneurs *expect* to obtain from the corresponding level of employment; and this is the level of employment which will be chosen by the entrepreneurs because, that 'day', they expect it to maximize their profits. When, two pages after defining effective demand, Keynes defines the 'equilibrium level of employment' (*GT*, p. 27), he defines it, on the contrary, as that level of employment that *actually* maximizes the entrepreneurs' profit, that is that level where there is coincidence between *Z* and *actual* expenditure: it is the level, in other words, where *Z* crosses what one may (following Casarosa, 1981) call the *expenditure function*, given by actual consumption expenditure plus actual investment:

> demand to gravitate toward the point of intersection of the *Z* curve and of what Casarosa calls the 'expenditure function', *C + I*: this latter point is the short-period equilibrium. Asimakopulos (1982, p. 20, n. 7) argues against Casarosa that an assumption of given expected prices would make such a construct redundant, since 'Its role ... is simply to determine the point on the aggregate supply function that maximises the entrepreneurs' expectations of profits, given the expectations of price. But this can be done directly... by noting that the aggregation of the profit-maximizing proceeds for each firm (given each set of expectations about prices) determines a single point on the aggregate supply schedule'. This is an unconvincing criticism, because the way Keynes uses the *D* schedule appears precisely to be 'to determine the point on the aggregate supply function that maximises the entrepreneurs' expectations of profits', that is the point of effective demand. Parrinello (1980, p. 70, n. 7) had earlier argued that 'a given state of expectations at the micro level cannot mean (under conditions of competition) a given concave demand function expected by each individual entrepreneur; only a point in the price-quantity space of the firm is relevant in this context'. But there is no need to assume given concave *demand functions* expected by each entrepreneur in order to derive the individual concave *demand price* curves (actually, expected total proceeds functions) whose aggregation should yield the *D* schedule: with given expected prices, demand price curves are linear functions of output. When re-drawn as functions of a variable factor, such as labour, they become concave if the marginal product of the variable factor is decreasing. What then remains of Parrinello's argument is the same argument advanced by Asimakopulos, and criticized above. But these divergences as to the way Keynes defines the *D* schedule do not appear to imply a disagreement among these authors on the substance of Keynes's analysis. They all accept that, according to Keynes, the 'daily' decisions will be revised in the light of realized results, that the short-period equilibrium is what the economy will gravitate toward as a result of this revision of short-period expectations, and that it is given by the intersection of the aggregate supply schedule and the 'expenditure function' (Casarosa's name for what is commonly called the aggregate demand curve).

... employers would make a loss if the whole of the increased employment were to be devoted to satisfying the increased demand for immediate consumption. Thus, to *justify* any given amount of employment there must be an amount of current investment sufficient to absorb the excess of total output over what the community chooses to consume when employment is at the given level ... [;] given what we shall call the community's propensity to consume, the equilibrium level of employment, i.e. *the level at which there is no inducement to employers as a whole either to expand or to contract employment*, will depend on the amount of current investment (*GT*, p. 27; italics added).

It was soon noticed that in Keynes the distinction is not as clear as one might have wished it to be, and that terminology is not consistently adhered to throughout:

Mr. Keynes in fact oscillates between using 'aggregate demand price' to mean what he has defined it to mean, viz. what entrepreneurs *do* expect to receive, and using it to mean (p. 30, line 5) what they 'can expect' to receive, i.e. what they can legitimately expect to receive, because that, whether they expect it or not, is what they *will* receive (Robertson, 1936, p. 171).

The oscillation between the two definitions is undeniable. After writing: 'The relationship between the community's income and what it *can* be expected to spend on consumption, designated by D_1' at the bottom of p. 28 of *GT*, Keynes proceeds to write at the beginning of the next page: 'D_1, the amount which the community *is* expected to spend on consumption' (italics added). Clearly, Keynes is assuming here that the expectations behind the aggregate demand function are correct. The same must hold for the passage where he writes: 'Thus, given the propensity to consume and the rate of new investment, there will be only one level of employment consistent with equilibrium; since any other level will lead to inequality between the aggregate supply price of output as a whole and its aggregate demand price' (*GT*, p. 28). Here Keynes may appear to define *equilibrium* as equality between Z and D, and thus he may appear to identify the point of effective demand, and equilibrium; but, in a letter to D.H. Robertson dated 13 December 1936, Keynes makes it clear that this is not what he meant: 'I do not remember attributing the disappointment of entrepreneurs "to a divergence between aggregate demand price and aggregate supply price". I attribute their failure to produce *more* to this; but their disappointment, if any, I attribute (like you) to a divergence between aggregate demand price and income' (*KCW*, XIV, p. 89).

Thus here aggregate demand price is the *expected* magnitude, income the *realized* magnitude. The passage quoted above from *GT*, p. 28, must then clearly be interpreted as follows: if 'any other level' of employment were established by the entrepreneurs, it would mean that they expected income to be different from what it turns out to be; and this would *lead* to a revision of short-term expectations and hence to a shift of the aggregate demand curve, which would cause the latter not to cross any more the aggregate supply curve at that level of employment. The implication is that the *equilibrium* level of employment is the one at which there is no need to revise one's (static) short-term expectations, and thus, at least at that level of employment, the aggregate demand curve D has the same value as the expenditure function. Short-term expectations are given when determining 'to-day's employment' but this employment is an equilibrium level of employment only if the expectations as to the forthcoming demand are correct. Thus, in equilibrium, short-term expectations are not given, they have adjusted so as to be correct.

Now, Keynes does not assume that short-term expectations are always correct; see, for instance, his analysis of the effects of a reduction of money wages, in ch. 19 of *GT*, from which a quote will be given shortly. When short-term expectations are disappointed, they are modified in the direction suggested by realized results ('producers' forecasts are more often gradually modified in the light of results than in anticipation of prospective changes', *GT*, p. 51); indeed, they are governed by realized results to such an extent as often to make it possible to omit express reference to them:

> Express reference to current long-term expectations can seldom be avoided. But it will often be safe to omit express reference to *short-term* expectation, in view of the fact that in practice the process of revision of short-term expectation is a gradual and continuous one, carried on largely in the light of realised results; so that expected and realised results run into and overlap one another in their influence. [...] the most recent results usually play a predominant part in determining what these expectations are (*GT*, p. 50–51).

Precisely this convergence of short-term expectations to realized results appears to be the reason why Keynes often speaks of effective demand as if it coincided with equilibrium expenditure.

That, in the process of convergence to the Keynesian short-period equilibrium, short-term expectations will be modified is certainly not a novel point; but it has not been used, as far as I am aware, to stress the difference in *data* between Keynes's notion of (short-period) equilibrium, and the TGE notion: the latter notion depends not only on given long-term expectations but also on *given* short-term expectations (or expectation functions); as a corollary, there is no guarantee that, in a TGE, price expectations, even relative to the immediate future, will turn out to be correct, while in Keynes's short period equilibrium short-term expectations *are* correct.

This difference in the treatment of short-term expectations derives from Keynes's conception of the equilibrium as something the economy gravitates around and towards, as a result of the revision of expectations in the light of realised results; thus, in the discussion of money wage reductions already referred to, Keynes writes: 'Thus the proceeds realised from the increased output will disappoint the entrepreneurs and employment will fall back again to its previous figure' (*GT*, p. 261). The methodology implicit in this treatment of expectations, fully in accord with the traditional method, is perhaps most clearly expressed in this passage from a letter to Kalecki, dated 12 April 1937:

> I hope you are not right in thinking that my *General Theory* depends on an assumption that the immediate reaction of a capitalist is of a particular kind. I tried to deal with this on page 271 *[? probably 261, F.P.]*, where I assume that the immediate reaction of capitalists is the most unfavourable to my conclusion. I regard behaviour as arrived at by trial and error, and no theory can be regarded as sound which depends on the *initial* reaction being of a particular kind. One must assume that the initial reaction may be anything in the world, but that the process of trial and error will eventually arrive at the conclusion which one is predicting (*KCW*, XII, p. 797).

(In this letter, clearly the process of trial and error is not an infinitely fast tâtonnement: Keynes never conceives of such a fairy-tale process.) Kregel (1976) has noticed the following passage where Keynes reiterates the same idea: 'The main point is to distinguish the forces determining the position of equilibrium from the technique of trial and error by means of which the entrepreneur discovers where the position is' (*KCW*, XIV, p. 181).[30]

True, only *short*-term expectations are determined endogenously by Keynes as correct in equilibrium, while long-term expectations are taken as exogenous. The justification is that Keynes judges long-term expectations to be generally fairly independent of the current level of employment: 'My own feeling is that present income has a predominant effect in determining liquidity preference and saving which it does not possess in its influence over the inducement to invest' (Letter to J. R. Hicks, 31 March 1937, in *KCW*, XIV, p. 81). '... it is of the nature of long-term expectations that they cannot

---

30. Kregel (1976, p. 224) appears, though, to identify the length of the 'day' when Keynes writes of 'to-day's employment' decisions (in *GT*, p. 50, and in *GT*, p. 47, n. 1), with the length of Keynes's short period, which may include wide fluctuations of output and prices, see *GT*, pp. 10, 12, 93, 97 (incidentally, this is one more demonstration of the illegitimacy of the assimilation of Keynes's short-period analysis to a TGE). Perhaps because of this mistake, Kregel does not notice the difference between 'to-day's employment' and equilibrium employment in Keynes, and the consequent difference between the data concerning expectations in Keynes's equilibrium and in a TGE.

be checked at short intervals in the light of realized results' (*GT*, p. 51). Therefore the data relative to long-term expectations are, according to Keynes, sufficiently persistent relative to the convergence of the economy to the short-period equilibrium.

It might be objected that this sufficient persistence of long-term expectations is not so clear in Keynes, because Keynes sees these expectations as based on flimsy foundations which make them to an extent conventional and hence subject to sudden changes.[31] But as the two preceding quotations in the text show, these changes in long-term expectations were not seen by Keynes as very frequent. On the whole Keynes's treatment of long-term expectations appears to be, again, within the traditional method of connecting them to objective phenomena; they are taken as given when determining the short-period equilibrium, but only because, as already said, they are judged to be generally sufficiently independent of the current level of employment. But their dependence on objective causes is neither denied nor left unanalysed; some of the objective causes considered may be, according to Keynes, short-lived; some may be impossible to predict; but Keynes appears to think one can say quite a lot about the causes affecting changes in long-term expectations. A clear proof is that one can – see chapter 22 of the *General Theory* – reach an explanation of the trade cycle, an explanation in which long-term expectations are endogenously determined by the functioning of the economy. Thus the stress of some post-Keynesians on the unpredictability and erratic nature of expectations appears to have little basis in Keynes's *General Theory*. Thus it is true that for example Keynes writes that, in a slump,

> it is not easy to revive the marginal efficiency of capital, determined, as it is, by the uncontrollable and disobedient psychology of the business world. It is the return of confidence, to speak in ordinary language, which is so insusceptible to control in an economy of individualistic capitalism (*GT*, p. 317),

but, on the other hand, in the sequel of the analysis he makes it clear that this only means that it will be difficult to restore optimism earlier than would otherwise be the case, but still, optimism *will* in the end be restored owing to objective reasons. The elimination of surplus stocks, the reduction even of fixed capital if the slump has been very serious and long-lasting, will in the end revive the marginal efficiency of capital (*GT*, pp. 317–9). Keynes does not seem to differ here, at the level of *method*, from the tradition of studies of accumulation and trade cycles of the Marshallian school or, for that matter,

31. See especially his 1937 article in the *Quarterly Journal of Economics*, 'The general theory of employment' (*KCW*, XIV).

of the classical period.[32] The choice to take long-term expectations as given when analysing the forces determining the short-period equilibrium appears therefore to express a procedure of analytical separation of forces and mechanisms, not unlike the separation to be found in Ricardo or Marx between the determination of prices and the determination of quantities; a separation which is of course only a first step toward more concrete, applied analyses in which this 'ceteris paribus' assumption will be relaxed or qualified.

In the treatment of expectations, then, we see a clear difference between Keynes's analyses and the TGE method. Keynes is concerned with defining an equilibrium which is a centre of gravitation of the economic system, that is such that realistic dynamic adjustment processes, based on trials and errors happening in real time, may bring the economic system toward it. Consequently, short-term expectations are not data of the equilibrium but rather determined endogenously; and long-term expectations, although given in the short period, are not left as an unexplained *deus ex machina*, but become in turn endogenous in the analyses of the trade cycle and of accumulation (except for an element of dependence upon political and other non-economic circumstances, a dependence which, I would think, must be admitted as effectively present in real economies, and prevents economic developments from being entirely predictable). Thus Keynes's treatment of expectations appears to be exempt from the indefiniteness problem.

(A full discussion of Keynes's treatment of long-term expectations falls outside the concerns of this Appendix, and indeed of this book; in order to stress the difference between Keynes and neo-Walrasian equilibria it suffices to notice the difference relative to short-term expectations. I therefore limit myself here to stating my persuasion that what distinguishes Keynes from earlier authors on the determinants of long-term expectations is, not a

---

32. 'In traditional theory, both the long-period position, and the gravitation towards it, were generally explained without introducing price expectations. It may be objected that a particular treatment of price expectations was in fact always implied: that, for example, Smith's argument about the tendency of the market price to fall when it exceeds the natural price implies that producers should expect the high market price to last long enough for them to reap an extra profit by acting now in order to produce more of the commodity later. But the important point of Smith's procedure is precisely that this effect upon the minds of people of a market price exceeding the natural price appeared to be so inescapable as to permit proceeding directly to its objective consequence, increased production. This would seem to be the procedure to be aimed at with respect to 'expectations' in the theory of value: to relate them uniquely to objective phenomena, so as to bypass them and relate the facts explaining the expectations directly to the actions of the individuals' (Garegnani, 1976, p. 140). This description appears fully to apply to Keynes's treatment of short-term expectations, and, I would claim, to that part of long-term expectations too, which depends on the functioning of the economic system itself (rather than on political events, wars, and so on).

characterization of their nature as erratic and unpredictable – as fundamentally exogenous relative to the economic mechanism – but rather a denial of their ready convergence to the ones required by full employment: a denial which appears to be, in the terminology of Garegnani (1976), a difference in *theory* rather than in *method*: a difference deriving, fundamentally, from Keynes's persuasion that the equilibrium position is indeterminate because it can be established at any of a range of values of the level of employment (and of the associated values of the rate of interest), and therefore the long-term expectations concerning the rate of interest and the marginal efficiency of capital can be self-confirming at any of a range of values rather than at a single value. It is because of this persuasion that, according to Keynes, in the determination of long-term expectations there necessarily enter conventional and customary elements that make them susceptible to sudden changes, but resistant to changes in money wages. Whether, given the rest of his analysis, and in particular Keynes's acceptance of the dependence of investment on the rate of interest, this aspect of Keynes's views on long-term expectations is acceptable is a different problem, on which we need not enter here; cf. however Chapter 7, and Garegnani, 1979a).

2A1.3. Keynes on the Endowment of Capital Goods

I turn now to Keynes's treatment of the data concerning the capital goods endowment, in order to show that there too he differs from neo-Walrasian equilibria.

Keynes distinguishes between durable capital on the one hand, and intermediate goods (goods-in-progress, working capital) and inventories (stocks, liquid capital) on the other. In a neo-Walrasian equilibrium, the endowments of *all* of these are data of the determination of equilibrium. In Keynes, they are all data only when what must be determined is the 'daily' decision of entrepreneurs, that is 'to-day's' point of effective demand, which, unless expectations are correct, is not an equilibrium; when the concern is the determination of equilibrium, then the amounts of goods-in-progress and of inventories are determined endogenously, and what is given is only the durable capital.

Thus Keynes writes of 'the increment of working capital corresponding to the greater output' (*GT*, p. 124), and, even more clearly:

However long the notice given to entrepreneurs of a prospective change in demand, it is not possible for the initial elasticity of employment, in response to a given increase of investment, to be as great as its eventual equilibrium value, unless there are surplus stocks and surplus capacity at every stage of production. On the other hand, the depletion of the surplus stock will have an offsetting effect on the amount by which investment increases. If we suppose that there are initially some surpluses at every point, the initial elasticity of employment may approximate to unity; then after the stocks have been absorbed, but before an increased supply is coming forward at an adequate rate from the earlier stages of production, the elasticity will fall away; rising again towards unity as the new position of equilibrium is approached (*GT*, p. 288).

This passage is strikingly clear in distinguishing the initial reaction of entrepreneurs to a change in demand from the 'new position of equilibrium' which is only gradually approached. It also clearly shows the variation of stocks during the adjustment.

Thus when, in chapter 18 of *GT*, Keynes summarizes his argument, and one finds '... the existing quality and quantity of the available equipment' (*GT*, p. 245) included among the 'given factors' that (together with the 'independent variables') determine what appears to be not simply the point of 'effective demand' but rather the equilibrium (cf. p. 249: 'the position of equilibrium', and the description of the multiplier on p. 248), it seems impossible that he intended to include working capital in the given 'equipment' in that sentence.[33]

This is further supported by how Keynes distinguishes the 'given factors' from the 'independent variables' two pages later. The first are '... the factors in which the changes seem to be so slow or so little relevant as to have only a small and comparatively negligible short-term influence on our *quaesitum*' (*GT*, p. 247), while the second are 'those factors in which the changes are found in practice to exercise a dominant influence on our *quaesitum*' (ibid.).

33. In most places in the *General Theory* Keynes appears to mean, by 'capital equipment', the durable or fixed capital only. For example, 'capital equipment' is distinguished from intermediate products when on p. 47 Keynes speaks of the expectations 'which led the firm to acquire the capital equipment and the stock of intermediate products and half-finished materials with which it finds itself at the time when it has to decide the next day's output'; on p. 48 he writes: 'equipment which will not be replaced will continue to give employment until it is worn out'; on p. 49 he writes of 'a change in the direction of consumption which renders certain existing processes and their equipment obsolete'. True, on p. 52 Keynes writes: 'capital equipment, which term includes both his [the entrepreneur's] stock of unfinished goods or working capital and his stock of finished goods'; but it seems clear that here Keynes is using the term in a special, extended sense which is convenient for the purpose of defining national income. The term 'capital equipment' is also used to mean only fixed capital in an early draft of the *General Theory* (*KCW*, XXIX, pp. 74, 87–9). By the way this – given durable capital only – would appear to be also the meaning of Marshall's given 'appliances' in the short period: of such given appliances Marshall writes, for instance, that in the short run 'there is not time for the supply to be reduced by gradual decay' (Marshall, 1920 [1970], V, v, 7, p. 313), and when discussing the short-period equilibrium of the fishing industry what he takes as given is the number and quality of boats and experienced fishermen, not the amounts of nets or hooks or bait. So he is referring to durable capital goods only.

The characterization of the given factors appears incompatible with working capital, which he had described on p. 124 (cf. above) as significantly affected by variations of output.

One may conclude, then, that also in the treatment of the capital endowment the Keynesian equilibrium differs from a TGE in that it does not take as given the endowments of circulating (intermediate) capital goods; thus Keynes is much less open to the methodological criticism (the impermanence problem) which can be advanced on this account against the TGE method. His equilibrium *can* be conceived as sufficiently persistent, relative to the presumable speed of convergence toward it, as to be able to function as the centre of gravitation of time-consuming adjustment processes.

The persistence of Keynes's equilibrium might be questioned on the basis of the dependence, which he admits, of investment itself upon variations of output, owing to the influence of variations of production on inventories and working capital (cf. the quotation above from *GT*, p. 288). So investment appears to change owing to the process itself, of adjustment toward equilibrium. But, although with less clarity – in the *General Theory* – than one might have wished, Keynes does distinguish between intended and actual investment, and takes only investment in durable capital as determined by the rate of interest. Thus he writes to H. D. Henderson on 28 May 1936: 'You must remember that, according to my theory, the rate of investment has to be kept at the level which equates the marginal efficiency of durable goods with the rate of interest' (*KCW*, XXIX, p. 223). We can therefore sketch Keynes's method as follows. The equilibrium level of aggregate production depends on the level of investment in durable capital goods, which will remain constant as long as the rate of interest and long-term expectations do not change. In fact, especially the latter do not remain constant long enough for the economy actually to reach the corresponding short-term equilibrium; the analysis of the short-term equilibrium corresponds therefore to an analytical separation of mechanisms, which in more realistic analyses must be considered in their mutual interactions; thus, the analysis of the trade cycle will include both an analysis of the fluctuations of income due to inventory cycles, and an analysis of – for instance – how long-term expectations are themselves influenced by the general optimism and general pessimism in different phases of the trade cycle. At each moment of the trade cycle, actual income is determined by the level of autonomous investment over a number of preceding periods, and is in pursuit, so to speak, of the equilibrium corresponding to the current level of autonomous investment.

On the level of *method*, then, Keynes appears to be fully within the tradition of Marshallian trade-cycle studies based upon the analysis of forces causing the economy to fluctuate around a 'central' position; his main difference is that his grasp of the principle of effective demand (that is of the role of income variations in bringing about the equality of intended investment and savings) allows him to consider 'central' positions which are not necessarily full-employment positions. This is something that previous marginalist authors *were analytically incapable of doing*, because they could not answer the question: 'suppose that investment (in durable capital) is constant and less than full-employment savings; will employment and output gravitate toward some definite level?'. But this is a difference of *theory*, not of *method*, between Keynes and previous marginalist authors.[34]

Thus, Keynes's analysis inherits the fruitfulness of the traditional method based upon the study of positions the economy gravitates around and towards by means of time-consuming trial and error. It is therefore not surprising that his analysis should have been the starting point for a literature rich in empirical applications.

34. Eatwell and Milgate (1983, p. 10) have even argued that the 'Keynesian short run ... is invoked [by Keynes] not in order to establish the possibility that complete adjustment to a long-run full employment equilibrium of the neoclassical kind will not occur, but rather in order to abstract from those more slowly working secular changes due to accumulation, technological progress and population growth or decline. This procedure ... is more directly analogous to that traditionally adopted for the construction of a long-period theory'. James Meade (1936–37, p. 98) had come very close to such a position when in order to formalize Keynes's theory he had defined the short period 'as the period of time in which the ratio between the output of new capital goods and the existing stock of capital goods is small, so that we can neglect changes in the stock of capital goods' (clearly he had in mind durable capital goods only).

APPENDIX 2A2. FRANKLIN FISHER AND DISEQUILIBRIUM

2A2.1. This Appendix motivates in greater detail the assessment of the contribution by Fisher (1983) presented in §2.2.1.

Fisher admits the necessity to examine disequilibria which involve the implementation of disequilibrium transactions and disequilibrium productions. He considers an economy with complete futures markets for the infinite future, but without an auctioneer. Agents know that they may face transaction constraints due to insufficient monetary purchasing power, or to quantity rationings; prices are proposed by the agents themselves, so that in general there is no uniform price for the same good throughout the economy at any given date; contracts are not provisional, and time goes on, such that there is disequilibrium all the time, and 'false price' transactions and production decisions are implemented; agents may speculate by for example purchasing a good forward because they think they will be able to re-sell it, once obtained, at a better price, or they may abstain from offering a (durable) good for sale because they think they can sell it at a better price in a subsequent period; and so on. Apart from the assumption of the existence of complete futures markets over an infinite horizon, Fisher's description of the choices and constraints open to agents is thus considerably more realistic than in the remaining neo-Walrasian stability literature. But he is able to prove that the economy will converge to *some* rest point (on the indeterminateness of these rest points, see below, p. 70) only by assuming, among other things:

- a given number of firms (an unacceptable assumption in any general equilibrium model, and even more so in intertemporal analyses);
- continuity of prices and of individual endowments with respect to time (no discontinuous jump in any price ever, and continuous flows of transactions; the latter assumption is very unrealistic, given the possibility in real economies of transferring the property of any basket of goods all at once, with a single contract; as to the absence of discontinuities in the time paths of prices, see below);
- continuity of the changes of expectations (expectations have a role in spite of the existence of complete futures markets, because equilibrium is not reached instantaneously, so prices on current and on futures markets keep changing, and speculation is possible);
- no discontinuities caused by bankruptcies, or by impossibilities of honouring contracts owing to mistaken predictions;

- the continuity in the prices of the solution to each agent's optimum problem, and the boundedness of all price, dividend and quantity 'profiles' (that is plans of agents).[35]

Even this series of highly restrictive assumptions would not get Fisher anywhere if he did not also make a very strong assumption which he admits is fundamental to the entire analysis. This assumption, termed *No Favourable Surprise*, stipulates that during the disequilibrium process things never turn out to be better for any household or firm, than she/he/it had expected. This assumption ensures that households' target utilities and firms' target profits are non-increasing through time, so their sum is a Lyapunov function which allows the demonstration of convergence to a rest point.

No Favourable Surprise means that mistakes in predictions can never be made in a pessimistic direction. For instance, it must never happen that a seller discovers that she can sell at a higher price than she had expected: something that comes extremely close to being an assumption of perfect foresight. Fisher admits that it is a quite unrealistic assumption:

> Imagine an exogenous favorable shock to the economy – say, an unanticipated invention. We wish to show that the effects of such a shock will be (quickly) arbitraged away. To do so, it is natural to examine those effects while assuming that further exogenous shocks do not occur. No Favorable Surprise, however, does more than this; it rules out favorable surprises which arise in the course of absorption of the original shock – endogenous shocks, as it were – as well as simply optimistic (possibly incorrect) changes in expectations. Yet the really interesting stability questions may lie in just how such 'endogenous' shocks disappear (Fisher, 1983, p. 91).
>
> ... there is no contention that No Favorable Surprise is an assumption that plausibly characterizes real economies ... It is a first necessary step towards a demonstration that a cessation of *exogenous* shocks leads to convergence. I discuss the details of No Favorable Surprise so as to be able to see just what is involved rather than to contend for its realism (ibid., p. 181).

---

35. See Fisher (1983, p. 204). Fisher tries to argue that the boundedness assumption does not exclude constant returns to scale, by arguing that, even with constant returns to scale, production plans cannot be unbounded because agents know that delivery of unbounded quantities of products is impossible and that the prices of the primary resources directly or indirectly demanded would rise. This clearly excludes price-taking from the analysis, consistently with the assumption that prices are proposed by the agents themselves. But constant returns to scale appear to be excluded anyway from the analysis because of the continuity assumption: it seems difficult to imagine perceived transaction constraints capable of preventing, in the presence of constant returns to scale, discontinuous jumps of production plans, when prices change so as to cause profits to pass from zero or negative to positive, or vice versa.

It is far from clear, however, why No Favourable Surprise should be a 'first necessary step'. One may think of many convergent adjustment processes not associated with 'further exogenous shocks' and yet contradicting No Favourable Surprise, for example, in macroeconomics, the dynamic multiplier during an expansion.

Furthermore, Fisher appears to underestimate how restrictive that assumption is; for example, he appears not to see that the claim he advances, that No Favourable Surprise is weaker than an assumption of perfect foresight or rational expectations, needs the assumption of no discontinuity in price changes. As noted by Madden (1984), discontinuous price changes, such as one usually observes in real economies, are perforce associated with advantages for one side of the market. If one admits discontinuous price changes, the only way to guarantee No Favourable Surprise is to assume that they were not unexpected, that is perfect foresight. Matters are not improved by the fact that, given Fisher's admission of price setting by individual agents, the assumption of continuous price changes appears implausible anyway: when the buyer and the seller of the same commodity each discovers the price proposed by the other (and the two prices are different) they must decide whether to exchange or not. Any agreement they might reach will generally entail a price discontinuity for at least one of them.

Furthermore the exclusion of any improvement in utility or profit levels when prices change, even with continuous price changes and no assumption of perfect foresight, imposes implausible restrictions on trade flows. For example, assuming no price dispersion and pure exchange (as in the Hahn Process which is the starting point of the analysis, see Hahn and Negishi, 1962, and Fisher, 1983, ch. 3), if the price of a commodity unexpectedly starts changing (at finite speed and continuously), the assumption of no improvement in utility implies that each trader must stay on the same indifference surface she started on, that is each trader must trade at exactly the right speed to remain always at the point of tangency of the moving price hyperplane with the initial indifference surface.[36] This is difficult to justify, since it is unclear why the trader should trade at all, as she achieves no advantage from doing so.

A final observation is that No Favourable Surprise would become even more difficult to justify if the assumption of complete futures markets were dropped and in its place one adopted a temporary-equilibrium framework, where expectations about future prices would become much more arbitrary.

---

36. As it is generally impossible for all agents to remain on the same indifference surface, one finds reasons here to conclude, again, that No Favourable Surprise will generally imply perfect foresight.

2A2.2. By directly ensuring that a Lyapunov function for the dynamic system exists, No Favourable Surprise powerfully ensures convergence, thereby allowing Fisher to remain very general on many aspects of the analysis. He is extremely vague, for instance, on how agents set prices; he does not even assume that when, on a market, supply exceeds demand, the price will decrease. Also, the analysis is compatible with flexible as well as with fixed prices, and Fisher makes no assumption restricting the possibilities in this respect. Nor does the analysis need specific hypotheses about expectation formation and change, beyond those mentioned above and needed to ensure the continuity of the dynamic process.

The result is that the rest points to which the economy might converge remain largely unspecified in their characteristics. What is clear is that they are not the equilibria associated with the initial endowments; apart from this, little can be said, since they are not necessarily Arrow–Debreu, nor necessarily full-employment, equilibria. This is so, not only because prices might be rigid for unexplained, exogenous reasons (there is therefore room for the results generated by fixprice, quantity-rationing models); but also because, in disequilibrium, one cannot be certain to be able to carry through all her intended transactions, since supply does not generally equal demand. Therefore agents must optimize, subject to perceived transaction constraints; and these perceived transaction constraints may cause the rest point to be of almost any kind.[37] Fisher has to admit, for example, that it is possible that the economy may get stuck in 'a trivial sort of fixed-price equilibrium which occurs because nobody believes he can transact anything and hence does not try it. We shall assume this does not happen' (Fisher, 1983, pp. 151–2). Also, although futures markets exist, agents may abstain from transacting in futures because they believe that it is more convenient to wait, or that they would not find partners to the transaction.

In the light of Fisher's honest admission of these indeterminacies, as well as of the little plausibility of the assumption of No Favourable Surprise, it is somewhat surprising that Fisher should end up by arguing that his result is an

---

37. On this issue, in the concluding chapter Fisher admits: '... the answer to the question of how perceived demand and supply curves change – which, as we have seen, is also the question of how prices are set – determines whether or not equilibria will be Walrasian ... it appears virtually certain that we cannot decide whether such positions are competitive or noncompetitive without a more detailed examination of the process of disequilibrium adjustment than has so far proved possible. Nor is this a matter of only microeconomic interest. The question of whether the economy converges to a quantity-constrained equilibrium, possibly with underemployment *à la* Keynes, has been seen intimately to involve the question of how perceptions of demand and supply change. Such questions cannot be answered by looking only at the existence of such equilibria; they depend on the specifics of the adjustment process – specifics that are sadly lacking in the present state of the art' (pp. 215–16).

important progress that asks for further research, and that the way forward from his results should consist in the development of more primitively based models, which allow No Favourable Surprise to be *inferred* rather than assumed to start with. As noted above, there is no reason to consider No Favourable Surprise a plausible assumption, and anyway it does not sufficiently restrict the possible end results. It is not surprising that, to the best of my knowledge, no further research has been done in the direction advocated by Fisher, not even by Fisher himself.

3. Long-Period Equilibria

3.1. THE LONG-PERIOD EQUILIBRIUM WITHOUT A RATE OF INTEREST, IN ECONOMIES WITH PRODUCTION BUT WITHOUT CAPITAL

3.1.1. This chapter illustrates the logic of the notion of long-period equilibrium, above all in order to dispel the frequent misunderstanding that the conception of capital as a single factor is only associated with aggregate production functions. It will be shown that a long-period general equilibrium needs the conception of capital as a single factor in spite of its complete disaggregation.

Two caveats are in order. The first is that the formalization to be presented is different from the historically proposed ones, and yet has every right to be considered a faithful rendition of the notion of long-period equilibrium. The only marginalist authors who attempted the complete formalization of a long-period general equilibrium where the composition of capital is endogenously determined were Knut Wicksell and some of his pupils, and they represented technology through production functions where the inputs are amounts of dated labour and dated land. The representation of the technological possibilities adopted here is, to the contrary, the usual one; however, it is shown in the Appendix to this chapter that the model presented here is simply a more general reformulation of Wicksell's model.

The second caveat concerns the fact that the model presented in this chapter neglects changes in relative prices over time. Today the dominant opinion appears to be that this treatment of prices is only legitimate in steady states; but this is *not* what traditional marginalist authors thought. The long-period equilibrium of traditional marginalists was definitely not conceived as being applicable only to steady-state situations. The neglect of the change that normal relative prices may be undergoing over time was only a simplification; and indeed, although historically this has not been done, it would seem that the formalization of long-period equilibria with non-constant relative prices would not present difficulties beyond those that already arise in cases with constant relative prices. The demonstration of these statements is postponed to Chapter 4; however now I offer some further reasons (besides those of §1.5.1) why it can be considered legitimate to neglect the changes that normal, or long-period, relative prices may be undergoing over time in spite of there being no assumption that these changes are in fact absent.

Even in a marginalist economy without capital goods, where production only utilizes labour and land, there may be gradual changes of relative prices over time, for either of the following reasons: there may be population growth that alters the relative scarcity of labour and land; or, since even in such an economy there may be saving and lending, there may be changes over time in the wealth of individuals as a result of the saving of some, and the dissaving of others, and this may alter the composition of demand. Now, it might be argued that the determination of the saving and lending decisions of individuals ought to take into account the changes that relative prices might undergo in the future. But the changes that relative factor prices might be undergoing over time for this type of cause will, in all plausibility, be so slow, that to neglect them will imply only a negligible error, of no importance for understanding the operation of the basic substitution mechanisms determining income distribution in any given year according to the marginalist approach (and also of no importance for the analyses, based on comparative statics, aiming at understanding the effects of changes in relative factor endowments, in taxation, and so on).

As long as one accepts the conception of capital as a single factor of variable 'form', when one turns to economies with capital goods the same type of consideration applies. The determination of a uniform rate of return on supply price in all employments of savings must take into account the possible changes in relative prices over time. There is now one further reason why relative prices may change over time: net savings may imply a change over time in the capital–labour ratio and hence in relative factor prices. Solow's growth model (1956) makes this clear, by showing the slow change of the returns to labour and to capital over time caused by the change in the K/L ratio outside the steady state. (As recalled at the end of Chapter 1, a long-period equilibrium is not a steady-state equilibrium. The latter is rather a *secular* equilibrium, requiring the consideration of time horizons much longer than those allowing adaptations in the composition of capital.) But again, it appears very reasonable that the speed of variation in relative factor prices due to this reason will be of a lower order of magnitude than the speed with which the composition of capital can adapt to the composition of demand. So here too the changes in relative prices caused by the slow changes in factor proportions can be presumed to be so slow as to be negligible at least in a first approximation.

The originators of the marginalist approach therefore saw no reason to abandon the assumption made by all earlier economists, that for the determination of normal long-period positions relative prices could be treated as if constant.

Modern economists are often confused by the fact that in Marshall, J.B. Clark and Wicksell, this treatment of relative prices goes together with an assumption of stationary state. It is frequently thought that the stationary-state assumption was made precisely in order to make legitimate the neglect of changes of relative prices over time. That this is a mistaken interpretation is clearly revealed, for example, by the fact that the same neglect of price changes is found in Smith, Ricardo, Marx or even Walras, all of whom were unambiguously *not* assuming a stationary economy. Wicksell was explicit that he considered the stationary state to be only a simplifying assumption; the reason for the stationary state assumption in J.B. Clark, Marshall or Wicksell was a different, essentially expository one, intended to present in the clearest way the factor substitution mechanisms determining distribution, leaving aside the complications connected with net savings. And what was assumed was not, anyway, a *secular* stationary state (where the absence of net savings results from the endogenous adjustment of the ratio between the capital endowment and the endowments of other factors) but rather a *static* state, where the endowment of capital is *given* and net savings are simply *assumed* to be zero. All this will be explained in Chapter 4.

3.1.2. The logic of a long-period general equilibrium with capital goods can be more clearly grasped if one contrasts it with the long-period general equilibrium with production, but with only non-produced, or primary factors of production. Here it is necessary to specify 'the *long-period* general equilibrium without capital goods', because some differences from the modern presentations of general equilibrium theory arise even before one introduces capital goods.

In order to concentrate on the issues central to this book, a number of simplifying assumptions will be made in what follows. Production takes one period, and each production cycle is self-contained; the equilibrium corresponding to one production cycle can be determined without any need to consider other production cycles. There is no joint production. The economy's endowment of labour (or of each type of labour, if there are distinct types of labour, each one treated as a different factor) is stationary.

Initially I assume that there is no interest rate because there is no saving nor dissaving, no borrowing nor lending.

A production function $q_i = f_i(x_{1i}, x_{2i}, ..., x_{ni})$ gives the output of good i at the end of the period, as a function of the amounts of factors x_{1i}, x_{2i} and so on, employed during the period in its production. There is free entry, and there are no fixed factors for individual firms (this is what one must of course assume if one intends to determine a long-period equilibrium). Then, as is well known, free competition implies that product prices will tend to equal minimum average costs, and as long as in each industry there is no product differentiation and the minimum efficient scale of firms is small relative to industry output, competition will oblige all firms in the same industry to adopt the same technical coefficients (that is the same inputs per unit of output), the ones yielding the minimum average cost.[1] Then, owing to variation of the number of firms, even when individual firms have U-shaped long-period average cost curves the industry will behave, with sufficient approximation, like a single price-taking firm with a constant-returns-to-scale technology. If factor rentals are given, the supply curve of each industry is therefore horizontal at the level equal to the minimum average cost.

Equilibrium then requires that product prices equal minimum average costs, and so we have as many 'price = minimum average cost' equations as there are products. Let p be the *row* vector of product prices, and let m be the number of products, so $p = (p_1, ..., p_i, ..., p_m)$.

Let v_j stand for the rental of factor j, $j = 1, ..., n$; let us assume that rentals are paid at the end of the production cycle, when the product comes out; and let

$$MAC_i(v_1, ..., v_n)$$

stand for the minimum average cost of producing good i, when factor rentals are $v_1, ..., v_n$. Because of constant returns to scale, in order to determine MAC_i it suffices to minimize the cost of producing one unit of output of good i. The resulting optimal factor employments per unit of output, which I assume are uniquely determined for each vector of factor rentals, can be called the *technical coefficients* of industry i; they are functions of (relative) factor rentals and will be indicated as $a_{ji}(v_1, ..., v_n)$, $j = 1, ..., n$. If we let A stand for the $(n \times m)$ matrix of technical coefficients (where the i-th column represents the inputs per unit of product of the i-th industry), and v stand for the *row* vector of factor rentals, then the price = average cost equations

$$p_i = MAC_i(v_1, ..., v_n), \qquad i = 1, ..., m$$

can be written in compact form as

$$p = vA(v), \qquad\qquad [3.1]$$

1. In order to keep the analysis close to tradition, I assume that the cost-minimizing technical coefficients are uniquely determined for each vector of relative factor rentals.

where $A(v)$ is the matrix of the functions $a_{ji}(v)$, homogeneous of degree zero in v, where $a_{ji}(v)$ is the technical coefficient of input j in the production of good i.

3.1.3. Let us note a difference between the traditional, long-period marginalist analyses of the equilibrium of a production economy, whose spirit is respected here, and the more modern presentations of general equilibrium. In many modern introductions to general equilibrium with production there is no free entry; it is assumed that there is a *given* number of firms, and it is often further assumed that the production functions exhibit sufficiently decreasing returns to scale for the existence of supply functions of firms. Then, owing to the adding-up theorem, in each firm the payment to factors of their value marginal products leaves a positive residue, a profit[2] that is distributed to consumers according to the given distribution of the ownership of shares. In the formulation of the consumers' budget constraint there also appears, therefore, income from share ownership.[3]

On the other hand, in traditional equilibrium analyses it was taken for granted that, owing to free entry, returns to scale for the industry were constant, and therefore, at given factor rentals, product supplies were not *functions* of product prices, being either zero (if the product price was lower than MAC) or infinite (if product price was higher than MAC) or indeterminate (if the two were equal).[4] Accordingly, the sole possible

---

2.   In this chapter, by profit, I mean the usual marginalist definition, not the classical one.
3.   The given distribution of shares among consumers is one more group of data of neo-Walrasian equilibria deprived of any persistence. This point has not been stressed in Chapter 2 because, as argued in Appendix 5A3, the sole acceptable assumption even in neo-Walrasian models (at least in intertemporal equilibria with complete futures markets) is zero equilibrium profits, and then the distribution of share ownership is irrelevant.
4.   That is, the supply curve of a product, at *given* factor rentals, was assumed to be horizontal at the price equal to minimum average cost. An upward-sloping long-period supply curve for a product could only be derived as a comparative-statics construction showing how the equilibrium price (= *MAC*) of a product changed if the composition of demand changed and factor rentals *changed* so as to re-establish equilibrium on factor markets. The logic behind such a derivation can be made clear by referring to an economy where $m > 2$ consumption goods are produced by two factors only, labour and land, supplied in rigid amounts. Let us suppose that good 1 is produced by techniques with a higher labour-to-land ratio than on the average in the economy. For simplicity in the rest of this footnote we will use 'labour intensity' to mean labour-to-land ratio. Starting from a full employment equilibrium, an expansion of the supply of good 1, with unchanged input proportions in all industries and unchanged proportions between the outputs of the *other* products, would entail an excess demand for labour or an excess supply of land. In order to maintain the equality between supply and demand for both labour and land, it is therefore necessary that in at least some industries the methods of production change in favour of less labour-intensive methods, and/or that, in the complex of the industries other than the first one, the average labour–land ratio be reduced by a contraction of the relative production of the more 'labour-intensive'

equilibrium prices were the prices equal to minimum average cost, that is zero-profit prices; supply had to be assumed to adapt passively to demand at zero-profit prices; and in the treatment of consumers' endowments there was no need to consider rights to shares of the profits of firms.

In the modern treatments, it is true, it is usually added that the analysis must be able to encompass the case of constant returns to scale, and some attention is then given to this case, explaining that unfortunately it raises some mathematical complications, because it gives rise to supply correspondences instead of supply functions; but in this way the traditional treatment of production in general equilibrium analyses becomes, in the modern presentations, something of a special case, and students are habituated to raise no qualms about hypotheses, for example the given number of firms, that traditional marginalist authors would have unanimously judged indefensible.

We can see here some first effects of the modern shift to very-short-period notions of equilibrium: without such a shift, it seems clear that the exclusion of free entry would have been unanimously found indefensible.[5]

among the remaining $m - 1$ goods. Both processes require that labour become more expensive relative to land (which is exactly what would result from an initial attempt to increase the supply of good 1); this will not only induce the adoption of less labour-intensive methods where there are alternative methods available, but also, by making labour-intensive goods more expensive relative to less labour-intensive goods, it will plausibly – or so it is argued – induce the required shift in the composition of the demand for the other consumption goods, away from the more labour-intensive ones. And since by assumption the good in question is labour-intensive, the result of the higher labour wage will be that the good becomes more expensive relative to a good produced with the average labour–land ratio. Thus a higher output of the good requires a higher price of the good in question, relative to a numeraire good produced with the average labour–land ratio. (Obviously this derivation requires that the 'indirect' substitution mechanism works 'well', and that it is not upset by backward-bending supply curves of factors.) The supply curve thus derived is then a locus of quantity-price combinations derived from a comparative-statics exercise of comparison of general equilibria differing in the marginal utility, and thus in the demand, and hence in the equilibrium supply, of the good in question. The more usual textbook derivation of an upward-sloping supply curve of a product in a partial-equilibrium short-period context, that is under an assumption of some fixed factor for the industry or for the firms in the industry, will upon reflection reveal itself to be no more than a special case of the above general-equilibrium derivation, in which there is a factor (or a number of factors: the fixed plants) specific to the production of the good in question: cf. §5A3.3.2.

5. In Appendix 5A3 it will be argued that even in a very-short-period framework the assumption of a given number of firms, as well as the assumption of decreasing returns to scale (and hence of positive profits in equilibrium) for individual firms, are hardly defensible. There is no reason why the number of firms should not be variable even in the shortest period (how much time does it take legally to set up a firm, and to purchase or hire already-existing capital goods?); and it is unclear why even in the very short period a firm should not be able to consider the replication of plants and managers, purchasing them from other firms if necessary (a firm can always sell its fixed factors to other firms, so no factor

3.1.4. Let us now deal with the determination of the quantities produced. We have seen that, owing to free entry, profits must be zero in equilibrium, and that therefore, for each given vector of factor rentals, prices must be assumed to be equal to minimum average costs, and supplies must be assumed to adapt to the demands forthcoming at those factor rentals and related product prices.[6]

The demands are derived from consumer decisions in the standard way, so we need not enter into a formalization of the consumer problem. Each consumer is endowed with given endowments of the several factors of production, and maximizes her utility subject to a budget constraint stating that the value of her purchases cannot exceed the value of the income earned by the factors of production she supplies. For each vector of (ratios of) factor rentals and product prices, each consumer's demands and supplies are (under an assumption of strict convexity of indifference curves) uniquely determined, and therefore aggregate product demands, and factor supplies to firms, being simply the net sums of the consumers' demands and supplies, are well-determined functions of relative prices.

Because it helps intuition to formulate demand = supply equations in which one side is determined by the decisions of consumers and the other by firms, I shall for simplicity assume that consumers only demand produced goods (alternatively one may assume that the aggregate factor supplies considered below are to be intended as the aggregate *net* factor supplies of consumers as a whole, that is the supplies to firms).

By assumption, firms do not own factors; if the owners of a firm contribute some factors to the firm's inputs, one logically separates their role as owners, from their role as consumers and factor suppliers. In this sense, firms have neither endowments nor inventories,[7] only production functions.

In a long-period equilibrium the endowments consist only of factors of production. Under the present hypothesis of absence of produced means of production, it is therefore possible to distinguish in two categories the objects

should be considered fixed *for firms*). But this criticism only means that the logic of short-period analysis was inadequately grasped by some of the modern general equilibrium theorists; still, without a shift of the analysis to a short-period framework, those assumptions could never have become so widespread; free entry is inevitably part of long-period analyses. In fact it is with Hicks's abandonment of long-period analysis in *Value and Capital* that the assumption, of a given number of firms endowed with decreasing-returns-to-scale production functions, appears for the first time in a treatise on general equilibrium theory (Hicks, 1946, pp. 100–101).

6. This adaptation of product supplies to demands raises awkward problems in neo-Walrasian stability analyses the moment free entry of firms is admitted, problems which are discussed in Appendix 5A3.
7. On inventories, cf. §1.4.3.

traded in the economy: (services of) factors of production, and products, that is consumption goods.

Then let q be the *column* vector of productions, $q = (q_1, \ldots, q_m)^T$, and let $Q(p,v) = (Q_1(p,v), \ldots, Q_m(p,v))^T$ be the *column* vector of aggregate demand functions for consumption goods, derived from the consumers' utility maximization on the basis of their given tastes and given endowments of factors. Q depends only on relative prices, that is it is homogeneous of degree zero in (p, v). The conditions of equality between supply and demand for products are, in compact form,

$$q = Q(p, v). \qquad [3.2]$$

Given q and v, the firms' demands for factors are determined by their technical choices, represented by the matrix of technical coefficients $A(v)$. Let $x = (x_1, \ldots, x_n)^T$ stand for the *column* vector of firms' aggregate factor demands; these demands are determined by $x = A(v)q$.

Finally, let $X(p,v) = (X_1(p,v), \ldots, X_n(p,v))^T$ stand for the column vector of consumers' net aggregate supply functions of (services of) factors to firms, homogeneous of degree zero in (p, v). The last group of equations imposes that these supplies must not exceed the firms' demands for factors; if for brevity we replace these demands x with the expression determining them, $A(v)q$, we obtain:

$$X(p,v) \geq x \equiv A(v)q, \text{ and if } X_j > x_j, \text{ then } v_j = 0. \qquad [3.3]$$

3.2. THE RATE OF INTEREST IN ECONOMIES WITHOUT CAPITAL

3.2.1. Let us now introduce loans, and thus interest, to this economy (still without capital). Traditional marginalist authors do not offer formalizations of this case (the rate of interest is introduced together with capital), but we can attempt such a study now in the spirit of long-period analysis, and it will be useful as a benchmark, in order better to understand (i) the contrast with neo-Walrasian models, and (ii) the difference made by the introduction of produced means of production.

Initially, issue (i) attracts our attention: we must explain why the consideration of loans does not require the introduction of dated commodities.

Let us assume that there is only one type of loan, for one period, and in real terms, that is in terms of a consumption good chosen as numeraire.

As in a pure exchange economy, it will be possible for some consumers to save, and transfer purchasing power into the future, only if some other consumers dissave. Indeed, consideration of the pure exchange economy is sufficient to make the point that interests us now. Let us therefore consider for a moment a pure exchange economy with savings and loans.

As noted in §1.2.7, in an exchange economy it is unrealistic to assume that, after any change in the data, the equilibrium is reached immediately. 'False-price' exchanges – to use the term proposed by Hicks[8] – are inevitable, and prices and quantities will converge, if at all, to an equilibrium only if one allows agents to learn and modify their actions over a succession of periods. Furthermore, the details of disequilibrium are impossible to determine. What economic theory can legitimately aim at determining is therefore only the position towards which the economy tends. But the determination of these final-rest positions is only legitimate if these positions are sufficiently persistent relative to the presumable speed of convergence; otherwise the processes of learning and error-correction would have no basis. Thus the equilibrium of an exchange economy can only be useful if it refers to a situation of constant, or nearly constant data, period after period. Now, the data of each period's equilibrium are the number of consumers, their tastes, their endowments, and their debts or credits. The first three groups of data must be assumed constant, or changing slowly enough that one may neglect the change. The debts and credits of individual consumers, to the contrary, might be changing endogenously (*exogenous* changes in the data are of course to be analysed via comparative statics) and sometimes quickly. It would, however, be an exceptional case indeed, if these changes, in economies with many consumers, were to cause more than very slow changes in the aggregate excess demands for the several goods; thus for the purposes of the analysis (which is after all interested only in aggregate excess demands), the dependence of the aggregate excess demands on relative prices and on the rate of interest can be presumed to change, if at all, only with a speed of the same order of magnitude as, for example, population.

Then there is no need to assume complete futures markets, nor exogenously given price expectations. Equilibrium prices are either constant or changing slowly enough that their changes can be neglected. The constant or nearly constant relative prices also make it possible to speak of 'the' rate of interest. The introduction of future variables as distinct variables into the excess demand equations for current goods is therefore unnecessary.[9] The

8. See Hicks (1946, p. 128).
9. One must bear in mind that it is not the purpose of long-period value theory to analyse the changes brought about over time by changes in population or by net savings; the latter changes pertain to the study of accumulation. It might be objected that there are certain investment decisions which take into account such a lengthy time horizon that the expected changes in relative prices acquire clear relevance; for example purchases of houses as an investment often take into account the expected rise in time of their value. Where the trend

consumer's problem can be formulated as including a decision as to how much to save, in terms of a representative basket of consumer goods, depending on current prices and the rate of interest. This makes it possible to arrive at an aggregate excess supply of savings, which must be zero in equilibrium.

Such an approach may also claim the advantage that it needs much less stringent assumptions as to the rationality and the computing capabilites of consumers vis-à-vis intertemporal decisions: considering the absence of complete contingent futures markets, the existence of ineliminable uncertainty (for example about future technical progress), the irrational element in decisions involving true uncertainty or gambling, and the all too human desire not to dwell on how much longer one will live, there is much to be said in favour of an approach that only assumes that it is possible to postulate an aggregate excess demand for loans as a function of current variables only.

3.2.2. Thus, already the pure exchange economy allows us to understand why in the traditional marginalist authors, including Walras, the net supply of savings coming from consumers is considered a function of current variables only, and the notion of 'the' rate of interest also appears. The very sensible idea that the equilibrium must be a situation the economy gravitates towards in real time, through trial and error, and that it must therefore be persistent, avoids the unhappy dilemma which arises in neo-Walrasian general equilibrium analyses, between the implausible assumption of complete futures markets over an infinite horizon, or the inclusion of unobservable and unpredictably changing expectations among the data.

In relation to the determination of the rate of interest, we are now ready to appreciate what little difference it makes, for the determination of the rate of interest, to admit a-capitalistic production. Let us envision the functioning of the economy as follows. All consumption goods require one period for their production, and for all of them the production is in cycles, starting at the beginning of the period (just after the big market fair which will be described presently) and reaching completion at the end of the period. All consumption goods are perishable. At the beginning of each period, soon after the

of the relative price in question was clear and there was no reason to expect that it changed, a long-period equilibrium might have included the rate of change of that price among the data determining the agents' decisions; but for the purpose of clarifying the basic forces determining quantities and distribution, it seems clear that such cases could be neglected. Furthermore, such cases could be considered at a second level of approximation, on the basis of more historically specific data such as the observed trend in incomes, in changes of tastes, and the expectations as to government policies and so on. These considerations explain, I would suggest, why these cases are not considered in the traditional presentations of (long-period) general equilibria.

productions of the previous period have been completed, consumers are paid – *in kind*, I shall assume, because I do not wish to introduce money explicitly here[10] – the previously agreed rentals on their factor supplies of the previous period, and debts are paid. After these payments, consumers find themselves with an endowment of factors and an endowment of consumption goods. The big market fair then occurs, where goods are exchanged, factors are lent out to firms for the period's production cycle, and loans are made. Loans again give some consumers the possibility to consume more goods than their endowments of goods would allow; but it remains true that the only way for a consumer to save is to find other consumers in that same market fair who want to dissave.

The only formal modifications to the system of equations [3.1]–[3.4], required by the existence of savings and loans, are therefore the following. First, in equations [3.2] and [3.4], the demand functions for goods and supply functions of factor services now become functions of the rate of interest r as well:

$$q = Q(p,v,r), \qquad\qquad [3.4]$$

$$X(p,v,r) \geq x \equiv A(v)q, \text{ and if } X_j > x_j, \text{ then } v_j = 0. \qquad [3.5]$$

(The price = cost equations do not require modification because factor rentals are assumed to be paid at the end of the production cycle: the rate of interest does not enter costs of production because no anticipation of capital is necessary.) Second, the appearance of one more unknown, the rate of interest, is counterbalanced by a new equation, the condition of equilibrium on the loans market. Let $S(p,v,r)$ represent the aggregate *net* supply of savings by consumers, valued in terms of the numeraire commodity. Then equilibrium on the loans market requires that this net supply be zero:

$$S(p,v,r) = 0. \qquad\qquad [3.6]$$

3.3.   THE INTRODUCTION OF CAPITAL GOODS

3.3.1. If one admits produced means of production among the factors, that is if one admits capital goods, it is no longer true that aggregate (net) savings must be zero.

If for instance one imagines that there is only one product, corn, which is both a consumption good and a (circulating) capital good (seed), then at the

---

10. On the role of money in long-period equilibria, cf. Appendix 5A1.

beginning of each production cycle the corn produced in the previous cycle is an endowment, it is a datum of the analysis. It belongs to some consumer or other, having gone to them either as gross repayment of interest on capital, or as wages or rents or – if there was disequilibrium – as entrepreneurial profits. Consumers decide how much of this corn to consume in the aggregate, and how much to save; their aggregate gross savings (that is their aggregate supply of corn to firms, netted of the loans to other consumers) are offered to firms, and, if accepted, become the capital stock of the period. Thus it is now possible for the aggregate of consumers to postpone consumption, because the corn not consumed goes to increase future production and thus makes it possible to consume more in the future.

In such an economy the stock of capital supplied to firms is endogenous, what is given is the stock of corn available after the harvest both for consumption and for use as seed-capital. But in the great majority of cases in real economies capital goods and consumption goods are generally different goods; a decision to consume less or more will only affect the flow of savings,[11] and although the stocks of most individual capital goods can be very quickly altered, the aggregate stock of 'capital' (for the moment we are not questioning this notion, we want to clarify the logic of long-period marginalist equilibria) is only slowly altered by net savings; therefore the aggregate capital stock can legitimately be taken as given when determining a long-period equilibrium, just like the stocks of (the several kinds of) labour and land.

3.3.2. We can now proceed to formalize the long-period equilibrium with capital goods. I shall remain close to Walras and to the modern treatments, by treating the several capital goods as distinct factors of production in the firms' production functions, rather than adopting an 'Austrian' representation of technologies (on the latter, cf. Appendix 3A).

We can approach the formalization of the equilibrium by discussing the modifications to be introduced into the system of equations [3.1]–[3.4]–[3.5]–[3.6].

Let us now assume that the technically distinct factors are $n + 1$, the first n of them being capital goods, that is produced means of production. The last factor of production is homogeneous labour. (The neglect of land is obviously unrealistic, but the problems which this book wants to discuss arise even when land is free, and then simplicity suggests that land be left out.)

---

11. The marginalist approach, which we are intent upon clarifying, assumes the full employment of resources; Keynesian effects of changes in the propensity to consume upon aggregate output and employment are excluded here.

Some of the products of the economy are capital goods. For simplicity and as an aid to intuition, I assume that capital goods and consumption goods do not overlap: the *m* consumption goods are useless as means of production, and the *n* capital goods yield no direct utility. Thus the economy produces (or may produce) *m* + *n* products.

Production is of the point-input, point-output type, taking one period in all industries, with factor rentals paid at the end of the period. This assumption makes it easier to link the analysis, now to be presented, with those of Wicksell, and of Sraffa.

I also maintain the hypothesis of technological constant returns to scale for the industries. I further assume absence of joint production except for the existence of durable capital goods; but for simplicity the need to treat partially worn-out durable capital goods as joint products will be circumvented through the all-too-common assumption (also in Walras) that durable capital goods deteriorate radioactively, as if by evaporation, that is that utilization for a period causes each capital good *i* to lose a constant proportion d_i (specific to itself and independent of the methods of production in which it is used) of its efficiency, as if it had shrunk in size.

Let us follow Walras in imagining that capital goods are not bought, but only rented, by firms, which pay the rentals at the end of the production cycle. The capital goods, as they are produced, are bought by consumers with their savings. The first *n* factor rentals $v_1, ..., v_n$ are therefore rentals on capital goods. The rental of labour – the wage rate – can, as usual, be indicated as *w*.

Then equations [3.1], price = minimum average cost for the consumption goods, need no modification, but to them one must add *n* more equations establishing the equality between selling price and minimum average cost for the newly produced capital goods.

Let us then re-define *p* to be the *n* + *m* row vector (p_k, p_c) whose first *n* components, the sub-vector $p_k = (p_1, ..., p_n)$ represents the purchase prices of the newly produced capital goods, and the last *m* components, the sub-vector $p_k = (p_{n+1}, ..., p_{n+m})$ represents the prices of consumption goods. Let us analogously re-define *A* to be the $n \times (n + m)$ matrix of technical coefficients of the non-labour inputs, the first *n* columns representing the technical coefficients of the capital-goods industries and the other columns representing the technical coefficients of the consumption-goods industries; let ℓ now stand for the row vector of technical coefficients of labour inputs. Technical coefficients are functions of relative factor rentals (that is they are determined by cost minimization). Then we can write

$$p = vA(v, w) + w\ell(v, w). \qquad [3.7]$$

This set of equations expresses the same price = cost conditions as equations [3.1], but it applies now also to the newly produced capital goods.

Let $q = (q_c, q_k)$ be the $n + m$-vector of quantities produced, the first n of them (the sub-vector q_c) being quantities of newly produced capital goods, and the last m of them (the sub-vector q_k) being quantities of consumption goods.

Let $Q(p,v,w,r)$ be the $n + m$-vector of demand functions for consumption goods, derived from consumer choices, and by assumption equal to zero for the first n goods which are pure capital goods. (As we shall see, capital must be conceived as a single factor 'capital' embodied in the several capital goods and capable of changing 'form'; the given capital endowment of each consumer will accordingly be measured in the same units in which the total 'capital' endowment of the economy is measured; we shall see that 'capital' must be measured as an amount of value; the given endowment of 'capital' of each consumer can therefore be taken to be a given amount of value; if the reader finds this perplexing, she/he is right, but this is precisely the weak spot of the theory we shall insist upon later, so for the moment the reader is asked to suspend disbelief and accept this given value endowment so as to be able to follow the logic of the theory.) r is the rate of interest.

Finally let k be the $n + m$-vector of investment demands, that is of demands for newly produced capital goods, whose determination is discussed later, and whose last m elements are zeros.[12] Then in equilibrium we have $n + m$ production = demand equations; in vector notation the equations, which correspond to equations [3.4], are:

$$q = Q(p,v,w,r) + k \qquad [3.8]$$

Now let X be the n-vector of endowments of capital goods (which are not given, they are variables to be determined by the equilibrium, for the reasons explained in Chapter 1); and let L stand for the given endowment of labour, a scalar. These endowments are, for simplicity, assumed to be entirely offered. The demands for capital goods and for labour are determined by the quantities to be produced q, and by the technical coefficients A, ℓ. Here too, for brevity, I replace the vector x indicating the demands for factor inputs with the expressions determining them. The demands for the endowments of capital goods are given by Aq, the demand for labour by ℓq. The equality between supply and demand for factors gives us $n + 1$ equations; in matrix notation the equations corresponding to equations [3.5] are:

---

12. For simplicity I am leaving aside inventories; thus there is no investment in inventories of consumption goods.

$$X = A(v,w)q, \qquad L \geq \ell(v,w)q \quad \text{and if} >, \text{then } w = 0. \qquad [3.9]$$

The reader is reminded that the capital endowments are *variables*, assumed to adjust to the demands for them; this is why, differently from the case in equations [3.3] or [3.5], all equations $X = Aq$ hold as equalities, possibly with zero on both sides if a capital good is not demanded at all; the inequality sign not found in traditional authors can hold only for labour.

Let us now add the condition of URRSP, Uniform Rate of Return on Supply Price. This was universally formulated – even by Walras – by neglecting the slow changes over time that normal relative prices may be undergoing. Then, if r is the rate of return or (neglecting risk, for simplicity[13]) the rate of interest, it must be

$$r = \frac{v_i - d_i p_i}{p_i}, \qquad i = 1,...,n \qquad [3.10]$$

which gives us n more equations.

Thus so far we have $(m+n)+(m+n)+(n+1)+n$ equations, in the following vectors of unknowns: p, q, X, v, w, k, r. The unknowns are $(n+m)+(n+m)+n+n+1+n+1$, that is $n + 1$ more than the equations. One of the supply = demand equations is derivable from the others due to Walras' Law, but we are only interested in (and indeed the equations can only determine) relative prices. Thus, after choosing one price as numeraire we still have $n + 1$ more unknowns than independent equations.

Of these degrees of freedom, n derive from the fact that so far nothing has been said about the determination of the k_i's. Traditionally, it was assumed that the economy be stationary; I show in Chapter 4 that this was only a simplifying, non-essential assumption, but for the moment let us accept this traditional assumption; for example we may suppose that tastes are such that consumers want to perform zero net savings whatever the prices and the rate of interest.[14] This yields the condition that the demand for new capital goods must just replace the rate of deterioration of their endowments:

13. In order to obtain the net rentals of capital goods, Walras subtracts from the gross rental v_i not only the value of depreciation but also an insurance charge which is one way to take into account the risk premium by which the rate of return on risky investment must be higher than the rate of interest on safe loans. Here for the sake of simplicity I neglect this complication and assume that rate of return (or of profits) and rate of interest can be treated as equal.

14. Such a stationary equilibrium would have been called *static* or *statical* by Marshall or J.B. Clark, in order to distinguish this kind of stationary state, in which the *given* aggregate factor endowments are *assumed* not to change over time in order to highlight certain forces as clearly as possible, from a *secular* stationary state in which factor endowments (capital, population) have themselves reached an equilibrium; cf. Chapter 4.

$$K_i = d_i X_i, , \qquad i = 1, ..., n \qquad [3.11]$$

This gives us n more equations. *There remains one and only one degree of freedom.* Its nature can be grasped by treating r, the rate of interest, as a parameter, as illustrated below.

3.3.3. For each level of the rate of interest, assuming uniqueness of the solutions, the system of equations from [3.7] to [3.11] will endogenously determine the vector X of capital endowments required for equilibrium. This derives from the implicit function theorem; it is, however, useful to stop and regard the economic logic embedded in the mathematics. There is a group of equations, determinining the relative prices of products, which can be considered in isolation: equations [3.7] and [3.10]. We can inquire into their properties by noting that they are equivalent to Piero Sraffa's price equations, with the sole difference that here depreciation is radioactive. Note indeed that equations [3.10] imply $v_i = (r + d_i) p_i$. So we may re-write equations [3.7] as

$$p = (r + d) p A(r) + w\ell(r) \qquad [3.7^*]$$

where d is the vector of deterioration coefficients.[15] Sraffa's equations when all capital goods are circulating capital goods (so that all the depreciation rates d_i are equal to 1) can be written as[16]

15. If $d = (1, ..., 1)$, then equations [3.7*] become identical to Sraffa's price equations for the case of circulating capital goods (Sraffa, 1960, p. 11) with the sole difference that Sraffa's price equations refer to the total quantities produced, while here they are in terms of technical coefficients that is per unit of product. Note that equations [3.7*] can also be interpreted as describing instantaneous-flow production, with r the instantaneous rate of interest and d the vector of instantaneous rates of radioactive deterioration; the formal identity hides a difference, though, which is particularly important for a correct appreciation of the meaning of a common rate of deterioration equal to 1 in the latter case. If production is a continuous flow, and capital goods deteriorate radioactively, then if a quantity x of a capital good starts being utilized at time 0, at time t that quantity will have become equivalent to a quantity xe^{-dt} of the same capital good; therefore in this case of continuous-flow production and analysis in continuous time a rate of deterioration equal to 1 does *not* mean that after one period of use a capital good will have 'disappeared', that is will have lost all its productive capacity. One unit of a new capital good after one period of use will still be equivalent, in efficiency units, to e^{-1} units of it when new. This difference has escaped Nikaido (1983, 1985), who in his study of the gravitation of relative prices to long-period prices has used Sraffa's price equations for circulating capital, but within a continuous-time instantaneous-flow production model, without realizing that the model had therefore to be interpreted as with radioactive deterioration at a rate $d = 1$.
16. Sraffa (1960, ch. II, p. 11). Actually Sraffa formulates his equations without using unit technical coefficients: in order to stress the dependence of technical conditions on the quantities produced and possibly on the stage reached by the exploitation of increasing

$$p = (r+1)pA(r) + w\ell(r), \qquad\qquad [3.7**]$$

and with an assumption of radioactive depreciation they would become equations [3.7*].

(This is as announced in §1.2.13; nor should it be surprising, because Sraffa's equations assume a uniform rate of return in all industries and assume a good to have the same price as an input and as an output; they therefore make the same assumptions on prices as in a marginalist long-period equilibrium. As an aside, we have here some elements for a first appreciation of Sraffa's price equations. They aim at studying, in isolation, the equations determining long-period relative prices, and to derive some properties of how these prices, and technical choices, change with distribution. They also aim at showing that the sole data necessary for the determination of those prices are the technical conditions of production and the value of one of the two distributive variables, so that the marginalist supply = demand conditions are something added to a theory of prices which may be separated from those conditions and combined with a different theory of what determines distribution and the quantities produced.)

Sraffa's equations have stimulated a series of studies that allow us to confirm the correctness of some insights of traditional analyses, insights that had not been formally proven before. Standard results on the existence and uniqueness of cost-minimizing Sraffa prices in the presence of choice of techniques[17] ensure that these equations [3.7*] will be capable of a cost-minimizing solution for each assigned level of the rate of interest within the interval compatible with a non-negative wage rate, a solution unique in the relative prices and wage rate,[18] and – assuming no co-existence of equally profitable methods of production – also unique in the technical coefficients.[19] Thus, under the latter assumption, equations [3.7*], that is [3.7] and [3.10], uniquely determine, for each level of the interest rate r, both the cost-minimizing technical coefficients (A, ℓ) and, once a numeraire is chosen, also the vectors p, v and the wage rate w. Once a numeraire is chosen we obtain therefore vector functions $p(r)$, $v(r)$, and a scalar function $w(r)$: the last one is the well-known decreasing *w–r curve* or wage curve or factor-price frontier, which has played an important role in the Cambridge

returns to scale, he prefers to write the price equations in terms of total quantities produced and total quanties of inputs used in each industry. It is however immediate to derive technical coefficients from his formulation.

17. Cf. Kurz and Salvadori (1995, chs 5, 7). Remember that I am assuming absence of joint production.

18. The sole exception is discussed in Kurz and Salvadori (1994) and concerns the case when $w = 0$.

19. With differentiable production functions all the standard equalities of value marginal products and input rentals will be satisfied.

controversies. Then in equations [3.8] the consumption demands can be seen to depend only on r, and we can use equations [3.8] and [3.11] to re-write equations [3.9] as

$$X = A(r)(Q(r)+d(r)X),$$
$$L = \ell(r)(Q(r)+d(r)X).$$

[3.9*]

Of these $n+1$ equations in the $n+1$ variables $X_1, ..., X_n, r$, only n equations are independent due to Walras' Law, so they determine the capital endowment vector X as a function of r. Thus we obtain a vector function $X(r)$ which determines the capital endowment vector required by firms to produce what is demanded, at the prices, and demands for consumption goods, implied by each given rate of interest.

Now the role becomes clear of the conception that the several capital goods are embodiments of 'capital', a homogeneous factor variable in 'form', that is composition, but given in quantity, and the demand for which is a decreasing function of the rate of interest. The equilibrium interest rate can then be determined as the one bringing the supply of and the demand for 'capital' into equality; that is, equilibrium will obtain when the rate of interest implies such a desired vector of endowments of the several capital goods that the amount of 'capital' embodied in them equals the given endowment of 'capital' of the economy under study.

3.3.4. The question that now arises is: in what units is this endowment of 'capital' (and thus also the demand for it) to be measured?

We can arrive at the answer by reflecting on the process by which 'capital' is conceived in this approach to change 'form' without changing 'quantity'.

According to the marginalist conception, at any given moment the capital of an economy will be 'fixed or tied-up in production, such as buildings, ships, machinery, etc.' (Wicksell, 1935, p. 192); but this capital wears out and, in order to ensure its maintenance, a part of the productive resources of the economy must be dedicated to producing capital goods. Of course, an economy can change the 'form' of its stock of capital goods by utilizing the resources, which *might* be employed for the reproduction of the capital goods worn out by the production process, by employing them in the production of different capital goods.

If because of a change in tastes the demand for fruit juices, for instance, increases and the demand for tobacco decreases, then some of the factors previously destined to replace worn-out means of production of the tobacco industry will be reallocated to produce more means of production for the fruit juice industry. Since factor prices do not appreciably change for small changes in the composition of production, and since product prices equal the value of the factors employed in their production, the capital goods produced in place of the ones whose production has been stopped will have the same value as those that are no longer produced; the suggestion therefore is that the *value* of the total stock of capital of the economy does not change while its 'form' does. Indeed, the value of the flow of services of the resources which might reproduce the worn-out capital goods is seen to be paid out of the flow of depreciation funds, which are viewed as 'free capital', or 'mobile capital in its free and uninvested form' (Wicksell, 1935, p. 192).[20] Capital is therefore conceived as a sum of purchasing power, of value, which at any moment is crystallized in the specific capital goods produced by the flow of services in whose purchase it was employed, but which gradually becomes 'free' (in the form of flows of depreciation allowances) to be re-employed in the purchase of productive services producing the same or different capital goods. Actually, in an economy with net savings, the flow of 'free capital' consists not only of the flow of depreciation allowances but also of the flow of net savings; it consists therefore of the flow of gross savings, an amount of value like the incomes of which they are part.

Here we can also perceive the connection between capital conceived as a single factor of variable 'form', and investment and savings. Gross savings constitute the supply of 'mobile capital in its free and uninvested form'; gross investment, the demand for it. The point has been put forward synthetically by Garegnani, as follows:

> Beneath the variety and, at times, the vagueness of the indications given in this respect [3.the unit of measurement of capital, F.P.] by the marginal theorists, there lies a common idea. The capital goods, and hence the quantity of capital they represent, result from investment; since investment is seen as the demand for savings, 'capital' emerges as something which is homogeneous with saving. Its natural unit is therefore the same as we would use for saving, i.e. some composite unit of consumption goods capable of measuring the subjective satisfaction from which (according to these theorists) consumers abstain when they save. 'Capital' thus appears as past savings which are, so to speak, 'incorporated' in the capital goods, existing at a given instant of time (Garegnani, 1978, p. 33).

Thus, for example, we find Wicksell writing:

> The accumulation of capital consists in the resolve of those who save to abstain from the consumption of a part of their income in the immediate future. Owing to

20. He adds: 'free capital will not really have any material form at all – quite naturally, as it only exists for a moment' (ibid.). On 'free capital' cf. §1.3.2. The notion is already in Jevons (1871 [1970], p. 239).

their diminished demand, or cessation of demand, for consumption goods, the labour and land which would otherwise have been required in their production is set free for the creation of fixed capital for future production and consumption and is employed by entrepreneurs for that purpose with the help of the money placed at their disposal by savings (Wicksell, 1935, pp. 192–3).

The issue of the measurement of 'capital' is clinched by the following reasoning. In equilibrium, different quantities of the same factor must earn rentals proportional to the respective quantities, because unit rentals are the same throughout the economy for all units of the same factor. Thus, if α and β are two fields of land of identical quality, and if α earns a rent twice as big as β's rent, we can deduce that α's surface is twice the surface of β. But now let α and β represent two different capital goods, or two baskets of capital goods of different composition. If we want to see the (net) rentals earned in equilibrium by α and β as paying the productive contributions of a *common* factor 'capital' embodied in them, then if α earns, as net rentals, twice as much as β we must conclude, as a matter of logical necessity, that α embodies twice as much 'capital' as β. But in a long-period equilibrium α's value will also be twice the value of β, because the net rentals constitute the interest on the value of the capital goods, and the *rate* of interest on the value of capital is the same everywhere. Hence if we want to see the net rentals of capital goods as payments to a common factor 'capital' embodied in them, it follows as a matter of logical necessity that *the amount of 'capital' embodied in different capital goods must be proportional to their equilibrium values*. It suffices then to choose as unit of 'capital' the amount of 'capital' embodied in a capital good of unitary value, and the value of the aggregate capital stock of the economy will measure the amount of 'capital' with which the economy is endowed.

But it also follows that nothing but the value of capital will do as a measurement of the endowment of 'capital', because no technical aggregable measure of capital goods – such as their weight[21] – would satisfy the proportionality with their value.

21. Two further and connected reasons why 'technical' units of capital such as the weight, or the volume, of capital goods cannot be satisfactory measures of the aggregate endowment of 'capital' may be recalled here. First, the 'quantity' of capital so measured could not be assumed given while its 'form' were treated as endogenously determined: it would be impossible to find general reasons why, as the composition of the demand for capital goods changed, and the composition of the capital endowment changed to adapt to demand, its total weight or volume should not change. Second, no reason exists why the aggregate demand for 'capital' measured in tons or cubic metres should be a regularly decreasing function of the interest rate: as the rate of interest increases, the change in optimal methods of production may imply changes in the total weight of capital goods in any direction and of any magnitude; the basis for a tendency toward a supply-and-demand equilibrium would be

Measuring is of course a comparison and is therefore meaningless except for purposes of comparison; so the meaning of the above conclusion of a necessary proportionality between value of, and 'capital' crystallized in, a capital good, can be made clearer in the following manner. If, in a certain economy, more capital goods are added to the previous vector of endowments of capital goods, without any change in relative prices having intervened, the increase in the 'capital' endowment of the economy must as a matter of logical necessity be taken to be proportional to the increase in the total value of the vector of endowments of the capital goods. And for the same reason if we have two different economies, where relative prices are the same because the rate of interest and the coefficients of production are the same, but where the vectors of endowments of capital goods are of different composition, then the ratio between the endowments of 'capital' of the two economies must equal the ratio between the values of the two endowments (once a common numeraire has been chosen).

It will not come as a surprise, then, to discover that all the traditional marginalist authors who adopted the conception of the several capital goods as embodying a single factor 'capital' measured the endowment of 'capital' as a given quantity of value.[22] Thus Wicksell speaks of 'the amount of capital of the community, reckoned in terms of money' (Wicksell, 1934, p. 174); J.B. Clark speaks of capital as a 'quantum of productive wealth' (1899, p. 119), measured in money, which is invested in capital goods; Knight writes:

> For theoretical analysis, the essential matter is the distinction between such objects or 'capital goods', and 'capital', i.e., productive capacity, viewed in

totally lacking. Both reasons derive from a common cause, the absence of any univocal connection between the quantity of 'capital' measured in weight or volume, and the cost of its employment. This lack of univocal connection makes it impossible to derive from cost minimization any regular connection between the demand for 'capital' in terms of such units, and the rate of interest or the rentals of capital goods. On the insufficiencies of the average period of production, cf. Appendix 6A1. For a discussion of the sole case in which a 'technical' capital aggregate might be envisaged to exist, cf. §6.4.4.

22. On the role of the conception of capital as an amount of value, Garegnani (1960, 1990a) has however pointed out that there is a difference between two groups of traditional marginalist theorists. Authors like J.B. Clark, and Marshall and his school, showed little hesitation to speak of capital as a single factor, capable of a treatment strictly analogous to that of technically homogeneous factors although measured as an amount of value, even when speaking of the production function of a single firm or industry: a procedure only legitimate if relative prices could be considered constant as factor prices varied. Other marginalist authors like Böhm-Bawerk and Wicksell avoided this mistake, and adopted a disaggregated representation of capital in the production functions (although in terms of dated inputs of primary factors rather than as here), but nonetheless they had to resort to a value measurement for the total endowment of capital of the economy.

abstract quantitative terms, as subject to increase or decrease, hence transferable from one use to another through change in form, i.e., decrease of one kind and increase of another. Thus the problem is one of measurement or quantification of productive capacity. This, in turn, is a matter of valuation, since value is the only common denominator between different economic forms (Knight, 1946, p. 389).

3.3.5. The residual degree of freedom of the equations of long-period general equilibrium is then 'closed' by the condition that the value of the vector of capital goods demanded by firms must equal the given value of the 'capital' endowment of the economy:

$$\Sigma_i X_i p_i = K^*, \qquad i=1,..., n \qquad\qquad [3.12]$$

where K^* is the given endowment of 'capital' of the economy, an amount of value.[23] Equations [3.7] to [3.12] are the equations of the long-period equilibrium.

We will presently discuss the legitimacy of such a conception and measurement of capital. What is important at the moment is to be clear that this conception of capital is *indispensable* to the determination of the fully disaggregated general equilibrium, as long as the latter aims at being a *long-period* equilibrium. The endogenously determined proportions among the endowments of the several capital goods require that the total endowment of capital goods, measured as a single quantity, be given and set equal to the demand for it. Thus the presence of a quantity of capital measured as a single number co-exists with a treatment of the equilibrium that is as disaggregated as found in Arrow–Debreu. The difference is not in the degree of aggregation in the treatment of technology (as mistakenly thought by those economists who identify aggregate capital with the use of aggregate production functions), but in the fact that the composition of capital is among the variables that the equilibrium must determine.

This inability of the traditional marginalist approach to do without the conception of capital as a single quantity has been obscured in recent decades by the widespread confusion of long-period equilibria with steady-state (stationary or steady-growth) equilibria, where the quantity of capital itself becomes endogenously determined and therefore does not appear among the data of the equilibrium. I will discuss this misunderstanding in Chapter 4.

---

23. In the factor endowments of consumers too, from which their demands and supplies are derived, the given endowment of capital of each consumer will have to be measured as an amount of value. Thus the given total quantity of 'capital' K^* of equation [3.12] should be seen as the sum of the given endowments of value 'capital' of each consumer.

3.4. THE PROBLEM WITH THE VALUE MEASUREMENT OF THE ENDOWMENT OF CAPITAL

3.4.1. Let us now ask whether or not this conception of capital as a factor of production consisting of an amount of value is defensible.

Two problems arise in this respect. The first one is, so to speak, a 'supply-side' problem: does it make sense to take as given an endowment of a factor conceived as an amount of value, when the purpose of the theory is to determine values? The second is, whether the factor substitution mechanisms, on which the plausibility of the marginalist approach rests, can be conceived to operate also for a factor measured as an amount of value; in this light it can therefore be seen as a 'demand-side' problem. The second problem remained unappreciated up to the Cambridge controversies on capital theory during the 1960s. By contrast, the first problem was acutely felt by a number of marginalist economists as early as the 1920s, and is largely responsible for the birth of the neo-Walrasian versions. For this reason now we tackle the first problem only, postponing a discussion of the second one to Chapter 6.

The economic meaning of the equation that imposes a value of the capital goods employed in the economy that is equal to a given number K^* can only be, it would seem, the following. For any real economy, let us assume that one might in principle collect data, as to its technology and tastes, its endowment of labour,[24] and the value K^* of its capital stock, sufficient to build a long-period general equilibrium model including equation [3.12]. Then one might (assuming existence and uniqueness) determine the long-period equilibrium of this economy, by treating these observations as data. But since, in the real economy, the value of the existing capital stock in terms of the chosen numeraire depends on income distribution,[25] and since it would

---

24. Endowments of labour, if labour is heterogeneous; and endowments of land too, if we do not wish to assume for simplicity that land is overabundant and hence free. There is no need to aggregate different kinds of labour (or of land) into one factor, because the several endowments are sufficiently persistent to allow each of them to be treated as given. This is not the case with capital goods.

25. Cf. §6.1.3. This will not be true for the normal value of the existing capital stock only if relative prices do not change with distribution – the strict labour-theory-of-value case – or if the numeraire is a composite commodity with the same composition as the existing capital stock. But in this second case, besides the obvious arbitrariness of this choice of numeraire, there is the further difficulty that, since it takes time to reach equilibrium and during the disequilibrium adjustments the composition of capital will change, after a short time the numeraire will no longer have the same composition as the capital stock, and the dependence of the value of the capital stock on distribution will reassert itself. Furthermore, the observable value of the existing stock of capital goods will also depend on the deviations of market prices from long-period prices.

have been different – and by percentages depending on the numeraire chosen – had income distribution been different even if neither technology nor the composition of production had differed, the number K^* and therefore the equilibrium one obtains comes to depend on what the observed income distribution is. An explanation or prediction of the trend of the observed income distribution on the basis of the one thus theoretically determined would mean engaging in a circular argument.

Let us indeed consider a stationary economy with full employment of labour, a rate of interest r_1, and a perfectly adjusted capital stock. The value of this capital stock in terms of a chosen numeraire is K_1. Now, for example, due to labour immigration, the real wage decreases, relative prices change, the value of the – for the moment physically unaltered – capital stock changes to K_2. Which number, K_1, K_2, or some other, should we put into equation [3.12] in order to determine the new long-period equilibrium of this economy corresponding to the new supply of labour? The choice is clearly arbitrary. But then the explanation of the original rate of interest r_1 as determined by, among other things, the given endowment of 'capital' K_1 is illegitimate; in fact, the same capital goods would be worth a different total value if for any reason (for example a state intervention imposing a change in the rate of interest) the rate of interest became r_2, and relative prices adapted to the corresponding new long-period values; therefore the value of any given vector of capital goods must be seen as *determined by* the rate of interest, rather than being one of the determinants of the latter.

Or let us consider two economies sharing the same technical knowledge, and where the non-substitution theorem holds,[26] but where consumer tastes are different so that, when the rate of interest is the same, relative prices are the same in the two economies but the composition of consumption per unit of labour is different and therefore also the vector of endowments of capital goods is different. It has been seen above that, for two such economies, the relative 'capital' endowment must be given by the ratio between the respective values of the capital stock in terms of a common numeraire. But the latter ratio will depend on relative prices, that is on the rate of interest, even if nothing physical changes in either economy, because that ratio is simply the relative price of the two composite commmodities made up of the two stocks of capital goods, and will therefore change with distribution just like any other relative price (outside the pure-labour-theory-of-value case). Therefore, even if changes in distribution alter neither technology nor quantities produced, and even if we always change the rate of interest in the

26. That is, where long-period relative product prices are given once the rate of interest is given, independently of the composition of demand. This requires that there be no primary factor besides labour, and no joint production (apart from durable non-transferable capital). Cf. Appendix 6A3.

same way in the two economies such that we compare the two economies at a common rate of interest, and assuming all relative prices are at the respective long-period values, still we are unable to ascertain, independently of the level of the rate of interest, by how much the 'capital' endowments of the two economies differ.

3.4.2. As evident as all this may seem, marginalist economists did not admit the problem for a long time. For instance Wicksell, probably the most rigorous marginalist economist, showed no doubts about the legitimacy of taking the value of capital goods as given in his first book on capital and distribution (Wicksell, 1893).[27] Only later, when he abandoned the average period of production as a measure of capital intensity, did he also start nurturing doubts about the value measurement of the capital endowment. In his *Lectures* he admits: 'it may be difficult – if not impossible – to define this concept of social capital with absolute precision, as a definite quantity. In reality, it is rather a *complex* of quantities' (Wicksell, 1934, p. 165, italics in the original). Here the 'complex of quantities' is the several amounts of labour and of land saved up for different lengths of time and embodied in the capital goods, according to the representation of production possibilities adopted by Wicksell (and explained in the Appendix at the end of this chapter). There are several passages in Wicksell's *Lectures* where the same idea appears; namely, that one should try as much as possible to conceive of capital as a vector, or complex, of quantities of labour and of land, saved up for different periods of time. But unless that 'complex of quantities' – quantities which, by his own admission (cf. the quotation below), cannot be taken as data because the composition of capital must change with relative prices – can be translated into a single magnitude capable of changing 'form' without changing its 'quantity', and whose endowment can be included among the data of the equilibrium, Wicksell's system of equations (indeed, any possible formulation of marginalist long-period equilibria) is indeterminate.

Thus Wicksell oscillates between treating the amount of capital as a single quantity – an amount of value – and as a vector of 'given quantities of original factors of different years' (p. 201). But he then admits that neither conception allows one to treat the endowment of capital as given before the equilibrium is established:

> But it would clearly be meaningless – if not altogether inconceivable – to maintain that the amount of capital is already fixed before equilibrium between production and consumption has been achieved. Whether expressed in terms of one or the

27. The reason for this position was his acceptance of Böhm-Bawerk's view of capital as a subsistence fund, cf. Appendix 3A.

other, a change in the relative exchange value of two commodities would give rise to a change in the value of capital, unless its component parts underwent a more or less considerable change. But even if we conceive capital genetically, as being a certain quantity of labour and land accumulated in different years, a change in the value of commodities would also alter the conditions of their production and thus necessitate a larger or smaller change in the composition of capital (Wicksell, 1934, p. 202).

The 'genetic' conception of capital treats capital as consisting of a 'complex of quantities', a series of dated amounts of saved up labour and saved up land. The main interest of this last part of the quotation is Wicksell's admission that the *composition* of capital cannot be taken as given when the problem is the determination of distribution, because that composition will itself depend on distribution. According to this argument, therefore, the 'quantities of original factors of different years' cannot be 'given' when the problem is the determination of income distribution. But in the first part of the quotation Wicksell admits that the quantity of capital conceived as an amount of value cannot be known either, before the equilibrium is established. Nor is help to be found in the clause 'unless its component parts underwent a more or less considerable change', because we do not know *which* 'amount', or value, of capital would have to be left unaltered by such a change: the one preceding, or the one following the change in relative prices? And in terms of which numeraire?

But the logic of the theory was implacable and, in the end, lest he admitted defeat and the inconsistency of the whole approach, Wicksell had to measure the endowment of capital as a single quantity of variable 'form' and hence as an amount of value. He put this into writing two pages after the passage just quoted: 'If, for example, we now wish to impose the condition that in equilibrium the sum total of capital shall have a certain exchange value, measured in terms of one of the products ...' (ibid., p. 204), a quite hesitant formulation when compared with the kind of statement one might have expected from an author convinced by what he was doing, and which would have sounded more like 'What we must obviously do now is add the condition that in equilibrium ...'. Interestingly enough, Wicksell refrained from explicitly writing down the corresponding equation, thus confirming his unease – an understandable disquiet, given what he had admitted a few pages earlier.

It would seem then that in the latter part of his life, although too deeply permeated by the marginalist approach to be able to abandon it, and therefore still ultimately clinging to the notion of 'capital' as a single factor of production, Wicksell nonetheless admitted that he did not know how to determine its endowment in a satisfactory manner.[28]

The conclusion is clear: the marginalist notion of long-period equilibrium is unacceptable, because it is impossible to specify one of its data, the endowment of 'capital'.

28. Also see Wicksell (1934, pp. 148–9). Wicksell even suspected that, owing to the changes in the value of capital brought about by changes in distribution, it might not be certain that an increase in the value of the 'capital' employed would be always associated with a rise in the wage rate, that is with a lower rate of interest (ibid., p. 183); thus he was not totally blind to the demand-side problem posed by the conception of capital as a value factor, but his suspicions were not further explored until Sraffa did so.

APPENDIX 3A. WICKSELL AND THE AVERAGE PERIOD OF PRODUCTION

3A.1. The Average Period of Production

3A.1.1. This Appendix has two purposes.

The first purpose is to show that the measurement of the capital endowment as an amount of value also characterizes the versions of the marginalist approach relying on the 'average period of production'. I show that the average period of production represented a measure, not of the economy's endowment of capital, but of the *capital intensity* of production techniques (that is of the capital–labour ratio, if labour is the sole other factor), and as such its role was to determine the *demand* for capital as a decreasing function of the rate of interest, with capital conceived as a quantity of value of variable 'form'. Thus the 'supply-side' problem discussed in Section 3.4 arises also in the 'Austrian' versions of the marginalist approach; and it is not surmounted by the justification of the given capital endowment based on the conception of capital as a 'subsistence fund', found in Böhm-Bawerk and in the early Wicksell.

The second purpose is to show that the formalization of long-period equilibrium proposed in Chapter 3 is faithful to the history of economic analysis in spite of being different from the formalizations actually found in the literature. This will be done by showing that Wicksell's mature general equilibrium model, the one of his *Lectures* (1934), is only a special case of the one presented in Chapter 3.

This Appendix also aims at supplying a basic understanding of the notions of 'average period of production' and 'roundaboutness', notions with which some younger readers may be unfamiliar, but that have been very important in the development of the marginalist approach, and that are very often encountered in older authors. Readers already familiar with these notions may jump to Section 3A.1.6.

3A.1.2. Historically, the 'average period of production' was an attempt to give precision to the notion of *capital intensity* of production techniques (that is proportion between 'capital', viewed as a single, homogeneous factor of variable 'form', and labour[29]), and hence also to the notion of marginal product of 'capital'. The capital intensity of the integrated production process of a good was measured by the average number of time periods elapsing

---

29. In this exposition, it will be assumed that labour is the only primary factor. In fact, the average period of production can only be defined if there is only one primary factor; see Garegnani (1960, pt. II, ch. 5), and, fn. 45.

between the payment of direct and indirect labour inputs, and the sale of the product.[30]

In this approach, the existence of capital goods is seen as a manifestation of the fact that entrepreneurs adopt production techniques[31] that are optimal at the given rate of interest, and that require some time elapse between the moment when non-reproducible ('primary') factors are utilized and the moment when the desired final product is obtained: that is 'indirect' or 'roundabout' production techniques that, instead of producing the product directly and in very little time with only rudimentary tools besides the services of primary factors, first produce capital or intermediate goods and only afterwards, with these capital goods aiding the further services of primary factors, produce the desired product. The capital goods that enter the production of a good are resolved into the services of the primary factors which produced them, services that remain invested for a certain time duration from their application to the emergence of the final product: the average length of this time duration, in other words, the average period of production (to be defined below), is considered an index of the relative 'roundaboutness', and then also of the relative quantity of 'capital', requested by different production techniques. This is due to the fact that the adoption of more roundabout production techniques is seen as requiring the

30. A first version of this approach can be found in Jevons. It was then taken up and developed by Böhm-Bawerk; a more rigorous development, to be followed by an abandonment, is found in Wicksell (1893, 1934). In Lindahl (1939) and Kuenne (1963) there is no advancement relative to Wicksell; rather, we find a less clear consciousness of the problems in the approach. For recent introductions, and bibliographical references, see Orosel (1987), Hennings (1987a, 1987b), Ahmad (1991). The important inquiry on the subject by Garegnani (1960) is summarized in Garegnani (1990a, pp. 23–29).

31. By production *process* of a certain good I mean the vector of technical coefficients of means of production and labour directly producing the good in question. To determine the average period of production of a good, it will be seen that knowledge of its productive process is not sufficient: one also needs to know the production processes of all goods directly or indirectly entering its production, that is of all goods produced in its *subsystem* (defined below). By *production technique of a good* I mean a matrix of production processes, one for each good, of the goods produced in the subsystem of that good: the production technique of corn changes even if the production process of corn has not changed, if the production process of one of its direct or indirect means of production, for example of tractors, changes. The *integrated* production process, or Sraffian *subsystem*, of a good or basket of goods is a hypothetical ensemble of industries having the same technical coefficients as the corresponding industries of the original economy, and taken in such dimensions that the net product of the subsystem consists only of the given quantity of the good or basket of goods. If the subsystem producing a unit of a good were lodged under a big tent, no input would need to go into the tent except labour, in order for the given net product of the good to come out of the tent at every production cycle. (All the remaining production exactly replaces the means of production used up in that production cycle.) The live labour employed in one production cycle by the subsystem equals the labour embodied in the net product.

giving up of immediate consumption for a longer period, that is entailing some net savings, which increase the value of the capital stock.

To make concrete the intuition behind this approach, let us consider an example. Let us suppose that the sole product of an economy is potatoes, which are produced by potato tubers constantly present in the ground, yet which produce potatoes of different dimensions, and after a different time period, depending on the quality of the soil achieved by tilling. Thus a unit of labour can be employed to produce potatoes (land is overabundant and free) in a number of different ways:

1. by digging spontaneous potatoes in wild fields, which is not very productive. With this technique the application of labour is to all effects contemporaneous with the emergence of the product, and in particular, if labour is wage labour (with wages paid in arrears), wages are paid out of the revenue from the sale of the product, so no capital advance is required;
2. by dedicating first one half of each unit of labour to till and clean the soil, which assists the growth of potatoes such that they become bigger but take a year to ripen[32]; and then, after a year, by dedicating the other half to digging up the potatoes. By means of this technique, half the wages must be paid a year before the revenue is obtained from the sale of the product; here, a vertically integrated firm therefore needs to borrow capital;
3. by dedicating first one half of each unit of labour to till and clean the soil in a different way, that causes potatoes to take two years to ripen, but to grow bigger. Thus, for a year no labour is applied, and then in the third year, the other half unit of labour digs out the potatoes;
4. similarly to the preceding case, but with potatoes now taking three years to ripen;
5. .....

With the first technique, the time elapsing between the application of labour (and the payment of wages) and the emergence of the product is zero; with the second technique, half of the labour employed (and of the wages) is anticipated for a year; with the third technique, half of the labour employed is anticipated for two years; and so on. The time elapsing between payment of wages and completion of the production process, for half the labour employed, becomes longer and longer. It seems clear therefore that, however precisely defined, the degree of roundaboutness or average period of production cannot but become greater and greater as one passes from the first

---

32. This assumption that no potatoes are required to start the production process of potatoes, unassisted labour being the only initial input, avoids the complications due to infinite regress. In Sraffian terminology, we are assuming that there are no basic commodities.

to the subsequent techniques. The precise definition of this average will be given later.

Let us use this example to show the role of savings. Let us assume that untilled land is overabundant and hence free, and that digging up potatoes is not an instantaneous process, but rather, it requires a year (the potatoes become available at the end of the year), and the same is true for the tilling of the ground. Wages are paid at the end of the year. Let us consider an economy endowed with one unit of labour, which produces only potatoes, initially with the first technique. The unit of labour produces q potatoes per year; wages are the only cost, so in competitive conditions $w = q$. To transfer some of the labour to producing with the second technique requires giving up some immediate consumption of potatoes in favour of future consumption, because dedicating labour to tilling implies giving up the potatoes that that labour might have harvested with the first technique. Let us suppose that the economy decides to pass to the second technique. This may be done, one year, by dedicating half a unit of labour to tilling. Production of potatoes that year becomes $q/2$; but let us assume that workers are still paid a real wage equal to q, out of potatoes which had been stored from previous harvests. The year after, the economy will employ half a unit of labour to dig out the potatoes planted one year earlier, and the other half to till the ground (still, by assumption, with the second technique). And then in the same way year after year. Let us assume that with the second technique the production of potatoes per unit of labour embodied is $2q$. By giving up $q/2$ potatoes for one year, the economy obtains $2q$ potatoes forever after. The rate of return on the sacrifice of production requested to pass from the first to the second technique is 200 per cent. If the rate of interest is less than 200 per cent, producing potatoes with the second technique is less costly than with the first, because, with w the real wage in terms of potatoes, the cost of production of q potatoes with the first technique (assuming wages paid at the end of the production cycle) is w, with the second technique it is $[3.(1 + r)/2 + 1/2] w/2$, which is greater or less than w according to whether r is greater or less than 200 per cent.

After the transition, at the beginning of each year the economy finds itself with a capital consisting of tilled land, of a value which is equal to the wages just paid to the half labour unit which tilled it. If the wage is $w = q$, then the value of the economy's capital equals the net savings originally performed, $q/2$.

Let us continue the example by assuming that now the economy passes from the second to the third technique, which we assume produces $3q$ per unit of labour employed. The first year in which half a unit of labour is employed to produce with the third technique (on land until then unused), the production of potatoes does not diminish (because that year's harvest consisted of the potatoes planted a year earlier with the second technique).

However, in the second year there will be no production of potatoes at all unless the economy assigns half a unit of labour to dig up potatoes grown by the first technique (obtaining $0.5q$), while the other half-unit is used to till the ground using the third technique. If this is what the economy does, then from the third year, and forever afterwards, half a unit of labour digs $3q$ while the other half tills the ground with the third technique. In this way the sacrifice of $1.5q$ potatoes for a year obtains an increase of production of $1q$ (from $2q$ to $3q$) in perpetuity, with a rate of return of 66.6 per cent.[33]

Actually, the rate of interest at which the two techniques are equally convenient, and below which the third technique becomes less costly than the second, is approximately 78 per cent, or rigorously $(-1 + \sqrt{17})/4$, as one can verify by noting that the cost of production of q potatoes with the third technique is $[3.(1 + r)^2/2 + 1/2] \, w/3$ and by setting this expression equal to the one given above for the second technique. That the rate of return obtained above is lower derives from the fact that in that example half a unit of labour is employed for a year with the *first* technique, which is less productive, in order to go back as soon as possible to a constant stream of consumption. A switch as fast as possible to the third technique, while maintaining the full employment of labour, would require the acceptance of zero production in the second year, and an irregular stream of production afterwards and forever. Then in the second year the unit of labour can be entirely dedicated to tilling the ground according to the third technique. In the third year one can employ 1/2 labour to dig up the $3q$ potatoes planted the first year, and employ the other 1/2 labour to till the ground according to the third technique. In the fourth year one can employ the whole unit of labour to dig up the $6q$ potatoes planted in the second year, and no labour would be left to till. The fifth year would be like the third, but in the sixth there would be no potatoes to dig up: the whole unit of labour can be employed to till the ground according to the third technique; and so on. The stream of production starting from the first year would therefore be $2q$, zero, $3q$, $6q$, $3q$, zero, $3q$, $6q$, $3q$, zero ... which means a repeated 4-year variation, from the previous perennial production stream of $2q$, given by $(-2q, q, 4q, q)$ which can be shown to imply a rate of return of 78 per cent. The avoidance of irregular

---

33. The example is misleading to an extent, in that, through its assumption of absence of basic commodities, it hides one complication of the transition from one long-period position to another. In general, different production processes use different capital goods, and the transition may require the temporary adoption of production processes later to be abandoned, necessary to produce with the existing capital goods (some of which may be destined to disappear) the new capital goods best adapted to (directly or indirectly) produce themselves. Thus the first iron tools cannot have been produced with iron tools, but once created they have supplanted, in the production of iron tools, the wood and stone tools which first produced them.

streams of production will in general only be possible with smooth factor substitutability.

However performed, the passage to the third technique requires some net savings.

3A.1.3. Now, according to this approach, even in more complex economies something of this kind continues to hold true: the production of final products via more 'roundabout' techniques, requiring a longer average investment time or 'average period of production' between the application of labour and the emergence of the final product, will often, at least up to a point, yield a higher amount of final net product per unit of labour directly and indirectly employed; but it is only the abstinence from immediate consumption which makes it possible for society to dedicate the resources thus freed to producing via more roundabout techniques.[34] Thus abstinence

34. The attempt, to depict these transitions to the second and then to the third technique as induced by decreases of the rate of interest caused by increases of the supply of savings, is an interesting exercise which will disclose some difficulties, too often overlooked (but cf. Garegnani, 1979a, p. 44, fn. 23), of this traditional marginalist thesis. When consumers decide to allocate a smaller fraction of their income to consumption, inequalities of demands and supplies will necessarily arise unless entrepreneurs have correctly foreseen this decision and produced fewer consumption goods (and more capital goods, to be then sold to those who borrow the income not spent on consumption goods). Entrepreneurs will not normally be able to foresee such changes: they must first *observe* that the composition of demand has changed, in order to be induced to alter the composition of production. Thus it seems inevitable to admit that, according to this perspective, there must be *first* a decrease of demand for consumption goods, and an increase in the supply of loanable funds; *then* a decrease of the rate of interest, and of the prices of consumption goods; *then* an increase of demand for capital goods, and of their prices; *then finally*, an increase in the production of capital goods. The danger of course is that the initial decrease of demand for consumption goods, in the absence, initially, of an increased demand for capital goods, may provoke a decrease of the production of consumption goods without any offsetting increase in the production of capital goods, that is a decrease of national income, which may annul the initial increase in savings, so that the increase of the demand for capital goods never comes into being. In our example, owing to the assumption of yearly production cycles the problem emerges very clearly: the switch from the first to the second technique must be caused by the appearance of positive savings out of the income of workers, which is the sole income as long as only the first technique is employed (there being no advanced capital, there is no interest payment to capitalists). Yet the fact that workers have decided to start saving half of their income will be noticed by the firms employing them only *after* they have worked; so firms have no incentive to employ them differently until it is too late. If, for example, one assumes that wages are paid out of the revenue from the sale of the product that is *after* the harvest is sold (one is then assuming that wages are kept unspent by workers until the next harvest), then what happens if workers decide to save is that the firms do not discover it until after the harvest has been produced with the old method, the savings simply cause an inability to sell the potato harvest at the cost-covering prices, and wages cannot be paid: firms go bankrupt.

from immediate consumption yields an increase of future consumption, that is yields a rate of return on savings, and we have the elements for a supply-and-demand determination of the rate of interest. The intermediate goods resulting from the earlier production processes, or stages, of a roundabout technique are capital goods;[35] in an economy with a constant flow of production, in each period those capital goods will be present in the economy that have not 'ripened' yet into the final product. Therefore, passing to a more roundabout technique, and increasing the 'amount' of capital in the economy are, in this perspective, two different ways of saying the same thing, since the more roundabout process adds further 'layers' of intermediate goods and/or 'thickens' the existing layers. Thus, in the stationary economy, if we adopt the second technique, we find that at the beginning of each year there are present (although hidden in the ground) the intermediate goods (the half-grown potatoes whose growth has been favoured by tilling) resulting from the half-unit of unassisted labour employed the year before. At the beginning of the year these goods will be worth $w/2$ which is their cost of production with wages paid in arrears. In the stationary economy adopting the third technique, at the beginning of each year there are present the partly-grown potatoes resulting from the half-unit of unassisted labour employed the year before, and again worth $w/2$, and in addition the semi-ripe potatoes resulting from the half-unit of unassisted labour of two years before, and worth, at the beginning of the year, $(1 + r)\, w/2$. The passage to the third technique has resulted in a second layer of capital goods being added to the first one.[36]

Since the capital goods existing in an economy exist because some of the services of primary factors are not destined to immediate consumption, the capital goods are seen as the results of acts of abstinence from consumption, that is acts of net savings, which create capital goods of the same value as the non-produced consumption goods. The quantity of capital is therefore a fund of value, the value of the consumption goods which have been given up in order to produce the capital goods. As the analysis attempts the determination of a long-period equilibrium, this 'capital' fund is allowed to take the 'form' which prices and technical convenience dictate. If for instance there is an increase in the supply of labour, society can 'spread' its 'capital' over the increased total amount of labour services, by employing them, on an average, with techniques that are less roundabout. (In our

35. In the example of potatoes, the intermediate or capital goods are the half-grown potato plants with their half-developed potatoes buried in the ground.
36. Let us note that the adoption of more roundabout techniques can result in all capital goods being different, so the image of the 'addition' of further 'layers' of capital goods is only an aid to intuition. What will normally happen is that at the same time the capital goods in each layer will change with the change in technique.

example, if the process of transition from Technique 2 is reversed to Technique 3, the economy finds itself with a potential increase in consumption, which may be saved, that is, employed to pay the first year of wages to further workers using Technique 2, so that the economy finds itself employing more workers than before, but all employed in Technique 2, and therefore yielding a smaller net product per unit of labour.)

If the employment of more 'capital' per unit of labour, that is the lengthening of the average period of production, increases the product per unit of labour but less and less so at least after a point, one may conceive the optimal average period of production to be a decreasing function of the 'price' of 'capital', that is of the rate of interest. The average period of production has, in this perspective, the function of measure of the 'capital' intensity of production techniques: a higher wage rate and hence a lower rate of interest will induce the adoption of more roundabout techniques, which will entail a higher demand for 'capital' if the employment of labour is given.

3A.1.4. Let us now see how these ideas are made precise in the version of marginalist theory propounded by Wicksell in his first book on value and distribution (Wicksell, 1893).

Let us assume that all production is in yearly cycles, with wages paid at the end of each cycle. We also assume that there is no joint production, no durable capital goods (there are only circulating capital goods, entirely consumed in a single yearly production cycle), no primary factor apart from homogeneous labour. Let us also, very importantly, assume that the *simple*, rather than the compound, interest rate prevails, that is, the interests maturing in each period on a capital invested for more than one period do not yield further interests in the subsequent periods: so that, if r is the yearly interest rate, an investment of value K is worth, after t years, not $K(1 + r)^t$, but rather $K(1 + tr)$.

Then if h_i is the labour embodied in the i-th good, and if therefore, in the subsystem[37] producing one unit of that good as its net product each year, one must pay wages of value wh_i, the price or cost of production p_i of the good is given by:

$$p_i = wh_i + rwh_iT_i$$

where T_i is the average period of production, defined as follows. Let h_i be the labour embodied in the good; this labour embodied can be seen as the sum of a series L_0, L_{-1}, L_{-2} and so on of dated direct and indirect labour inputs,

---

37. Cf. fn. 31 for the definition, and further on in the text for a demonstration that the total labour employment of a subsystem coincides with the labour embodied in its net product.

whose terms indicate the live labour employed in the direct production of the good, the live labour employed in the production of the means of production of the good, the live labour employed in the production of the means of production of the means of production, and so on, so that $\Sigma_t L_{-t} = h_i$ (where t goes from 0 to, if necessary, infinity); then:

$$T_i = \frac{\Sigma_t \left(tL_{-t} \right)}{h_i}.$$

The reason is as follows. As shown by Sraffa (1960, ch. 6), knowledge of the production conditions of a good and of its means of production (in the absence of joint production) allows one to re-write its cost of production as the sum of the wages paid to direct labour L_0, plus the (interest-augmented) wages paid to the direct labour employed in the production of its means of production L_{-1}, plus the (interest-augmented) wages paid to the direct labour L_{-2} employed in the production of the means of production of those means of production, and so on, where 'interest-augmented' means that to each one of these wage payments one must add the interest maturing on them from the time of their payment to the time when the good is finished and sold. If for instance the good is good 1, whose price equation is (with wages paid in arrears, and with a_{ij} ($i, j = 1, ..., n$) the technical coefficient of good i, and ℓ_j the labour technical coefficient, in the production of good j):

$$p_1 = (1+r)(p_1 a_{11} + p_2 a_{21} + ... + p_n a_{n1}) + w\ell_1 = w\ell_1 + (1+r) \Sigma_j a_{j1} p_j,$$

then in this equation one may replace, in the cost-of-production expression on the right-hand side, the prices $p_1, ..., p_n$ with their own cost-of-production expressions, and obtain, by rearranging:

$$p_1 = w\ell_1 + (1+r)w\Sigma_j \ell_j a_{j1} + (1+r)^2 \left(p_1 \Sigma_j a_{1j} a_{j1} + p_2 \Sigma_j a_{2j} a_{j1} + ... + p_n \Sigma_j a_{nj} a_{j1} \right) =$$

$$= wL_0 + (1+r)wL_{-1} + (1+r)^2 \left(p_1 \Sigma_j a_{1j} a_{j1} + p_2 \Sigma_j a_{2j} a_{j1} + ... + p_n \Sigma_j a_{nj} a_{j1} \right).$$

Here ℓ_1 is the term L_0 and $\Sigma_j \ell_j a_{j1}$ is the term L_{-1} of the series of dated quantities of labour producing directly and indirectly good 1. By repeating the same operation, one adds further terms of type $(1 + r)^t wL_{-t}$ while the residue of value of means of production of means of production of means of production ... becomes smaller and smaller. In this way one can 'reduce' the price of a good to wage payments plus the interest on them as follows:

$$p_1 = wL_0 + (1+r)wL_{-1} + (1+r)^2 wL_{-2} + ... + (1+r)^t wL_{-t} + ... = w\Sigma_t \left[(1+r)^t L_{-t} \right]$$

for t going from zero to plus infinity.

But if we assume simple instead of compound interest, this expression becomes:

$$p_1 = wL_0 + (1+r)wL_{-1} + (1+2r)wL_{-2} + ... + (1+tr)wL_{-t} + ... = w\Sigma_t\left[(1+tr)L_{-t}\right] =$$

$$= w\Sigma_t L_{-t} + rw\Sigma_t(tL_{-t}) = wh_1 + rwh_1T_1 = wh_1(1+rT_1) \qquad [3.13]$$

where $w\Sigma_t L_{-t} = h_1$ by the definition of labour embodied, and T_1 is defined by $h_1T_1 = \Sigma_t(tL_{-t})$, that is $T_1 = \left[\Sigma_t(tL_{-t})\right]/h_1$, which is what we needed to show.

The interpretation of T_1 is not difficult: it is that length of time such that, if all wages wh_1 directly and indirectly paid for the production of good 1 had been advanced for that length of time, the interests matured on them (with simple interest) would have been the same as the ones actually to be paid, that is the cost of production of the final good would have been the same.

T_1 is also *the labour embodied in the capital goods employed per unit of labour in a subsystem producing as net product one unit of good 1*. The demonstration is the following. The *subsystem* associated with a good or basket of goods is an economy composed of the several industries in such proportions that the net product consists only of that good or basket of goods. Formally, let y be the column vector representing a basket of goods (possibly with all elements equal to zero but one), and let (A, ℓ) be, respectively, the matrix of technical coefficients of capital goods inputs (each column an industry), and the row vector of labour technical coefficients. Assume all capital goods are circulating capital, with all processes taking one period; then the subsystem associated with y is an economy producing a (column) vector of total quantities x such that the net product is y, that is $x - Ax = y$ or $x = (I-A)^{-1}y$. In this subsystem the vector of capital goods employed (and reproduced) is $k = Ax = x - y$. The row vector of labours embodied is defined by $h = hA + \ell$, that is $h = \ell(I-A)^{-1}$. Hence the labour embodied in the capital goods of the subsystem is hk, and the labour embodied in the capital goods employed per unit of labour is hk/hy, since $hy = \ell(I-A)^{-1}y = \ell x$ is the total labour employment in the subsystem. To show that $hk/hy = T_y$, since $T_y = \left[\Sigma_t(tL_{-t}(y))\right]/hy$, we must prove that the infinite sum at the numerator equals hk. This sum is given, in matrix terms, by

$$\ell Ay + 2\ell A^2 y + 3\ell A^3 y + ... + t\ell A^t y + ... = \ell(A + 2A^2 + 3A^3 + ...)y.$$

The value of $(A + 2A^2 + 3A^3 + ...)$ can be determined as follows:

$$(A + 2A^2 + 3A^3 + ...) = -I + I + A + A^2 + A^2 + A^3 + 2A^3 + A^4 + 3A^4 + ... =$$

$$= -I + (I + A + A^2 + A^3 + A^4 + ...) + A(A + 2A^2 + 3A^3 + ...) =$$

$$=(I-A)^{-1}-I+A(A+2A^2+3A^3+...).$$

From the first and last term of this series of equalities one obtains

$$(A+2A^2+3A^3+...)=(I-A)^{-1}\left[(I-A)^{-1}-I\right].$$

Hence the numerator of the expression for T_y is

$$\ell(I-A)^{-1}\left[(I-A)^{-1}-I\right]y=h\left[(I-A)^{-1}y-y\right]=hx-hy=hk. \qquad \text{QED}$$

Thus the labour, embodied in the capital goods assisting on average one unit of labour in the subsystem producing y as its net product, is also the length of time such that, if all wages wh_i directly and indirectly paid for the production of good i had been advanced for that length of time, the interests matured on them (with simple interest) would have been the same as the ones actually to be paid.[38]

---

38. Some intuition for this result is provided by Garegnani (1990a, pp. 25–6). Imagine the subsystem as a reservoir of labour time, much like a water reservoir with water coming in and an equal amount of water going out: each period hy units of labour enter the subsystem by getting embodied in the goods produced in the subsystem, and hy units of labour go out with the net product in which they are embodied. Just as the average time spent in the water reservoir by each gallon of water is given by the ratio between the water contents of the reservoir and the inflow (and outflow) of water (if the reservoir is empty and a flow of water of x gallons per time unit starts flowing in and an equal flow starts going out only after m time units, m is the average time spent in the reservoir by each water molecule, and the reservoir contains mx gallons of water). Thus, the average time one labour unit spends in the reservoir is given by the ratio between the total labour time embodied in the goods present in the subsystem and the flow of live labour. This ratio is given by hk/hy: now, surprising as it may seem, this expression implies that the labour time embodied in the goods present in the subsystem does not include the labour embodied in the net product; this is because, the final purpose of the calculation being the determination of costs of production, one must assume that direct labour becomes embodied in goods the moment it receives its wage (plus interest, if it is not direct labour but rather indirect labour, that is capital goods), that is *at the end* of the production cycle in which it is employed since wages are paid in arrears. (What one wants to determine is actually the 'wages embodied' and the average time *the wage payments* spend in the subsystem.) Thus for consistency the indirect labour must also be seen as embodied in its product at the end of the production cycle, because only at that moment does its (augmented) wage enter the product's cost of production. Thus, while the net product embodies no labour time up to the moment it is completed, that is also the moment it gets out of the subsystem. So the average time the hy wages 'entering' the subsystem every year remain in the subsystem and must therefore earn interest is hk/hy. Due to the simple interest assumption, interest is only paid on the wage cost of capital goods. (This is very clear if one imagines that production processes are 'Austrian', in the more restricted sense in which this term is sometimes used, to mean that the reduction to dated quantities of labour only involves a finite number of steps because there are no basic goods.) Moreover, interest is paid t times on a wage advanced t periods (that is which remains t periods in the subsystem), so total interest payments are $rwhk=rwhyT_y$.

3A.1.5. T thus defined is a function of technical coefficients only. Furthermore, under simple interest, the relative convenience of two techniques changes monotonically with distribution: if a good can be produced with either of two techniques 1 and 2, with associated labours embodied h_1 and h_2 and periods of production T_1 and T_2, with $T_1 < T_2$, then, measuring prices in labour commanded units that is putting $w = 1$, the relative cost of production is given by $[h_1(1+rT_1)]/[h_2(1+rT_2)]$, a monotonically decreasing function of r. Production techniques with a greater T tend to become relatively more convenient as the rate of interest decreases, in perfect analogy with the case where labour and land are the only factors of production. The reversal in the direction of the movement of relative prices as distribution changes, which makes reswitching possible, cannot happen here. Indeed, if there is choice of techniques with smooth substitutability, it is possible to formulate a sort of 'production function':

$$q = f(L, T) \qquad [3.14]$$

which yields the *net* product q of the subsystem of the given good as a function of the *total* labour employment L in the subsystem, and of the average period of production of that good. One can then determine the marginal product of T; a hypothetical entrepreneur owning the entire subsystem will choose T so as to maximize profits, but the same result will emerge from separate firms, so, assuming a given employment of labour, and choosing that product as numeraire, the problem is $max_T f(L,T)-w(1+rT)L$. The first-order condition is

$$\frac{\partial f}{\partial T} = wr. \qquad [3.15]$$

Because of competition, profits are zero so the value of the net product, which is q, because we have set $p = 1$, must satisfy

$$q = whq(1 + rT). \qquad [3.16]$$

Thus we have three equations in the four variables q, T, w, r: the real wage in terms of the net product is determined once r is assigned (or vice versa), and it is a decreasing function of r, because as r increases, w must decrease if T is constant; and even if T decreases, it cannot decrease as much as required for w to remain constant, because that would imply that the technique at the lower and the technique at the higher level of r are equiprofitable (this is easy to verify by reverting to labour-commanded prices that is to $w = 1$), but this would contradict the demonstrated monotonicity of the relative profitability of alternative techniques.

Let us now use the above considerations to arrive at the condition of equilibrium between supply and demand for capital. In the subsystem having one unit of good 1 as its net product, the value of the net product is p_1 and this must be divided between wages and interest: total wages are wh_1, total interest is rwh_1T_1. Interest is earned as a rate of interest on capital, so the *value* of capital K_1 must be given by $rK_1 = rwh_1T_1$, that is $K_1 = wh_1T_1$ is the value of capital which it is necessary to employ in order to produce as net product one unit of good 1: it is therefore the demand for capital (in value terms) associated with the production of one unit of good 1 as net product when the period of production is T_1. As the labour embodied in the net product of a subsystem is also the actual labour employment in the subsystem, the value of capital *per unit of labour* is wT_1. (Note that if the real wage is chosen as numeraire, that is $w = 1$, then the value of capital per unit of labour is T_1, and the marginal product of the average period of production is set equal to r.)

Now, assuming the supply of labour to be fully employed, the overall demand for capital will be given by the sum of the demands for capital implied by the technical choices and by the amounts of the various goods in the net product of the economy. The net product vector of the entire economy can be treated as a single composite good, with the entire economy being its subsystem, and to it one can apply the procedure outlined above for good 1. Thus one finds T^*, the average period of production of the net product of the entire economy, a function of technical choices (that is of the rate of interest) and of the composition of the net product.

For example, if one assumes a rigid labour supply L^* and two consumption goods, 1 and 2, and a stationary economy, then, given the technical possibilities, one derives $T_1(r)$ and $T_2(r)$, the respective periods of production of the techniques for the production of goods 1 and 2. The economy-wide average period of production will be a weighted average of T_1 and T_2 with the distribution of the total labour employment between the two subsystems as weights: $T^* = [q_1h_1T_1 + q_2h_2T_2]/(q_1h_1 + q_2h_2)$, where $q_1h_1 + q_2h_2 = L^*$: the total labour employment must equal, in equilibrium, the labour supply.

Let us for simplicity leave aside the issue of the determination of the composition of the net product, by assuming a stationary economy with only one consumption good, whose production constitutes therefore the net product of the economy. Then the above three equations refer to the entire economy, if only we let $L = L^*$. One can therefore determine T^* as a function of the rate of interest. If $w^*(r)$ is the real wage implied by the rate of interest r, the demand for capital in value terms is determined by $w^*(r)L^*T^*(r)$. Therefore the system of equations [3.14]–[3.16] is 'closed' by a final equation similar to equation [3.12]:

$$w*L*T* = K*$$ [3.17]

where $K*$ is the supply or endowment of capital, a given number, the given value of 'capital' in terms of the consumption good. This is how Wicksell (1893) determines the rate of interest.[39]

3A.1.6. The framework is that of a long-period equilibrium, with the composition of capital determined endogenously: as the rate of interest changes, the optimal T changes and, with it, techniques change and the vector of capital goods existing in the economy changes. The latter vector does not appear explicitly in the equations, but it is implicit in the derivation of the series of dated quantities of labour, from which one derives T; the 'form' of the capital endowment of the economy is thus left free to adapt itself to demand and to technical choices.

The average period of production is therefore an attempt at finding a synthetic measure of the *capital intensity* of production, capable – once labour employment is assigned – of determining the *demand* for 'capital', conceived as a single factor of endogenously determined 'form'. The demand for 'capital' must equal, in equilibrium, the given endowment of 'capital', inevitably measured here too as an amount of value.[40]

39. Wicksell actually makes the simplifying assumption that the employment of labour is evenly spread over a production period of finite length (the production process requires only unassisted labour to be started), so that the *average* period of production is one half the length of that production period, cf. equations (12) and (13) in Wicksell (1893, p. 121). Wicksell admits however (p. 125) the need for a more general formula, which, given his assumption of simple interest (p. 121), will be our equation [3.13]. This simplifying assumption on the average period of production causes his equations not to coincide with ours, but the reader should have no problem in verifying that his equation (13) corresponds to our [3.16], his (14) correspond to our [3.15], our [3.14] is implicitly assumed by him in his verbal discussion, and his equation (15) corresponds to our [3.17]. Our formalization basically follows Garegnani (1990a).

40. Garegnani has argued that, under the very restrictive conditions making the period of production a correct measure of capital intensity, 'the measurement in value terms of the existing capital is not *essential* to the theory' (1960, p. 127, italics in the original; our translation), because both the demand for and the supply of capital in value terms might be replaced by a measurement in terms of the labour embodied in the capital goods. Since $TL*$ measures the labour embodied in the capital goods of the economy, the equation $w*L*T* = K*$ might be replaced by $L*T* = K'$ with K' the given labour embodied in the capital stock of the economy, a quantity independent of relative prices (Garegnani, 1960, p. 128; 1990a, p. 28). This is one of the rare instances where I cannot agree with him. It does not seem possible to assume that the capital endowment so measured is given *before* the economy has found the equilibrium technical coefficients: this is made clear by considering the one-good case (corn produced by corn-seed and labour according to a variable-coefficients production function), in which capital is a physically homogeneous factor, its measurement in technical units therefore encounters no obstacles, the change in the capital–labour ratio induced by, for example, an alteration in labour supply leaves the capital stock

Thus the impossibility to include a given endowment of 'capital' among the data of a long-period equilibrium holds for the Austrian variants of those versions as well.

In fact, under the present hypotheses the dependence of the value of a given physical vector of capital goods on distribution is particularly clear: let us suppose that technical coefficients are fixed, and that the physical vector of capital goods is adapted to a full-employment demand which is rigid in composition; then the value of capital is given by $w^*L^*T^*$, and L^*T^* is invariant as r varies, so the value of capital is not given, it is a linear function of w^*. And it may be noted that in the case in which the correctly determined – that is determined with compound interest rate – long-period value of a given stock of capital goods does not change with changes in distribution, that is in the case of uniform 'organic composition of capital' and no technical choice (then relative prices do not vary with distribution, the labour theory of value holds), the assumption of simple rate of interest would nonetheless cause the value of capital to vary with distribution in spite of unchanged technical conditions (unless the real wage were chosen as numeraire).

3A.1.7. These considerations make it possible briefly to appraise the 'subsistence fund' conception of capital.

Böhm-Bawerk appears to have justified his taking the endowment of capital as given in value terms, through the conception of capital as a 'subsistence fund', that is as representing a potential fund of consumption goods that may be used to anticipate subsistence to workers in advance of the coming out of the final products. The basic idea is that capital is created by net savings, and net savings consist of renouncing direct consumption in order to allow the advancement of wages to workers; the labour of these workers creates capital goods of a value equal to the value of the net savings. If the average advancement of wages to workers is to be maintained, the capital must be re-employed in production as soon as it is recuperated out of the sale of the final product; it is thus a revolving fund which allows the continuous re-advancement of wages. Wicksell (1893) accepts such a conception.

Thus we read in Böhm-Bawerk: 'in any economical community the supply of subsistence available for advances of subsistence, is ... represented by the total sum of its wealth' (Böhm-Bawerk, 1891, p. 319); 'all goods

unaltered in physical form, and yet the labour embodied in the capital stock changes owing to the changed technical coefficients. Indeed in a footnote of his 1960 book Garegnani admits that his argument pre-supposes given technical coefficients (1960, p. 130, fn. 17); but then it is unclear how he can advance this argument for Wicksell (1893), who admits variable coefficients.

which appear today as the stock or parent wealth of society ... will, in the more or less distant future ... ripen into consumption goods, and will consequently cover, for a more or less lengthy time to come, the people's demand for consumption' (ibid., p. 322). And in Wicksell (1893, p. 22): 'Following the precedent of [Jevons], he [Böhm-Bawerk] conceives the true role of capital in production as merely an advance of means of subsistence which makes possible the adoption of longer, but more fruitful, processes of production'.[41]

But in order for this conception to justify taking the value of capital[42] as a datum of equilibrium, it is essential that this fund of consumption goods to which the given capital corresponds 'will, so to speak, be there at the disposal of the community in a sufficiently definite amount, independently both of the methods of production to be used, and of the ruling rates of wages and interest' (Garegnani, 1990a, p. 36).

Surprisingly, neither Böhm-Bawerk nor the early Wicksell notice that, according to their own theory, this condition is not satisfied. The given capital, since it consists of capital goods and not of consumption goods, can only correspond to consumption goods as an amount of *value*. But the value of capital in terms of consumption goods depends on distribution according to their own theory, and indeed in a more evident way than with compound interest. For example, let us assume that the net product y of an economy where all capital is circulating capital, $y = x - Ax$, consists of a single consumption good which is also the numeraire and the sole subsistence good. The vector x is the social product[43] and the entire economy can be viewed as the subsystem of y; labour employment is $L^* = \ell x$; the vector of capital goods employed is $k = Ax$ and the value of the capital stock is (with simple interest) $wL^*T^* = whk$ (because $T^* = hk/hy = hk/L^*$), that is it is the value of the wages paid to the labour *embodied* in the capital goods. Thus capital does not *consist of* wage goods, it is only *of equal value to* the wage rate times the labour *embodied* in the capital goods, and if w increases, the value of capital in terms of the consumption good increases even if physically nothing has changed: thus, to what amount of subsistence goods can a given

41. Jevons had written: 'Capital, as I regard it, consists merely of those commodities which are required for sustaining the labourers of any kinds or class engaged in work' (Jevons [1871] 1970, p. 223; also cf. pp. 226, 229, 240–41).
42. In terms of the same basket of consumption goods that measures the real wage.
43. The *social product* is the term proposed by P. Garegnani to indicate the (value of the) sum total of goods produced by an economy in a period, including the production of intermediate goods which replace intermediate goods used up during the period (and which is excluded from the usual definition of gross national product). For example in a Leontief–Sraffa circulating-capital economy where the physical net product is determined by $y = x - Ax$, the social product is the value of the vector x, while the gross national product, as defined by modern national accounts, coincides with the net national product, that is with the value of y.

stock of capital goods be considered to be equivalent, since it will correspond to a different amount for each different level of w and thus of r?

It can therefore be concluded that the 'subsistence fund' conception of capital in no way justifies the given value endowment of capital, even granting the assumptions necessary to the average period of production.[44]

3A.2. Wicksell's Theory of Capital in the Lectures

3A.2.1. Wicksell eventually grew dissatisfied with the assumptions needed for the average period of production, and in the *Lectures* (1934 [1901]), in order to be able to use compound interest and to admit land besides labour as a second primary factor,[45] and yet not to lose sight of the delay between application of original factors and final production which he still considered the key to the role of capital, he turned to a representation of production possibilities in terms of differentiable production functions whose inputs

---

44. Friedrich A. Lutz thus wrote: 'the subsistence fund, in the sense of a given value magnitude, cannot be taken as a datum but is itself one of the unknowns, so that the system of these writers [Böhm-Bawerk, Wicksell, and other 'Austrian' authors, *F.P.*] lacked one equation for determining the equilibrium' (Lutz, 1967, p. 69; it would have been more precise to say that one of the equations was illegitimate). He proposed therefore to follow the route indicated by Hayek (cf. Chapter 5), treating capital as a vector of given endowments.

45. When land is a second primary factor besides labour, then one might – under the hypothesis of simple interest – define an average period of production for the dated land inputs, but then one would have two periods of production, one for labour and one for land, and, with T_L the labour period of production, β the rate of rent, T_B the land period of production and h_B the 'embodied land', the price of a product would now equal $wh(1+rT_L)+\beta h_B(1+rT_B)$, which when applied to the entire economy's net product becomes

$$p = wL^*(1+rT_L)+\beta B(1+rT_B)$$

where B is the supply of land. This expression can be re-written

$$p = (wL^* + \beta B)+r(wL^*T_L+ \beta BT_B),$$

and in order to pass to a single period of production T, that is in order to pass from the term $r(wL^*T_L + \beta BT_B)$ to a term $r(wL^* + \beta B)T$, the single period of production T must satisfy $T = (wL^*T_L + \beta BT_B)/(wL^* + \beta B)$ which means it will depend on w/β, so it will not depend only on technical coefficients, but also on distribution. (In his 1893 book, Wicksell was able to admit land only through the hypothesis that the average period of production is the same for labour and for land.) Another restrictive assumption, the absence of durable capital, is maintained by Wicksell even in the *Lectures*; he later wrote that it is 'just as absurd to ask how much labour is invested in either one or the other annual use [of a durable capital good] as it is to try to find out what part of pasture goes into wool and what part into mutton' (Wicksell, 1923, p. 260), implying that in the presence of joint production it is impossible to determine, independently of relative prices, the series of dated quantities of labour. As in this book durable capital and more generally joint production are not discussed, the limits of validity of this statement, and of Wicksell's subsequent study of fixed capital, will not be examined.

were dated quantities of labour, and dated quantities of land. The efficiency conditions were now that the value marginal product of each dated factor had to equal its rental multiplied by the appropriate power of $(1 + r)$. For example, if the production of a consumption good c employs labour and land saved up for up to two periods only, let L_0 and T_0 stand for labour and land employed in the current period (that is paid at the moment the product comes out), and L_{-j}, T_{-j} stand for labour and land employed j periods before; the CRS 'Austrian' production function for the consumption good c is then

$$c = \varphi(L_0, T_0, L_{-1}, T_{-1}, L_{-2}, T_{-2})$$

and the efficiency conditions, with factor rentals paid in arrears, are

$$\varphi_{L0} = w, \qquad \varphi_{T0} = v$$
$$\varphi_{L-1} = w(1+r), \quad \varphi_{T-1} = v(1+r) \qquad\qquad [3.18]$$
$$\varphi_{L-2} = w(1+r)^2, \quad \varphi_{T-2} = v(1+r)^2$$

where w is the wage rate in terms of the consumption good, v the rent rate, φ_i the physical marginal product of factor i.

It should be evident that this representation of technical choices can always be seen as *derived from* the more usual representation adopted in §3.3.2. The labour and land that have been employed two periods earlier must produce some intermediate capital goods which are then utilized, jointly with labour and land employed one period earlier, to produce other intermediate capital goods, which are finally combined with current labour and land to produce the consumption good. If one represented separately each one of these one-period industries and their efficiency conditions, these, plus the condition that all intermediate capital goods are sold at their costs of production inclusive of a uniform rate of interest r on all capital goods, would imply conditions [3.18]. Conversely, if conditions [3.18] hold, then the intermediate goods, if in fact sold on markets, earn zero pure profits, that is are sold at their costs of production, and when employed as means of production earn rentals which yield a rate of return equal to r on their costs of production, hence the URRSP condition holds. The efficiency conditions of Wicksell are simply the efficiency conditions embodied in equations [3.7]–[3.11], as they would appear if firms were vertically integrated.[46]

3A.2.2. Actually, a 'production function' in terms of dated quantities of land and labour *cannot* generally be obtained when there are capital goods that

---

46. One example of this 'translation' of Wicksell's representation of technical choice into the more usual one is in Petri (1978).

enter directly or indirectly into *their own* production, because then it is generally impossible to change only one dated input.[47] For example, if corn is produced by the use of direct labour (paid in arrears) and of corn seed employed one period earlier, one may consider corn as produced by dated quantities of labour employed (or better, paid) zero, one, two, three, and so on periods earlier. However, it is impossible to change only one of these dated labour coefficients, because what one can change is the direct labour and/or the corn seed technical coefficients, but such a change will change *all* dated labour coefficients (apart from, at most, the first one, that is, the direct labour one). So the representation of production conditions adopted in §3.3.2, that is the more usual representation, is more general than Wicksell's model. The latter must be seen as assuming an 'Austrian' structure of production in the following precise sense: technology is such that, for all goods, if one proceeds backwards from its capital inputs to their capital inputs and so on, after a finite number of these backward steps one reaches capital inputs which are produced by unassisted primary inputs only (in Sraffian terms: there must be no basic goods).

Consequently, since Wicksell (1934) assumes the equality between supply and demand for labour, land and capital and for all consumption goods, and measures the capital endowment as an amount of value (cf. §3.4.2), it is evident – since it is not necessary here to recount his entire model (for this the reader may turn for example to Garegnani (1990a)) – that the model of Wicksell's *Lectures* is only a special case of the model presented in Chapter 3.

In conclusion, there can be no doubt that the long-period general equilibrium model represented by equations [3.7]–[3.12] in the main text of Chapter 3 correctly captures the logic of long-period equilibria, as more or less explicitly conceived by all the founders and early developers of the marginalist approach (with the sole exception of Walras, who will be discussed later). That formulation, which renders explicit the presence of capital goods, has been preferred to Wicksell's formulation not so much because it is more general, but rather because it makes for a readier comparison with Walrasian and neo-Walrasian treatments of capital, rendering clearer the fact that the essential difference lies in whether the composition of the physical capital endowment is or is not part of the data of the equilibrium.

47. I owe this point to Professor Neri Salvadori.

4. Must Long-Period Equilibria Be Stationary? With Initial Observations on Investment

4.1. SECULAR STATIONARINESS VERSUS STATIC STATIONARINESS

4.1.1. The shift away from long-period equilibria toward neo-Walrasian intertemporal or temporary equilibria started in the late 1920s and early 1930s; and its justification – particularly clearly in Hicks's *Value and Capital* – was the necessity of overcoming the limitations of the traditional notion of equilibrium. Traditional equilibrium was criticized as only being valid for stationary economies, and therefore unhelpful for the analysis of real economies, which are always undergoing change.[1] Hicks put the accusation in very drastic terms, by describing the 'method of Marshall' as:

> a plausible theory of a stationary state; unfortunately it is only a theory of a stationary state ... Once we leave that special case, a crowd of new complications need to be considered ... many of which are supremely important ... The stationary state has positively impeded the development of the theory of interest ... it can tell us nothing about anything actual at all (Hicks, 1946, p. 119).

This accusation was in fact mistaken, but it has been widely accepted, and it has contributed to the current mistaken but widespread belief, that the neglect of the changes that normal relative prices may undergo over time is only legitimate in stationary or steady-growth economies.

In this chapter I explain why the accusation was mistaken. In Chapter 5 I will point out the real reason for the shift toward neo-Walrasian formulations.

4.1.2. In equations [3.7]–[3.12] (§§3.3.2–3.3.5) relative prices are treated as if constant over time. The neglect of the changes that relative prices may be undergoing over time is evident in equations [3.10], where the net rental of

---

1. Also cf. Section 5.3.

capital goods does not include the possible variations in the relative values of capital goods due to causes different from deterioration. This becomes particularly clear if one assumes that capital goods do not deteriorate, $d_j = 0$; then equations [3.10] imply that the rate of return on a capital good does not take into account any appreciation or depreciation of the capital good relative to other goods.

It is often thought nowadays that it was the stationariness assumption which made it possible to assume constant relative prices. It has already been noted (§3.1.1) that this is a misconception: the same neglect of the slow changes over time that long-period prices may be undergoing can be found in the earlier classical authors and in Marx, who were far from assuming a stationary economy. The reason for that neglect is, rather, to be found in the slowness with which normal long-period prices can be generally assumed to be changing, relative to the presumable speed of adjustment of market prices to costs of production.

For example, in the marginalist perspective with which we are here concerned, in a situation in which the proportions between capital goods have already been allowed to reach an equilibrium, the reasons for endogenous changes over time of normal relative prices are only the slow changes which distribution may be undergoing, owing to the slow variations in the proportions between labour, land and 'capital', due to the possible changes over time in the supply of labour and of 'capital'.[2] This slowness is mentioned by, among others, Marshall and Knight:

> For the general fund of capital is the product of labour and waiting; and the extra work, and the extra waiting, to which a rise in the rate of interest would act as an incentive, would not quickly amount to much as compared with the work and waiting, of which the total existing stock of capital is the result (Marshall, 1920 [1970], VI, ii, 4, p. 443).

> In the case of capital, the normal case is a growing total stock; but this is so large that the net production in a short period of time will not make an appreciable difference in the demand price (Knight, 1946, p. 400).

However it will be shown below that the analytical structure of the marginalist approach creates a certain complication for the analysis of non-

2. The assumption of constant prices is even more justified in a classical approach where, owing to the absence of the full employment assumption and to the different explanation of distribution, a growth rate of labour supply different from the growth rate of output does not necessarily imply a change of production methods or of distribution as time goes on. Sharp changes of normal relative prices, as caused for example by technical progress or by exogenous and considerable changes in income distribution, are of course to be analysed via comparative statics.

stationary economies, a complication connected with the way the demand for 'capital' translates into a demand for loanable funds and hence into aggregate investment. But it will be argued that this complication did not make the stationary-state assumption indispensable to the formulation of long-period equilibria, even though it did inspire the adoption of the static stationary state assumption as a simplifying assumption that could more simply highlight the forces determining distribution according to the marginalist approach.

4.1.3. At the outset it is important to avoid a frequent misconception; namely, that the stationary state assumed by J.B. Clark or Marshall or Wicksell was a *secular* stationary equilibrium, in which tastes are assumed to be given and the amount of 'capital' is *endogenously determined* at the level associated with such levels of income and of the rate of interest (assuming they exist) as to induce zero net accumulation (cf. Robbins, 1930).

This *secular* stationary equilibrium can easily be characterized in terms of the model of Chapter 3: the degree of freedom, introduced by the fact that in equation [3.12] the number K^* is now treated as a *variable*, is 'closed' by dropping the assumption that net savings will be zero whatever the prices and distribution. The supply of savings is considered a function, derived from consumer choices, of their endowments and of prices and distribution.[3] It is assumed that endowments, prices and distribution must be such as to induce zero net savings. In other words, in equations [3.7]–[3.12] K^* is now treated as an unknown *variable* to be determined endogenously. Aggregate gross savings are assumed to be a function $S(p, w, r)$ of prices and distribution, and a further equation is added, that establishes the equality between aggregate gross savings and the value of replacement investment implied by equations [3.11]:

$$pk = S(p, w, r). \qquad [4.1]$$

This is precisely how Hicks in *Value and Capital* (1946, pp. 117–19)[4] and

3. Much as in equation [3.6], §3.2.2.
4. Hicks appears to have been influenced by Lindahl, who interprets the stationary state assumption of Wicksell as implying 'that all factors determining prices are to the requisite degree adapted to stationary conditions' (1929, pp. 311–12), that is that the quantity of capital has become the one inducing zero net savings. Lindahl includes a given 'quantity of capital' among the data of the long-period equilibrium, but this is because he reasons as follows (1929, p. 302): let us suppose that an economy has reached a secular stationary equilibrium; in this economy the endowment of 'capital' will be some ascertainable quantity (assuming it to be measurable), and the endowment of labour will be another ascertainable quantity; let us include these endowments among the data of the equilibrium: the fact that we know that the economy is stationary authorizes us to include the stationary conditions among the equations of general equilibrium. The root of Lindahl's position appears to lie in an insufficient attention to the way in which the determination of equilibrium prices was

in *Capital and Growth* (1965, p. 47) misinterpreted the assumption of stationary state made by Marshall (he might also have cited Wicksell or J.B. Clark) when determining a long-period general equilibrium.

In this way, as noticed by Garegnani (1976), Hicks was killing two birds with one stone. First, the need for a given endowment of 'capital' does not arise in this secular stationary equilibrium because the quantity of 'capital' is determined endogenously. (Actually equation [3.12] can be eliminated, and the variable K^* with it, so the equilibrium can be determined without mentioning 'capital' the single factor at all.) Thus Hicks could avoid discussing the problems with the assumption of a *given* endowment of 'capital', a given amount of value – an assumption he himself had made in his earlier, Marshallian *Theory of Wages* (1932) where he was fully within the long-period method and spoke of capital as a single, homogeneous factor. Second, he could dismiss the traditional long-period method (in its marginalist application), as necessarily based on a notion of equilibrium of very little use, and he could thus present his new method of temporary equilibria as the only way to avoid sterility.

Indeed, if Marshall, Wicksell, or J.B. Clark had been referring to a secular stationary state when assuming the economy to be stationary in their discussion of general equilibrium, the relevance of their analyses to the explanation of distribution would have been very doubtful, since the objection would have arisen that distribution in actual economies could be considerably unlike the one associated with the capital endowment required to ensure the cessation of accumulation. Furthermore, a truly rigorous secular stationary state would have required that population and technical progress should have come to a halt too, because the speed of change of total 'capital' is so slow as to make it impossible to leave out of consideration the changes in population and in technical knowledge intervening during the gravitation to the secular equilibrium (Garegnani, 1960, appendix E; Knight, 1917–18, pp. 94–6).[5] Thus Hicks would not have been far wrong in claiming that 'the

traditionally supposed to help understand economies constantly in disequilibrium. This insufficient attention, reflected by the absence in his analyses of any discussion of this issue, was probably responsible both for Lindahl's belief that the traditional stationary-state assumption referred to a secular stationary state (with a consequent lack of relevance for actual economies), and for the absence in his writings of any attention to the impermanence, indefiniteness and substitutability problems arising with the shift to intertemporal and temporary neo-Walrasian equilibria.

5. This condition, of a state in which population too has reached an equilibrium, was indeed the Ricardian and the Marshallian conception of a secular stationary state. In Marshall one finds the other notion, of statical stationary state, for example when he writes: 'In the stationary state all the conditions of production and consumption are reduced to rest: but less violent assumptions are made by what is, not quite accurately, called the *statical* method. By that method we fix our minds on some central point: we suppose it for the time to be reduced

method of the Austrians ... stationary theory ... can tell us nothing about anything actual at all' (1946, pp. 117, 119).

4.1.4. But there is no doubt that, as had already been noted by Lionel Robbins (1930) (an article which Hicks surprisingly neglects to mention – it is hardly credible that he had not read it), this conception of a secular stationary equilibrium was *not* the one that not only the Austrians, but also Marshall or J.B. Clark, were referring to when assuming *static* conditions in order to explain distribution.[6] They were only assuming, for purposes of simplicity, that the existing quantities of factors, and in particular the existing quantity of 'capital', whatever they were, were not changing, so as to be able to illustrate the forces determining distribution with the maximum clarity, and by so doing, to keep to a minimum all unnecessary complications. J.B. Clark, for instance, described the static state as 'an imaginary state' which 'reveals facts of real life' because it exhibits laws that 'continue to act in a dynamic one ... We are, then, studying the realities of the modern progressive state when we examine the characteristics of the imaginary static one' (1925, p. 60). And even more explicitly, Wicksell wrote:

> The real theoretical difficulty is ... to explain how, under stationary conditions, the possession of capital can remain a permanent source of income. The application to

to a *stationary* state; and we then study in relation to it the forces that affect the things by which it is surrounded, and any tendency there may be to equilibrium of these forces' (Marshall, 1920 [1970], pp. 306–7: V, v, 3).

6. A similar mistake is made by those authors, for example Marglin (1984), who interpret a long-period equilibrium as a steady-growth position with full employment of labour, and then 'close' the model by adding, instead of an equation like [4.1], an equation imposing that, given the saving propensities of individuals, the growth rate of the economy must be equal to the exogenously given growth rate of the labour supply (obviously it is assumed
. that there are no scarce natural resources). The sole difference from the secular *stationary* state is that now the rate of interest must be low enough to induce just enough net savings as required for that growth rate; the 'quantity of capital' is again endogenously determined. This solution again avoids the need to take as given the quantity of 'capital' only by turning to the determination of a steady state whose connection with the actual distribution and prices of non-steady growth economies is at best unclear, even accepting the marginalist approach to distribution. It is enough to think of Solow's typically marginalist one-good growth model (Solow, 1956) to see that steady growth factor ratios and income distribution may be considerably different from those in the initial situation. The sole usefulness that it might be possible to claim on behalf of neoclassical steady states for understanding concrete economies would be, at best, as a guide to the *very* long-run, or secular, tendencies of economies. But such a role would require the validity of the notion of long-period equilibrium, and of its role as centre of gravitation, because one would need to prove the tendency to the steady state of the *actual* path of economies not continuously in equilibrium, and to such an end, one would need the persistent forces only derivable from long-period analysis.

non-stationary conditions offers no difficulty in principle. [...] Both logically and for purposes of exposition it would seem right to begin by examining the effects of a given supply of capital already accumulated, and *then* to inquire the causes which influence, and eventually alter, this supply. [...] Böhm-Bawerk neglected to base his argument on the fundamental simplifying assumption of stationary economic conditions, though he did not really achieve any greater degree of generality (Wicksell, 1934, pp. 154–5, italics in the original).[7]

But after stating that the extension of the theory to non-stationary conditions offers 'no difficulty in principle', Wicksell passes to other issues, so the statement remains undemonstrated. Evidently he thought it so obvious as not to need explicit demonstration. But in the light of the frequent misunderstandings on this issue, an attempt will now be made to describe how the legitimacy of such an extension might have been defended by traditional marginalist authors (granting, for the sake of argument, the conception of 'capital' as a single factor of variable 'form').

Readers who feel they do not need to be convinced that Wicksell was right may skip Section 4.2.

4.2. LONG-PERIOD POSITIONS WITHOUT CONSTANT RELATIVE PRICES, AND NON-STATIONARY LONG-PERIOD EQUILIBRIA WITH CONSTANT RELATIVE PRICES

4.2.1. A first thing to get clear is that long-period relative prices need *not* be constant. The defining characteristic of a long-period position is that there is a uniform rate of return on supply price, URRSP, that is that it is *not* the case that some capital goods are present in the economy in so abundant an endowment that it is not convenient to produce them because their demand price is less than the supply price (or cost of production). The latter situation would be indicative of a misadaptation of the composition of capital relative to demand, entailing quick changes of relative capital stocks and hence of rentals and prices. The prices corresponding to such a situation could not therefore be seen as centres of gravitation of market prices, they would be changing with a speed of the same order of magnitude as market prices. But the condition of URRSP does not exclude changes of relative prices over time, changes with which we are all familiar from intertemporal equilibrium models: what it adds to the condition of 'no arbitrage' (uniform rate of return on all possible forms of investment) characteristic of Arrow–Debreu models is that the uniform rate of return must be *on supply price*.

7. Equivalent statements are in Wicksell (1893, pp. 21–2, 113).

Thus in the first periods of a McKenzie–Arrow–Debreu equilibrium[8] the URRSP condition will not generally be satisfied, because of the arbitrary initial endowments of capital goods which may well give rise to the situation illustrated above, incompatible with the URRSP condition. The uniform rate of return (in terms of a chosen numeraire) will be on supply price only for the investments in the purchase of newly produced capital goods. But if the McKenzie–Arrow–Debreu equilibrium extends over a sufficient number of periods, there will be a future period of the equilibrium where, the capital stocks having had time to adjust, the URRSP condition will be satisfied (although relative prices may still be changing over time), because all capital goods in use are by that time newly produced ones. Relative prices may however still be changing, for example because there is gradual extension of cultivation to inferior lands as accumulation proceeds. All subsequent periods will of course also satisfy the URRSP condition.

Any period of a McKenzie–Arrow–Debreu intertemporal equilibrium, where the URRSP condition holds, gives us one possible picture of a long-period equilibrium with non-constant relative prices. If one leaves aside the first couple of periods satisfying the URRSP condition, where changes in the composition of capital might still be fairly quick, then, as long as the exogenous data (supplies of non-reproducible factors, technical knowledge, tastes) do not undergo quick changes from one period to the next, the subsequent periods will exhibit nearly constant relative prices.

On this basis, the *non-stationary long-period equilibrium* corresponding to the current (period 0) state of a given economy can be conceived as the current situation that would be observed in the economy, if it had been foreseen sufficiently in advance; it might be determined by assuming that the period from date 0 to date 1 (in discrete-time analysis) is an intermediate period of an intertemporal equilibrium established many periods before and extending into the future, and such that the amount of 'capital' at date 0 is equal to the given endowment of 'capital' of the given economy. In this way the composition of capital at date 0 would be endogenously determined as the one that would result from all adjustments having had sufficient time to operate; the URRSP condition would be satisfied in period 0; and the influence of accumulation and of the slow change in distribution on economic decisions at date 0, would be captured.

8. I use this name to refer to an intertemporal equilibrium with complete futures markets (up to the last period considered by the model) but without contingent commodities (that is without markets for promises to deliver future goods conditional on the realization of some event, for example 'one umbrella 452 days from now *if* that morning it rains' – the further extension of the interpretation of intertemporal equilibria proposed by Debreu so as to be able to encompass certain kinds of uncertainty).

The implicit assumption of correct foresight would here be to some extent justified by the long-period nature of the analysis, that is by the fact that we are not pretending to determine the actual values of prices and quantities in period 0, but only the trend values around which market magnitudes are gravitating (assuming the correctness of the theory, of course). We are asking what the situation (including the composition of capital) would be now (period 0), if people had had enough time to grasp the trends of relative prices and of quantities, so as to have become (already some time ago) so adept at foreseeing the future as to have no regrets now as to the decisions they took relative to the capital stocks to be held at time 0.[9]

But having assumed that there has been equilibrium for a sufficient number of periods before period 0, then even if in the past the composition of capital was maladjusted, by period 0 it has had time to adapt to demand. Thus relative factor and product prices, and the quantities produced, are only slowly changing in the equilibrium of period 0. Let us then ask whether a neglect of the changes that relative prices are undergoing in the formulation of the equilibrium conditions for period 0 would entail significant errors.

In all likelihood the error would be negligible with respect to consumer decisions, and thus with respect to:

a. the division of income between consumption and savings (and thus between consumption and investment, once one assumes that investment adapts to savings), and
b. the composition of consumption;

so the only possibility of relevant mistakes concerns the *composition* of investment.[10] The latter composition is only relevant for the determination of equilibrium in so far as it influences the relative demands for factors and hence distribution. But in view of the likely limits to the variability of that

9. For example, the trend in the value of houses and of land in the centre of urban areas would be correctly forecast. The historical experience of ample fluctuations in the rates of change of these values shows how far-fetched such an assumption is; this goes a long way toward explaining why economists have traditionally deemed it better not to introduce rates of change of relative prices into their determination of long-period positions, and to study the effects of non-constant relative prices at a lower level of generality, when a specific need arose. Cf. Petri (1999) for a refutation of a possible further objection, based on the so-called 'Hahn problem' (Hahn, 1966), to the determinability of a long-period equilibrium when the assumption of constant relative prices is dropped.
10. Consumers are indifferent between different investments, as long as these yield the same rate of return (or yield own-rates of interest which, if relative prices are changing, just compensate for the rates of change of relative prices so that the rates of return in terms of the same numeraire are again the same); therefore in the absence of futures markets consumer choices cannot determine the composition of investment once the assumption of URRSP is made.

composition, established by the reproduction needs of the economy,[11] that influence can be considered of secondary importance in most situations. Hence one can take the composition of investment as simply exogenous (and explained in a separate analysis according to the specifics of the situation), or perhaps – if there is reason to believe that the change in the composition of investment is slow – one can assume an equal rate of change for all capital stocks.

We conclude that what may be called the *static non-stationary long-period equilibrium* (to be formalized presently), in which relative prices are treated as constant although net savings are not zero, can be considered a good approximation to the non-stationary long-period equilibrium with non-constant relative prices, determined at time 0 by the hypothetical intertemporal equilibrium discussed above. The *stationary* long-period equilibrium is, in turn, an approximation to that approximation, which misrepresents somewhat the share of investment in the total product. However, in general, the latter distortion will be negligible, if the purpose is that of illustrating in a simple way the result of the forces that determine normal distribution and normal prices in a non-stationary economy according to the marginalist approach.

Formally, in order to arrive at the static non-stationary equilibrium, the stationary-equilibrium equations [3.7]–[3.12] (§§3.3.2–3.3.4) are modified as follows. Equations [3.7]–[3.10] as well as equation [3.12] remain unaltered. The only change concerns the n equations [3.11] which express the stationary-state assumption; these are now replaced by equation [4.1] (§4.1.3) which determines aggregate investment, and by $n-1$ conditions determining the composition of investment, for example, assuming an equal rate of change of all capital stocks:

$$\frac{k_i - d_i X_i}{X_i} = \frac{k_n - d_n X_n}{X_n}, \qquad i = 1, ..., n-1. \quad [4.2]$$

4.3. INVESTMENT AND DEMAND FOR CAPITAL

4.3.1. If a static non-stationary long-period equilibrium could have been formalized without difficulty, why did traditional authors refrain from explicitly discussing the notion? My hypothesis is that they wanted to avoid

---

11. For example, Marshall (1970, VI, vi, §6, p. 492) writes: 'The flow of investment of resources from their common source in production consists of two streams. The smaller consists of new additions to the accumulated stock. The larger merely replaces that which is destroyed'. This was the premise to the second quotation from Marshall in ch. 1, fn. 29.

the complexities arising from their approach when dealing with how investment would adapt to savings in a non-stationary economy. I shall now attempt to explain why the issue was complex.

I shall build upon the connection between demand for 'capital' and the marginalist approach to aggregate investment, as clarified by Garegnani (1978). As Garegnani has pointed out that connection remains largely implicit in traditional marginalist authors but can be reconstructed, given the logic of the theory, as follows.

As explained in Chapter 1, the marginalist view was that 'capital' was a single factor, whose 'form' was variable and would change according to the 'capital'–labour ratio imposed by income distribution; thus for example a decrease in the 'capital'–labour ratio in digging would imply the use of smaller spades. Obviously, such a conception admits that at any given moment the existing 'capital' is not free instantaneously to change its 'form', being for the greatest part 'congealed' in the existing capital goods. The change in the 'form' of 'capital' can only take place by changing the destination of the resources that might reproduce the used up capital goods, to the production of capital goods different in kind although of the same value. Accordingly, one finds in all these authors the distinction between capital of fixed form, and 'mobile capital in its free and uninvested form' (Wicksell, 1935, p. 192; also cf. ch. 1, fn. 29): the latter notion refers to the flow of purchasing power, resulting from the sum of depreciation allowances plus value of the consumption of intermediate goods plus net savings, and indicates the value of the flow of new capital goods purchasable with this non-consumed gross income – a flow of as yet undetermined composition. If there were no desire to change the 'form' nor the 'amount' of 'capital', firms would simply wish to replace the used up capital goods, thus generating a flow of demand for new capital goods – a flow of gross investment – of a value equal to the 'gross depreciation' of the existing stock of 'capital'.[12]

4.3.2. I propose to call *long-period investment function* the schedule connecting this investment demand to the rate of interest:[13] it is the function connecting the interest rate with the replacement investment (a value flow) necessary to maintain unaltered the optimal long-period amount of capital associated with that interest rate; that is it is the gross depreciation associated with each optimal long-period amount of capital. For example, if all capital

12. By 'gross depreciation' I mean depreciation of durable capital, plus the value of used up intermediate goods: this latter value is excluded from income, saving and investment in modern national accounting, but it is useful to be clear that it was treated as part of the flow of 'free' capital, capable of changing (and needing to change) 'form' as much as fixed capital.
13. Garegnani (1978) introduces the notion but does not use this term.

goods are circulating capital goods, and all production takes a year (which is the time-unit), the long-period investment function coincides with the demand-for-'capital' schedule. Otherwise it is derived from the demand-for-'capital' schedule in a way depending on the depreciation of the several capital goods, a way which may be very complex and in which we need not enter, the important thing being that anyway it will represent a fraction of the demand for 'capital'. Since the demand for 'capital' was assumed to be a decreasing function of the rate of interest, and since it was thought hardly possible that the fraction of that demand, represented by depreciation, changed significantly in a direction opposite to the demand for 'capital' when the rate of interest changed, the long-period investment function was thought to be downward-sloping because the demand-for-'capital' schedule was downward-sloping.

As traditional marginalist authors explicitly stated that different 'capital'–labour ratios implied different 'forms' of capital, their theory implied that the choice of new optimal 'capital'–labour proportions due to a change in distribution[14] could only apply to the combination of this flow of 'free' 'capital' with the flows of other factors 'released', so to speak, by the closure of old plants. If distribution, or technical knowledge, or tastes changed and thus the optimal 'form' of 'capital' changed, 'free' capital would be used to purchase capital goods differing in kind and/or in proportions from the used-up ones to be replaced. Given the nature of technology implicit in this view, essentially of the 'putty-clay' type,[15] the market where the real rate of interest was determined could only be the market where the demand for (the flow of) 'free' capital met its supply (also a flow); the rate of interest determined the optimal combination (and 'form') of the flow of this free 'capital' with the flow of other factors 'released' by the closure of old plants; the capital 'congealed' in already existing capital goods only received residual quasi-rents.

4.3.3. In a situation in which a change in the rate of interest caused the existing stock of 'capital' no longer to be the optimal one, the long-period

14. Or to technical progress.
15. A putty-clay technology is defined as one in which factor proportions cannot be changed at all once initially adopted: the inputs become perfect complements. Here, by the expression 'essentially putty-clay', I mean that physical capital goods, once built, cannot be 'transformed' into different ones. They can only be replaced by different ones. The two assumptions are of course not equivalent, but the second would appear to come very close to implying the first, when remembering (i) Hicks's observations cited in Chapter 1 on the low elasticity of the employment of labour once the 'form' of capital is fixed, and (ii) the full utilization of capacity (absence of Keynesian problems) assumed in marginalist equilibrium theory. Thus in the rest of this Section I will assume a fixed utilization of labour on a given fixed plant, so long as the plant is not closed down.

investment function would accurately indicate the (flow) demand for investible resources at each moment of time if it could be assumed, not only that other factors are fully employed, but also that (a) the age distribution of capital and the flow of 'release' of other factors due to the scrapping of old plants are constant and not affected by changes in the rate of interest; (b) prices – including rewards of factors other than capital – 'adapt without appreciable delay to the equilibrium compatible with the new rate of interest' (Garegnani, 1978, p. 35).

It could have been argued by traditional marginalist authors that the latter assumption is not too much at odds with reality, because prices and distribution are *determined on the basis of marginal products and costs in new plants*. The idea here is largely independent of the marginalist approach: when there is a change of technology, it is quite plausible that the average price of a good will start oscillating around its new long-period value much before *all* old plants producing the good are replaced by new plants embodying the new optimal technology. It suffices that some new optimal plants be built in an industry, and their lower cost of production will impose itself in the industry as the new normal price. The technology determining income distribution[16] can therefore be taken to be the one adopted in new plants, long before the old plants have been all scrapped.

Then – traditional marginalist authors could argue – the flow of gross savings is absorbed by the building of new plants adopting the new optimal 'capital'–labour ratio, and in which therefore the return to investment is equal to the one in the stationary economy corresponding to that flow of savings, even though the capital stock is not yet the stationary one. Given sufficient time, if the rate of interest remains constant at a given level, the corresponding investment flow causes the capital stock gradually to reach its new optimal level.

Even with irregular age distribution of capital and non-constant 'release' of other factors, and non-instantaneous price adjustment, the long-period investment function would still reflect the persistent tendency of the average demand for gross savings or 'free capital'.

4.3.4. The basic insight can be made clear by thinking of a case where capital can be measured in technical units. Let us imagine a putty-clay, one-good, marginalist economy, where the single output, produced as an instantaneous

---

16. In a classical approach where the real wage rate is given, it will be the rate of profits that will be determined by the technology adopted in new plants. In the traditional marginalist approach, both the rate of wages and the interest rate will be determined by the marginal products of labour and of 'free' capital in new plants. In both approaches, the value of older plants will be determined by capitalization of quasi-rents at the new rate of profits or of interest.

flow by capital and labour, can be either consumed or reinvested, and if reinvested it instantaneously becomes clay capital, with an economic life of ten years and constant efficiency during those ten years whatever the technical K/L ratio: the latter ratio, which is variable *ex ante* according to a standard differentiable production function $Y = F(K, L)$, cannot be varied once adopted.

If the economy is initially stationary, with a continuous uniform age distribution of capital, the (given and constant) labour supply is 'released' by the closure of old plants at a constant rate, such that the flow of labour 'release' takes a period of ten years to sum up to the total labour supply L; and if the equilibrium interest rate is r' when the total capital stock (measured in technical efficiency units, that is in the physical units of output which have gone to create it, independently of age) is $K(r')$, the flow of (gross) savings and investment per year is $S' = I' = K(r')/10$.[17] Thus each year $L/10$ units of labour 'freed' by the closure of old plants are combined with I' units of output-capital, and the physical capital–labour ratio is the same on all plants. For each level of the rate of interest one may derive the optimal long-period capital–labour ratio[18] and thus, given the fixed labour supply L, assuming a continuous uniform age distribution of capital, one may derive the demand for capital (measured in efficiency units, that is in the physical units of output which have gone to create it, independently of age) $K(r)$. This demand-for-capital function indicates the stock of capital one would observe in this economy if the latter were stationary with a rate of interest r.

If we now assume that at time t^* the flow of gross savings unexpectedly increases 10 per cent (because of a change in tastes) and then stays (and is expected to stay) at the new level,[19] the supply of savings becomes greater than the demand, and the rate of interest will decrease until it becomes convenient for entrepreneurs building new plants to combine a 10 per cent greater amount of capital with each unit of 'released' labour. Thus the rate of interest will have to jump down to the level r' (which we will assume to exist) such that the optimal capital–labour ratio becomes 1.1 times what it was, so that – since the flow of labour 'release' is unaffected – $I'' = I' \cdot 1.1$, that is, given our assumptions and measurement units, such that

17. In value terms, the ratio S/K or I/K would be greater than $1/10$ because old capital goods gradually lose value as they approach the end of their economic life: but for our purposes it is unnecessary to specify the correct formula.

18. Again, we need not enter here the way the marginal product maximum-profit conditions would have to be reformulated in this case in which capital consists of machines of constant efficiency lasting 10 years. It is a problem of choice of techniques with durable capital which is known to be soluble.

19. For simplicity, I am assuming that the absolute physical level of savings remains constant, whatever the rate of interest, and in spite of the subsequent gradual change in the capital stock and in output.

$K(r'') = K(r') \cdot 1.1$ if the economy were given time to become stationary again. With our assumptions and units in which capital is measured, the investment function is an exact scale copy of the capital demand function. What will happen to investment and to the physical capital stock is shown in Figure 4.1.

For ten years after t^*, old plants embody less capital than the new plants gradually taking their place, so the capital stock increases every year; only after ten years does the economy become stationary again, with a capital stock equal to $K \cdot 1.1$. But the equilibrium interest rate (and hence the wage rate too) starts gravitating toward the one appropriate to the new stationary state *immediately after* t^*: the distributive variables are determined by factor proportions on *new* plants, so their gravitation toward the new equilibrium values starts immediately after the change in savings. The real wage in old plants is rendered by competition equal to the one in the new plants, while the quasi-rents on old plants are determined residually.

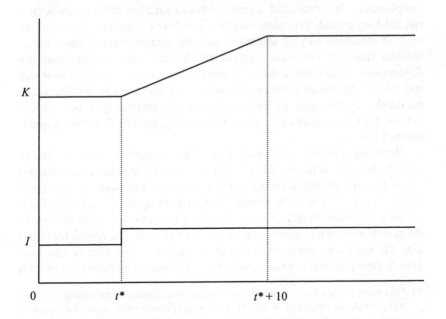

Figure 4.1 Capital and investment when in t *the rate of interest decreases*

4.3.5. Fundamentally the same connection between 'capital' demand function and long-period investment function can be shown to exist under more complicated hypotheses as to the nature of technology and capital, and with a value measurement of 'capital' and investment. The necessary measurement of 'capital' and of investment in value terms destroys the simplicity attainable when, as in the previous example, a physical measurement is available, but does not fundamentally alter the 'scale copy' character of the investment function. Thus, if in the previous example one measured capital and investment in value terms, this would imply that the investment schedule would not be a 1:10 scale copy of the 'capital' demand function because of the influence of depreciation on the value of existing capital: older units of capital would be worth less than new units, so investment in value terms would be more than 1/10 of capital in value terms, and the ratio between value of investment and value of capital would depend on the interest rate. If, furthermore, the average durability of capital in the several industries, as well as the proportions between industries, were to depend on the rate of interest, then the ratio between value of investment and value of capital would depend on the interest rate for these reasons too; but even with all these complications the traditional 'capital' demand function still implies what I call the long-period investment function, which is a reduced-scale copy (the scale of reduction varying somewhat with the interest rate) of the 'capital' demand function. For each level of the interest rate, this indicates the depreciation of the optimal stock of 'capital' associated with that interest rate and labour employment (under a hypothesis of uniform age distribution of the durable capital goods in that capital stock). Its decreasing shape therefore derives from the decreasing shape traditionally attributed to the 'capital' demand function.

Obviously it would be admitted that in real economies things are not so smooth, but the belief in the gravitation toward long-period equilibrium made it plausible that such an analysis correctly exhibited the *persistent* forces at work.[20] It must be stressed that such an approach made the long-period equilibrium highly relevant also for the analysis of situations where the rate of interest had undergone a significant change. The reason for this is that the putty-clay conception of capital suggests that, after a transition period, the equilibrium capital–labour ratio determined by the rate of interest

20. 'The theory implies that such circumstances as delayed adjustments in the markets for labour and products, or irregularity in the age distribution of fixed capital, do not fundamentally alter the terms of the question. As a result, the interest elasticity of the sequence of demands for investment would reflect, on average, the elasticity of the demand for capital as a stock. Hence the significance of a demand for capital as a stock which exhibits, in a clear form, the basic tendencies which must emerge from the multiplicity of forces acting in any given moment of time' (Garegnani, 1978, p. 35). The simplicity of the example in the text is largely due to the assumption that the amount of gross savings in physical terms does not change from t^* onwards in spite of the gradual increase in income due to the gradual increase of average labour productivity.

and by the demand-for-capital schedule would obtain on average on new plants. Moreover, the associated prices would tend to impose themselves in the whole economy, even though a possibly large part of the existing plants (the old but still active ones) would be unchanged in 'form' and would be using non-equilibrium methods of production.[21] The same reasoning would apply to changes in the optimal technical choices due to technical or labour supply changes.

4.3.6. We can now see why the long-period static non-stationary equilibrium leaves unclear the way investment is brought into equality with non-stationary savings.

The idea of the marginalist approach is that savings correspond to a supply of loanable funds, while investment corresponds to a demand for loanable funds. The decreasing shape of the investment function will generally ensure that the equilibrium on the market for loanable funds is stable; this equilibrium will determine the rate of interest at a level which, by equalizing demand for and supply of loanable funds, at the same time ensures the equality of savings and investment (at least, if financial intermediaries do not cause disturbances, discussed, for example by Wicksell in his famous 'cumulative process'). If net savings are not zero, the equilibrium on the loanable funds market will obtain at a rate of interest different from the stationary one. The economy will therefore be in a situation in which the rate of interest does *not* reflect an equilibrium between demand for 'capital' and *existing* aggregate stock of 'capital', because the stock of 'capital' has not yet become the one corresponding to the new level of the rate of interest.

The static non-stationary long-period equilibrium on the contrary determines the rate of interest as the one which ensures the equality between supply and demand for 'capital', and simply *imposes* the assumption that investment be equal to savings. It does not explain why investment is not at the level ensuring the constancy of the stock of 'capital'. It would be spontaneous to object: if the rate of interest ensures that entrepreneurs are satisfied with the existing stock of 'capital', how can they desire to effect a non-zero net investment? How can they simultaneously be satisfied with the existing stock of capital, and desire to *alter* the stock of capital?

The answer implicit in the logic of the theory is that, in most situations, the difference between the stationary rate of interest, and the rate of interest establishing equilibrium on the loanable funds market, cannot but be small,

21. In value terms this non-equilibrium element would not be visible because the value of old fixed plants would be obtained by capitalizing the residual quasi-rents accruing to the plant, and therefore the rate of return on the new value of old fixed plants would be the same as on new plants.

and therefore negligible at least in a first approximation, because the ratio between the flow of labour 'freed' by the gradual closure of old plants, and the flow of gross savings or 'free' capital, generally changes only slowly.[22] Thus we find Wicksell writing that it is not far-fetched to 'consider society as a whole, and regard its average economic conditions as *approximately* stationary' (Wicksell, 1934, p. 209; italics in the original).

4.3.7. It should now be clearer why traditional marginalist authors thought the stationary-state assumption was a legitimate simplification. It implied some further distortion, relative to the static non-stationary long-period equilibrium, in the determination of investment's share in income, and of the composition of investment. But both distortions could be considered of secondary importance, for the reasons indicated; all the more so, since the aim of the stationary long-period equilibrium was not centrally that of determining the amount nor the composition of investment, but rather that of illustrating, essentially, the forces determining distribution. (Let us remember the lines by Wicksell quoted in §4.1.4: 'The real theoretical difficulty is ... to explain how, under stationary conditions, the possession of capital can remain a permanent source of income.')

The complementary analysis, required for the determination of investment in non-stationary situations, was implicit in the connection between demand-for-'capital' schedule and investment schedule. Therefore the determination of the demand-for-'capital' function remained fundamental. It was the basis for indicating how investment would develop in non-stationary situations:[23] the rate of interest had to be such as to ensure that the flow of gross savings was absorbed by the flow of gross investment; the latter would be gravitating, for any given rate of interest, toward the level and composition determined by the long-period investment function. Traditional marginalist economists could argue that the path of a non-stationary economy could therefore be well approximated by assuming the level and composition of its investment to be on an average appropriate to the successive stationary equilibria implied by the successive levels of the rate of interest.

22. The logic of the theory requires that any abrupt change in the rate of interest, due for example to state intervention, to extensive malfunctioning of financial intermediaries, or to a sudden and significant change in saving propensities, would have to be studied at a lower level of generality, admitting for example the possibility of inflationary effects or of difficulties with maintaining the full employment of labour. The theory also requires, for its plausibility, that the demand functions for factors be significantly elastic, which implies that gradual changes in factor proportions cause very slow changes in relative factor prices.

23. Cf. Wicksell (1934, p. 164), for an attempt at studying the possibility that during the transition associated with a change in the rate of interest, due to an innovation making long-term investment more profitable, the real wage may initially fall. The basis for this study is the determination of the long-period stationary demand for, and structure of, 'capital'.

The above sketch of the analysis of investment in non-stationary economies explains why traditional marginalist authors did not feel the need for an explicit formulation of the static non-stationary long-period equilibrium. The stationary equilibrium, and the long-period investment function derived from the demand for 'capital', were all that they needed in order to understand the forces determining distribution and accumulation. But the fact that they did not formulate the static non-stationary long-period equilibrium does not mean that its formulation was impossible.

This confirms that the stationary-state assumption is not a possible basis for criticism of traditional long-period equilibria.

We can conclude that it is not in the stationary-state assumption that one can find reasons to reject the traditional versions of marginalist theory that relied on the long-period method.

However, we have seen that these traditional versions suffer from another crucial weakness: the need to specify the endowment of 'capital', a single quantity, and the impossibility of so doing. It is therefore time to examine the alternative specification of general equilibrium proposed by Walras, where that need – and with it, at least apparently, the need to conceive capital as somehow a single factor – is avoided by having recourse to a formulation which treats the endowments of *each* capital good as data of the equilibrium.

5. Walras, the Shift to Neo-Walrasian Equilibria, and some Confusions

5.1. INTRODUCTION

5.1.1. The reconstruction of the evolution of the supply-and-demand or marginalist approach to value and distribution requires, after the presentation of the notion of long-period equilibrium, an explanation of why this notion is no longer the recognized foundation of the approach.

Even the fact that the notion of long-period equilibrium was for many decades the unquestioned foundation of the marginalist approach is not often clear to contemporary theorists. For this reason, the chapter starts with a discussion of Walras (the sole early marginalist economist who treated the composition of the capital endowment as given rather than endogenously determined by the equilibrium), in order to show that Walras too aimed at determining a *long-period* general equilibrium and for a long time believed he had succeeded in this task. As will be shown, only with the fourth edition (1900) of his treatise, that is near the end of his intellectually productive life, did Walras admit that the long-period condition of a uniform rate of return on supply price (URRSP) could not be generally satisfied by his system of equations. In that edition he introduced several changes (among them the famous device of 'tickets' or *bons* allowing recontracting without actual exchanges or productions) to try, as best he could, to overcome the inconsistencies he had just discovered in his analyses.

The reason why modern readers should pay attention to the differences between Walras' early and later analysis is that the implications, of the conclusion that Walras too was trying to determine a long-period equilibrium, are important. One implication is that Walras' current high reputation should be reconsidered: Walras was *less* clear than the other founders of the marginalist approach on the logical requirements of the notion of equilibrium he was trying to determine. Another implication is that *all* founders of the marginalist approach shared the belief that their approach had to be seen capable of determining a *long-period* equilibrium if it was to be acceptable. A third implication is that, in the decades when the marginalist approach became dominant, the general belief was that the approach *was* in fact capable of determining a long-period equilibrium. The sole other early

136

formalization of a general equilibrium including capital goods was by Wicksell (1893, cf. appendix 3A), and he too believed he had succeeded in satisfactorily determining a long-period equilibrium. The inconsistency of Walras' theory in the first three editions of his treatise, or the impossibility of relaxing the restrictive assumptions of Wicksell's 1893 theory, were first noticed by their respective authors; but when they admitted that their theories were meeting some difficulty (Walras in the fourth edition of the *Eléments*, Wicksell in his *Lectures*), they did so almost *en passant*, without in the least suggesting that the entire approach might be jeopardized.[1] As a result, their reticent admissions long remained unnoticed. It was therefore nearly impossible for economists at the turn of the century not to believe that there were sufficient demonstrations showing that the marginalist approach *was* capable of determining a long-period equilibrium. The opposite was in fact the case. Economic theory might easily have taken a very different turn had this truth been immediately recognized.

5.1.2. This chapter then discusses Lindahl, Hayek and Hicks, who started from the long-period versions but in the years around 1930 realized the illegitimacy of a given value endowment of 'capital' and, in order to avoid it, started groping toward notions of very-short-period intertemporal or temporary general equilibria, where the equilibrium's data include *given* endowments of each capital good. But the rejection of a given value endowment of capital was not accompanied by any doubt as to the 'demand-side' roles of the conception of capital as a single factor of variable 'form' (cf. §1.3.3). By then the marginalist approach had become so deeply ingrained in the economists' minds that it was taken as obviously true in its conclusions, independently of the precise specification of the theory.

Also, the advocacy of short-period general equilibria was accompanied by a mistaken identification of long-period equilibria with secular (steady-state) equilibria, that helped the profession to lose touch with the logic of its own theory. The 'Patinkin controversy' (discussed in the first Appendix to this chapter) offers proof of a widespread inability of economic theorists to understand traditional analyses as early as the 1940s; the confusions have persisted up to the present day, as confirmed by the other Appendices to this chapter,[2] and are one main reason for the schizophrenia of present-day neoclassical theory.

---

1. Also, these books (both dated 1900), written respectively in French and in Swedish, were for many decades not available in translation.
2. Also cf. Appendix 6A3, and the arguments of Chapters 7 and 8; also Petri (2003a).

5.2. WALRAS' INCONSISTENCY

5.2.1. Let us then discuss Walras' approach to capital. Walras takes the endowments of the several capital goods as data of the equilibrium.[3] But he also assumes the uniform rate of return on supply price which is the distinguishing element of long-period prices: he assumes that for all capital goods the demand price, equal to the present value of the future net rentals, equals the supply price (cost of production) of a new capital good of equivalent efficiency.[4]

The equations of the general equilibrium with capital goods presented in Chapter 3, from equations [3.7] to [3.10] (cf. §3.3.2) are also valid for Walras, except that the decisions of consumers, from which their excess demand functions are derived, must now be conceived as derived, for each consumer, from factor endowments that include a given *vector* of endowments of capital goods, and not a given value endowment of 'capital'. But with respect to equations [3.11] and [3.12], which impose respectively a stationary condition on investment, and the equality between the total value of the several capital endowments and a given value endowment of 'capital', an important difference arises. Besides obviously not assuming an equation like [3.12] (cf. §3.3.5) due to the different treatment of the capital endowment, Walras does not assume that the economy is stationary.[5] This is understandable in view of the fact that he is taking the endowments of the several capital goods as given: had he maintained equations [3.7]–[3.11] in spite of treating the variables X_i ($i = 1, ..., n$) as given, he would have obtained a clearly overdetermined system of equations, because he would have obtained $n-1$ more equations than variables. Walras is therefore obliged not to assume equations [3.11], and to endogenously determine the value of gross savings as depending on the given tastes of consumers, and on prices and so on; he therefore introduces a condition of equality between gross savings, and gross investment (that is, the value of the production flows of new capital goods), which we can formulate[6] as identical to equation [3.19] of §4.1.2:

---

3. This is made clear for example when he specifies that the data on which the choices of each consumer are based include given endowments of the several capital goods: cf. Walras (1954, §201, p. 238): 'let us single out an individual who has at his disposal ... q_k of (K) ...'; also cf. ibid. (§234, p. 269).

4. Cf. Walras (1954, §233, p. 269) and Section 5.2. The summary of Walras' theory of capital presented in this chapter has been greatly influenced by Garegnani (1960, 1962, 1990a). Cf. also Kuenne (1963).

5. Cf. Walras (1954, §234, p. 269): 'the case of a progressive economy, which is the only case we shall consider'.

6. In fact Walras has an intermediate step here: he imagines that consumers with their savings purchase a perpetual bond which pays one unit of numeraire per period, and whose price is

$$pk = S(p,w,r) \qquad [4.1]$$

except that, again, the function $S(p,w,r)$ must now be seen as deriving from consumer choice problems in which each consumer has a given *vector* of endowments of the several capital goods. Walras' general equilibrium can therefore be represented by the following equations:[7]

$$p = vA(v,w) + w\ell(v,w). \qquad [3.7]$$

$$q = Q(p,v,w,r) + k \qquad [3.8]$$

$$X = A(v,w)q, \qquad L = \ell(v,w)q \qquad [3.9]$$

$$r = \frac{v_i - d_i p_i}{p_i}, \qquad i = 1,...,n \qquad [3.10]$$

$$pk = S(p,w,r). \qquad [4.1]$$

Relative to the stationary long-period equilibrium consisting of equations [3.7]–[3.12] there are n fewer equations (the $n + 1$ equations [3.11], [3.12] have been replaced by the single equation [4.1]) but also n fewer variables, the initial endowments X_1, ..., X_n of the several capital goods which are now given quantities. So the number of unknowns is equal to the number of equations.

The economic meaning of Walras' equations is best appreciated against the system of equations of the static non-stationary long-period equilibrium presented in §4.2.1. In the latter equilibrium, equations [3.11] (the stationary-state conditions on investment) are absent, while equation [3.12] (the equality between demand and supply of value capital K^*) and equation [4.1] are both present, and the number of equations remains equal to the number of variables because there are only $n - 1$ conditions [4.2] on the composition of investment (the conditions of equal rate of growth of all capital stocks) in place of the n stationary conditions [3.11]. Relative to the latter equilibrium,

the reciprocal of the rate of interest (Walras, 1954, §242, p. 274). He then puts the value of the production of new capital goods equal to the value E of the purchases of this bond, what can be interpreted as the bond being sold by firms to consumers and the resulting income utilized to purchase new capital goods (but Walras also adds that it amounts to the same thing to assume that consumers themselves purchase the new capital goods and then lease them to firms). The economic meaning is simply the equality between gross savings and gross investment, so for simplicity I have left this perpetual bond out of the analysis.

7. Equations [3.10] are simplified relative to Walras, in that for simplicity we have omitted the costs due to insurance premiums, which Walras subtracts from gross rentals net of depreciation in order to arrive at the net rentals. Equation [3.9] should now admit inequalities both for labour and for the endowments of capital goods, but Walras does not introduce inequalities.

what Walras can be seen to be doing is: he drops equation [3.12] and the $n - 1$ conditions [4.2] on the composition of investment, thus obtaining n fewer equations; and he turns n variables – the n endowments of capital goods – into data.

5.2.2. However, the equality between number of equations and number of unknowns hides a problem: the impossibility, in general, to satisfy equations [3.10]. If the number and productive capacity, say, of steel plants is given, and thus not generally adapted to demand, why in the world should we expect that the demand price of steel plants should equal their current supply price (cost of production)? The demand for steel may, for instance, have fallen considerably, relative to the demand expected when the plants in existence were built, causing an underutilization of existing steel plants which will make their demand price lower than the supply price of a new steel plant. In other words, there is a contradiction between the given vector of capital endowments, and the URRSP condition.

Up to the third edition of the *Eléments* (1894), there is no indication that Walras was aware of this contradiction. The reason would appear to be that he had not fully realized the implications of his taking the endowment of each capital good as a datum of the equilibrium.

Up to that edition, Walras relies on the thesis that the equality of rates of return on the supply prices of the several capital goods will be reached because when a higher-than-average rate of return induces an increased production of a capital good, the increase in the production of that capital good will decrease the rate of return on its supply price *above all because it will appreciably decrease its rental* (Walras, 1988, p. 396: §253 [second edition]; also cf. Walras, 1954, p. 594, Jaffé's collation note [n]; Garegnani, 1962, pp. 23–4, fn. 3). This idea clearly derives from the traditional reasoning which allows the production of new capital goods to affect their rentals by affecting their *endowments*; that is, it expresses the traditional argument which sees the equality of rates of return occur due to variations in the relative endowments of different capital goods.[8]

As noticed by Garegnani (1962, p. 23, fn. 1), the traditional reasoning survives in one passage of the fourth and fifth editions: at the beginning of para. 238 of the definitive or fifth edition, Walras writes the lines already

8. For instance, in a stationary economy, a higher rate of production of a capital good means a greater endowment of that capital good. In Walras' own model, on the contrary, changes in factor rentals can only derive from changes in the composition of demand, but an increase in the rate of production of only one capital good will mean only a very limited change in the composition of aggregate demand and will therefore in all likelihood entail only a negligible change in that capital good's rental – as Walras would later admit.

quoted in §1.2.11 and reproduced here for the reader's convenience (it should be remembered that 'selling price' is Walras' term for demand price):

> Capital goods proper are artificial capital goods; they are products and their prices are subject to the law of cost of production. If their selling price is greater than their cost of production, the quantity produced will increase and their selling price will fall; if their selling price is lower than their cost of production the quantity produced will diminish and their selling price will rise. In equilibrium their selling price and their cost of production are equal (Walras, 1954, p. 271; 1988, p. 353).

The traditional nature of Walras' notion of equilibrium is crystal-clear here: equilibrium is here defined as a situation in which cost of production and 'selling price' (that is demand price) of capital goods are equal, that is URRSP; and such equality is seen as brought about by changes in the quantities produced which cause changes in the *demand* prices, evidently due to changes in the stocks (which cause changes in the rentals).

That Walras thought he was determining a *long-period* position is confirmed by his neglect of the changes that equilibrium relative prices may be undergoing over time: the demand price of a new capital good is obtained by capitalizing the rental of the existing capital goods of the same type, that is there is an implicit assumption that that rental is not going to change in subsequent periods, or that the change will be sufficiently slow as to be negligible. Such an assumption is of course illegitimate if the relative capital endowments are arbitrary rather than endogenously determined, because then they might change very quickly, and their rentals with them.

Confirmation that Walras was not clear as to the contradiction between the kind of equilibrium he wanted to determine, and his treatment of the capital endowment, comes from Walras' description of the tâtonnement up to the third edition: the *tâtonnement* is *not* described as going on in a 'congealed activity' situation (that is while all productions and exchanges are suspended) and as based on provisional promises or bons; rather, it is conceived as a process going on in real time, with disequilibrium exchanges and production decisions being actually implemented.[9]

In the fourth edition Walras introduces the 'bons' and thus a 'suspended activity' tâtonnement. The most plausible explanation for this change is that

9. This is uncontroversial among Walras scholars: for example, cf. Jaffé's collation, in Walras (1954), of notes [h] to lesson 20 (pp. 582–3), [a] to lecture 21 (p. 583), and [f] to lecture 24 (p. 590); and Walker (1987, 1996). When in the preface to the fourth edition Walras describes the changes with respect to the previous editions, he writes: 'In the part concerning production, I have supposed the preliminary tâtonnements for the establishment of equilibrium to be done no longer effectively, but *by means of bons*' (Walras, 1988, p. 6–7, my translation; italics in the original; cf. Walras, 1954, p. 37: the reader may check how different Jaffé's translation is from my own literal translation).

when he started working on a revision of the third edition, he realized that a tâtonnement involving actual productions would alter the endowments of capital goods, contradicting his treatment of the capital endowment.[10]

This explanation is supported by the fact that, in that same fourth edition, Walras also changes the explanation of the mechanism tending to establish a uniform rate of return on supply price, in a way that shows that he now sees that he cannot rely on changes in the relative endowments of capital goods. He does not change the equations, but changes the reasoning justifying the URRSP assumption, in the following direction. Assume that the production of new capital goods is bought by the consumers themselves with their savings. If a newly produced capital good yields a higher rate of return on its supply price than other capital goods, in the tâtonnement with provisional 'tickets' the amount of this capital good that firms intend to produce will increase, because consumers will increase their demand for it. This will cause an increase in the rentals of the factors which are used in relatively higher proportions in the production of that capital good (Walras, 1954, §257, pp. 292–3); the consequent rise in its relative cost of production will tend to lower the ratio of its rental to its cost of production,[11] on which its rate of return depends. Thus, the tendency toward equality of rates of return on supply price operates through changes in the composition of investment; the argument therefore also explains what determines the composition of investment, which is not directly determined by any equation in Walras' system of equations.

But Walras keeps neglecting changes in relative prices over time, when the justification for such neglect – the slowness of changes in the data – is now clearly absent. If up to the third edition he was simply unclear as to the implications of a given vector of capital endowments, now he implicitly admits that the composition of investment might be such as to cause quick changes in the composition of capital; and that the relative rentals of the several capital goods may therefore easily undergo rapid change.[12] This

10. Walker (1996, pp. 201–3).

11. This effect is actually not guaranteed, because it may happen that the capital good utilizes itself as a factor of production in a higher-than-average proportion to other factors: then an increase in its production makes its endowment relatively more scarce, raising its relative rental. This may well raise the rate of return on that capital good, thus generating a tendency for the mechanism determining the composition of investment (as conceived by Walras), to increase rather than decrease the divergences among rates of return on supply price. This problem (first pointed out by Garegnani, 1960) of Walras' approach to the determination of the composition of investment will not be further explored here, because it is overshadowed by other more radical problems.

12. Investment may easily become concentrated on only one or very few capital goods, owing to the limited capacity, in general, of changes in the composition of investment to affect the relative costs of production of capital goods. This implies a high likelihood of quick changes

means that the determination of the composition of investment is itself implausible, because it does not take into account the presumable subsequent changes in the relative rentals of capital goods.

5.2.3. And yet even this implausible determination of the composition of investment is unable to achieve the establishment of a URRSP. To demonstrate this, it suffices to note that the gross rental of a capital good might be and might remain at zero, whatever the composition of investment: this will happen if marginal products may become zero, and if the existing stock of a capital good is so abundant that its marginal product is zero whatever the composition of production. In this case the rate of return on that capital good cannot be positive so long as its cost of production and its rate of depreciation are both positive (its net rental is then negative). In this case the rate of return on supply price cannot be uniform, if it is positive for at least one other capital good.

But even without going to such extremes, it is easy to imagine cases[13] where the rate of production of a capital good yielding a low rate of return may reach zero, without its cost of production having decreased sufficiently to guarantee the same rate of return on its cost of production as for other capital goods.[14] Traditionally the equality of rates of return on supply price was always viewed, not by chance, as brought about by changes in the relative *amounts in existence* of the capital goods.

Thus Walras unintentionally confirms the need for a notion of capital as a factor of endogenously determined 'form' for the determination of long-period general equilibria. If the composition of capital is given, URRSP is generally not obtainable, and those capital goods, which keep yielding a rate of return on supply price lower than for other capital goods even when their rates of production reach zero, will not be produced. They will not be produced until their deterioration or scrapping, which decreases their stocks

in the relative scarcities of capital goods and hence in their relative rentals. The substitutability problem discussed in Chapter 2 reinforces this conclusion.

13. For example cases in which the different capital goods are produced with similar factor intensities; or cases where a capital good, whose rate of return on supply price is out of line with the average rate of return, is produced by factor proportions very close to the average, so that changes in its rate of production are incapable of significantly affecting relative factor rentals.

14. Also cf. Eatwell (1987). The likelihood that variations in the composition of investment may succeed in bringing about URRSP by altering the relative rentals of existing capital goods is obviously greater, when the amount of gross savings is greater. If gross savings were nearly zero, or if the variability of the composition of investment were very small (for example because net savings are zero and the reproduction needs of the economy leave little freedom to the composition of investment), Walras' mechanism would be unable to operate. In all likelihood, this is why Walras assumes a 'progressive economy', that positive net savings.

and thereby raises their rentals, raises their rates of return on supply price to the same level as for the other capital goods.[15]

With the fourth edition, Walras has realized this problem and concedes that the equations imposing a uniform rate of return on supply price may well not admit solution; in such cases, he writes, only the capital goods will be produced for which the 'rate of net income' (Walras' term for the rate of return on supply price) is highest. The following passage first appears in that edition:

> If we suppose that old fixed capital goods proper of the types (K), (K'),(K''), (K''') ... are already found in the economy in quantities Q_K, $Q_{K'}$, $Q_{K''}$... respectively [...] it is not at all certain that the amount of savings E will be adequate for the manufacture of new fixed capital goods proper in just such quantities as will satisfy the last 1 equations of the above system. In an economy like the one we have imagined, which establishes its economic equilibrium *ab ovo*, it is probable that there would be no equality of rates of net income. Nor would such an equality be likely to exist in an economy which had just been disrupted by a war, a revolution or a business crisis. All we could be sure of, under these circumstances, is: (1) that the utility of new capital goods would be maximized if the first new capital goods to be manufactured were those yielding the highest rate of net income, and (2) that this is precisely the order in which new capital goods would be manufactured under a system of free competition. On the other hand, in an economy in normal operation which has only to maintain itself in equilibrium, we may suppose the last 1 equations to be satisfied (Walras, 1954, p. 308: §267 [fourth and fifth editions]; for the French original cf. Walras, 1988, pp. 430–1).[16]

This passage has induced some authors (for example Morishima, 1964, 1977; Zaghini, 1986, 1993; Donzelli, 1986, p. 267) to reject the evaluation that

---

15. Among the capital goods existing at a certain moment there may be capital goods that are simply going to disappear without replacement, because all the processes that utilize them are not optimal. In a long-period equilibrium this would be shown by the fact that their equilibrium (endogenously determined) endowments would be zero. Therefore URRSP must be intended as uniformity of the rates of return on supply price, not for all known capital goods, but only for those that would be utilized in a completely adjusted long-period position.

16. The same idea is announced earlier, in a passage which again first appears in the fourth edition: at the end of the discussion of how the equality of 'rates of net income' is reached, Walras concludes that the system of equations imposing such equality 'will be satisfied for those equations which survive after the elimination of those new capital goods which it is not worth while to produce' (Walras, 1954, p. 294; §258 [fourth and fifth editions]; translation modified on the basis of Walras, 1988, p. 401). The passage is hardly comprehensible at that point of the exposition, because the idea that there may be capital goods 'which it is not worth while to produce' has never appeared up to then, and the passage is not accompanied by any explanation. This indicates that the changes introduced in the fourth edition were rushed, as will be shortly argued in the text.

Walras' approach is contradictory, first advanced by Garegnani (1960, 1990a). These authors argue that the non-existence of solutions to Walras' original system of equations is surmountable via a reformulation of Walras' theory, that, although admittedly not to be found in Walras, is nonetheless argued to be in a direction pointed out by Walras himself, and can therefore claim to represent what Walras aimed to achieve. This passage, it is argued, shows that equations [3.10] should be reformulated by introducing inequalities in place of the equalities establishing the uniformity of rates of return on supply price. The inequalities should express the condition that the rate of return on the supply price of each capital good cannot exceed the rate of interest, with the added side condition that only the capital goods yielding the highest rate of return (equal to the rate of interest) should be produced. The resulting system of equations, it is argued, can be seen as characterizing a *temporary* equilibrium, differing from the modern formulations essentially by the fact that no expectation functions are introduced in order to determine expected prices. This is attributed to an implicit assumption of stationary price expectations: Walras is interpreted as assuming that agents expect current relative prices to remain unaltered in subsequent periods. Walras, it is argued, was not trying to determine a *long-period* equilibrium; he was trying to determine a *temporary* equilibrium, and the absence of inequalities in his equations relating to the uniformity of rates of return, simply reflects his general inability to introduce inequalities into the mathematical formulation of the general equilibrium model. But Walras – the argument continues – had clearly seen the need for inequalities, as shown by the passage just quoted.

Such an argument overlooks the development of Walras' theory. We have indicated that there is clear evidence that up to the third edition of his *Eléments* Walras conceived the equilibrium in the traditional way. Additional evidence is supplied by the fact that at least until the third edition (1896) of the *Eléments*, Walras did not assume the entire production function of a firm to be known by the entrepreneur in advance, but rather assumed that the marginal products of factors had to be discovered by actual experimentation of variations of factor employments. Walker (1987, p. 771) cites a letter dated 1895 from Walras to Barone where such a thesis is unambiguously spelled out, since Walras writes that 'the entrepreneur does not know' the production function. This is consistent with the tâtonnement as described in the first three editions, which included actual productions and thus admitted experimentation. It is on the contrary incompatible with the device of recontracting with '*bons*', introduced in the fourth edition, which made experimentation impossible and therefore required a complete knowledge of the production function.

The role attributed to the notion of equilibrium is also, unambiguously, the traditional one; Walras does not eliminate from the fourth nor the fifth edition passages from the earlier editions such as:

> It never happens in the real world that the selling price of any given product is absolutely equal to the cost of the productive services that enter into that product, or that the effective demand and supply of services or products are absolutely equal. Yet equilibrium is the normal state, in the sense that it is the state towards which things spontaneously tend under a régime of free competition in exchange and in production (Walras, 1954, pp. 224–5).[17]

> Such is the continuous market, which is perpetually tending toward equilibrium without ever actually attaining it, because the market has no other way of approaching equilibrium except by groping, and, before the goal is reached, it has to renew its efforts and start over again, all the basic data of the problem, e.g. the initial quantities possessed, the utilities of goods and services, the technical coefficients, the excess of income over consumption, the working capital requirements, etc., having changed in the meantime. Viewed in this way, the market is like a lake agitated by the wind, where the water is incessantly seeking its level without ever reaching it. But whereas there are days when the surface of a lake is almost smooth, there never is a day when the effective demand for products and services equals their effective supply and when the selling price of products equals the cost of the productive services used in making them. The diversion of productive services from enterprises that are losing money to profitable enterprises takes place in various ways, the most important being through credit operations, but *at best these ways are slow* (ibid., p. 380, emphasis added; 1988, p. 580).[18]

17. Note how in this passage again Walras defines the equilibrium as a situation of equality between 'selling price' (that is demand price) and cost of production, without any qualification relative to non-produced capital goods.
18. It might be suspected, on the basis of the first sentence in this quotation, that the need to avoid changes in the endowments of capital goods was not the only reason why, in the fourth edition of his *Eléments*, Walras introduced the tâtonnement with 'bons', other reasons being the difficulties with the assumptions of given tastes or technology, and of given 'initial quantities possessed' (that is given endowments of non-labour factors of production for each consumer). Such a suspicion would be ill-founded: the passage is there from the first edition. This shows that here Walras was simply illustrating the traditional argument that a real economy cannot be expected ever actually to reach its long-period equilibrium, but only to be, so to speak, always chasing it. But this may be the place to say something more on the assumption of given 'quantities possessed'. The non-labour endowments of a consumer may change because of net savings or dissavings, but then the change will normally be sufficiently slow as to pertain to the study of accumulation; but they might also change because of exchanges of assets, such as sale of a piece of land and purchase of a building; these exchanges of assets may be seen as a possible cause of impermanence of the distribution among consumers of the 'initial quantities possessed', which might affect long-period equilibria too. The neglect of this problem by traditional marginalist authors (including Walras, who never mentions this problem, not even in the discussion of the

In these passages Walras clearly attributes to the notion of equilibrium the traditional role of describing the normal situation toward which the economy continually gravitates, although without ever reaching it: the normal situation is clearly conceived as persistent, or changing only slowly, like the level of a lake; the processes causing the gravitation are explicitly conceived as 'slow'.

5.2.4. Thus, there can be no doubt that Walras' intention was to determine a long-period equilibrium; since he also took the endowments of the several capital goods as given, Garegnani's accusation of contradiction is fully justified. The passage from Walras (1954, p. 308) quoted in §5.2.3, p. 144 is part of a series of changes in the fourth edition suggesting that Walras had finally and precisely become conscious of the contradiction of which Garegnani accuses him, as well as of the associated need to assume that the reaching of equilibrium must go on in a 'suspended activity' situation, lest the endowments of the several capital goods changed during the groping toward equilibrium. It is precisely this contradiction that explains the changes of the fourth edition.

The changes are far from amounting to a consistent shift to a notion of temporary equilibrium. The neglect of price changes shows the persistence of the traditional conception of equilibrium.[19] There remain numerous other analytical aspects which only make sense in a long-period equilibrium: the absence of debts of firms, and more generally of past binding contracts tying factors to a firm; the absence of a fixed factors/variable factors distinction; the absence of a distinction between modern and obsolete capital goods; also, in the theory of money, the treatment of the money endowment of each consumer as constant.[20] And the role attributed to the notion of equilibrium remains the traditional one; as mentioned earlier, the passages quoted at the end of §5.2.3 had appeared in earlier editions but survive in the fourth and fifth edition. It does not testify in favour of Walras the theorist that he does not appear to notice the contradiction between this conception of the equilibrium's role, and his specification of the capital endowment. But

exchange economy in the fourth or fifth editions, where he might, but does not, have recourse to the 'bons' to prevent disequilibrium exchanges from redistributing the endowments among consumers) suggests that they thought – with reason, it would seem – that the endogenous changes in the distribution of the property of capital and land attributable to disequilibrium transactions could be safely assumed to be generally so slow as to be negligible in their economy-wide effects in a general theory. The study of their effects could therefore safely be left for a second stage of the analysis, through comparative statics, if the specific case so required (for example in hyperinflations).

19. Walras never mentions expectations; the thesis that he assumes stationary price expectations is only a projection of later theory onto his analysis, he simply never worried about this issue.

20. Cf. Appendix 5A1, fn. 59.

anyway those passages are hardly compatible with viewing Walras as the founding father of the neo-Walrasian versions of general equilibrium.

A more correct perspective should view Walras as simply less clear than the other founders of the marginalist approach, about the need to treat the composition of capital as endogenously determined, if the equilibrium was to be characterized by a URRSP and was to have the role traditionally attributed to it. Walras was brought by the logic of the marginalist approach – which needs given endowments of factors measured in technical units – to treat each capital good as a distinct factor of production with a given endowment, without realizing that in this way he was formulating an inconsistent system, and forgetting that his own reasons for assuming a URRSP implied that those endowments had to be considered endogenously determined. For almost 30 years he believed he had satisfactorily determined a long-period equilibrium. Suddenly, probably in 1899, he realized that something was wrong with his treatment of capital, and he then tried to paper over the cracks as he could – but he could not suddenly change his entire conception of equilibrium.

That Walras realized in 1899 or not much earlier that his analysis was imperfect is suggested by the fact that he first introduced the tâtonnement based on 'bons' in 1899, in a brief note appended to an article entitled 'Equations de la Circulation'. I take this information from a useful book by Donald A. Walker (1996, p. 323, fn. 1);[21] Walker also notes that by then Walras had been suffering for years from the mental fatigue that had led him to retire from his chair at Lausanne in 1892, at the early age of 58; in the subsequent months his health showed no improvement; less than a year later, in 1900, he published the fourth edition of the *Eléments*; afterwards he produced no more theoretical contributions of any significance.

The changes introduced in the fourth edition are therefore the product of a period when Walras' capacity to work was limited; they were nonetheless published very quickly; afterwards, Walras was probably incapable of further reflection on them. Thus those changes should not be considered the solid result of years of ponderate reflection. True, Walras was often unrigorous in his reasonings even before; but some of those changes look more like acts, I dare say, of desperation, motivated by the need to salvage a theory in deep trouble. It would be otherwise difficult to understand how Walras could

21. Walker (1996) does not notice Walras' change in the description of the process supposedly bringing about a URRSP, nor Walras' admission that a URRSP will not generally be achieved and therefore some capital goods will not be produced. He only discusses Walras' changed description of the tâtonnement, which occurs for the first time in 1899. Thus, further research would be necessary in order better to ascertain how and when Walras realized the need for the other changes. But it is likely that the changes, being all strictly connected with a better realization of the implications of the given endowments of the several capital goods, were decided by Walras in the same period.

accept, for example, the new tâtonnement based on 'bons', which contradicted his aspiration to describe the actual groping of real economies, and which made it very clear that the equilibrium could hardly be conceived as the situation the economy actually groped toward.

Therefore I fully agree with Professor Walker that Walras' '... written pledges model ... was extremely unrealistic; it was an incomplete afterthought; his presentation of it was sketchy; and he forced it into the structure of the *Eléments* without eliminating or revising the older theorizing that contradicted it' (Walker, 1996, p. 205). I also agree that that 'model' cannot claim to be a guide to the behaviour of actual economies. However, I cannot agree with Walker when he characterizes Walras' recourse to that 'model' as a 'weakening of his creative powers' due to ill health and age (ibid.; cf. also ibid., pp. 321–3). It must rather be attributed to the need to surmount the contradiction Walras had discovered in his theory. Professor Walker himself admits that the realistic description of the tâtonnement in the second and third editions, when applied to the economy with capital formation, implies that 'the model is path-dependent ... the equilibrium values cannot be deduced from the equations' (Walker, 1996, p. 203) because the disequilibrium actions change the data relative to the endowments of the several capital goods. The consequence is the same that we have already pointed out in Chapter 2 for neo-Walrasian equilibria: the 'model' is unable to determine the state toward which the economy tends, or even to determine whether the economy does tend toward a definite position of rest. The theory turns out to be barren of definite results, that is a failure. Once Walras realized this problem, he *had* to abandon the 'realistic' tâtonnement.[22]

This examination of the evolution of Walras' analyses allows us to reach the following conclusion. The traditional method of explanation of market prices as gravitating toward long-period prices (the latter being what the analysis had first of all to determine) was *universally accepted* – by Walras as well – at the time marginalist theory became dominant. The marginalist economists who left the proportions between the endowments of the several capital goods to be determined by the equilibrium, and had therefore to treat the capital endowment as a single quantity capable of changing 'form', simply saw better than Walras the implications of the traditional method, and in particular of the hypothesis of a uniform rate of return on supply price, for the treatment of the relative proportions of capital goods in equilibrium. It

22. Why, instead of choosing this way out, did not Walras abandon the given vector of capital endowments and turn to the conception of the capital endowment as a single quantity of variable 'form'? This question deserves further study; it would anyway seem that Walras never perceived such a possibility, and was for example unable to understand this aspect of Böhm-Bawerk's approach to capital.

should not then cause surprise that Walras' theory of capital formation found few adherents.[23]

5.3. THE SHIFT TO VERY-SHORT-PERIOD EQUILIBRIA: HAYEK, LINDAHL, HICKS

5.3.1. Although initially Walras' treatment of the capital endowment as a given *vector* encountered little success, later its fortunes changed radically. What made such a change possible was the acceptance of explicitly very-short-period notions of equilibrium. However this development had little to do with Walras (nor is this surprising, because as we have seen Walras had not clearly abandoned the conception of equilibrium as a long-period notion). The impulse toward the shift to intertemporal and temporary equilibria as the basis for the marginalist approach to value and distribution arose among economists who were internal to the long-period tradition based on the conception of capital as a single factor of variable 'form'; and it arose because these economists (Hayek, Lindahl, Hicks) realized the untenability of the treatment of the 'capital' endowment as a single quantity, an amount of value. They then turned to the very-short-period treatment of the capital endowment as a given vector, utilizing to this end notions which had been initially developed (nearly independently of any reference to Walras) for the purpose of studying the trade cycle.[24] Hicks, for example, in *Value and*

23. Wicksell (1934, p. 171) and Hicks (1934) expressed negative judgements on Walras' theory of capital formation, although without grasping its real inconsistency. Vilfredo Pareto, the successor to Walras' chair in Lausanne, after initially following Walras, must also have come to have doubts on the correctness of Walras' theory of capital formation, because he completely left the equations of capital formation out of his *Manuel d'Economie Politique* (Pareto, 1909). The influence of Walras on Irving Fisher did not extend to the theory of capital formation, because Fisher's first book (1892), heavily influenced by Walras, presented a general equilibrium model restricted to production without capital goods, and it contained no theory of interest; his subsequent theory of the rate of interest (1907, 1930) assumed given current and expected prices, an assumption incompatible with variations in the rate of interest (see Hagemann, 1987; Alchian, 1955, p. 942) unless the economy produces only one good which can be either consumed or reinvested, so that Tobin could characterize Fisher's approach as follows: 'he proceeded as if there were just one aggregate commodity to be produced and consumed at different dates' (Tobin, 1987, p. 167). We will see later in the chapter that the modern preference for a 'Walrasian' treatment of the capital endowment did not originate from a return to Walras, or more precisely, not from a return to his approach to capital formation.

24. After Garegnani (1976) first drew attention to the change in the notion of equilibrium by focusing on Hicks's *Value and Capital*, the issue has been studied by Milgate (1979, 1982), who drew attention to Hayek and Lindahl; and then by others among whom particularly relevant are Currie and Steedman (1989, 1990) and Gehrke (2003). The reader is invited to

Capital (1946, pp. 119, 129), mentions Marshall's analyses of short-period equilibration, not Walras, as the basis which he tries to generalize.

(Thus, it is only with hindsight that we can see how these developments surmounted the inconsistency, present in Walras, between the long-period uniformity of rates of return on supply price, and the treatment of the several capital endowments as given. In order to develop more consistent notions of very-short-period equilibrium it was necessary to drop the long-period elements persisting in Walras' theory. The greater consistency was acquired by dropping the URRSP condition, and by admitting that in a very-short-period situation the changes of relative prices over time are going to be significant, and cannot therefore be left out of the picture when one attempts to determine the agents' decisions. The intertemporal-equilibrium way to take them into account was by assuming that agents have correct forecasts of subsequent prices, or that these prices are determined, already in the initial period, in complete futures markets. The alternative was to assume that agents act on the basis of given (and possibly mistaken) expectation functions, and then one obtains the temporary equilibria proposed by Lindahl and Hicks.)

For our purposes, the important element in this story is the essential role played by dissatisfaction with the conception of capital as a single factor, in the advocacy of the notions of intertemporal and temporary equilibrium as an alternative foundation for the marginalist approach to value and distribution. The authors who first proposed such a shift, in the late 1920s and early 1930s, were Lindahl and Hayek; Hicks followed in their steps and, with his widely acclaimed *Value and Capital*, probably had the greater influence on subsequent generations.[25] For all three authors, there is clear evidence of dissatisfaction with the notion of homogeneous capital. This is evident, for example, in Hayek's contributions to the capital theory debates of the 1930s, which culminated in a 1936 article that contains statements such as:

> *It is not proposed, and is in fact inadmissible, to reduce the description of the range of periods for which the different factors are invested to an expression of the type of a single time dimension such as the average period of production* (Hayek, 1936, p. 362, italics in the original).

consult in particular Gehrke, for details on the problems (monetary problems and trade cycle problems, essentially) that stimulated the birth of the notions of intertemporal and temporary equilibria, initially independently from any doubt about the traditional conception of capital. Hayek appears to have been the first to formulate the notion of intertemporal equilibrium, in Hayek (1928), but without motivating it as a way to avoid the notion of capital as a single factor; it was Lindahl who first advanced this motivation, in 1929; he was also the first to propose the notion of temporary general equilibrium.

25. Cf. Weintraub (1983, pp. 19–20).

The Böhm-Bawerkian theory in particular went astray in assuming, with the older views that Professor Knight now wants to revive, that the quantity of capital (or the 'possibility to wait') was a simple magnitude, a homogeneous fund of clearly determined size (ibid., p. 374).

All the other attempts to state the assumptions as regards the supply of capital in terms of a definite fund and without any reference to the time structure, whether this is attempted by postulating given quantities of 'waiting', or 'capital disposal', or a 'subsistence fund', or 'true capital', or 'carrying powers' are just so many evasions of the real problem ... they are just so many empty words ... And the concept of capital conceived as a separate factor of determinate magnitude which is to be treated on the same footing with 'land' and 'labor' belongs to the same category (ibid., p. 377).

... it would be erroneous to assume that this given 'factor' [the existing 'capital'] is given as a definite quantity of value, or as any other determinate quantity which can be measured in terms of some common unit ... the only exact way of stating the supply condition of this factor would be a complete enumeration and description of the individual items... (ibid., p. 382).

These lines not only illustrate the conception of capital as a single factor prevalent at the time, and indicate Hayek's rejection of that conception, but also propose to replace it with 'a complete enumeration and description of the individual items' composing the capital stock of an economy.

Lindahl had earlier written, in his 1929 article 'The place of capital in the theory of price':

By this I do not mean that the problem when the volume of capital can be regarded as unchanged is solved through the ordinary concept of capital as a sum of values. In some cases, it is true it is possible to manage with this concept or the closely related 'weighted average time of investment.'*[26] But sometimes it seems impossible in the nature of the case to determine any fixed points for a comparison between different stationary situations. What is for instance meant by saying that two separate communities with different populations, on different cultural levels and with different technique and consequently quite different price relations, have the same quantity of capital? To regard this as being the case if the circulating capital has the same value (estimated in some common money term) or if the weighted average investment period is equal in the two communities is evidently a purely conventional idea. For this reason the possibilities of an analysis of the pricing problem on these lines are somewhat limited.

The difficulties here mentioned are associated with the stationary setting of the problem. On account of its artificial and very special assumptions the static problem has little or no connection with the phenomena determining prices in the

26. [*Fn. by F.P.*] Lindahl attaches here a footnote *, which is quoted and commented upon in the next footnote below.

real world. Therefore the attempt must be made to build up on this foundation an improved analysis which will have more general validity (Lindahl, 1929, pp. 316–7; also see ibid., pp. 247, 312–3).[27]

The 'improved analysis' is sketched by Lindahl in the subsequent chapters and it rests on the formulation of a 'dynamic' analysis (at first, an intertemporal equilibrium with perfect foresight; then, a temporary equilibrium) that assumes a given vector of endowments of capital goods (cf., for example, 'During the initial period in the dynamic process under observation, all existing capital equipment in the community can be regarded as original' (Lindahl 1929, p. 320)). (On the reference to stationariness in the above quotation, cf. Chapter 4, fn. 4.)

5.3.2. Hicks was less explicit than Hayek or Lindahl, but in his case too there is no doubt that the advocacy of the temporary equilibrium method was largely motivated by misgivings with the traditional treatment of capital. One might not get this impression from *Value and Capital*, because in that book the criticism is concentrated on the limitations of the static method (equilibrium analysis where commodities are not dated), which according to Hicks is unable to consider the influence of expectations (1946, p. 117). In the presence of capital goods (or rather, as Hicks prefers to put it, of a necessity to date commodities) the static method – he argues – is only legitimate in a stationary state, because only in a stationary state prices are expected not to vary and therefore expectations can be neglected. Of course this was a misrepresentation of traditional analyses, which, as we have

27. Currie and Steedman (1990, pp. 86–7, fn. 9) criticize Milgate's interpretation (according to which Lindahl proposes a temporary-equilibrium analysis essentially to avoid the problem of defining the quantity of capital as a single factor) by claiming that 'Lindahl does not seek to circumvent the problem of measuring capital'. Their only supporting evidence is unconvincing: they quote the following lines from the * footnote Lindahl appended *in 1939* to the passage quoted in the text: 'Both these methods of measuring capital [...] have the disadvantage, that the measure of capital is made dependent on the prices of the services invested and on the rate of interest – which belong to the unknown factors of the problem. [...] Since no better method seems to be available, we must, however, choose one of these two measures of capital'. But Lindahl's footnote continues as follows: 'And in the algebraic treatment of the problem given above, we have preferred to use the second, which seems on the whole to be less influenced by unexpected changes in prices or in the rate of interest'. Given that the footnote does not contradict the very clear admissions in the main text, it seems more convincing to interpret it as motivating why (in order to remind readers of the logic of static analysis and of the role within it of the conception of capital as a single factor) Lindahl has preferred to measure 'capital' in terms of the average period of investment rather than as an amount of value (the more usual way); thus he shows no intention of denying that that analysis is based on debatable assumptions which justify the search for a different approach.

argued in Chapter 4, did not need an assumption of strict constancy of relative prices and assumed a stationary state only for reasons of simplicity and clarity. The misrepresentation is compounded by the interpretation of the traditional stationary state assumption as referring to a secular stationary state, in which not only the composition but also the 'quantity' of capital is not given but instead is endogenously determined by the condition that, given the tastes of consumers, 'the rate of interest must therefore be fixed at a level which offers no incentive for net saving or dis-saving' (Hicks 1946 , p. 118). In this way, as already pointed out (§4.1.3), Hicks could avoid admitting that traditional marginalist analyses, including his own earlier analysis in *The Theory of Wages* (Hicks, 1932 [1963]), relied on a given quantity of capital of variable 'form'. An explicit admission that there were some problems with traditional marginalist treatments of capital only appears in a footnote:

> Of course, people used to be able to content themselves with the static apparatus, only because they were imperfectly aware of its limitations. Thus they would often introduce into their static theory a 'factor of production' capital and its 'price' interest, supposing that capital could be treated like the static factors. (Cf. J. B. Clark's 'free capital' and Cassel's 'capital disposal'.) That some error was involved in the procedure would not have been denied; but the absence of a general dynamic theory, in which all quantities were properly dated, made it easy to underestimate how great the error was (Hicks 1946, p. 116, fn.).

But in the text the sole 'error' explicitly indicated is the neglect of expectations; no mention is made of the problem of how to measure this factor of production 'capital' or its variations, even in stationary states.

However, as pointed out by Garegnani (1976), Hicks's turn to the temporary equilibrium method comes little after a harsh review of *The Theory of Wages* by the Cambridge economist Gerald Shove (1933 [1963]). Shove, at the end of a series of critical comments, had pointed out a true mistake in Hicks's book, caused by an insufficient appreciation of the peculiarity of capital. Hicks had argued that a rise in wages would cause a lower demand for labour owing to a shift to more capitalistic methods of production, even without changes in the rate of interest. Shove points out that if the rate of interest does not change, a rise in wages will only raise all costs, and hence prices, in the same proportion, leaving relative prices (and the real wage) unchanged and therefore inducing neither direct nor indirect factor substitution[28]. And this criticism starts with: 'Unfortunately "capital" is not

---

28. Hicks had not realized that the relationship between rate of interest and wage is different from the relationship between land rent and wage. If in a labour–land economy the wage–rent ratio rises because the rate of money wages rises while the rate of money rent remains

defined and we are not told how quantities of it ... are to be measured' (Shove, 1933 [1963], p. 264).

Two years later, at the beginning of the article where Hicks first proposes the temporary equilibrium method (Hicks 1935b [1963], p. 268, fn. 1) there appears the admission that some inconsistencies of the notion of capital adopted in *The Theory of Wages* had been correctly pointed out by Shove. The proposal of the temporary equilibrium method is motivated by a criticism of traditional marginalist capital theory: both J.B. Clark's theory, and Böhm-Bawerk's and Wicksell's theory, are accused of being 'built upon the hypothesis of a stationary state, quite satisfactory under that hypothesis, but incapable of extension to meet other hypotheses, and consequently incapable of application' (pp. 268–9).

Clearly, Shove's harsh review had obliged Hicks to reflect upon the conception of capital he had been uncritically using, and he believed he had found what was wrong with it. We cannot accept his diagnosis, but what is relevant now is that in Hicks's case too, the shift to very-short-period equilibria was largely, if not essentially, motivated by dissatisfaction with the traditional treatment of capital. However, differently from Hayek or Lindahl, in Hicks there never appears an explicit admission that it is impossible to measure the quantity of capital independently of relative prices. The statement in Hicks (1935b [1963]) that at least in the stationary state traditional capital theory is 'quite satisfactory' suggests that Hicks was less clear about this problem than the other two authors. Still, he was evidently unable to restate traditional capital theory in a way that he felt would spare him further harsh criticisms.

The harshness of Shove's review (which persuaded Hicks to let his book go out of print for 30 years) can also help us to understand why Hicks hurriedly jumped to advocate the temporary equilibrium method, in spite of the several problems he could see in it. We have quoted in §1.3.2 his 1932 rejection of the notion of a short-period marginal product of labour; in Petri (1991) it is shown that the impermanence problem and the indefiniteness problem too were recognized by Hicks before or while writing *Value and Capital*. Little wonder, then, that in later years he would be unable to repress his doubts about the legitimacy of neo-Walrasian notions of equilibrium, coming to reject his own earlier advocacy of the temporary equilibrium method (Petri, 1991). In the meantime, however, many other economists had adopted neo-Walrasian notions of equilibrium.

unchanged, the real wage rises and relative prices change in favour of goods or methods utilizing less labour per unit of land. On the contrary, if the rate of interest remains unchanged, changes in the rate of money wages cannot alter the real wage, and relative prices do not change: once the rate of interest is given, relative prices are given (cf. Chapter 6).

5.4.   THE CO-EXISTENCE OF THE TWO APPROACHES TO CAPITAL

5.4.1. A systematic study of the diffusion of neo-Walrasian notions of equilibrium in the 1940s and 1950s (and of the resistances they met) remains to be done.

What seems clear is that the doubts about homogeneous 'capital' expressed by Lindahl, Hayek and Hicks did not cause doubts about the correctness of the marginalist approach; even the doubts about homogeneous 'capital' were not explicitly endorsed by other authors. For example, Knight's 1946 survey for *The Encyclopaedia Britannica* on capital and interest (quoted in §3.3.4 and §4.1.2) makes no mention of those doubts, and upholds the validity of the conception of capital as somehow a single factor.

No doubt the reason Hayek's, Lindahl's and Hicks's misgivings about 'capital', the homogeneous factor, had little impact, was the fact that not even these three authors had been induced by their misgivings to doubt the marginalist description of the basic forces at work in market economies. Neither Hicks, Hayek, nor Lindahl showed any suspicion that their criticisms of traditional marginalist analyses based on 'capital', the value factor, might have destructive implications for the whole of the marginalist approach. All three authors apparently believed that the tendency of the 'real' forces of a market economy toward full employment and toward a determination of wages and interest as reflecting the productive contributions respectively of labour and of abstinence from consumption, the tendency traditionally argued to exist on the basis of long-period arguments, could still be argued to exist if one did away with 'capital', the homogeneous factor, and adopted neo-Walrasian notions of equilibrium and a treatment of capital as a set of heterogeneous goods.

But what this meant was that the traditional conception of capital–labour substitution continued in fact to be accepted, although somewhat less explicitly. For example, the continued belief in the tendency of investment to adapt to savings rested on the belief that investment was a decreasing function of the rate of interest: a belief necessarily based on the idea that a lower rate of interest would induce a greater demand for loanable funds[29] –

29. In Walras too (cf. Walras, 1954, §253, p. 287) the demand for savings, that is the value of investment, is claimed to be a decreasing function of the rate of interest. The justification is that the price of new capital goods is a decreasing function of the rate of interest because it is the capitalized value of their rentals, that are treated as independent of the level of the interest rate. We need not stop here to discuss the shortcomings of this justification in any detail; it should be evident that it is inconsistent with the dependence of all relative prices and rentals on the rate of interest, implicit in the URRSP assumed by Walras. Here again,

this, in turn, due ultimately to a greater convenience of more value-capital-intensive processes as the rate of interest decreased.

In Hicks's case – arguably the more influential one – the persistence of the traditional conception of capital is particularly clear. In the article where he first proposes the temporary equilibrium method, Hicks (1935a) assumes an economy where there are heterogeneous capital goods and a single consumption good, but he then proceeds to argue that 'In our simplified economy there are thus two prices: a rate of wages and a rate of interest' (1935a, p. 70). He completely neglects the prices of capital goods, as if capital (which he calls 'equipment' in this article) were in fact homogeneous with the product. In the Commentary added to the reprint of *The Theory of Wages* which he finally authorized in 1963, Hicks even reaffirms his faith in the possibility of conceiving capital as a single factor in some *physical* sense (1932 [1963], p. 345), and in the existence of capital–labour substitution induced by variations in income distribution (ibid., p. 366).

How does this continuing faith in the fundamental soundness of the traditional conception of capital surface in the proposal of the temporary equilibrium method in *Value and Capital*? Precisely in the passages concerned with the 'demand-side' role of that conception. When, in order to criticize it, Hicks describes the (secular) stationary state he attributes to the Austrians, he states (1946, p. 118):

> ... when we look at this stationary economy ... How will the quantity of intermediate products – the quantity of capital – be determined?
> It turns out to be determined through the rate of interest. A fall in the rate of interest would encourage the adoption of longer processes, requiring the use (at any moment) of larger quantities of intermediate products.

No objection is advanced by Hicks against this negative relationship between rate of interest and 'quantities of intermediate products'.[30] What Hicks

Walras reveals a superficiality of analysis that suggests that the high reputation he enjoys is misplaced.

30. Note how Hicks here speaks of 'larger quantities of intermediate products', neglecting the changes in the types of capital goods associated with changes in technology, and thus clearly betraying the belief that it is possible to conceive the different vectors of capital goods associated with different rates of interest as representing in fact different quantities of a single factor 'capital'. Garegnani (1990a, p. 56) has noticed that exactly the same belief emerges in Walras, who 'did attempt to analyse changes by comparing equilibria defined on the basis of capital stocks taken as data or independent variables. In fact, as revealed by expressions such as "increase in the quantities of capital goods proper" (Walras 1954, for example p. 387) which he used in those comparisons, Walras treated the several stocks of capital as if they constituted a *single* composite physical quantity of capital' (Garegnani, 1990, p. 56). According to Garegnani – and we agree with him – this confirms the inescapable need, in the marginalist approach, for the conception of capital as a single

objects to is only the *usefulness* of using such a relationship in order endogenously to determine the secular-stationary-state quantity of capital, since actual economies are far from a secular equilibrium. Indeed, later in the book Hicks tries to confirm the validity of that traditional relationship by arguing (1946, ch. XVII, pp. 214–7; also p. 328) that, when investors entertain *given* price expectations, then a general decrease of interest rates (increase of discount rates) will induce firms to 'tilt' the time shape of net returns, by increasing present inputs at the expense of future inputs, and increasing future outputs at the expense of current outputs. This increases the average time lag, in some sense, between inputs and outputs, that is encourages 'the adoption of longer processes, requiring the use (at any moment) of larger quantities of intermediate products'. Consequently investment can be considered a decreasing function of the rate of interest.[31] Here Hicks self-indulgently neglects, not only free entry,[32] but also the effect of changes in interest rates on relative prices and price expectations. Surprisingly, it does not seem to occur to him that, since the rate of interest is a cost of production, its changes will affect relative costs and therefore also expected relative prices – such that no conclusion can be derived from his reasoning as to the true effect of changes in interest rates on investment. However, Hicks's lack of attention to these problems would seem to confirm his faith that, in the field of investment, traditional reasonings were correct.

5.4.2. Lindahl, in spite of his doubts as to the conceivability of capital as a single quantity, did not doubt 'the basic thesis of the modern theory of capital

'quantity' of variable 'form', if one wants to analyse changes in distribution and prices by means of comparisons.

31. This conclusion relative to investment remains implicit in the book; indeed *Value and Capital* contains no explicit discussion of aggregate investment. However the discussion of the period of production and of 'tilting' in ch. XVII would be difficult to explain without the implicit aim of reaching such a conclusion. And indeed, the general thrust of the subsequent chapters, in particular the discussion of the trade cycle (ch. XXIV) as a fluctuation around a state of full employment due to irregularity in the flow of innovations, imply that investment is viewed by Hicks as determined, on an average over the trade cycle, by full-employment savings – what would be difficult to explain without the negative elasticity of investment with respect to the rate of interest, which Hicks does not question in his review of Keynes's *General Theory* in 1936 and explicitly posits when formulating the IS–LM model in 1937. Even in his late years Hicks maintains that investment is a decreasing function of the rate of interest (see, for example, Hicks, 1973, p. 51).

32. Since Hicks assumes price-taking firms, he can avoid discontinuous jumps of firms' planned production to plus infinity or zero the moment a change of an interest rate (with all other prices unchanged) causes non-zero profits, only because he has assumed a *given* number of *decreasing-returns-to-scale* firms: disconcerting assumptions in an analysis aiming at general conclusions. Other examples of Hicks's self-indulgence as a theorist can be found in Petri (1991).

..., namely that with an increased amount of capital and a falling rate of interest longer investments are on the whole increased in a greater degree than the short ones' (Lindahl, 1929, p. 310).

Hayek's views on savings and investment in the 1930s are well known, partly owing to Sraffa's (1932) scathing review of Hayek's *Production and Prices*. It suffices here to observe that Hayek starts from Wicksell, remains within a fundamentally 'Austrian' perspective (similar to Hicks's) as to the influence of the rate of interest on the average length of production processes, and, because of this, takes it for granted that, when monetary policy or financial intermediaries do not interfere in the loanable funds market, accumulation corresponds to the consumers' wishes, that is investment adapts to full-employment savings.

Thus Hicks, Lindahl and Hayek, although criticizing the measurement of the endowment of capital as an amount of value, did not really abandon the conception of capital that was most clearly expressed by that measurement. As insisted upon by Garegnani (1990a, 2000; cf. Section 4.3), the fundamental role of that conception was to present in a synthetic form the forces that were assumed to manifest themselves concretely on the savings-investment market, and thus to justify the belief in the capacity of the rate of interest to bring about the equilibrium between supply and demand for savings, by influencing the desired (value)-capital-to-labour ratio in new plants. The latter belief is never questioned by these authors, in spite of their doubts abut the possibility of conceiving capital as a single quantity. They had marginalism and its conception of capital–labour substitution in their blood, and were unable to suspect that the circular reasoning, involved in the measurement of the capital endowment as an amount of value, might be only the most evident manifestation of an inconsistency affecting *all* applications of that conception of capital.

5.4.3. The subsequent development of marginalist, or neoclassical, theory is less surprising when these limitations of the criticisms put forth by Hayek, Lindahl and Hicks are considered. The debates on capital of the 1930s[33] must have appeared a storm in a teapot to economists in general, since the contenders did not derive from their differences on capital theory any fundamental difference in the analysis of the 'real' forces determining distribution and employment. The disagreements and uncertainties on how to include capital into a general formulation of the supply-and-demand approach to distribution[34] did not question that, for example, the

---

33. Cf. Kaldor (1937) for a survey of those debates.
34. The uncertainty about how best to introduce capital into general equilibrium is clear in the treatise on general equilibrium by Robert E. Kuenne (1963). Kuenne includes a detailed discussion of Walras, but concludes that the nature of capital and of the origin of a positive

accumulation of net savings would tend to depress the rate of interest, or that higher wages would tend to lower the demand for labour. (Keynes's *General Theory* too, which absorbed a great share of the theoretical energies in subsequent years, accepted a negatively sloped investment function and a negatively-sloped labour demand curve, notions difficult to justify without an ultimate acceptance of the marginalist conception of capital–labour substitution – cf., Chapters 7 and 8.) It cannot then cause surprise that, some years later, the hypothesis of a single capital good homogeneous with the product was proposed by Solow and Swan as the basis for the theory of growth: that hypothesis could be seen as a simple way to highlight the basic 'real' forces at work in a market economy, forces on which there was no disagreement.[35]

One can therefore date to the 1930s the beginning of a period (that still continues![36]) of co-existence of neo-Walrasian disaggregated analyses with analyses where capital is treated like a single factor, on the basis of the belief that the 'unrigorous' analyses of the second type are nonetheless legitimate, because their conclusions can also be reached through more 'rigorous', disaggregated analyses.

rate of interest are best discussed in terms of stationary economies; however he is then unable to choose between the different views of J.B. Clark, Böhm-Bawerk, Fisher, Knight, Wicksell, Metzler and so on.

35. The faith in the existence of these forces independently of the precise specification of the theory continues today; it is evident for example in the position of some 'neo-Austrian' economists. These have insisted on the need to go back to more realistic analyses of competition as a process going on in real time, with no auctioneer, and with a crucial role being played by free entry, see, for example, Kirzner (1981, pp. 116–17). But they have not been induced by their criticisms of the neo-Walrasian specifications of equilibrium to doubt the marginalist 'vision' of capitalist economies. According to Kirzner, the Austrian perspective 'sees the edifice of neoclassical economics as built upon essentially sound foundations ... The required task of reconstruction does not, in the Austrian view, call for a radically different set of *fundamental* insights (as would be required, for example, by a Marxist view)' (ibid., pp. 111–12). The reference to the need for a 'reconstruction' confirms that what is proposed is not a return to the conception of capital as a single factor; modern 'Austrian' economists know that Hayek rejected that conception. But then, since Kirzner also rejects neo-Walrasian equilibria with their need to assume instantaneous equilibration, what can the 'sound foundations' for the marginalist 'fundamental insights' consist of? A sentence by Joan Robinson applies very well here: 'It seems that he has sawn off the bough that he was sitting on, but expects to remain in the air all the same' (Robinson, 1971).

36. Milton Friedman did not feel the need to distinguish Wicksell from Walras (nor, more probably, from neo-Walrasian theories) when writing: 'Thanks to Wicksell, we are all acquainted with the concept of a "natural" rate of interest and the possibility of a discrepancy between the "natural" and the "market" rate ... This analysis has its close counterpart in the employment market ... The "natural rate of unemployment", in other words, is the level that would be ground out by the Walrasian system of general equilibrium equations' (Friedman, 1968, pp. 7–8). More recently, one finds a reference to 'substitution of capital for labour' in Malinvaud (1995, pp. 125–6, quoted in §7.1.2).

5.4.4. That belief was in fact deprived of foundations: neither Hayek, nor Lindahl, nor Hicks had offered any proof that such was the case. But its survival was favoured by a loss of familiarity with the traditional long-period method, which becomes noticeable shortly after Hicks's *Value and Capital*.

This loss of familiarity emerges for example in the first of Tjalling Koopmans' well-known *Three Essays on the State of Economic Science* (1957). This essay summarizes the work on general equilibrium theory carried out by Arrow, Debreu, Gale, Nikaido and other mathematicians in the immediately preceding years. That work had remained within the confines of the 'atemporal' equilibrium *without* capital goods (only primary factors and consumption goods) and had made no attempt to investigate the modifications of that model, considered necessary by Walras (or by Wicksell) in order to encompass capital; indeed, I am not aware that any serious study was dedicated to the history of marginalist capital theory by these mathematical economists in those years. The starting point of their mathematical investigations had been the work of Abraham Wald, who had demonstrated the existence of equilibrium for a reformulation of the so-called Walras–Cassel model (a simplified general equilibrium model of a production-and-exchange economy with fixed coefficients, formulated by the Swedish economist Gustav Cassel in 1918, where no mention was made of capital goods). Walras was hailed by these economists as the founder of modern general equilibrium theory simply because he had been the first to formulate the production-and-exchange equilibrium model in completely disaggregated form. But these economists implicitly argued that that model was all that general equilibrium theory needed, because it could be re-interpreted as an intertemporal equilibrium in terms of dated commodities and discounted prices, and through this re-interpretation it was capable – it was argued – of also encompassing production with capital goods.[37] The resulting intertemporal equilibrium was a very-short-period equilibrium because the re-interpretation required viewing the list of initial factor endowments as including given endowments of each capital good; but apart from this similarity, Walras' approach *to capital* had no influence on these developments; it is nowhere discussed in the writings of these theorists.

---

37. Thus it is in the early 1950s that the first rigorous formulation of intertemporal equilibria was born. Cf. Weintraub (1983) and Ingrao and Israel (1990) for a history of this development. Interestingly, both these works identify general equilibrium theory exclusively with Walras and the neo-Walrasian developments, ignoring the existence of the long-period general equilibrium models of Wicksell and his pupils. For *temporary* equilibria the first rigorous formalizations arrived even later, with Morishima (1964), Stigum (1969) and Arrow and Hahn (1971, ch. 6). Hicks had offered no formalization of the notions of temporary or of intertemporal equilibrium.

One might have expected some more discussion of older approaches to capital in Koopmans' essay, intended as it was to introduce a wider public to the new results in general equilibrium theory. But Koopmans limits himself to presenting the intertemporal re-interpretation of the atemporal production-and-exchange model. Interestingly, Koopmans does note that this re-interpretation poses serious problems. He admits the implausibility of assuming that consumers know when they will die, or of assuming that producers know future technical improvements. He also notes that the finite number of periods covered by the equilibrium leads to a difficulty with the last period's saving decisions. But no suspicion is advanced that these difficulties might point to a fundamental deficiency of the attempt to deal with capital within the constraints of formalizations originally conceived for economies without capital goods. No attempt is made to compare this approach with more traditional ones, as if marginalist capital theory had no history before Lindahl and Hicks (the sole antecedents mentioned). Nor does Koopmans show any awareness of the once-total dominance of long-period notions of equilibrium. The absence of any discussion of the role of capital as the single factor in traditional analyses, as well as of the new problems – the impermanence problem, the substitutability problem – arising with intertemporal equilibria, confirms Koopmans's lack of familiarity with the traditional notion of equilibrium and with its role.

5.4.5. The Appendices to this chapter and to the next one show that Koopmans is representative of a general situation that arose in the 1940s and that continues to the present day – a central point in the argument of this book. The familiarity of the generation of Knight, Hayek, Lindahl and Hicks with marginalist analyses internal to the long-period method was rapidly lost. There resulted an inability of subsequent neoclassical economists to understand the traditional formulations of their own theory, or to realize that certain traditional analyses became illegitimate in the neo-Walrasian formulations; even the consciousness that a shift had occurred in the notion of equilibrium was generally missing. The 'Patinkin controversy' (or Classical Dichotomy controversy) in monetary theory (cf. Appendix 5A1), which started in 1948 (but really with Oskar Lange in 1942) and went on up to the early 1960s, shows that already in the 1940s many economists were unable to understand traditional analyses, because they were only acquainted with neo-Walrasian notions of equilibrium and unaware that older analyses were based on a different notion of equilibrium. The inability to escape neo-Walrasian conceptions of equilibrium is also illustrated in Appendix 5A2 by reference to Arrow, who in 1959 admits that disequilibrium adjustments take time, that production goes on while prices adjust, and that therefore equilibrium is a 'long-run' notion, but does not translate these admissions into doubts about the meaningfulness of the formalization of equilibrium he advocates. Appendix 5A3 points out the problems arising for the auctioneer, and for the determinacy of temporary equilibria, when there are constant returns to scale or free entry, and argues that the problems are underestimated due to an implicit but illegitimate reference to the traditional descriptions of the long-period adjustment of quantities: these descriptions relied on actual, time-consuming adjustments which neo-Walrasian theory cannot admit; we see therefore here an example of illegitimate survival of ways of theorizing which are no longer justified in the neo-Walrasian framework. Another example is supplied in the fourth Appendix, which shows an inconsistency in Christopher Bliss' analysis (1975b) of the stability of Solow's growth model, an inconsistency deriving from an inability to accept to the bitter end the implications of the neo-Walrasian framework. (Still other examples of confusions due to the lost familiarity with the long-period method can be found in Appendices 6A2 and 6A3.)

The most important effect of this development was and is an inability to appreciate the indispensable role of the conception of capital as a single factor in the marginalist approach. To this day, the distinguishing features of neoclassical analyses of real-world economies remain the beliefs that the demand for labour appreciably increases if real wages[38] decrease; that the investment schedule is a decreasing (and appreciably elastic) function of the rate of interest; and that these functions are sufficiently persistent as to allow for the tendency toward a definite full-employment equilibrium to impose itself on average over the cycle,[39] in spite of the undeniable occurrence of disequilibria and disturbances both on individual markets and at the aggregate level (that is, in spite of the absence of anything vaguely resembling the auctioneer). What since the end of the 1940s is no longer clearly perceived is the fact that those downward-sloping schedules were originally derived from long-period marginalist theory, based on 'capital' conceived as a single factor, and lose their foundation if one rejects that conception of capital – as the neo-Walrasian versions claim they do. This will be demonstrated in subsequent chapters. And the main reason for the inability to grasp this fact is the lack of understanding of the way the theory was originally formulated, and thus of its inner logic and contradictions.

5.4.6. With hindsight, we can realize now the great importance of Hicks's (and Lindahl's) mistaken identification of long-period equilibria with secularly stationary equilibria.[40] This identification had an advantage that

---

38. Per unit of effort, in the effort-based theories of efficiency wages.
39. Of course, unless impediments, for example a downward inflexibility of real wages, obstruct the operation of such a tendency.
40. Cf. §§4.1.3, 5.3.1, 5.3.2. Hicks was much more influential than Lindahl.

probably favoured its rapid acceptance: it avoided the unpleasant need to admit that nearly the entire profession had been guilty of using equilibria whose endowments included a given value of heterogeneous capital, when relative values were what the equilibrium had to determine. The result was the disappearance of the true notion of long-period equilibrium from the notions of general equilibrium discussed by economists. The sole notions left were short-period equilibria, and stationary equilibria (later generalized to steady-growth equilibria).

This obscured not only the supply-side role of the conception of capital as a single 'quantity' of variable 'form', but also its demand-side roles. Since that conception of capital was (at least apparently) dispensed with in the writings of Hayek and Hicks, younger economists, when they met a statement such as 'A fall in the rate of interest would encourage the adoption of longer processes, requiring the use (at any moment) of larger quantities of intermediate products' (Hicks, 1946, p. 118), had to conclude that the reasons were other from the conception of capital–labour substitution as analogous to labour–land substitution. Similarly for the demand curve for labour: in 1932 Hicks had written that in order to determine a useful notion of labour demand one had to allow the 'form' of capital to change with the real wage; the decreasing shape of the resulting labour demand curve was then clearly to be attributed to the decreasing marginal product of labour when combined with a *given* quantity of capital conceived as a single factor. Now this conception was (at least apparently) abandoned, but the thesis that lower wages would increase employment was maintained: younger economists had to conclude that this thesis could be given a foundation different from the traditional one.

Thus the generation of mathematical economists who worked on general equilibrium theory after *Value and Capital*, and who were greatly influenced by that book,[41] inherited (i) the misrepresentation of the long-period method as the study of secularly stationary or steady-growth economies, (ii) the conclusion that the only way to study non-steady-state economies was through very-short-period equilibria, and (iii) the lack of clarity as to whether or not the supply and demand forces basic to the marginalist approach needed the conception of capital as ultimately a homogeneous factor.

41. Two examples: 'Hicks's *Value and Capital* made the biggest impression on me' (Arrow, letter to Weintraub, 1981, cited in Ingrao and Israel, 1990, p. 276); 'I began studying economics with his *Value and Capital* and was solaced by reading it in the gun room of Ohmura air base of the Imperial Navy when I was called up for active service in the war' (Morishima, 1969, p. vi). A clear indication of Hicks's influence is the assumption made by Arrow and by Debreu of a given number of producers.

Hopefully the previous chapters of this book have dispelled the confusions under (i) and (ii); the issues under (iii) will be discussed in the next chapters.

APPENDIX 5A1. A REINTERPRETATION OF THE PATINKIN OR 'CLASSICAL DICHOTOMY' CONTROVERSY IN MONETARY THEORY[42]

5A1.1. Introduction

This Appendix discusses what is probably the longest and most confusing controversy in monetary theory of modern economics: the so-called 'Patinkin' or 'Classical Dichotomy' or 'Neoclassical Dichotomy' controversy, which raged from about 1948 to 1965 and beyond.

The reason why this topic is discussed in this book is that the birth as well as the length of this controversy were due to an insufficient awareness of the change undergone by the notion of equilibrium, and of its implications for monetary theory. This will emerge from an examination of the contributions of Hicks, Lange, Patinkin, and others: although the controversy has been associated with Patinkin's name, his basic argument was taken from Lange (1942), and its roots can be traced to certain little-noticed contradictions in Hicks (1946). When the notion of long-period general equilibrium (LPGE in the remainder of this Appendix) and the method based on that notion are fully understood, then Lange's criticism of traditional monetary theory is easily perceived to be misplaced; and even Archibald and Lipsey's fundamental contribution (1958) reveals some important deficiencies.

Thus, the main purpose of this Appendix is to adduce a convincing proof of the assertion that in the 1940s a large part of the economic profession had adopted neo-Walrasian notions of general equilibrium without clearly understanding that a shift in the notion of equilibrium – with relevant analytical implications – had occurred. As a side effect, this Appendix clears up a number of points which to this day remain confused in the 'Patinkin controversy', particularly about shifts of meaning of the term 'demand for money', and about the role of the stationary-state hypothesis.

42. This Appendix is an abridged version of Petri (1982). It does not constitute an exhaustive review of the contributions to the controversy. A fairly complete bibliography up to 1964 can be derived from Patinkin (1965); also see Jossa (1963a, 1963b), Mauer (1966), Clower (1969, pp. 345–6), Lloyd (1970), Patinkin (1972), Nagatani (1978), Niehans (1978, pp. 8–12).

5A1.2.   The meaning of the 'Classical Dichotomy': the implicit treatment of the money endowment in long-period equilibria

5A1.2.1. The object of discussion in the Patinkin controversy was the logical consistency of the 'Classical Dichotomy', that is of systems of general equilibrium equations[43] purporting to determine both relative and monetary equilibrium prices, where *relative* prices are determined without any consideration of money, and then a separate 'money equation', for example a Fisherine equation $MV = PT$ determines the price level.

Patinkin's thesis was that the Classical Dichotomy was illegitimate, because (for example in an exchange economy) the excess demands of consumers depend on their money endowments, which he treated as given, that is as data of the equilibrium. My basic point is that Patinkin's argument rested on a misunderstanding: the 'real' equations of 'Classical Dichotomy' equilibria intended to describe the real behaviour of agents under the hypothesis that their money endowments were not given, but rather endogenously determined as the ones appropriate to the carrying through of the intended equilibrium transactions;[44] and therefore the price level too was implicitly assumed to be the equilibrium one, that is the one compatible with the simultaneous appropriateness of the money balances of all agents. This is because the equilibrium of traditional analyses was a long-period equilibrium, and the tranquil[45] and repetitive behaviour associated with such a notion of equilibrium could only come about if the price level was the equilibrium one and the money balances too had reached an equilibrium distribution among the agents.

The issue can be most simply clarified by assuming the long-period equilibrium to be stationary and the supply of money to be constant and of the 'outside' variety only.

Let us then consider an economic agent, say, a consumer, facing given prices, and with given factor endowments constant through time, whose maximizing behaviour follows a pattern that repeats itself indefinitely. The agent maximizes her utility by choosing certain supplies and demands of goods and services per period. She also decides (what is not normally shown in standard consumer theory) a time pattern of her purchases and sales;

43. 'Classical' was used in this controversy in Keynes's sense, that is as referring to the marginalist tradition (cf. Chapter 1, fn. 1). This is confirmed by the fact that the term 'Neoclassical Dichotomy' was also occasionally used. Thus, the equations determining relative prices considered in the controversy were always derived from the marginalist theoretical framework.

44. Obviously traditional analyses did not assume the existence of the auctioneer; exchanges were assumed to be against money and dispersed in time.

45. For this meaning of 'tranquillity', cf. Robertson (1957–59: vol. I, p. 95; II, p. 11; III, p. 9).

associated with it, there will be a function which represents the amount of money held by the agent as a function of time. Let us indicate it as $h_i(t)$. The graph of this function will show a pattern that repeats itself again and again. Clearly, behind the pattern of $h_i(t)$ there is an optimization performed by the agent, an optimization concerning the distribution over the period of her expenses, and the money to be held at each instant; but it is not necessary here to discuss this optimization in any detail. It will suffice to assume that money is only held for transaction purposes (no precautionary nor speculative money balances), and that the rate of interest is zero (idle money is not converted into bonds). Then $h_i(t)$ will represent the minimum money balance an agent needs for her transactions at each moment of time, a balance which will be given once the real equilibrium transactions of the agent, their time pattern, and money prices, are all given (Ellis, 1937–38); its graph will reach the value zero at least once in each 'transaction cycle' of the agent.

This minimum money balance $h_i(t)$ constitutes a first possible meaning of 'demand for money' of the agent i at the instant t.[46] If at the given money prices one can determine the maximizing behaviour and transactions time pattern of all agents, then the sum of all agents' demands for money in this sense can be seen as the total 'demand' for money. Clearly the word 'demand' must be treated with caution here: $h_i(t)$ is not an amount of money demanded by offering something in exchange; it is rather *a prerequisite of long-period maximizing behaviour*. The usual equations determining the consumer's optimal behaviour will not include any supply of goods or services to offset the value of this 'demand for money'; but if the agent held at any moment more or less money than shown by $h_i(t)$, then her behaviour would not be the one determined by the 'real' equations.

It follows that the determination of a long-period equilibrium *cannot* include, among the *data* of the equilibrium, the distribution of the given total money stock among the various agents. The money endowment of each agent (both at each moment and on average) must have adapted so as to be that amount which is a prerequisite for the equilibrium behaviour.[47] Equilibrium behaviour, since it requires the money balances to be the appropriate ones, does not depend on them but rather *determines* them as a function of money prices (and of one additional element not usually included in the theory of consumer choices: the time structure of transactions).

An implication not grasped, for example, by Lange (1942), is the following: from the fact that the agents' excess demand functions for goods

---

46. This is for example the meaning of 'demand for money' in Hicks (1935a).
47. The analogy is evident with the treatment of the composition of capital, which is also endogenous in long-period equilibria.

(a term which, for brevity, will be used in this Appendix as also including services) depend only on relative prices it does *not* follow that it is sufficient to look at relative prices to establish whether there is equilibrium in the markets for goods. Those relative prices, which solve the equations expressing equilibrium on the goods markets, are *necessary but not sufficient conditions for equilibrium* on those markets.

Equilibrium requires in addition three conditions:

1.   that the time pattern of transactions decided by each agent be compatible with the time pattern decided by the other agents;
2.   that the price level be such as will make the total 'demand for money' equal to the economy's money endowment;
3.   that the economy's money endowment be distributed among the agents in the proportions required by each agent's equilibrium behaviour.

Even if only the third of these three conditions is not satisfied, then, even if relative and money prices are those of the equilibrium, still some agents will find it not optimal, or impossible, to behave as equilibrium would require.

It is not easy to find *explicit* stress on the third condition in traditional marginalist monetary theory: but the reason is, clearly, that it was thought obvious: for example it was clearly implicit in the discussions of forced savings.[48] Furthermore, the existence of a tendency of the distribution of the total money endowment among the agents toward the equilibrium could be derived from the same mechanism envisaged by the quantity theory of money to be at work to push the price level toward the equilibrium level, that is the mechanism based on the 'real balance effect':

> Let us suppose that for some reason or other commodity prices rise while the stock of money remains unchanged, or that the stock of money is diminished while prices remain temporarily unchanged. The cash balances will gradually appear to be too small ... I can rely on a higher level of receipts in the future. But meanwhile I run the risk of being unable to meet my obligations punctually, and at best I may easily be forced by shortage of ready money to forgo some purchase that would otherwise have been profitable. I therefore seek to enlarge my balance ... through a *reduction* in my *demand* for goods and services, or through an *increase* in the *supply* of my own commodity ... the universal reduction in demand and increase in supply of commodities will necessarily bring about a continuous fall in all prices.

---

48. The discussions of 'forced savings' imply disequilibrium redistributive effects, with possible permanent further effects, of initial non-equilibrium distributions of money: see, for example, Wicksell (1935, p. 165), Hayek (1932), Saulnier (1938, pp. 63–73, 147, 243–4). Also see Fisher (1922, p. 166).

This can only cease when prices have fallen to the level at which the cash balances are regarded as *adequate* (Wicksell, 1936, pp. 39–40, italics in the original).[49]

Wicksell's aim here is to illustrate the mechanism which changes the general price level, but the basis is a change in each individual's behaviour, owing to her need to adjust her money balance, and this change will also redistribute the money endowments so as to make them accord with individual needs.

5A1.2.2. Another possible definition of 'demand for money' of the individual is the *average* money balance, implicit in the time path of $h_i(t)$ over the individual's 'transaction cycle', that is over a period of such length that her behaviour repeats itself unaltered from one period to the next:

$$d_i = (t_2 - t_1)^{-1} \int_{t_1}^{t_2} h_i(t)dt$$

where $t_2 - t_1$ is an interval equal in length to the length of the 'transaction cycle' of the agent or to an integer multiple of it (Ellis, 1937–38). (This second definition is more useful in that it allows for random variations in the path of expenditures and sales.) What was said above, about the peculiar meaning of the word 'demand' if applied to $h_i(t)$, holds for d_i too.[50]

The connection between these definitions of demand for money and the Fisherine equation $MV = PT$ is that the sum, over all agents, of their respective d_i's yields the demand for money for the economy as a whole – let us indicate it with the symbol M_D – that is, in terms of the Fisherine equation $MV = PT$, it yields $M_D \equiv PT/V$. In terms of the Cambridge equation $M = kPY$, the corresponding expression is $M_D \equiv kPY$.

With the additional assumption that all intended transactions 'match', that is that to every intended sale there corresponds an intended purchase (as would be the case if relative prices are equilibrium prices and the timing of transactions is congruent as between agents), if the various $h_i(t)$'s are all well-defined then the same M_D might also be obtained by summing over all $h_i(t)$'s calculated at the same instant, no matter which instant were chosen, because the deviations of the various $h_i(t)$'s from the respective d_i's, under that assumption, sum up to zero.

---

49. Also see Wicksell (1935, p. 64); Fisher (1922, pp. 153–4); and obviously Pigou (1943). The possibility of permanent effects of an initial non-equilibrium distribution of money was not denied, see the preceding footnote.

50. The endogenous determination of the average money balance is for example clear in this passage by Marshall: 'let us suppose that the inhabitants of a country ... find it just worth their while to keep by them on the average ready purchasing power to the extent of a tenth part of their annual income, together with a fiftieth part of their property ...' (Marshall, 1923, p. 33). Also see Fisher (1922, p. 152).

In the traditional discussions of the quantity theory of money, of course, comparatively little space is dedicated to the individual's demand for money; the attention is generally given directly to the economy-wide aggregate demand for money, and the reason is that

> Each man's adjustment is, of course, somewhat rough, and dependent largely on the accident of the moment; but, in the long run and for a large number of people, the average rate of turnover, or what amounts to the same thing, the average time money remains in the same hands, will be very closely determined (Fisher, 1922, pp. 152–3).[51]

This passage is interesting because, with reference to the velocity of money, it illustrates the traditional opinion that, as long as one clearly stated one was speaking about averages over time and over many individuals, it was not necessary to assume that the economy actually *was* in equilibrium, in order for the theoretically determined equilibrium to be useful for explanations and predictions; accidental or stochastic deviations from average behaviour would generally sufficiently compensate one another as between individuals and over time. This conception also explains the comparatively small space traditionally devoted to discussing the individual's 'demand for money' in comparison with the economy-wide demand. What was considered important was the sum resulting from the aggregate of individual agents, a sum that, as the above quotation shows, was believed to be more stable than the behaviours of single individuals.

Equilibrium then required that the total money demand thus obtained be equal to the (given) quantity of money M° existing in the economy: this equation $M_D = M^\circ$ established the price level.

When one enlarges the picture, introducing bonds, and so on, and one considers further motives for holding money besides the transactions motive, as, for example, in the so-called Cambridge approach,[52] then the desired money balance (at each moment as well as on average) will also result from, for example, the choices of the agent between money and bonds, and therefore will depend on the rate of interest too. But it remains true that, in order to obtain a repetitive behaviour pattern of each agent, the money balance held on average as well as at each moment by an agent must have adjusted itself, and its equilibrium value will therefore depend on the 'real' behaviour and wealth of the agent.

---

51. Also see Wicksell (1936, p. 41; 1935, p. 62); Pigou (1917–18, p. 53; 1943, p. 76); Fisher (1922, p. 80). It is noteworthy that most studies of the individual's transaction demand for money still concern themselves with the average demand (see, for a survey, Nagatani, 1978, ch. 4).
52. See for example Pigou (1917–18).

5A1.2.3. Some formalization may be helpful. For simplicity, let us consider an exchange economy *à la* Patinkin (1965, pt. I), without bonds. The consumers' given endowments of goods are constant through time. There are *n* commodities, and the length of the period *T* is chosen such that for all agents it includes a finite integer number of 'transaction cycles', if the economy is stationary. *Money is needed in order to purchase goods.*

Let us then consider a consumer at the beginning of one such period, with a randomly given initial endowment of money m_0. The consumer, in formulating her plans as to purchases and sales, must take this constraint into account. She can perform many successive transactions within the period, and, depending on the possibility to vary the time pattern of her transactions, she may or may not succeed in avoiding the constraint almost entirely. What she definitely cannot do is to buy when she has no money,[53] thus the only constraint we can be certain of is that the value of her purchases in the entire period cannot exceed the value of her sales plus the value of her initial money endowment. In order to say more, we would have to know the constraints on the variability of the time patterns of transactions (for example whether the goods the consumer intends to sell can or cannot be sold before the purchases she intends to make). But it is not necessary for our purposes to enter into this issue. (All we need is to assume that purchases are only against money, and are not simultaneous, so that at least for some time all consumers must hold positive money balances, and for at least some consumers it is convenient to start the period with positive money balances; thus at least some consumers will want to end the period with positive money balances.) I assume our consumer knows all she needs to know, and also has expectations about the future evolution of money prices, and accordingly she formulates certain excess demand functions for goods over the time interval constituting the period, e_{jt} for commodity $j = 1, ..., n$ and for t going from 0 to T. The transactions implied by these excess demand functions will entail a certain time pattern $m(t)$ of her money balances, with t going from 0 to T, and ending in m_T which is the initial money endowment of the subsequent period – the money endowment the consumer finds optimal to have at her disposal at the beginning of the next period in the light of her expectations of next period's (and the subsequent periods') money prices. If we indicate with e_j the total excess demand for good j of our consumer over the current period, and with e the vector of these excess demands, and if p is the vector of current period prices and p_E the vector of expected prices for the next periods, we can write

$$e = e(p, p_E, m_0) \qquad [5.1]$$

53. By assumption I am excluding credit, at this stage.

$$m_T = m(p, p_E, m_0) \qquad\qquad [5.2]$$

where the two are connected by:

$$m_T = m_0 - \sum\nolimits_{j=1}^{n} e_j p_j. \qquad\qquad [5.3]$$

Standard assumptions about consumer behaviour imply that functions [5.1] and [5.2] are homogeneous, respectively of degree zero and one.

Even if the consumer expects that the next periods' prices will be the same as this period's, she will not in general decide to end the period with the same money endowment she started with: if at the very end of the previous period she won a big lottery prize, she will very probably want to end the period with less cash than she commences the period with. A stationary behaviour requires (besides an expectation of future prices equal to current prices) an endogenous determination of the initial money endowment as that m_0 which causes

$$m_T = m(p, p_E, m_0) = m_0. \qquad\qquad [5.4]$$

Assuming such an m_0 to exist, it will be a function of money prices, homogeneous of degree zero. Let $m_0^*(p)$ represent this function. Then equation [5.1] becomes (remembering the assumption that $p_E = p$):

$$e^* = e\big(p, m_0^*(p)\big) = e^*(p) \qquad\qquad [5.5]$$

which is homogeneous of degree zero in p, because when p is multiplied by a scalar, p_E and m_0 are multiplied by the same scalar. The vector e^* indicates the long-period excess demands, the ones associated with fully adjusted money endowments. It is a function of relative prices only.

Equation [5.5] shows the rationale of the traditional '(Neo)Classical Dichotomy'.[54]

Clearly, the excess demands determined by the 'real' equations of 'dichotomous' models were *not* intended to describe the choices of agents when the price level, and/or the distribution among the agents of the money endowment of the economy, were not those of the equilibrium.

---

54. Equation [5.5] conclusively shows that Samuelson (1968, p. 187) was wrong when, as late as 1968 and in spite of Archibald and Lipsey's contribution (to be discussed below in the text), he denied that it is perfectly correct and adequate, within the LPGE framework, to write down excess demand functions for goods and services which depend on relative prices only, and then to determine the price level via a Fisherine or Cambridge equation.

What was explained for a pure exchange economy carries over to economies with production in an obvious way which it does not seem necessary to enter into.

In sharp contrast with the above analysis, neo-Walrasian equilibria are conceived as depending very specifically on the accidents of the moment when they are established, for example on the amounts in existence of even the most quickly variable inventories of goods at that moment. It is not surprising that, within a framework in which the equilibrium must be imagined as reached instantaneously on the basis of such flimsy data, also the endowments of money of the several agents should be conceived as given, and that the excess demands for goods of an agent should be therefore conceived as in equation [5.1] rather than as in equation [5.5]. Also, the need to imagine the equilibrium as reached instantaneously obscures the role of money as a medium of exchange. It is not surprising that some confusions emerged, as shown in what follows.

5A1.3. Hicks

5A1.3.1. In *Value and Capital* Hicks was conscious of the novel need introduced by the changed framework: 'to suppose that price-changes are negligible during market hours on the Monday, when the market is open ... This implies that the market (indeed, all markets) proceeds quickly and smoothly to a position of temporary equilibrium' (Hicks, 1946, p. 123), and he admitted in an Additional Note to the second edition of 1946 that this supposition amounted to a 'hypothesis of essentially instantaneous adjustment' (ibid., p. 337). But then, when markets open on the Monday of Hicks's 'week' and the equilibrium is to be instantaneously reached, *it becomes natural to consider the money endowment of each individual agent as given*, and as influencing the agent's decisions.

Hicks does not explicitly state that the initial money endowment of each agent is given and among the data influencing his behaviour;[55] but the thing is implicit in the analysis. When discussing the case of an individual who 'plans to spend, in every future week, the same amount as he receives', Hicks concludes:

> Then, if he is perfectly confident that he can carry out this plan, his demand for money will be nil. All the money he receives will be paid out again, at once; he will need to keep over from one week to another no money balance at all to finance his transactions (Hicks, 1946, p. 240).

55. Nor does Lange (1942); only Patinkin (1948, and subsequent articles) says so explicitly.

Here the 'demand for money' of an agent is the money balance 'he will need to keep over from one week to another', that is the amount of money the agent wants to hold *at the end* of the 'week'. Since the equilibrium is conceived as also determining this 'demand for money', at the beginning of the next 'week' the agent's initial money balance is given: thus it must be treated as given in the initial 'week' too. The excess demands for goods and services in a 'week' must then be conceived as consistent with equation [5.1] of §5A1.2.3.

5A1.3.2. Hicks contributes to the subsequent debate not only this implicit treatment of the money endowment of each agent as given, but also some confusions, due, it would seem, to the artificial assumption that equilibrium for the entire 'week' is reached, essentially instantaneously, at the beginning of the 'week', with all contracts signed at that initial moment – an assumption that obscures the role of money as a medium of exchange.

In fact, in order to conceive of a transactions demand for money, Hicks assumes that 'receipts ... come in, not every week, but, say, every fourth week; then, even if receipts and expenditures balanced over the four weeks taken together, the money balance could only fall to zero in the week just before the month's receipts were due to come in' (Hicks, 1946, p. 240).[56] It is implicit here that if in a 'week' the receipts and expenditures of an agent balance, the agent has no need to start the 'week' with positive initial money holdings for transactions purposes; in other words, purchases and sales within a 'week' are cleared against each other, with no need for money except for the excesses of expenditures over receipts. It is very much as if there were an auctioneer acting as a clearing house.

It is then understandable that Hicks should define the 'demand for money' of an individual as the amount of money the individual wants to end the 'week' with. The aggregate 'demand for money' so defined equals the aggregate supply of money when in the aggregate the agents want to end the 'week' with the same amount of money they started with, that is when the aggregate value of their receipts in the 'week' equals the aggregate value of their expenditures. Hicks calls 'money equation' this condition of equality between aggregate 'demand for money' so defined, and aggregate supply of money. Clearly, if there is equilibrium in the markets for goods and for bonds, this 'money equation' is satisfied:

56. Even more surprisingly, Patinkin (1965), in his Part I model, where there is no room for a speculative demand for money, explains the holding of positive money balances as due to uncertainty as to the timing of payments in the 'week', thus suggesting that, if the timing of payments of the following 'week' were known with certainty, the desire to end the 'week' with positive money balances would be inexplicable.

> To say that the net acquisition of money by trading is zero, taken over the whole community, is the same thing as to say that the demand for money equals the supply of money. Consequently, if there is equilibrium in the markets for goods and services, and in the market for loans, there must also be equilibrium in the market for money (ibid., p. 157).

Hicks proceeds to argue that any one of the $n + 1$ equations establishing the equilibrium for the $n - 1$ goods, for (the single type of) securities, and for money, being derivable from the other ones, can be eliminated. For instance, he writes, one can eliminate the 'money equation', and he describes the implication as follows:

> If we decide to eliminate the money equation, then we can think of prices and interest being determined on the markets for goods and services, and the market for loans; the money equation becomes completely otiose, having nothing to tell us (ibid., p. 158).

This means that the remaining n equations suffice to determine *money* prices: this implies that the excess demands for goods and for loans must depend not only on relative prices, but also on the price level, that is on money prices (as in our equation [5.1]). But Hicks promptly contradicts the implications of his own statement, by writing a few lines below:

> Thus, whenever the money equation is used as an effective part of the mechanism of price-determination it must be implied that some other equation has been selected for elimination. In the more developed versions of the quantity theory of money, where the money equation is used to determine the price-level, it must be supposed that the relative values of other goods and services are independently determined, the money equation being needed to determine their money values only (ibid.).

Here Hicks admits that in the 'more developed'(?) versions of the quantity theory of money the excess demands for goods and services depend only on relative prices. What Hicks does not notice is that, in this case, the 'money equation' as defined by him *cannot* determine the price level. By definition, his 'money equation' is satisfied if there is equilibrium on all markets for goods and securities; but if equilibrium on all these markets is a function of relative prices only, then, as long as relative prices on all these markets are those of the equilibrium, the 'money equation' is satisfied, whatever the price level. Thus the price level is indeterminate. Lange (1942) starts off precisely from here.

5A1.4. Lange, Patinkin, Valavanis

5A1.4.1. Lange (1942) introduces a peculiar interpretation of Say's Law and of its consequences for price theory, and a further change in the meaning of 'demand for money', but within Hicks's framework. For simplicity I will leave bonds out of the analysis.

By Say's Law, Lange means the following. Define ΔM as 'the total increase of cash balances (in excess of a possible increase of the quantity of money) desired by all individuals' (Lange, 1942, p. 152). This – apart from the possibility of variations, within the period, of the total quantity of money in the economy, a complication which may here be left aside – is the same as Hicks's *aggregate* desired 'net acquisition of money'. ΔM will equal the aggregate value of excess supplies of goods and services. Lange takes Say's Law to mean that the aggregate value demand for goods and services is always equal to their aggregate value supply; in Lange's scheme, this must mean that in the aggregate the agents plan to spend as much as they earn and therefore plan to end the period with, in the aggregate, the same amount of money balances they started with; so Lange takes Say's Law to mean that $\Delta M = 0$ *always* holds true, that is whatever the relative as well as absolute prices:

> Thus, Say's Law implies a peculiar nature of the demand for money, namely, that the individuals in our system, taken together, are always satisfied with the existing amount of money and never wish to hold either more or less. There is never a desire to change the total cash balances otherwise than to adapt them to changes in the amount of money available. Under these circumstances, purchases of commodities are never financed from cash balances nor do sales of commodities serve to increase cash balances (Lange, 1942, p. 153).[57]

This passage is the key to Lange's position. Lange never comes down to discussing the individual; he always remains at the level of total demand and supply functions for goods and money. But from this passage it is clear that he is interpreting these demand and supply functions as deriving from individual choices that *should* normally be affected by the agents' money holdings, and are not so affected only if one makes the peculiar assumption that 'There is never a desire to change the total cash balances'. In other words, Lange is thinking in terms of individuals who are deciding their demands and supplies for goods and services on the basis of *given* initial

---

57. Strictly, the last sentence of this passage is false, because 'changes in the amount of money available' are not excluded by Lange, and this means that some agents (those who create money) are financing purchases from (newly created) cash balances. But this is secondary to our purposes and the connected complications have been left out of the discussion.

money endowments; it is then natural to find that 'Say's Law' (as defined by him) is an extreme hypothesis: it would render Friedman's helicopter unable to affect nominal expenditures whatever amount of cash it poured into the economy.

It is unnecessary to show here how wrong the attribution of this hypothesis is, to Say, Ricardo, and so on.[58] Rather, it is useful to trace the root of the mistake: although Lange always remains at the level of all individuals 'taken together', *his mistake lies in interpreting Say's Law as consisting of the introduction of a balanced-budget constraint upon individual choices, while at the same time assuming that the individuals' initial money endowments are given*, an assumption made natural by the temporary equilibrium framework.[59] In terms of the formalization developed above in §5A1.2.3, Lange's confusion can be characterized quite simply: Lange thought that traditional theory added the balanced-budget constraint (equation [5.4]) to equations [5.1]–[5.2] where m_0 was *given* rather than a variable.

It is then easy to understand why he concludes: 'The money prices of commodities are indeterminate in a system in which Say's Law is satisfied' (Lange, 1942, p. 165). The balanced-budget constraint suffices to make the excess demands for goods and services depend on relative prices only (ibid., p. 164). Hence the equilibrium equations for goods and services cannot determine the price level; nor – Lange continues – can the price level be

58. Becker and Baumol (1952) were quick to point it out; but they were not as clear on the meaning of traditional analyses, see below.
59. In Petri (1982, appendix) it is pointed out that Walras' theory of money in its final form did make both these assumptions (thus Lange may have been misled by this fact), but within a model which is different both from 'dichotomous' LPGE models and Hicks's (and Lange's) temporary equilibrium, and where the price level is not indeterminate. Briefly (also cf. Kuenne, 1963), Walras assumes that at the beginning of the period all money balances are with the consumers, who keep part of it (their '*encaisse désirée*') for their own purchases during the period, and lend the remainder (against one-period promissory notes) to entrepreneurs who need it for their day-by-day payments during the period; the need for an exchange medium derives from the imperfect synchronization of expenditures and receipts. Monetary equilibrium requires that this beginning-of-period supply of working money balances by consumers to entrepreneurs be equal to the demand for them; since the former decreases and the latter increases with the price level, the equilibrium price level is uniquely determined. At the end of the period the promissory notes are repaid to consumers, and since by assumption entrepreneurs make zero profit, firms are left with no money: all money balances are back with the consumers, who indeed are assumed to plan to end the period with the same money balances they started with. Here again, Walras maintains a traditional long-period assumption (the constancy of the money balance of each consumer) within a framework where it is no longer justified: he states explicitly that the initial money endowments of the several consumers are 'random' (Walras, 1954, p. 318), that is of any magnitude; then it would be absurd to exclude the possibility that consumers may want to start the following period with a different amount of initial money balances.

fixed by a Fisherine (or Cambridge) equation, because the latter implies that the demand for money increases with the price level, while Say's Law implies that it does not, remaining always equal to the existing amount of money. Therefore, to introduce both a Fisherine equation, and 'Say's Law', would mean to make contradictory assumptions about the agents' behaviours (also cf. Patinkin, 1972, p. 280).

On this specific issue, Patinkin (1948, 1949, 1950–51, 1951, 1954) added nothing to Lange,[60] except some impressive but essentially superfluous mathematics. The purpose of his efforts was formally to prove that 'Say's Law' in Lange's sense, and a Cambridge-type equation, imply contradictory statements about the behaviour of the demand for money. This he achieved by showing that 'Say's Law' implies that the demand for money (in a sense to be explained presently) is homogeneous of degree zero in absolute prices, while a Cambridge-type equation implies that the demand for money is homogeneous of degree one in absolute prices. As has been shown, Lange (1942, pp. 163–7) had already said it all.

5A1.4.2. The adoption of the Hicksian framework prevented Lange from grasping the meaning of the 'demand for money' which appears in a Fisherine or Cambridge equation. Lange's definition of the demand for (and supply of) money is different even from Hicks's, and dominated the subsequent controversy. Treating money simply as the n-th commodity in a system of n demand = supply equilibrium equations of the type $D_j(p_1, p_2, ..., p_n) = S_j(p_1, p_2, ..., p_n)$ (j being the index of commodities, the price of money being $p_n=1$), Lange (1942, p. 150) defines the demand for money as:

$$D_n = \sum_{j=1}^{n-1} p_j S_j$$

and the supply of money as:

$$S_n = \sum_{j=1}^{n-1} p_j S_j.$$

These definitions were adopted by Patinkin: 'the only way people can obtain money is by selling goods, hence the demand for money is identical with the supply of all goods' (Patinkin, 1949, p. 1), and they were a major source of confusion in the subsequent debate.

60. Patinkin admits this in Patinkin (1951, p. 139, n. 15).

Hickman (1950) and Leontief (1950) accepted Patinkin's definition of 'demand for money' without distinguishing it from the traditional meaning, and on the contrary identifying the two.[61]

Becker and Baumol (1952) accepted the validity of Patinkin's argument, that is, they accepted the fact that real money balances should appear among the data influencing the agents' excess demands for goods, and did not discuss (did not perceive?) Patinkin's shift in the meaning of 'demand for money', nor – in spite of their historical perspective – the shift in the notion of equilibrium. Their criticisms were only aimed at showing that the 'Classics probably *[!]* never held views like those ascribed to them' (Becker and Baumol 1952, pp. 355–6), but only to conclude that Patinkin's own equilibrium model (with initial money endowments among the data of each agent's decisions) was closer than the 'Classical Dichotomy' model to what the 'Classics' meant.[62]

Valavanis (1955) started by repeating Hickman's argument, that from a purely formal viewpoint a Cambridge-type equation is not inconsistent with demand-and-supply equations for goods and services embodying Say's Law in Lange's sense and hence determining relative prices only. Also, no inconsistency is created by the further addition to these equations of Patinkin's $D_n = S_n$ 'money equation',[63] that is of the equation stating that the demand for money (as defined by Lange) must equal the supply of money (again, as defined by Lange), an equation that Valavanis appropriately defined the 'mirror-image equation for money' because it does no more than mirror the money side of transactions of goods against money. This equation – Valavanis correctly observed – is necessarily satisfied, precisely due to its mirror-image nature, if the supply-and-demand equations for goods and services are satisfied; so the price level is not determined yet. Thus, a Cambridge–type equation (a 'technological restriction' on the agents' planned transactions, according to Valavanis), which determines the price

61. Hickman used the same symbol to indicate the demand for money in Patinkin's sense and in the 'Cambridge-equation' sense; see his equations (b.4), p. 12, and (e.1), p. 13, in Hickman (1950); also see Patinkin (1951, p. 139 n. 14, and p. 150 n. 31). For Leontief, see Leontief (1950, p. 21). Later, Encarnaciòn (1958) tried to refute Lange's demonstration of the existence of a contradiction in the 'Classical Dichotomy' (as interpreted by Lange); his apparent success (see Johnson, 1962, p. 21) was due to a minor slip by Lange, who wrote down an identity as if it were an equation: as Lange's text makes clear, equation (8.3) in Lange (1942, p. 166), is an *identity*; it *defines* ΔM, and should therefore have been written with the $\equiv$ symbol.

62. Later, Baumol (1960) claimed that he had always been clear on the distinction between the two notions of equilibrium and the different treatment of the money endowment associated with them. His 1952 contribution does not support this claim.

63. Actually, in Patinkin (1948, 1951), $D_{n+1} = S_{n+1}$, because he assumes n goods and services instead of $n-1$ as Lange does.

level, does not over-determine the system nor contradict any other equation of the model. But this observation did not answer Lange's and Patinkin's charge of inconsistency against the 'Classical Dichotomy': the latter charge, as clarified in Patinkin (1951), was about a supposed contradiction in the assumptions concerning individual behaviour which lie behind, on one hand, the aggregate demand and supply equations for goods (these depend on relative prices only, because of the balanced-budget constraint which, on Lange's and Patinkin's interpretation, implies that individuals are always satisfied with their initial money balances), and on the other hand, the Cambridge-type equation (which implies people are not always satisfied with their money balances). A satisfactory reply to Patinkin required pointing out that in dichotomous models the balanced-budget constraint implies that the agents' excess demands presume adjusted initial money balances, and not given initial money balances. But Valavanis was not clear on this. When discussing a model by Brunner (1951) (which need not detain us here), Valavanis (1955, p. 358) accepted Brunner's assumption that the initial money endowment of each agent was given (Brunner, 1951, p. 170). Small wonder that Patinkin felt entitled to dismiss Valavanis as someone who had advanced 'the obscure contention ... that money, alone of all goods, must have two equations (termed by Valavanis the 'mirror image' and 'technological restriction', respectively) to describe its behaviour' (Patinkin, 1965, p. 629, fn. 45; also see Hahn, 1960, p. 40).

5A1.5. Archibald and Lipsey

Eventually Archibald and Lipsey (1958, 1960) pointed out that Lange and Patinkin had mistakenly taken the 'Classical' separation between the determination of the price level and of relative prices as intended also for situations in which the money balances held by individuals were not the long-period equilibrium ones. But even Archibald and Lipsey were not totally clear on the meaning of 'demand for money', and on the connected issue of the possibility of having, in an equilibrium system of equations, two different 'demands for money'.

Archibald and Lipsey distinguish between the individual's 'weekly' equilibrium, which they also call disequilibrium, and the 'full equilibrium' (which is obtained when the individual's money balance at the end of the 'week' is the same as the beginning), which they also call simply equilibrium.[64] The 'weekly' equilibrium is determined on the basis of utility

64. This terminology, already present in Hicks's *Value and Capital*, suggests that only a 'full equilibrium' is properly an equilibrium, and thus reveals that the authors were still influenced by the traditional method. But, as will be illustrated below – see footnote 68 – the traditional notion of long-period equilibrium is distorted by the notion of 'full equilibrium'.

maximization with given initial money balances among the data, and with end-of-the-week real money balances influencing utility. In general, therefore, the consumer will choose to increase or decrease her money balances. Only with a certain price level will she choose to maintain her money balances unaltered. For full equilibrium, that is in order for this price level to be the same for all individuals, the distribution of money balances among individuals must be endogenously determined.

They correctly contend that the 'Classical Dichotomy' only applies to comparative statics exercises where situations are compared in each of which all agents are in full equilibrium. Since in full equilibrium the balanced-budget constraint (over goods and services only, that is what is often called Say's Identity) holds, the individual's demands and supplies of goods in full equilibrium depend on relative prices only, and therefore so do the aggregate demands and supplies. And there is no formal inconsistency in adding a Cambridge equation to determine the price level.

They must then answer the charge that this addition of a Cambridge equation is illegitimate because, as they put it in their own words:

> assume that the system is in equilibrium; double all money prices; since relative prices are unaffected, the goods markets are still in equilibrium; thus either the system leaves money prices undetermined, in the absence of a stock demand for money, or, if there is a stock demand, there are two inconsistent excess demand functions (Archibald and Lipsey, 1958, pp. 10–11).

To this Archibald and Lipsey answer that 'the model has no economic interpretation when it is out of equilibrium' (ibid.), and add that in their model the fact that doubling all prices from the equilibrium solution creates an excess demand for 'money to hold', that is an excess 'demand for money' in the Cambridge equation,

> is in denial of Walras' Law. Although there is an excess demand for money to hold, there is no excess supply of goods. In fact, *Walras' Law does not hold in this model at all*. This raises a problem of interpretation {...} Walras' Law says that goods can only be demanded if goods or money are offered in exchange. It is therefore a relationship which must obtain if a model is to make economic sense. When the classical model is in equilibrium the relation does obtain, i.e. the excess demand for both goods and money to hold are zero. Hence the equilibrium solution to the system makes sense. The relationship does not, however, hold out of equilibrium, i.e., is not an identity in this model. Hence, out of equilibrium, the system does not make economic sense. It does not describe a possible form of disequilibrium behaviour (ibid., p. 16; italics added).

Although not wrong in their basic message (which is made clear in the very last sentence), Archibald and Lipsey are clearly wrong in the statement I have italicized.[65] As already noticed by Valavanis (1955, p. 355), Walras' Law as intended by them *does* hold, it is formally an identity in 'Classical Dichotomy' models: as each agent's actions satisfy a balanced-budget constraint, the form taken by Walras' Law is that the 'mirror-image' excess demand for money is always zero.

One must conclude that even Archibald and Lipsey were unable clearly to distinguish the excess 'demand for money' which appears in a Cambridge-type or Fisherine equation, from the 'excess demand for money' shown by the 'mirror-image' money equation, which is the one for which Walras' Law holds.[66] As already said, the first one is not a 'demand' in the sense that something (goods) is offered in exchange; it rather indicates a *prerequisite* for the behaviour shown by the LPGE excess demands for goods. When these are all zero, the 'mirror-image' excess demand for money is also zero but we still do not know whether that prerequisite can be satisfied, that is whether the price level is compatible with the quantity of money existing in the economy; in other words, whether the money balances, which agents would need to hold in order to behave as shown by the goods equations, total the available quantity of money. If the price level is not so compatible (and this will show up in the Cambridge-type equation), then in the actual economy people will not behave as the goods equations would tell us, and that is all.

5A1.6. Criticisms, based on Positive Net Savings, of the 'Full Equilibrium' Notion

Another point on which Archibald and Lipsey were not able to re-establish the meaning of traditional analysis is not simply a point of monetary theory, but rather, more generally, a point about the long-period method and the role, inside the marginalist application of that method, of the assumption of stationariness. Their shortcomings on this score brought them to admit – in response to a criticism to be discussed presently – that, when one introduces production, bonds and the possibility of accumulation into the model, then the concept of 'full equilibrium' loses interest because it only makes sense

---

65. Baumol (1960, p. 29, n. 2) follows them on this question.
66. Hahn (1960) is apparently unable to understand all this, since he repeats that 'there is only one excess demand function for money' (p. 40). It is also inaccurate to state, as Archibald and Lipsey do, that 'out of equilibrium, the system does not make economic sense'. Systems of equations can make sense in a variety of ways. What is true is that, if the price level is out of equilibrium, the goods-markets equations do not describe actual planned behaviour; but the conclusion we can derive from the system, that equilibrium behaviour would require, at the given price level, total money balances greater (or smaller) than the actual total money endowment of the economy, does make sense, and from it one can derive further sensible inferences.

for stationary economies; so that 'Patinkin had in fact no alternative but to consider weekly equilibria in the production model' (Archibald and Lipsey, 1960, p. 56). Thus the final victory effectively remained with Patinkin.[67]

The criticism which prompted Archibald and Lipsey's concession to Patinkin came from Ball and Bodkin (1960). They argued that, if production and the possibility of accumulation are allowed, then, unless everybody's propensity to net savings is zero, a 'full equilibrium' cannot even be *defined*, because the holding of bonds of at least some individuals will be changing every 'week' and, with it, the desired proportions between goods, money and bonds, and hence the desired holdings of real balances. The relevant passage is worth reporting in full:

> If saving is positive, individuals will be adding to their stock of bonds, but this will cause a rearrangement in the structure of their assets. An increase in an individual's bond holdings will alter, in the succeeding period, both his wealth and his money income (by the amount of the additional yield), which with given prices will cause some re-shuffling between goods, bonds, and money. The individual (short-period) demand for money will depend on prices, income, and initial money holdings as before – but also on the initial stock of bonds held. Changes in the holdings of bonds therefore imply changes in the holdings of real balances (Ball and Bodkin, 1960, p. 48).

They concluded that:

> the only type of equilibrium that is meaningful in a production model with positive saving and investment, is the traditional short period type of equilibrium. Full equilibrium, in the sense that the authors use the term, cannot even logically be considered ... In order that the system may come to rest, it is necessary (among other conditions) that the flow of new bonds cease. This in turn implies that there must be zero saving and investment in the economy (Ball and Bodkin, 1960, p. 45).

Archibald and Lipsey were wrong in conceding the correctness of this argument, and in so doing they revealed an imperfect grasp of the traditional logic which they had tried to describe with their distinction between a 'weekly equilibrium' and a 'full equilibrium'.[68] Their mistake lies in not

67. See, in fact, Patinkin's reiteration of the superiority of his approach in Patinkin (1972).
68. It must be noted that anyway in Archibald and Lipsey the 'weekly' equilibrium is reached instantaneously, with no 'false tradings': the notion of long-period equilibrium only re-surfaces deformed, as a sequence of identical 'weekly' equilibria, each one instantaneously established by the auctioneer. The role of the long-period equilibrium, of being an indication of average magnitudes in an economy perennially in disequilibrium, is thereby obscured.

realizing that there is no need to define a 'full equilibrium' as a succession of identical temporary equilibria, that is as describing a stationary economy.

The issue has little to do with the existence of money. If full equilibrium is *defined* as a succession of identical temporary equilibria, that is as stationary, then the simple existence of a propensity to net savings obviously suffices to disprove its possibility.

The question, therefore, is whether a 'full equilibrium', in the more restricted sense of a situation where also the distribution of the average money endowment among agents has reached an equilibrium, must necessarily be stationary. We can utilize here what has been said on the stationariness issue in Chapter 4.[69] It was argued there that a long-period general equilibrium need not be stationary; its defining characteristic is not stationariness, but only the adaptation of the composition of the capital stock to demand, so as to yield a uniform rate of return on supply price, an adaptation which is perfectly compatible with non-stationary situations.

Let us remember that the foundation for this argument is that the speed with which the composition of capital can adjust to changes in distribution or in the composition of demand is high relative to the speed with which accumulation may be changing income distribution. Thus we find Marshall and Wicksell considering the effects of accumulation only in their discussion of the very-long-run tendencies of the economy, *after* discussing the long-period equilibrium on the basis of the simplifying assumption of stationariness.

The mistake of Ball and Bodkin lies in having lost sight of this difference between long-period forces and very-long-run tendencies: long-period forces

69. As in Chapter 4, here too the problem caused by heterogeneous capital for the determinability of the capital endowment of a long-period equilibrium will be neglected, in order to concentrate on whether the logic of traditional analyses was well understood by the contributors to this controversy. This problem did not arise in the controversy because most of the controversy was in terms of models without capital; Archibald and Lipsey (1958, 1960) utilized a one-good model to discuss how the introduction of production affected the distinction between 'weekly' and 'full' equilibrium; Patinkin (1965, pt. II) also utilized a one-good model. Incidentally, not the least reason for the popularity of Patinkin's 1965 book was probably the fact that his macroeconomic analysis, although worded in temporary equilibrium terms and therefore in line with the trend in value theory at the time, was actually based on such 'simplifying' assumptions as to make its comparative static results indistinguishable from those that could have been reached within a long-period marginalist framework, thus probably preserving, in the eyes of many, that relevance to real-world analysis which is often admitted to be lacking in neo-Walrasian models. Patinkin assumed a world with a single product homogeneous with the single capital good, and further assumed, for most of his analysis, no 'redistribution effects'. Thus the lack of permanence of the data of temporary equilibrium, relative to the composition of capital, was eliminated, and the lack of permanence of the data relative to the initial distribution of the total money endowment was rendered irrelevant.

are those which tend to establish a uniform rate of remuneration for all units of the same factor and a URRSP, which means an endogenously determined composition of capital; these forces are sufficiently faster than the very-long-run forces connected with accumulation, such that one may legitimately assume the former to have come to rest while the latter have not.

Analogously, one may distinguish the long-period forces from the very-long-run forces acting on the average distribution of the money endowment among agents. The long-period forces will tend to make the average money balance of each agent the one appropriate to her wealth and to her normal transactions; the very-long-run forces will tend slowly to redistribute these average money balances among agents as normal economic conditions slowly change, some agents accumulate wealth faster than others, and so on.

The right to neglect the slow changes entailed by accumulation in the determination of a long-period position means that one can legitimately determine the individual agent's average demand for money under an assumption of stationary conditions. Anyway one should not forget the lines by Irving Fisher quoted in §5A1.2.2: namely, that the economist is only interested in the *average* velocity of circulation, resulting from the actions of many agents for each of whom the 'adjustment is somewhat rough, and dependent largely on the accident of the moment'.

In conclusion, the traditional marginalist dichotomy between the study of relative long-period prices and distribution, and the study of the determinants of the price level, was perfectly legitimate. This was not understood in the (Neo)Classical Dichotomy controversy only because of an inability to understand that the traditional dichotomy reflected the attempt to determine the *long-period* result of the equilibration of the 'real' forces contemplated by the marginalist approach. And even when, with Archibald and Lipsey, the basic mistake (relative to the treatment of the money endowment of each agent) was corrected, an important mistake persisted: the identification of the 'full equilibrium' with a stationary state.

APPENDIX 5A2. IF EVERYBODY IS A PRICE-TAKER, WHO SETS PRICES? ON ARROW'S CONCEPTION OF EQUILIBRIUM

5A2.1. A well-known problem, arising out of the assumption of price-taking, is: who changes relative prices if all agents are price-takers?

This is one of the problems with neo-Walrasian competitive equilibria, which the assumption of the existence of the auctioneer conveniently takes care of. And it is a problem specific to *neo-Walrasian* competitive equilibria only, because, within the traditional conception of equilibrium, there was no need to assume that agents are price-takers whatever the prices, that is also in disequilibrium; agents could be thought of as price-makers, and yet obliged by the process of competition (especially by free entry) sooner or later to bring their prices to the equilibrium levels.

The limited purpose of this Appendix is to point out that a well-known discussion of this problem, the one by Arrow (1959), reveals the persistence of the traditional conception of equilibrium, without apparently a realization of the incompatibility of that conception of equilibrium with the data of Arrow–Debreu equilibria.

Arrow notes that 'perfect competition can really prevail only at equilibrium' (p. 41) because, if the market price is at a level such that supply exceeds demand:

> the individual firm cannot sell all it wishes to at the market price; i.e., when supply and demand do not balance, even in an objectively competitive market, the individual firms are in the position of monopolists as far as the imperfect elasticity of demand for their products is concerned ... [Therefore] Under conditions of disequilibrium, there is no reason that there should be a single market price, and we may very well expect that each firm will charge a different price (Arrow, 1959, p. 46).

An analogous situation of downward-sloping demand curves for individual firms exists, Arrow continues, when demand exceeds supply: in either case one may expect to observe each firm setting its own price, and then changing that price as its (perceived) demand curve shifts, owing to buyers moving from one firm to another or proposing higher (or lower) prices because they realize that supply is not equal to demand.

Arrow's sensible observations also imply that time is required to discover what amount one can sell at a certain price: 'The demand curve for the particular entrepreneur under consideration is thus shifting upward at the same time that he is exploring it' (p. 46). During this time, Arrow notes, there may be an accumulation or a decrease of inventories if sales have not been correctly foreseen. The variation of inventories, Arrow adds, will indicate in which direction to revise prices (p. 48). For our purposes, this is a further highly important observation, because 1) it implies that the variation in inventories is considered actually to take place, which again needs time; 2) it implies that there is something like a desired level of inventories, which is then presumably part of the definition of equilibrium, but, in order for the desired level of inventories to be re-established once the actual level has fallen below this desired level, production must be allowed to take place. Consequently there can be little doubt that Arrow is granting that *disequilibrium adjustments take time and that production is going on while prices adjust.* He realistically concludes:

> Thus the whole adjustment process is apt to be very irregular. Although the broad tendency will be for prices to rise when demand exceed supply, there can easily be a considerable dispersion of prices among different sellers of the same commodity, as well as considerable variability over time in the rate of change of prices (ibid., pp. 46–7).

5A2.2. Arrow's basic message is clearly realistic, and plausible (given the belief in supply and demand curves); but, in fact, it does little more than remind the profession of the traditional explanation handed out to all beginners, of why price (hopefully) gravitates toward the level which equates supply and demand. If demand exceeds supply, sooner or later some buyers realize that they are not able to buy at the ruling price, and then offer a higher price, rather than go without the good: but then other buyers too, rather than be pushed out of the market, will offer a higher price, and so on. This implies a non-uniform price during disequilibrium adjustments, bilateral bargaining, agents who decide to wait for a little while and look around for other offers before deciding whether to accept a certain offer, and so on. Now, clearly the equilibrium approached in this way must have some persistence, since it may take a considerable time for the average of market prices sufficiently to approach the equilibrium price. Arrow admits this openly, since he writes that *an economy cannot be thought of as continuously in equilibrium: the equilibrium is a long-run notion*; it is a good indication only of the long-run tendency:

> There has been a position strongly held in recent years that the American economy is basically competitive, in that neither firms nor labor unions have, in fact, much control over prices, despite superficial appearances. The present model suggests that the evidence, to the extent that it is valid, relates only to equilibrium and, therefore, to long-run situations. Such long-run competitiveness is not incompati-

ble, on the present view, with considerable short-run monopoly powers in transitory situations (Arrow, 1959, p. 49).

Here one is provided with evidence that even some of the best economists were and are unclear on the nature of neo-Walrasian models. Arrow, in writing these lines, follows a methodological position on the meaning and role of equilibrium that is essentially traditional, where equilibrium is conceived as a position only approached in the 'long run', through time-consuming trial-and-error processes involving productions and exchanges at disequilibrium prices. The conception of this 'long-run' competitive equilibrium as what the economy gravitates toward is made clear by the reference to the existence of 'short-run monopoly powers' as 'transitory situations'. And yet, Arrow had been, before this article, and continued to be, afterwards, one of the great advocates and developers of neo-Walrasian equilibria, which are incompatible with that role. Clearly, he had not perceived at that time (nor, it would seem, later[70]) this incompatibility.

70. See, for example, Arrow (1989, pp. 167–8): 'Prices do not adjust rapidly ... There is much evidence of rigidities ... I believe there is no market clearing and for the short-run fluctuations of the economy it is a very important fact'.

APPENDIX 5A3. WHY THE AUCTIONEER MUST BE A CENTRAL PLANNER AND TEMPORARY EQUILIBRIA MAY BE INDETERMINATE: OR, NEO-WALRASIAN DIFFICULTIES WITH CONSTANT RETURNS TO SCALE

5A3.1. Introduction

This Appendix, like the previous one and that which will follow, intends to stress the illegitimate survival of traditional modes of reasoning in neo-Walrasian theorists. It examines some new difficulties that arise exclusively in the neo-Walrasian versions, and that are underestimated owing to an implicit reliance on traditional analyses no longer legitimate in the neo-Walrasian framework. The difficulties concern the following:

1. the role of the auctioneer in the tâtonnement when there are constant returns to scale for the industries (if not for individual firms);
2. the determinateness of investment decisions in temporary equilibria;
3. the possibility to avoid the assumption of complete futures markets by assuming perfect foresight.

The second and third of these difficulties appear not to have been widely noticed yet; the first, on the other hand, has been noticed, but has then simply been set aside, as if one were certain that there was some actual way to overcome this difficulty. This surprising inclination to neglect admitted difficulties becomes more understandable, I would suggest, as a result of the same confusion that is discussed in Chapters 7 and 8, apropos macroeconomic theory: namely, the persisting faith in the validity of conclusions reached by traditional marginalist analyses, while in fact the abandonment of the method of long-period positions, and of the treatment of capital required within the marginalist approach by that method, entails losing the very foundation for those conclusions.

5A3.2. Constant Returns to Scale and the Auctioneer

5A3.2.1. In this section it will be argued that the assumption of technological constant returns to scale, CRS, for each industry if not for individual firms,[71]

---

71. The assumptions on *technological* returns to scale (how the quantity produced by a firm varies with proportional variations in all its inputs) should not be confused with the assumptions on returns in Marshall's sense, which were the object of Sraffa's famous criticism, see Sraffa (1925, 1926, 1930). Under the heading of 'returns', Marshall's analysis discussed assumptions both on technological returns to scale for individual firms, and on

makes it very difficult to conceive how a competitive neo-Walrasian equilibrium might be reached by the auctioneer-guided tâtonnement based on provisional 'tickets'. The implication is that there are some logical problems with this fiction, that are not perceived only because of the illegitimate survival of traditional modes of reasoning.

In the modern formal studies of competitive general equilibrium theory, the traditional approach (still followed for example by McKenzie, 1987), which concentrates directly on industries, and assumes them to have Constant-Returns-to-Scale (CRS) technologies owing to free entry, is often replaced by the approach exemplified by Arrow–Debreu (see for example Debreu, 1959, p. 37), also adopted in Arrow and Hahn (1971). This approach assumes a *given* number of firms or producers, each with its own production possibility set.[72] It is not excluded – often it is even *assumed* (for example Hicks did so in *Value and Capital*) – that this production possibility set be *strictly* convex (decreasing returns to scale).[73] However it is conceded that the analysis must be able to encompass the case of CRS *firms* as well. In the latter case the analysis becomes formally identical to that of the first approach, because each industry will have a CRS production function, although now originating only in the expansion or contraction of the firms in that industry.

Thus, in spite of the difference between the two approaches, it seems to be universally admitted that general equilibrium theory must be able to encompass the case of CRS industries.

5A3.2.2. In this case, at the equilibrium prices the number of firms in each industry (if free entry is assumed), and/or their dimension (if CRS for individual firms are assumed), are indeterminate; thus both product supplies and factor demands at the equilibrium prices are indeterminate if no further

what would happen to input prices and to externalities as the *industry's* output expanded, cf. Garegnani (1990c).

72. There is a little-noticed problem here, due precisely to the absence of free entry of firms with the same minimum average cost as the incumbent ones. If the production possibility sets of different firms are not identical, then in general for given factor prices there will be, for each product, a price range within which only one producer – the most efficient one – does not make losses. Within that price range that producer is therefore a monopolist, and the assumptions of price-taking, and of zero profits in equilibrium if there are CRS, are unjustified. This problem by itself suggests that the approach is not appropriate for studying competitive economies.

73. The analytical advantage is that, assuming sufficiently decreasing returns to scale, one obtains supply functions for products and demand functions for factors, thus allowing a symmetrical treatment of consumers and firms. But analytical convenience should not justify assumptions without economic justification; belatedly this has been admitted by Hahn himself: 'though one can argue that it is reasonable to take the number of households as exogenous, this is not so when it comes to the number of firms' (Hahn, 1981a, p. 131).

conditions are imposed. Thus there is no guarantee that, at the equilibrium prices, productions will equal demands, nor that factor demands will equal supplies.

In other words, *equilibrium prices are now a necessary, but not a sufficient condition for equilibrium.*

Accordingly, general equilibrium specialists have reformulated the meaning of the demonstration of existence of equilibrium prices for the constant returns to scale case as follows. What is demonstrated is not that there are prices *determining* mutually compatible decisions, but rather that there exists a set of mutually compatible consumption and production decisions and of *supporting* prices (that is prices such that agents do not wish they had decided differently): 'The problem is no longer conceived as that of proving that a certain set of equations has a solution. It has been reformulated as one of proving that a number of maximizations of individual goals under independent restraints can be simultaneously carried out' (Koopmans, 1957, p. 60).

5A3.2.3. This creates problems for the story of how such an equilibrium might be brought about by the auctioneer-guided tâtonnement.[74]

With CRS for the industries, the auctioneer's task as usually conceived – initially announcing arbitrarily chosen prices, then collecting the agents' planned demands and supplies, calculating the excess demands, and altering prices accordingly, until the equilibrium prices are reached – won't work, and must therefore be conceived differently; but it appears then to require the performance of tasks not attributable to the market.

The problem comes from the indeterminate scale of industries at zero-profit product prices.[75] Finding these prices for *given* factor rentals is not a problem:[76] as long as the excess demand for a product is positive (zero supply) the auctioneer must increase its price, and as long as the excess demand is negative (it will then be infinitely negative, because supply will be infinite) the auctioneer must decrease its price. In this way the price can be made to equal minimum average cost, and clearly this is a necessary condition for equilibrium, because, at a different price, supply is either zero or infinite. But at this price the industry supply is indeterminate (so factor demands are indeterminate as well). It is not clear, then, what the firms' decisions in the tâtonnement can be. It seems as reasonable as anything else to assume that firms pick out a quantity to be supplied at random. Then,

---

74. Of course other adjustment processes have been proposed; but the purpose of this Appendix does not require their discussion.
75. In this Appendix 'profit' has the marginalist/neoclassical, not the classical, meaning.
76. I assume single-product industries. For the critical purpose of this Appendix, this assumption is sufficient.

except by an extraordinary fluke, supply will not equal demand, so even if the factor rentals are the equilibrium ones, the auctioneer cannot discover it. If announcing prices and collecting excess demands is all the auctioneer does, the tâtonnement will not stop at the equilibrium factor rentals.

The way out described by Arrow and Hahn (1971, pp. 280–81, 316–9) is as follows. For each given vector of factor rentals, the auctioneer is assumed to be able to determine the price equal to minimum unit cost of production of each produced good. Having randomly chosen an initial vector of factor rentals, and having determined the associated product prices, she jointly announces them. She then collects from households the demands for final goods and the supplies of factors at those factor rentals and product prices (households calculate their income assuming they will find purchasers for their supplies of factors). The assumption is then introduced that *industries adjust supply to demand for each produced good*: 'whatever is demanded is also supplied provided minimum unit costs are covered' (ibid., p. 319). The justification is very brief and runs as follows: 'Since minimum unit costs are exactly covered at all times in all lines of production, producers stand ready to supply whatever is demanded of the produced goods' (ibid., p. 317). Assuming uniqueness of optimal factor proportions in each industry, factor demands are derived from the demands for final goods. Then the auctioneer raises the relative rentals of the factors in excess demand, and/or tries again.

5A3.2.4. But there is one step in this procedure – the assumed adjustment of supplies of produced goods to demands – whose justification is unconvincing. Hahn (1982a, p. 48) has written: 'under constant returns to scale, firms must know not only prices but what will be sold'. More precisely, since there is product homogeneity in each industry, each firm must:

1. know the total demand for its industry's product,
2. know what will be offered by all other firms in the industry,
3. want to make up only and entirely the difference (if positive) between demand and the total supply of other firms.

But to assume point (3) contradicts the assumption that the firm, making zero profits, is indifferent as to scale and is a price-taker. As to point (2), it is not a problem of knowledge but of ex-ante co-ordination: even granting point (3), what a firm can sell depends on the total that the other firms in the same industry are deciding to supply. But this in turn depends on what the first firm decides to supply, so we have a vicious circle. Under constant returns to scale for the individual firms, each firm in the industry must know what *each and every one* of them *should* produce, but this problem, in the general case of (at least potentially) several firms per industry, is indeterminate: a decision must be reached but it cannot but be arbitrary. Thus the auctioneer, in order to be able to perform the tâtonnement procedure described above, must be endowed with the additional power to *impose* on each firm how much it shall produce at the announced prices. If there is free entry and firms have U-shaped cost curves, then the dimension of each firm is determinate; but if the auctioneer only announces the zero-profit prices, there is nothing to guarantee that the *number* of firms in each industry will be the number required by demand, and then again the auctioneer must intervene to ensure the correct number of firms, by *imposing* the decision whether to set up firms or not.[77]

Thus, in order to bring equilibrium about, the auctioneer story requires that firm owners or would-be firm founders *must not* freely and independently decide whether and how much to produce: the auctioneer must become indistinguishable from the central planner of a command economy, taking upon herself the additional task and authority to impose the creation or closure of firms and/or to assign to each firm its output.

The conclusion neo-Walrasian theorists should reach would seem to be that, in the price-taking case, the auctioneer-guided market economy is *incapable* of reaching a neo-Walrasian equilibrium. Incapable, that is, unless the auctioneer is truly a central planner in that he also imposes on firms the quantities of products they should produce and/or the setting up of firms – but then are we still in a market economy?

5A3.3.   Constant-Returns-to-Scale Adjustments in Traditional Analyses

5A3.3.1. Earlier marginalist economists, who tried to determine an equilibrium sufficiently persistent as to have the role of centre of gravitation for time-consuming adjustment processes, did not feel that the hypothesis of CRS industries posed any additional problem. To the contrary, they took that hypothesis as the natural one, because their equilibrium was endowed with sufficient persistence, and unaffected by the time-consuming disequilibrium processes assumed to cause the tendency toward it. Those disequilibrium processes could accordingly be conceived as happening in real time, and as involving *actual* productions and exchanges. This made an important difference relative to tâtonnement adjustments.

In the tâtonnement firms *promise* to supply quantities of products which require the utilization of factors in amounts which the firms are not certain they will be able to get; but there is nothing to prevent them from so doing,

---

77. The same indeterminateness of the number of firms would seem to arise if one assumes
    monopolistic competition with product differentiation and free entry.

since if the total demand for a factor comes out to be greater than the supply, the promises to deliver products are automatically invalidated and the tâtonnement continues. This is why as soon as profits are positive, the intended size and number of firms becomes infinite.

Traditional marginalist authors conceived equilibrium as the outcome of real-world adjustment processes. They accordingly conceived disequilibrium contracts to be binding. Changes in prices were seen as the byproduct of differences between quantities *actually* demanded and quantities *actually* brought to the market over a certain time period, differences that result in some agent being unable to implement her intentions to buy or to sell. And changes in supply were seen as factual, and thus resulting from changes in the factors actually employed by firms. A firm could only increase supply if it had first obtained increased amounts of factors.

In such a more realistic picture of the functioning of markets the problem of infinite supplies at positive profits and of indeterminate supply at zero profit did not arise. A price above minimum average cost did not make supply instantly infinite, because a CRS firm making positive profits and intending to expand could not become instantaneously of infinite dimension; it had first to obtain increased amounts of factors, something that would take time and would soon stop its expansion; and the same would be true for the industry.

Furthermore, it is only when adjustment takes time and involves the implementation of disequilibrium decisions that it is possible to reap the temporary profits deriving from the imperfect adaptation of supply to demand, and therefore, there is an incentive for supply to increase if price exceeds average cost. The thesis, that produced quantities adjust so that product prices tend to equal average costs, appears therefore necessarily to imply an adjustment in historical time.

5A3.3.2. It is perhaps a helpful digression to pause and consider why the very-short-period nature of neo-Walrasian models does not prevent the supply curve of products from being horizontal once factor prices are given. One might think that in the short period there are fixed factors that cause the marginal-cost curve of each firm to be upward-sloping. But Marshall described the industry's short period as characterized by a fixed supply *for the industry as a whole, not* for the individual firms, of some reproducible factor specific to the industry:[78] and rightly so, because 'fixed' factors, for example fixed plants, are not legally tied to a firm. They can be sold or

---

78. For instance Marshall (1970, V, v, 4, p. 308), when discussing the short-period equilibrium of the fishing industry, takes as given the number and quality of boats and of experienced fishermen *in the industry*, not the number of boats and experienced fishermen *of each fishing firm*.

leased by (the owners of) firms to other firms; in a neo-Walrasian equilibrium there must therefore be a market for each (type of) fixed plant, just as for each type of land. Nothing prevents a firm from wishing to employ an indefinite great number of fixed plants, in case these were available at the given prices and rentals. Therefore the existence of fixed plants, in a neo-Walrasian tâtonnement, will not prevent firms from desiring to become infinitely large, and therefore announcing to the auctioneer an infinite demand for factors (including fixed plants).

If on the contrary adjustments involve actual productions and, in order to produce more, firms must first obtain the necessary factors, then an increase in the price of a product will increase competition for the factors (including fixed plants) in limited supply for the industry, thus raising their implicit or explicit rentals until all profits are absorbed. Therefore, contrary to the usual textbook derivation, the partial-equilibrium short-period upward-sloping supply curve should not be seen as implying higher and higher profits as demand increases, but only higher and higher imputed rentals to fixed factors. And since there are no truly fixed factors *for a firm* because firms can buy or sell fixed plants, then the textbook individual firm's rising supply curve can only be salvaged by interpreting it as depicting a Marshallian 'representative firm', for example as representing on a reduced scale the cost/supply conditions of the entire industry. These cost/supply conditions reflect the increase in the rentals of the factors in limited supply for the industry as aggregate supply increases. It is only for the 'variable' factors, that is the factors which are not specialized and whose rentals therefore can be assumed not to be affected by variations of the industry's level of activity, that rentals can be assumed given in partial-equilibrium analyses. *When factor costs are correctly imputed, profits are therefore zero at all levels of the standard partial-equilibrium short-period supply curve.*

In a general-equilibrium context, the same reasoning applies, except that not even the rentals of *variable* factors can be assumed given: as the industry expands its output, there will be a rise in the relative rentals of the factors which the industry employs in a higher-than-average proportion, in order to discourage their employment in the rest of the economy. The general-equilibrium supply schedule of a product is therefore the result of a comparative-statics exercise in which one assumes the quantity of a product produced to be higher and higher, and one determines the change in the corresponding supply price of the product, resulting from the changes in factor prices necessary for adjustment on all other markets. However, the assumption of equilibrium on all other markets requires a mechanism bringing this equilibrium about, and here the auctioneer story runs into trouble. In traditional marginalist analyses, to the contrary, the admission that adjustment took time, made it possible to postulate the gradual adjustment on the factor and product markets which would ensure that equilibrium was actually reached. The price paid for this was the inconsistency of the treatment of capital as a single factor.

5A3.3.3. Thus the difficulty highlighted in section 5A3.2 was not present in traditional marginalist analyses, and only arose for marginalist theory with the shift to neo-Walrasian equilibrium analyses.

The scarcity of attention given to this difficulty by neo-Walrasian authors has probably been due, as in other cases (see section 5A3.4, and Appendices 5A2 and 5A4), to a difficulty with fully abandoning older (and more plausible) ways of thinking that are incompatible with the new models. In the present case, the difficulty is with abandoning the traditional conclusion that, with constant returns to scale, short-period price variations coupled with long-period variations in industry capacity would ensure that supply adapts to demand at the minimum-cost price.

5A3.4. Constant Returns to Scale may render Temporary Equilibria Indeterminate and Perfect Foresight Impossible

5A3.4.1. Even if one makes the extreme assumption about the role of the auctioneer, that the auctioneer imposes the creation or closure of firms and/or assigns to each firm its output, some little-noticed problems caused by CRS remain. I argue in this section, with the help of an example, that even such an auctioneer/co-ordinator is unable to avoid a certain indeterminateness of *temporary* equilibria. It will then be shown that the interpretation of intertemporal equilibria as sequential temporary equilibria with perfect foresight and intertemporal transfers of income, due to Arrow (1964)[79] and Radner (1972), is untenable.

So now there are only the current markets; let us assume the existence of the auctioneer/co-ordinator for the current markets, and that when the auctioneer announces the current prices, all agents forecast the same future prices.[80] Let us further assume that the auctioneer announces current prices

---

79. Arrow has implicitly reasserted in a recent interview that he views the intertemporal equilibrium model as interpretable as a perfect-foresight model: 'There is probably no sense in which an aggregate measure of capital will automatically follow the rate of interest, once there is a multiplicity of capital goods. Pasinetti was quite correct. The trouble is that with heterogeneous capital goods almost anything is possible. Now, I do not think this in any way interferes with the consistency of the general equilibrium theory of capital formation based on perfect foresight. You may not like the assumption of perfect foresight; that I can understand. But what I am saying is that there is no logical inconsistency in the perfect foresight model' (Arrow, 1989, p. 155).

80. With constant returns to scale, price-taking firms whose productions, requiring time, will be sold in subsequent periods will have either zero or infinite desired size unless expected

which are the Arrow–Debreu current-markets equilibrium prices, and that all agents then forecast with certainty for the future periods the Arrow–Debreu equilibrium prices. In other words, agents are confronted with the same array of current and future prices as would be established in intertemporal equilibrium if there were a complete set of futures markets (for the sake of argument I assume uniqueness of the intertemporal equilibrium). The accepted view is that, in this case, the temporary equilibrium will be the same as the initial-period equilibrium of the intertemporal equilibrium with complete futures markets. This view neglects a problem.

We have assumed constant returns to scale. We further assume that production takes time, one period at least. We already know that at the equilibrium current and future prices, which are zero-profit prices, the decisions of price-taking firms as to scale are indeterminate, and must be assumed to be random if one does not introduce further mechanisms of co-ordination. Then it makes a fundamental difference whether or not a future market exists. If the market exists, the auctioneer/co-ordinator can collect the firms' planned supply decisions and, if the excess demand is not zero, she can ask firms to increase or decrease the proposed supplies, and she can go on until an equilibrium is reached. If, to the contrary, the future market does not exist, the auctioneer cannot make sure that the planned supplies of firms at the correct future equilibrium prices will ensure the equilibrium between future supply and future demand. This is the key to the result below.

Uncertainty as to future states of nature will be left aside: it is assumed in what follows that future states of nature are perfectly forecasted.

5A3.4.2. Let us now come to the example. Assume an economy, for simplicity without capital, where the number of consumption goods is greater than the number of factors, say, three consumption goods produced by homogeneous labour and homogeneous land via constant-returns-to-scale single-product production functions which are the same for all the firms in each industry, but are different for the three products, implying different relative factor intensities at all factor rentals. Production goes on in yearly cycles, factors are hired in January and the products come out and are sold in December. Assume that this economy lasts only one year, from January to December. Assume also that, if forward markets for the consumption goods existed in January, the economy would have a unique intertemporal

product prices equal average costs, so expected product prices *must* be equal to average costs in order for an equilibrium to be possible on the current markets, so firms must necessarily all forecast the same future product prices (equal to minimum average costs) for all products whose production costs are, directly or indirectly, determined in the current markets. As is well known, shared expectations also avoid some of the causes of possible non-existence of temporary equilibrium.

equilibrium. But there are no forward markets for the consumption goods, so firms must decide in January how much of the factors to hire and how much of the goods to produce, on the basis of *known* factor rentals (agreed upon in January in terms of some basket of consumption goods and to be paid in December) but based on *forecasts* of the consumption goods' prices in December. Assume that in January, with the help of the auctioneer/co-ordinator, a temporary equilibrium is established on the factor markets, on the basis of perfect price foresight in the following sense: agents correctly predict the December prices which would be established if the forward markets existed (so they are zero-profit prices).

The point I wish to make is the following: there is no guarantee that the quantities of the three consumption goods that will be produced will be those which would have been produced, had the forward markets actually existed. The reason is that the given factor prices determine the factor proportions in the production of each good, but, since the number of consumption goods is greater than the number of factors, the equilibrium on the factor markets leaves the composition of production indeterminate.

Note that an extension of the perfect foresight assumption to the total quantities to be demanded in December would be of no help, for two reasons. First, firms would still not know the planned production of other firms (at least as long as one assumes that in competitive markets a firm does not know what each other firm is deciding with regard to what and how much to produce for future supply: a firm can observe the current markets and thus know factor prices and factor quantities exchanged, but in this economy this does not permit inferring the quantities produced by each firm). Second, even if a firm did know both the total future demand for the good its industry produces, and the supply of the other firms in the industry, if it were certain that the product price would be the zero-pure-profit one, its supply decision would in any case be indeterminate: there is no reason why it should want to equalize total supply and demand.

Still, the assumption of equilibrium on the current factor markets constrains the firms' decisions to those ensuring the full employment of all factors. But all full-employment compositions of planned production are compatible with temporary equilibrium.

Thus although the temporary equilibrium prices and quantities exchanged on the current markets are uniquely determined (and, under our assumptions, coinciding with those of the intertemporal equilibrium), the temporary equilibrium is nonetheless indeterminate in so far as the allocation of factors destined to future production among industries is indeterminate. The important implication is that the production decisions taken in conjunction with the establishment of that temporary equilibrium, but bearing fruit only in subsequent periods, are indeterminate. In other words, the next period's data are indeterminate: the future evolution of the economy is indeterminate.

Then a sequence of temporary equilibria is impossible to determine, and one completely loses the possibility of conceiving – doubtful as that may be for other reasons – a sequence of temporary equilibria as approximating in some tolerable way the behaviour of the actual economy.

5A3.4.3. For the problem just outlined to arise it is unnecessary that the expected future prices be exactly those which would be established with complete futures markets. Whatever the factor prices, as long as some composition of production for future sale exists ensuring equilibrium on current factor markets, then if there are more products than factors that composition will not be generally unique.

It is also clear that the problem extends to more complicated cases. If for instance in the current period there are stocks of consumption goods to be sold, and/or capital goods among the products, and/or the economy lasts more than two periods, the problem outlined above survives untouched. So long as there are factors supplied and demanded in the current period's temporary equilibrium, and so long as at least some part of the demand for them is motivated by production decisions which will produce goods that cannot be sold in advance, the possibility arises that the current period's equilibrium does not fully determine the composition of the production for future sale, in which case that composition remains indeterminate.

5A3.4.4. To avoid this indeterminateness one must assume both 1) that the number of goods to be produced is not greater than the number of factors, and 2) that no two different products have identical production functions.

I shall not discuss here how restrictive the second assumption is. The first one definitely is. For economies with capital goods, since all capital goods are factors but also products, the relevant comparison is between the number of non-reproducible factors and the number of consumption goods, and the latter number would appear to be the greater one in real economies. One may conclude therefore that the allocation of investment in a temporary equilibrium with production destined to missing future markets and with constant returns to scale for industries is in general indeterminate.

An implication of this result is that the correct foresight of future equilibrium prices is insufficient to cause those prices to come about. More precisely: the announcement of the current and future Arrow–Debreu intertemporal equilibrium prices, plus the shared certainty that those prices are actually Arrow–Debreu equilibrium prices, plus the intervention of the auctioneer/co-ordinator in the current markets to ensure the equalization of supplies and demands in these markets in spite of the indeterminacy caused by CRS,[81] is generally insufficient to ensure that supplies in subsequent periods will be the Arrow–Debreu equilibrium ones. Therefore there is no reason to believe that the Arrow–Debreu intertemporal equilibrium prices will actually rule in future periods, even if they are ruling in the current period.

For readers familiar with the notion of Radner equilibria (equilibria of plans, prices and price expectations) the implication will be clear: '*perfect foresight*', in the sense of correct calculation of Arrow–Debreu future prices coupled with the belief that those prices will actually prevail, turns out not to be a *correct* foresight except by a total fluke. Thus we have here one more reason why perfect foresight in the sense of self-fulfilling foresight is in fact an unacceptable assumption. The alternative interpretation of intertemporal equilibria, not as equilibria reached on the basis of the existence of complete future markets, but as sequential Radner equilibria with perfect foresight, comes out to be indefensible.[82]

Again, it is a fair guess that so far this problem has not been widely noticed due to the persistence of ways of thinking that originated in traditional analyses. These analyses allowed adjustments to take time and disequilibrium decisions to be implemented, so that constant returns to scale did not cause problems to the adjustment of supply to demand. This

81. This condition makes my argument different from the one independently advanced by Currie and Steedman (1989, 1990, pp. 76–7) who argue against Lindahl that perfect foresight is impossible because with CRS or free entry the correct foresight of equilibrium prices does not ensure equilibrium production decisions. My argument (advanced in seminars before the publication of Currie and Steedman's article and book) adds, first, that replacing perfect foresight with complete markets plus the usual auctioneer does not eliminate the problem: one needs an auctioneer/co-ordinator who is actually a central planner; second, that in the absence of complete future markets not even the existence of the auctioneer/co-ordinator ensuring equilibrium in the current markets will eliminate the problem.

82. Nor can one tautologically argue, that if equilibrium is not reached then foresight was not perfect and that therefore to assume perfect foresight means to assume that an equilibrium will be reached: one would then be assuming from the very start what the analysis should aim at demonstrating. Perfect foresight is only useful if it means a capacity to forecast the future values of certain variables, which causes such a behaviour as brings about those values. With CRS or free entry such a perfect foresight is impossible. If the tautological interpretation of perfect foresight is rejected, all that remains is the possibility to argue that the same path as the one of an intertemporal equilibrium with complete futures markets, might be *sustained* by a sequential equilibrium with 'perfect foresight': in other words, that the expectation of Arrow–Debreu prices would turn out to be correct if by an extraordinary fluke firms did in fact manage to produce the correct quantities. But what is the interest of this claim, if only an extraordinary fluke could prevent the expectation of Arrow–Debreu prices from being rapidly refuted by events? Again, the fact that this Appendix does not discuss the other difficulties with perfect foresight (caused for example by the non-uniqueness of equilibrium) or with temporary equilibria (caused for example by divergent expectations) must not be taken to mean that these other difficulties are judged not serious.

adaptation of production to demand in equilibrium, in the presence of CRS industries, is such a deeply ingrained conclusion that, in their models too, neo-Walrasian theorists implicitly take it for granted, without checking to find out whether it is a plausible hypothesis given their different framework.

APPENDIX 5A4. BLISS ON SOLOW'S ONE-SECTOR GROWTH MODEL

5A4.1. This Appendix discusses one more example of incomplete understanding of the implications of the adoption of a neo-Walrasian framework. It illustrates a case of persistence of habits of thought typical of analyses internal to the traditional method of long-period positions, in an author who takes it for granted that the only legitimate notions of equilibrium are the neo-Walrasian ones.

The example is the discussion in Bliss (1975b, pp. 312–15) of the stability of the (momentary) equilibrium of Solow's one-good growth model. Bliss argues that the various adjustment mechanisms proposed for Solow's one-good model are all more or less equivalent to the following one, where F_K, F_L are the partial derivatives of $Y = F(K, L)$, r is the instantaneous interest rate or profit rate, w the wage rate,[83] K and L are the demands for capital and labour, α_1, α_2 are positive coefficients, and the dot over the symbol of a variable indicates its time derivative:

$$\dot{K} = \alpha_1 (F_K - r)$$

$$\dot{L} = \alpha_2 (F_L - w)$$

$$\dot{r} = K - K^\circ$$

$$\dot{w} = L - L^\circ.$$

The adjustment is supposed to be sufficiently fast, relative to the processes of capital accumulation and population growth, as to legitimize the hypothesis that K° and L°, the endowments at the moment of analysis, are given. At first sight (but see below) the dynamic adjustment hypotheses appear reasonable: entrepreneurs increase the demand for a factor if its marginal product is greater than its rental, and the rental of a factor increases if demand is greater than supply. I will follow Bliss in using factor *price* to mean factor *rental*.

The dynamic system is non-linear because F_K and F_L are not linear: for instance if $Y = K^\theta L^{1-\theta}$, then $F_K = \theta K^{\theta-1} L^{1-\theta}$. Since Bliss wants to show that there may not be convergence, one example is enough, and the Cobb–Douglas case supplies it. He assumes (example 13.1, p. 315) that $\alpha_1 = \alpha_2 = 1$, and that (it only requires choosing units in an appropriate way) the (rigid) supplies of capital and of labour are both equal to one; also, he assumes

---

83. Bliss prefers to formulate the equations in terms of two generic factors X_1 and X_2, but then his discussion refers to capital and labour.

θ = 1/2 and initial conditions such that $K(0) = L(0)$ and $r(0) = w(0)$. Then the system yields $K(t) = L(t)$, $r(t) = w(t)$, $F_K = F_L = 1/2$ for all subsequent t; one can therefore restrict one's attention to the sole variables (K, r), that is to the two-equations' linear system

$$\dot{K} = 1/2 - r \qquad\qquad\qquad [5A4.1]$$

$$\dot{r} = K - 1 \qquad\qquad\qquad [5A4.2]$$

which yields constant-amplitude oscillations, anti-clockwise circles around the point (1, 1/2) in the plane (K, r); see Figure 5A4.1.

Bliss has achieved – or so he believes – his aim: the economy never reaches the full-employment equilibrium. He concludes: 'it is not obvious that an account of continuous full-employment equilibrium involving prices of inputs can be given which has any explanatory value with regard to the full-employment assumption' (Bliss, 1975b, p. 315).

I will now argue that 1) Solow has no reason to worry on *this* account, and 2) Bliss falls into inconsistent reasoning.

Let us note one fact: during one half of each oscillation K (and therefore L too) is greater than its supply. This is only possible because, as Bliss puts it: 'the process is a *tâtonnement*, i.e. no capital or labour is hired at disequilibrium prices' (ibid., p. 313).

Actually (see below) it is impossible to interpret the dynamic equations proposed by Bliss as descriptive of an auctioneer-guided tâtonnement. But, before coming to this inconsistency on Bliss' part, let us note that, if ever there was a neoclassical model that was *not* meant to depict an economy with auctioneer, but rather to describe the average trends which might be observed in actual economies where disequilibria do happen, this is the one-good

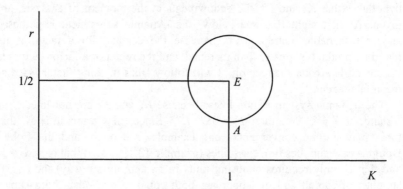

Figure 5A4.1 Oscillation in Bliss's tâtonnement for Solow's model

growth model (on this also cf. Appendix 9A). Let us then ask what kind of realistic adjustment process (that is *without* the auctioneer) the dynamic equations proposed by Bliss might be seen as formalizing. Let us then interpret equations [5A4.1]– [5A4.2] as signifying that an entrepreneur tries the harder to increase the amount of a factor he *actually employs*, the more the price of that factor is below its marginal product. Then, if the employment of the factor cannot be increased because the factor is already fully employed, an excess demand for the factor will cause its factor price to increase, but *the factor's employment cannot change*. Therefore, if, in Figure 5A4.1, one interprets K as *actual* employment of capital, then as the economy's motion reaches point A, it will go up vertically from that point along the line AE, thus tending to the full-employment equilibrium. So Bliss' difficulty is created by the shift to a neo-Walrasian framework; the traditional approach would be problem-free.

But, interestingly, the shift to a neo-Walrasian framework is incomplete. Bliss appears to find it hard to be consistent with his own assumptions: if there really were an auctioneer, then his dynamic equations would make no sense, because there would be no reason why the amounts of factors demanded should vary as indicated. The moment there were positive pure profits, factor demands should become infinite. The hypothesis of a finite velocity of adjustment of the demands for inputs can only make sense if they refer to the real world, where some time is necessary to alter the amounts *actually* employed. In an auctioneer-guided tâtonnement there is no reason why, with constant returns to scale, price-taking firms should not want to become infinitely large and/or infinitely numerous the moment prices ensure positive pure profits.

This contradictory argument by Bliss shows how difficult neo-Walrasian authors find it to accept, right to the bitter end, the disagreeable implications of the framework they have chosen.

6. Reswitching and Reverse Capital Deepening

6.1. THE VALUE OF CAPITAL DEPENDS ON DISTRIBUTION EVEN WHEN NOTHING CHANGES PHYSICALLY

6.1.1. In Chapter 5 we saw that Hayek, Lindahl and Hicks rejected the treatment of capital as a single value factor but did not reject the marginalist or neoclassical approach. This was explained as arising from their lack of any suspicion that *the entire approach* might depend on that treatment of capital. In particular, those authors continued to believe in the traditional conception of capital–labour substitution, in the form for example of an assumed capacity of the rate of interest to ensure the adaptation of the capital–labour ratio in new investments to the full-employment flow of savings. In the terminology of §1.3.3, the unease with the conception of capital as an amount of value only impinged upon the *supply-side* role of that conception, and was basically ignored in relation to its *demand-side* roles. This of course means that ultimately the traditional marginalist conception of capital was not really questioned; Hicks, who in 1963 declared his continuing faith in the possibility of conceiving capital as a single factor in some physical sense, was only the clearest representative of a general attitude.

This faith, as well as the demand-side roles of the traditional conception of capital, are radically questioned by Piero Sraffa's results on reswitching and reverse capital deepening; it is therefore appropriate to discuss them at this point of the book. The chapter starts with an explanation of these results, as a help to readers not yet acquainted with them;[1] readers who know what reswitching and reverse capital deepening stand for may go directly to Section 6.3. The chapter then goes on to assess the relevance of reswitching and reverse capital deepening, and ends with some consideration on why this relevance is still very imperfectly appreciated.

---

1. For more detailed discussions of the analytical aspects cf. Garegnani (1970), Kurz and Salvadori (1995, especially chs 3, 5), Schefold (1997, ch. 3).

6.1.2. To explain in simple terms what Sraffa (1960) was able to show, let us go back to the system of equations of §3.3.2 determining long-period prices as functions of the rate of interest

$$p = (r+d)pA(r) + w\ell(r). \qquad [3.7^*]$$

It was shown earlier that variants of this system of equations were implicit in Walras' or Wicksell's equations of general equilibrium. Sraffa, aided by his starting from a classical perspective, saw that these equations could be examined in isolation and important insights could be gained from such an examination.

System [3.7*] presupposes a variety of alternative techniques among which firms may choose on the basis of the cost-minimization principle. But an important result is achieved by concentrating at first on the given-technique case. Let us assume technical coefficients are given. Assume further that all production methods take one year and that all capital goods are circulating, that is are entirely used up in a single production cycle. Then the depreciation coefficient is $d = 1$ and we get:

$$p = (1+r)pA + w\ell \qquad [6.1]$$

Once a numeraire is chosen, by varying in the above system of equations the exogenously given value of one of the two distributive variables, r or w, one can study how the solution values of the other variables vary. Then on the basis of the results, one can study whether or not the changes conform to the predictions of marginalist/neoclassical theory. The results concern changes in the *long-period* values of variables, and therefore they are relevant for the correctness of the long-period predictions of neoclassical theory. The long-period predictions are clearly fundamental, because the long-period forces indicated by the theory are those on which one can with greater confidence base explanations and predictions, given the accidents and indeterminateness of what can happen in the short or, worse, very short period.

The equations, as written here, assume no scarce natural resources, homogeneous labour, and independence of technical coefficients from the quantities produced (constant technological returns to scale for industries).[2]

---

2. This is how the equations are to be interpreted if viewed as a subset of the system of equations of a long-period general equilibrium. Sraffa on the contrary assumes given quantities produced and makes no assumption about returns. This is because Sraffa's equations are first of all intended to recuperate the classical approach to value, and the latter approach, owing to its different structure, needs no assumption of constant returns to scale (cf. Garegnani, 1990b, 1990c). But Sraffa's equations are also compatible with the

These are obviously restrictive assumptions, but they are legitimate when the purpose is a critical one: if the theory under criticism does not stand up in this simple case, the same will be true for more complex cases.

6.1.3. A first thing Sraffa shows is that, as the rate of profits (or the real wage) is made to vary, both the normal relative prices, and the value of capital per unit of labour, have to change (the sole exception being the special case of 'equal organic composition' already noted by Marx – in which case prices are proportional to labours embodied, whatever the distribution of income). This is of course a well-known result, but it is possible to arrive at an extremely simple graphical representation (not found in Sraffa) of how the value of capital will change (in terms of whatever numeraire is chosen[3]) with changes in distribution when neither technology nor the quantities produced change. For readers not very familiar with the literature on the Cambridge controversies, it may be useful to report this graphical representation here, because it has been widely used and indeed it permits a quick grasp of many issues.

Suppose the quantities produced are given. Choose a vector of commodities y as numeraire, $py = 1$; then w indicates the purchasing power of the wage rate in terms of the bundle y. The price equations then define w and p as functions of r, and it can be demonstrated by use of the Perron–Frobenius theorems on non-negative matrices that, for viable economies,[4] the function $w(r)$ is downward sloping and its graph in the positive orthant (variously called 'w–r frontier' or '$w(r)$ curve' or 'wage curve', or also, illegitimately, 'factor price frontier'[5]) exists, and intersects both axes (see Figure 6.1) if there is at least one good, among those entering directly or indirectly into the production of the numeraire, which also enters directly or indirectly into the production of itself.[6] We assume this is the case. The $w(r)$ curve may be concave or convex or, if there are at least three commodities, it may have inflections, that is, it may alternate concave and convex sections.

interpretation adopted here, and must indeed be so interpreted for their second, critical, role vis-à-vis the marginalist approach.
3. Obviously the value of capital will not change if the chosen numeraire coincides with the given vector of capital goods employed by the economy. But this fact does not overcome the illegitimacy of taking as given the value of capital, cf. note 30 of Chapter 3.
4. That is, economies capable of a positive rate of growth if the wage rate is zero.
5. The question is whether the rate of profits or of interest *can* be seen as the price of a factor of production 'capital': calling such a curve 'factor price frontier', as most neoclassical authors do, implies that one has already answered in the positive.
6. If this condition does not hold (one has then an 'Austrian' structure of production, with all goods ultimately produced by unassisted labour), then, as the real wage tends to zero, the rate of profits rises without limit; the wage curve does not intersect the horizontal axis.

This is because it is a polynomial function, of degree equal to the number of commodities.[7]

In Figure 6.1 let W indicate the vertical intercept, corresponding to $r = 0$, and R the horizontal intercept, corresponding to $w = 0$. The vertical intercept W indicates the real wage per unit of labour in terms of the chosen numeraire, when profits (interest) are zero.

If we assume that the net product of the economy consists solely of the numeraire and is given, then W measures the net product per unit of labour. Let us make this assumption, because this is the assumption which allows us to understand the 'demand for capital' implicit in the production of a commodity or bundle of commodities as net product. Consequently, this is the assumption which allows us to understand the 'demand for capital' implicit in the persistent demand for a certain quantity of a consumption good, or in the production of a certain net product which is not quickly changing through time.

Let us further assume that the total labour employment of the economy (which is given because both technical coefficients and net products, and hence total quantities produced too, are given) is one unit: then y is also the net product vector per labour unit, and w is the total wage bill, which is also the share of wages in the value of the net product since we choose the physical net product vector as our numeraire, that is $p(r)y = 1$. Then the vertical intercept W is necessarily equal to 1, since, when $r = 0$, wages get the

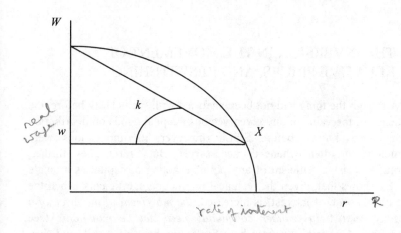

Figure 6.1   The value of capital derived from the w(r) *curve*

7. For mathematical treatments of these issues cf. for example, Kurz and Salvadori (1995). These are uncontroversial facts, so it seems unnecessary to reproduce the demonstrations here.

entire net product: $W = p(0)y = 1$. Assume that the net product goes either to wages, or to capital income, that is interests or, in classical terminology, profits. For $w < 1$, the difference $W - w = 1 - w$ measures the share of profits or interests in the net product per unit of labour; therefore for any given $r \leq R$, if we indicate with $k(r)$ the corresponding value of capital in the economy as a whole, total profits are given by $rk(r)$ and since it must be $1 = p(r)y = rk(r) + w(r)$, the following relation must be true:

$$k(r) = \frac{(1-w)}{r}$$

so $k(r)$ is the trigonometrical tangent of the angle wXW, that is the absolute value of the slope of the straight line XW connecting the vertical intercept W with the point X on the $w(r)$ curve corresponding to the given r.

By varying the rate of profit and studying how the angle wXW changes, one obtains how the value of the given vector of capital goods changes in terms of the net product, when neither quantities produced nor technology change. It is immediately obvious that k will remain constant only if the $w(r)$ curve is a straight line, what has been shown to be the case for arbitrary numeraires only if relative prices do not change with distribution: the pure labour-theory-of-value case.[8] Thus the dependence of the value of capital on distribution, even when physically the capital vector remains unchanged, can be grasped visually, and with it the untenability of a given endowment K^* of value capital.

6.2.   THE INVERSION IN THE MOVEMENT OF RELATIVE PRICES, AND RESWITCHING

6.2.1. Although the thing had not been analysed with such clarity before, the dependence of the value of any given vector of capital goods on distribution was of course known before Sraffa (however, its implications were conveniently forgotten whenever necessary!). But Sraffa goes further, supplying a decisive criticism of any possible notion of capital as a single factor. He shows that, given the technical production coefficients, when the rate of profits (rate of interest) is increased, *the movement of the price of a commodity relative to another commodity need not be monotonic* (see Figure 6.2). Let us first illustrate how Sraffa reaches this result, and then comment on its importance.

8.   When the pure labour theory of value does not hold, the $w(r)$ curve will be a straight line only if the net product consists of the Standard Commodity (see below), in which case the numeraire (the net product) has the same composition as the capital stock.

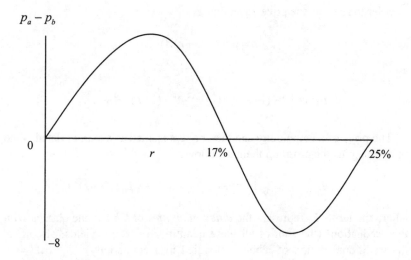

Source: Sraffa (1960, p. 38).

Figure 6.2   Sraffa's example of movement of the difference between two prices as r varies

Sraffa first shows that the price of a commodity can be obtained by 'reduction to dated quantities of wages', that is as the sum of an infinite series of terms, representing the wages paid, to direct labour, to the direct labour necessary to produce the means of production, to the direct labour necessary to produce the means of production of the means of production, and so on, each term multiplied, respectively, by $(1+r)$, by $(1+r)^2$, by $(1+r)^3$ and so on.[9] Formally, this is equivalent to utilizing the property (derivable from the Perron–Frobenius theorems on non-negative matrices) that, as long as the rate of profit r is less than the maximum rate of profits R, the following holds:[10]

$$\left(I-(1+r)A\right)^{-1} = I+(1+r)A+(1+r)^2 A^2 +(1+r)^3 A^3 +...$$

9. The procedure has already been illustrated in §3A.1.4.
10. For a non-negative real matrix A, one of the results of the Perron–Frobenius theorems is that the inverse of $I - \rho A$ exists and is non-negative and equal to $I + \rho A + \rho^2 A^2 + \rho^3 A^3 + ...$ if and only if the real scalar ρ^{-1} is greater than λ^*, the dominant eigenvalue of A, which is also a positive real number (less than 1 if the economy is viable that is capable of a positive growth rate if the real wage is zero). The maximum rate of profits R, that is the one associated with a zero wage, is equal to $(1/\lambda^*) - 1$, that is $1/(1+R) = \lambda^*$. Therefore as long as $\rho = (1+r) < (1+R)$, it is $[I - (1+r)A] - 1 = I + (1+r)A + (1+r)^2 A^2 + (1+r)^3 A^3 + ...$.

in order to re-write the price equations

$$p = w\ell(I - (1+r)A)^{-1}$$

as

$$p = w\ell\left[I + (1+r)A + (1+r)^2 A^2 + (1+r)^3 A^3 + ...\right].$$

The price of a commodity can then be represented as a sum of dated wage payments plus the profit on them as follows:

$$p_i = wL_{i(0)} + wL_{i(-1)}(1+r) + wL_{i(-2)}(1+r)^2 + wL_{i(-3)}(1+r)^3 + ...$$

where the terms L_{it} represent the *dated quantities of labour* one obtains with this 'reduction' (the sum of all these quantities of labour yields, of course, the traditional notion of labour embodied in a commodity): $L_{i(0)} = \ell I = \ell$; $L_{i(-1)} = \ell A$; $L_{i(-2)} = \ell A^2$, and so on.

Sraffa then considers the case of two commodities whose 'reduction to dated quantities of labour' generates identical dated labour terms except for three.

> One of them, 'a', has an excess of 20 units of labour applied 8 years before, whereas the excess of the other, 'b', consists of 19 units employed in the current year and 1 unit bestowed 25 year earlier. (They are thus not unlike the familiar instances, respectively, of the wine aged in the cellar and of the old oak made into a chest.) (Sraffa, 1960, p. 37)

This means that the difference between their prices is given by the equation

$$p_a - p_b = 20w(1+r)^8 - [19w + w(1+r)^{25}].$$

The two commodities 'a' and 'b' have the same price for $r = 0$, for $r = 17$ per cent and for $r = 25$ per cent, which is the value of the rate of profits at which the wage rate is assumed by Sraffa to be zero; commodity 'a' rises in price relative to 'b' as the rate of profits rises from 0 to $r = 9$ per cent, then falls between 9 per cent and 22 per cent, and then rises again from 22 per cent to 25 per cent. Sraffa's graphical representation of the difference $p_a - p_b$ as a function of r is reproduced in Figure 6.2. (The precise shape and height of the curve is obtained by taking as numeraire the composite commodity Sraffa calls the Standard Commodity,[11] but this is irrelevant to the

---

11. The Standard Commodity (that is the composite commodity of such composition that, if produced as net product, requires for its production a stock of capital goods of exactly the

increasing or decreasing shape of the curve, which would remain the same with any numeraire.)

Sraffa comments: 'The reversals in the direction of the movement of relative prices, in the face of unchanged methods of production, cannot be reconciled with *any* notion of capital as a measurable quantity independent of distribution and prices' (Sraffa, 1960, p. 38). Let us make sure we understand why. Let us consider the marginalist analysis of an economy without capital: let us assume that production only uses homogeneous labour and homogeneous land, and that there are two goods, say corn and meat, produced by fixed-coefficient technologies; and let corn production employ labour in a higher proportion relative to land than meat production. The unambiguous measurability, independent of distribution, of the factor proportions of the different production processes implies a monotonic relationship between the price (equal to cost of production) of corn relative to that of meat, and income distribution. The relative price of corn to meat will be a monotonically increasing function of the wage/rent ratio, because wages are a greater proportion of costs in the production of corn than in the production of meat. This is a fundamental result for marginalist theory, because it is the foundation of the mechanism of 'indirect' factor substitution through which consumer choice helps establish (apart from 'perverse' cases due to 'malfunctioning' of income effects) the existence of decreasing demand curves for factors of production: if the composition of consumption demand shifts in favour of the consumption good which becomes cheaper, then a rise in the wage/rent ratio unambiguously decreases the labour/land proportion in factor demand.[12]

The same measurability, independent of distribution, of factor proportions is also the basis of the mechanism of direct, or technical, factor substitution. Suppose that two fixed-coefficient methods are known for producing corn, with the second method employing less labour, and more land per unit of corn than the first. Then as the wage/rent ratio rises, the cost of production of corn with the first method will monotonically rise relative to the cost of production with the second method, and the tendency in technical choices will unambiguously be toward the adoption of less labour-intensive methods;

---

same composition) relative to a production technique described by the matrix of technical coefficients (A, ℓ) is given by the right eigenvector of A, that is by the solution of the eigenvalue problem $(1 + g)Ay = y$; the labour coefficients are irrelevant except possibly for the choice of the unit in which to measure the Standard Commodity (Sraffa chooses as his unit the amount of Standard Commodity whose production employs the same total labour employment as the economy under study). If the economy's industries are in the proportions which maximize the rate of growth when wages are zero and the product is entirely re-invested, then the product consists of Standard Commodity.

12. See Section 2.2.

hence again, a rise in the wage/rent ratio will unambiguously decrease the labour/land proportion in factor demand.

We see then that the monotonic correlation between changes in distribution, and changes in the relative price of consumption goods, or changes in the relative cost of production of the same good with different production methods, is the foundation of the factor substitution mechanisms upon which the entire marginalist approach to distribution is built.

The same monotonicity still holds if, in place of land, one has corn-capital, and the distribution of income is between wages and interest (or profits, in classical terminology).

But if we imagine corn and meat to be produced by labour and *heterogeneous* capital goods, then Sraffa's result means that we might observe that, as the real wage increases and the rate of profits (rate of interest) decreases, the (long-period) relative price of corn to meat first increases and then decreases. If we wanted to see corn and meat as produced by labour and 'capital', we would be obliged to conclude that corn is more labour-intensive than meat for certain values of the rate of profits, but more capital-intensive for other values, in spite of the fact that no production process has changed. Thus no measure independent of distribution of the 'capital' intensity of production methods exists, which might allow 'capital' to be seen as a factor of production analogous to labour or land, that is such that, when the price of its services increases, the goods produced by relatively capital-intensive methods become dearer.

6.2.2. In the last chapter of his book, Sraffa (1960, pp. 81–4) applies this result to argue that technical choices too may go counter to what neoclassical theory presumes. What was just said about two different commodities 'a' and 'b' may in fact be re-interpreted as referring to two different alternative production methods to produce the *same* commodity; the prices of the two commodities 'a' and 'b' will then be re-interpreted as the two different costs of production of the single commodity, according to which method of production, 'a' or 'b', is adopted; the cheaper price will then indicate which one of the two methods of production is cheaper and therefore tendentially imposed by competition.[13] The possible reversals in the direction of the

---

13. If the commodity's price enters, directly or indirectly, into the cost of production of all other commodities produced in the economy, then in order to be able to compare the two costs of production of the commodity with the two methods, one must choose one of the two production methods for the commodity as 'basic', that is, as the basis for prices, and calculate at those prices the cost of production of the commodity with the other method. It has been demonstrated that choosing one or the other method as 'basic' makes no difference as to which method is cheaper and therefore is tendentially imposed by competition. The reason why the comparison is described as between production *methods* rather than between

movement of the two relative prices mean now that, independently of distribution, it is impossible to establish which of the two alternative production methods for the same commodity is more capital-intensive.

One consequence is that in general the values at which in Figure 6.2 the $p_a - p_b$ line crosses the horizontal axis may be many, implying that it may happen that one production method is more convenient for more than one interval of values of the rate of profits, while the other is more convenient in between.

For instance, in the example of Figure 6.2 it would suffice to assume that the production coefficients, and therefore the dated quantities of labour, of commodity 'a' were all uniformly smaller by a common sufficiently small percentage, and the curve $p_a - p_b$ would be shifted downward a little,[14] such that it would cross the horizontal axis twice, a new intersection appearing now at a level of r close to zero; see Figure 6.3.

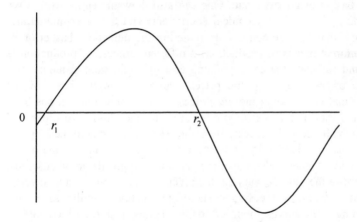

Figure 6.3 Sraffa's example modified to yield reswitching

production *processes* is because often a different production process (in one industry) requires the use of different specific capital goods, which would not be produced at all were that process not adopted: the adoption of that process then implies a change in more than one process in the economy, often a change in the number of capital goods produced and hence in the number of industries. A production *method* of a good is a *set* of production processes, one for the good in question and one for each of the other commodities directly or indirectly used as inputs of the good in question. The term *technique* is also used as synonymous with *method* in the above sense.

14. Sraffa's example can be interpreted as applying to two non-basic commodities (that is commodities which do not enter into the production of all other commodities), neither of which uses the other one as an input, and whose prices are determined relative to the common Standard Commodity (which only includes the basic commodities). Then a small reduction of the production coefficients of commodity 'a' means a small reduction of its cost of production p_a at all rates of profit; hence the downward shift of the curve $p_a - p_b$.

If we indicate these two levels as r_1 and r_2, we would find that as the rate of profits rose from 0 to r_1 method 'a' would be the more convenient; as r passed r_1, it would become convenient to switch to method 'b'; but as r passed r_2, it would become convenient to switch back to method 'a'. This is the so-called '*reswitching of techniques*'.

6.2.3. The same finding can also be presented in terms of $w(r)$ curves. As a preliminary, I remind the reader that it has been demonstrated[15] that when alternative production methods are available, long-period cost minimization implies that the economy will settle on the outer, or North-East, envelope of the $w(r)$ curves corresponding to all possible production methods of the numeraire. To make this result clearer, assume that, at a given rate of profits (interest), a given set of processes with the associated technical coefficients is adopted. Certain prices and a certain real wage rate (in terms of the chosen numeraire basket of goods) result. One can also draw the entire $w(r)$ curve corresponding to the given technical coefficients and the given numeraire. Assume now that for one commodity (entering the numeraire basket or its direct or indirect means of production) a different process of production is known,[16] and calculate the corresponding cost of production, at the already determined prices (that is at the prices determined on the basis of the technology matrix including the *old* process, not the new one). It has been demonstrated that, if the cost of production with the alternative process is lower than with the old process, then the $w(r)$ curve, determined by the technology matrix obtained by replacing the old process with the alternative one, will yield a higher real wage at the given rate of profits, in other words, it will be above the old $w(r)$ curve at the given rate of profits, and vice versa. On the other hand, if the two costs of production are the same, the corresponding $w(r)$ curves intersect (or are tangent) at the given rate of profits. Thus, if at the old prices an alternative process is less costly and is adopted, then at the new technology and prices the real wage rate is higher, and the old discarded process is confirmed to be more costly (there is therefore no switching back and forth from the old to the new method of production and back).

This result means that, if interpreted as referring to production costs of the same commodity with alternative production processes, Figure 6.3 has a corresponding graphical representation in terms of intersections of $w(r)$ curves (when the numeraire or its direct or indirect means of production include the commodity in question). Thus, let us suppose that the commodity

---

15. For a recent exposition cf. Kurz and Salvadori (1995, ch. 5).
16. For simplicity, I am assuming here that the alternative process does not require capital goods not contemplated in the old matrix; so its adoption only alters one column of the technology matrix.

is itself the numeraire, and 'a' and 'b' are two alternative methods to produce it. To them there will correspond two $w(r)$ curves, $w_a(r)$ and $w_b(r)$, and when for a certain level r' method 'a' is cheaper,[17] this will show in the wage curve diagram as $w_a(r') > w_b(r')$, that is in a neighborhood of r' the 'a' wage curve will be above the 'b' wage curve, and vice versa. So, when there are many alternative productive methods available for one or more commodities, in order to know which set of production processes will be finally imposed in the long period by the tendency to cost minimization it is sufficient to draw the $w(r)$ curves corresponding to all possible feasible combinations of known processes, one for each commodity. For each given rate of profits, the technology matrix (or, for brevity, the *technique*) associated with the outer envelope of the $w(r)$ curves, that is the one yielding the highest w for that value of r, will be the one the economy will tend to adopt.[18]

In other words, if two $w(r)$ curves derive from techniques differing for only one process, then for any r the outer curve indicates that at that r the corresponding process is the cheaper of the two; if we call 'a' and 'b' the two processes, if the outer curve in the wage curves diagram is curve 'a' then in the graphical representation of Figure 6.3 this corresponds to a negative value of $p_a - p_b$. Figure 6.3 might correspond therefore to Figure 6.4.

In Figure 6.4 we see the so-called *'reswitching of techniques'* in terms of wage curves. The name derives from the use of the term 'switch' to indicate

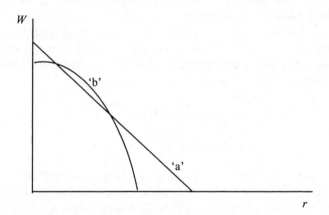

Figure 6.4 Reswitching of techniques in terms of w(r) *curves*

17. Remember that it is indifferent whether, in order to decide which method is cheaper, one chooses the wage rate and prices associated with method 'a' or with method 'b'.
18. For expository reasons, I have left aside the complications connected with the possibility that different processes use different specific capital goods, complications which do not invalidate the theorem but render its exposition more involved.

a change in technique due to a change in income distribution. In Figure 6.4 the economy will tend to adopt technique 'a' for $0 < r < r_1$, but it will 'switch' to technique 'b' if r increases beyond r_1, only to 'switch back', or 'reswitch', to technique 'a' as r, increasing still more, goes beyond r_2. The possibility of reswitching of techniques confirms that it is not possible to order production methods according to relative 'capital' intensity independently of distribution, in such a way that an increase in the rate of interest always causes an increased relative convenience of less capital-intensive methods. Thus, if, in neoclassical terms, one were to accept that, as the rate of interest increases, the switch in methods of production cannot but be toward less capital-intensive methods, one would have to conclude that the more capital-intensive method is 'b' at r_1 and 'a' at r_2.

6.2.4. Many numerical examples of reswitching have been produced. Sraffa's example is not one of them, but, as noted above, with a small modification it would become one. A mistaken attempt at refutation of the possibility of reswitching for indecomposable technology matrices by Levhari (1965) prompted a number of such examples in a Symposium in 1966 in the *Quarterly Journal of Economics*, where the possibility of reswitching was admitted by all sides to the controversy. One of these examples, by Samuelson (1966), is worth reporting for its simplicity.

Suppose that champagne can be produced by either of two methods. Method 'a' requires, per unit of product, the payment of 7 wages two periods before the sale of the product; method 'b' requires the payment of 2 wages three periods before, and of 6 wages one period before the product is sold. Therefore the price of champagne produced, respectively, with method 'a' and with method 'b' is given by

$$p_a = 7w(1+r)^2$$

$$p_b = 2w(1+r)^3 + 6w(1+r).$$

The reader can check that $p_a = p_b$ for $r = 50$ per cent and for $r = 100$ per cent, and that $p_b < p_a$ for $0.5 < r < 1$, while $p_a < p_b$ for $0 < r < 0.5$ and for $r > 1$. Thus as r increases from zero, initially the most convenient method is 'a', at $r = 0.5$ there is a switch to 'b', and at $r = 1$ there is a reswitch to 'a'.

6.2.5. Perhaps the simplest examples of reswitching are those obtainable for an economy where a single consumption good can be produced with a variety of different methods (or techniques), in each of which the consumption good is produced by labour and a different circulating capital good, and the capital good is produced by itself and labour.[19] The production processes last one year. There are constant returns to scale; α_i, β_i are the technical coefficients, respectively, of capital good of type i and of direct labour in the production of the consumption good according to technique i; a_i, b_i are the technical coefficients respectively of the capital good and of direct labour in the production of capital good of type i. For simplicity each capital good will be measured here in such units that its production needs one unit of direct labour, so $b_i = 1$, for all i. The coefficient a_i must be < 1 for the economy to be viable. The consumption good is the numeraire. Wages are paid at the end of the production period. The price-of-production equations for any technique i are, with w the rate of wages in terms of the consumption good and p_i the price of the capital good i:

$$1 = \alpha_i p_i (1 + r) + \beta w \qquad [6.2]$$

$$p_i = a_i p_i (1 + r) + w. \qquad [6.3]$$

These equations establish a functional dependence of w on r:

$$w = \frac{1 - (1+r)a_i}{\beta_i + b(1+r)(\alpha_i - a_i \beta_i)} \qquad [6.4]$$

such that, as long as $a_i > 0$ and direct or indirect labour is necessary to produce one unit of net product (assumed to consist of the sole consumption good), this function crosses the non-negative orthant with negative slope and positive intercepts on both axes, determined by:

$$R_i = \frac{1 - a_i}{a_i} \qquad [6.5]$$

$$W_i = \frac{1 - a_i}{\beta_i + (\alpha_i - a_i \beta_i)}, \qquad [6.6]$$

The $w(r)$ *curve* is the portion in the non-negative orthant of the function $w(r)$ defined by [6.4]. It can be shown that it is concave relative to the abscissa if $a_i > \alpha_i / \beta_i$, convex if $a_i < \alpha_i / \beta_i$, a straight line if $a_i = \alpha_i / \beta_i$.[20] If R

19. In such a hypothetical economy, the transition from one technique to the other would require the use of transitional technologies, capable of producing a capital good without already having it available for use as input, but no longer convenient the moment the capital good is available for use as input. The complications raised by this fact will not be discussed here. Anyway the analysis is only intended to highlight possibilities also existing in more realistic and complex economies. The model has been proposed by Samuelson (1962), discussed by Hicks (1965), and thoroughly examined by Garegnani (1970).

20. The relevant inequality is actually between a_i/b_i and α_i/β_i, but we have assumed $b_i = 1$.

and W are assigned but technical coefficients are not, then the $w(r)$ curve is not yet fully determined because the equations are two, [6.5]–[6.6], while the technical coefficients are three; therefore by varying for example α/β the curve can be chosen concave or convex. This means that one can easily build numerical examples where the $w(r)$ curve can be made convex or concave without altering the intercepts; therefore it is easy to produce numerical examples where two $w(r)$ curves i and j cross twice, by for example choosing a concave i curve and a convex or straight j curve such that their intercepts on the axes differ but little and $W_i < W_j$ and $R_i < R_j$. One can also build more complicated examples, with more than two alternative techniques, and some of the switches between techniques being below the outer envelope: for example in Figure 6.5 there are three techniques, with all couples of techniques yielding reswitching, but only three switch points on the outer envelope, two of them representing reswitching.

By the way, these several examples show that reswitching is *not* an extreme possibility requiring very peculiar and implausible characteristics of the alternative technical methods. It is simply a possibility that was never suspected owing to the illegitimate extension, to a factor measured as an amount of value, of properties only valid if all factors are measured in 'technical' units.

Two wage curves corresponding to alternative techniques may cross more than twice, if there are several capital goods. It has in fact been demonstrated that two wage curves may cross in the positive orthant up to as many times as there are distinct industries directly or indirectly producing the numeraire.[21]

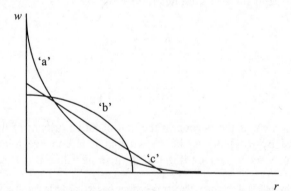

Figure 6.5   Multiple reswitching

21. Thus in the economy of this paragraph two wage curves may cross at most twice. But if one of the two techniques employs two capital goods (both specific to the technique) and has therefore three industries, then its wage curve, being a third-degree polynomial, may have inflections and then the wage curves might cross three times.

6.3. THE RELEVANCE OF RESWITCHING

6.3.1. Reswitching shows that there is no way of attributing a capital intensity (independent of distribution) to production methods, such that as the rate of interest decreases, the more capital-intensive methods become relatively more convenient.

Reswitching undermines therefore both the 'direct' and the 'indirect' factor substitution mechanism (cf. §§1.2.3, 1.2.4), and thus the foundation itself of the supply-and-demand approach to distribution.

Let us consider the 'direct' substitution mechanism. Consider the case illustrated in §6.2.2. Suppose some criterion is assigned for deciding (independently of distribution) which of the two methods 'a' and 'b' is more capital-intensive:[22] whichever the criterion, in one of the two 'switches' the change in technique will imply the adoption of the *more* capital-intensive method when the rate of interest *increases*. For example, if it is technique 'b' which is considered to be more capital-intensive, it will be the switch at r_1 that is associated with a direct relationship, instead of an inverse one, between change in distribution and change in capital intensity.

Let us now consider the 'indirect' substitution mechanism by considering the case illustrated in §6.2.1, assuming that corn and meat are both consumption goods. Suppose again that some criterion is assigned for deciding (independently of distribution) which consumption good is more capital-intensive. Suppose further that, when a consumption good becomes relatively cheaper, the composition of consumption shifts in its favour. Then, whichever the more capital-intensive good, there will be one or more ranges of values of the rate of interest, where an increase of the rate of interest makes the more capital-intensive good relatively cheaper, implying a shift of the composition of consumption in the direction of an increase, rather than a decrease, of the average capital-intensity of the demand for consumption goods.

Thus, if 'capital' is measured in units independent of distribution, there is no guarantee that changes in the rate of interest will always cause changes in the opposite direction in the amount of 'capital' per unit of labour employed by the economy.

Note that the above conclusion was reached independently of any income effect;[23] it is the *substitution* principle between 'capital' and labour that is

---

22. One such criterion might be the average period of production as traditionally defined, cf. Appendix 3A.

23. Indeed, in the case of the 'indirect' substitution mechanism, the assumption was that the composition of consumption would change in favour of the consumption good which became relatively cheaper; thus 'perversities' arising from income effects were explicitly excluded.

questioned, that is that principle which, differently from income effects, was thought to work unambiguously in support of the supply-and-demand approach to distribution, by always causing the composition of the demand for factors to shift in favour of a factor whose relative rental decreased.

6.3.2. The above considerations show the impossibility of a definition of capital intensity, and therefore of a measurement of the 'quantity of capital' employed by a production method, independent of distribution, and at the same time capable of salvaging traditional beliefs about substitution between 'capital' and labour. But it was shown in the preceding three chapters that 'capital', the single factor of variable 'form', was always conceived and had to be conceived as a quantity of value: therefore attention must also be paid to the behaviour of the demand for 'capital' measured as an amount of value (that is, as pointed out in §3.3.4, measured in terms of some composite consumption good capable of measuring savings, or the utility from which consumers abstain when they save). This is because it might be thought, precisely because a value measurement is not independent of distribution, that perhaps the substitution mechanisms work 'correctly' for value capital, so that the demand for value 'capital' (if one excludes 'perverse' income effects) might turn out to be a decreasing function of the rate of interest after all.

Now, even if this turned out to be the case, an immediate counter-objection would be that a long-period equilibrium would still be indeterminable, given the illegitimacy of a given endowment of value capital (cf. Section 3.4).

However, the current widespread acceptance of short-period or very-short-period analyses makes it worthwhile to discuss also the demand for value 'capital'. In fact, Section 4.3 indicated that the decreasing shape attributed to the demand for value 'capital' was the foundation of the marginalist belief in the capacity of the rate of interest to bring investment into equality with full-employment savings. And in Section 5.4, it was argued that one important explanation for the continuing faith in the marginalist approach, in spite of the admitted inconsistencies of a value endowment of 'capital', was (and is) precisely the continuing belief in a negative elasticity of investment vis-à-vis the rate of interest, which induced economists to think that analyses based on sequences of short-period equilibria would not yield results that differed very much from traditional analyses based on the gravitation toward long-period equilibria. If, to the already very grave problems of these short-period analyses highlighted in Chapter 2, one were to add the fundamental undermining of the above belief concerning investment and the rate of interest, then there would appear to be no remaining reason to continue to accept the supply-and-demand approach to value, distribution and employment.

In the remainder of this section, the question is discussed whether or not a negative elasticity of aggregate investment vis-à-vis the rate of interest can be derived from the demand for value 'capital' along the lines illustrated in Section 4.3. The next chapter will discuss other more recent derivations.

6.3.3. The graphical technique illustrated in §6.1.3 can be used to study how the value of capital per unit of labour varies with income distribution, when there are alternative techniques. Once again the result contradicts traditional neoclassical beliefs. As shown in Figures 6.6 and 6.7, the switches of technique may well be associated with what has been called *reverse capital deepening* or *capital reversal*, that is a positive, instead of negative, correlation between rate of interest and long-period value of capital per labour unit.

All we have to do is utilize the graphical device of Figure 6.1 for the case with many alternative techniques and therefore many wage curves in the same diagram. For each value of the rate of interest, the value of capital will be determined, in the way indicated in §6.1.3, by the $w(r)$ curve which at that rate of interest corresponds to the cost-minimizing technique, that is the one on the outer envelope of the wage curves. As the rate of interest changes, one finds at a switch point that the value of capital per unit of labour k jumps from the value associated with one curve to the value associated with the other curve. Thus when the rate of interest *increases*, a switch of techniques at a certain rate of interest will be associated with a *decrease* in k if the technique which becomes dominant has a *lower* vertical intercept than the

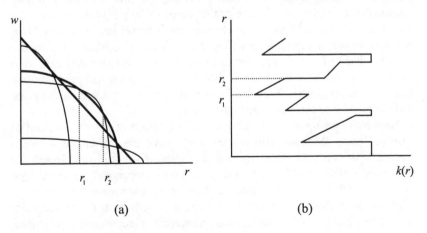

(a)   (b)

Figure 6.6 How the value of capital may change with distribution

abandoned technique, but it will be associated with an *increase* in k if the technique which becomes dominant has a *higher* vertical intercept. This second case, which goes against neoclassical traditional beliefs, will happen if the two wage curves had already crossed (once, or an odd number of times) at lower values of the rate of interest, and we have seen that this is definitely possible. For example, Figure 6.6(b) illustrates (in stylized fashion) the $k(r)$ curve corresponding to five alternative techniques generating the wage curves of Figure 6.6(a): following tradition, in Figure 6.6(b) the 'price' r is on the vertical axis while the dependent variable $k(r)$ is on the horizontal axis. There are seven switches on the outer envelope, and as r increases from zero, the second, fifth and sixth switches cause k to increase as r increases, owing to reswitching. The horizontal segments of $k(r)$ correspond to switch points (that is to values of r at which two techniques are equi-profitable), and are due to the fact that at those values of r the two techniques can be employed side by side and then, depending on which proportion of the net product is produced with either technique, k can take any value in between the values determined by each technique. The vertical or upward-sloping sections correspond to ranges of values of r where the technique is not changing, and they are upward-sloping when the corresponding wage curve is concave. (The jumps in the value of k due to a switch of techniques are sometimes called '*real Wicksell effects*', and the changes in the value of k, due to changes in distribution with a given technique, '*price Wicksell effects*'.) Note how little the $k(r)$ curve corresponds to traditional neoclassical ideas.

The possible concavity of wage curves means, by the way, that the $k(r)$ curve may have very non-neoclassical shapes even in the absence of any reswitching among wage curves (on, or below, the outer envelope). It may happen that as r increases, although the jumps of $k(r)$ at switch points (the 'real Wicksell effects') are all downward, the increase in the value of k in between switch points (the positive 'price Wicksell effects') due to the concave shape of some wage curves more than compensates the downward jumps at the switch points. There is then a resulting upward-sloping saw-like shape of the $k(r)$ curve (Figure 6.7), which again is incompatible with the traditional view of capital–labour substitution.

How little, owing to the possible combined effects of reswitching and of positive 'price Wicksell effects', the $k(r)$ curve may resemble a 'well-behaved' demand function for value capital has been confirmed by Garegnani (1970, pp. 431–5) by using the two-sector model presented here in §6.2.5 and by assuming that an infinity of alternative techniques is available, such that as distribution changes, the coefficients of the dominant technique change continuously, thus generating a continuous $k(r)$ curve.

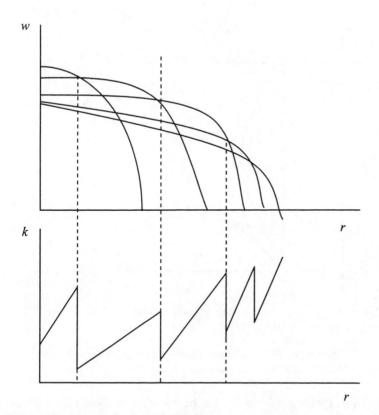

Figure 6.7 How the value of capital may change with distribution, in the absence of reswitching, owing to price Wicksell effects

Garegnani has proven that for such a model any continuous $k(r)$ function which starts at point Q and stays within the shaded area STQ0 of Figure 6.8 is possible. The $k(r)$ function might for example be constant (i.e. vertical), or increasing all the way up to the maximum r (assumed by Garegnani to equal 20 per cent), or serpent-like with numerous inflections.

It is then clear that analogous shapes might be exhibited by the long-period investment function defined in §4.3.2; we have reached what is perhaps the most important critical implication of Sraffa's results: *the behaviour of the long-period capital–labour ratio as a function of the rate of interest provides no foundation for the belief in a negative elasticity of aggregate investment vis-à-vis the rate of interest.*[24]

24. Cf. Appendix 6A4 for a comment on some attempts to minimize the relevance of reswitching and reverse capital deepening.

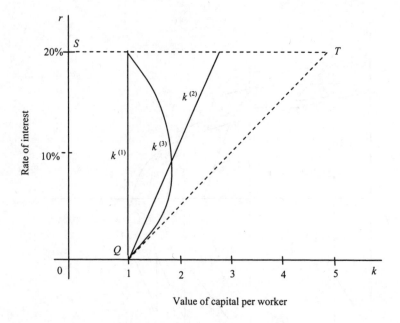

Figure 6.8 Garegnani's example: any function k(r) *that starts at point* Q *and stays within the* 0QTS *area is possible*

The next two chapters will expand on the relevance of these results for the analysis of aggregate investment, and of the labour market; but some implications can be grasped immediately, at least intuitively. The thesis, that the rate of interest is the price that brings about equilibrium on the savings-investment market, loses its supposed foundation in the neoclassical factor substitution mechanisms. Unless other foundations can be found for a negatively elastic investment schedule (and Chapter 7 will argue that no other foundation is within sight), it becomes extremely difficult to believe that investment tends to adjust to savings. Then the thesis of a tendency of the economy toward the full employment of resources loses its plausibility. The existence of unutilized resources, in particular, of labour unemployment, must be admitted as normal. One is then obliged to reconsider the functioning of the labour market and to admit the presence in it of forces capable of preventing an indefinite fall in wages whenever there is unemployment (a fall that not only does not correspond to anything observable, but, being generally unable to come to a quick end, would cause such disruptions as to render the economy incapable of functioning). These forces, ultimately responsible for the determination of income distribution, will have to be seen, not as somehow impeding the free working of competition, but rather as necessary components of its working, which, without those forces, would not be capable of determining income distribution. The adaptability of production to demand, made possible by the existence of unutilized resources, also undermines any necessary dependence of income distribution on the level of employment, so that the notion of a well-defined full-employment level of the real wage must also be abandoned. (These themes are developed in Chapter 9.)

These implications show how misguided is one frequent attitude vis-à-vis the non-uniqueness of neo-Walrasian equilibria demonstrated by the famous Sonnenschein–Mantel–Debreu results: namely, that what is needed is a theory of equilibrium selection. This attitude is based on the presumption that the economy tends to *some* neo-Walrasian equilibrium. But neo-Walrasian equilibria are full-employment equilibria. We see now that there cannot be any presumption that the economy tends toward the full utilization of resources. The implication is not that the forces of supply and demand as described by the marginalist approach exist but may result in a number of different outcomes; the implication is rather that the forces determining distribution must be other ones, capable of determining distribution independently of any assumption of full employment.

6.4.   WHY SO MANY AND SO PERSISTENT MISUNDERSTANDINGS?

6.4.1. The present section tries to explain why a large part of the profession has so far been unable to appreciate the implications of reswitching and reverse capital deepening. Three reasons will be suggested: (i) the confused state of capital theory at the time the Cambridge controversy started; (ii) the deficiencies, in the first two decades of debate, of the critical arguments themselves; (iii) the neoclassical ignorance of the more recent critical contributions on capital theory.

When Joan Robinson (1953–54) started the Cambridge controversies in capital theory, the universal practice in applications[25] was still to treat capital as a single factor, measured as an amount of value. However, as explained in Chapter 5, in the pure theory of value the reference was more and more to neo-Walrasian models, that is models without capital (whose interpretability as intertemporal equilibria was barely starting to be suggested). Also,

_____

25. Except of course in short-period analyses.

although these versions were still far from having won the field,[26] the prevalent (and unfounded) opinion was that completely disaggregated models would simply confirm the theses reached on the basis of models where capital was treated like a single factor; the analytical role of the conception of capital as a single factor of variable 'form' was rapidly slipping away from the consciousness of economists.

The confusions surrounding capital theory at the time could not but leave their marks also on the minds of most of the critics of the neoclassical conception of capital. Unfortunately the deficiencies of the critical arguments allowed many important misunderstandings to crystallize and perpetuate for many years, in particular:

- the belief that the Cambridge criticism only impinged upon the legitimacy of aggregate production functions;
- the consequent belief that neo-Walrasian general equilibrium theory was not affected by the criticism;
- the belief that, since general equilibrium theory survived the criticism, then the neoclassical approach to distribution, employment and growth did so too.

6.4.2. An important responsibility for the persistence of misunderstandings must be assigned to Joan Robinson. She was a central figure in the so-called Cambridge controversy in the theory of capital because she was a highly respected economist, owing to her book on imperfect competition; because of her repeated and caustic interventions; and because her 1953–54 article 'The production function and the theory of capital' had started the controversy.[27] Unfortunately that article was far from clear on the real issues at stake.

The article commences very provocatively, in a brilliant and vivacious style, with the correct accusation that when using an aggregate production function $O = f(L, C)$ (where O is output, and C capital), the neoclassical

---

26. It was noted in §5.4.3, fn. 34, that the 1963 treatise on general equilibrium by Kuenne still preferred to discuss capital within a stationary context, that is treating the composition of capital as endogenously determined. Earlier, Metzler (1950, p. 302) had expressed strong reservations on the treatment of the initial endowments of capital goods as so many different factors each earning a rent just like land. As late as 1970 Bent Hansen was still including in his *Survey of General Equilibrium Systems* a Wicksellian model of disaggregated long-period general equilibrium where the endowment of capital is measured as a given amount of value and its composition is endogenous (cf. Hansen, 1970, ch. 17).

27. Joan Robinson was later to admit (Robinson, 1970) that she had based that article on clues derived from conversations with Piero Sraffa and from his 'Introduction' to Ricardo's *Principles* (Sraffa, 1951). The controversy up to the end of the 1960s is surveyed by Harcourt (1972).

economist never makes it clear 'in what units C is measured' (Robinson 1953–54, p. 81). But the implications for the neoclassical approach, drawn from this observation, are not the ones that the reader of this book might have expected. Nowhere does Joan Robinson conclude that the neoclassical approach cannot determine income distribution because the economy's endowment of capital conceived as a single factor, necessarily an amount of value, cannot be determined before values – and hence income distribution – are determined.[28] Indeed a careful reading of the complete article shows that the criticism is not aimed at questioning the notion of a capital–labour ratio measurable independently of distribution and positively influenced by the real wage (that notion is in fact *accepted* in the remainder of the article). Robinson's aim is rather to argue that capital can be precisely measured only in a state of *realized expectations*, because outside such a state the value of capital goods depends on expectations of, among other things, future earnings and hence future aggregate demand. Therefore, Joan Robinson argues, the production function has been 'a powerful instrument of miseducation' (ibid.) because it has helped people forget the Keynesian arguments on the importance of uncertainty and expectations for the determination of the level of aggregate demand and of the pace of accumulation.[29] The main aim of the article, in other words, is a Keynesian

28. A statement like the following suggests, to the contrary, that, were it not for the occurrence of unexpected events, there would be little problem with the measurement of the capital stock: 'Equilibrium requires that the rate of profit ruling today was expected to be ruling today when investment in any plant now extant was made, and the expectation of future profits obtaining today was expected to obtain today. Thus the value of capital in existence today is equal to its supply price calculated in this manner. The heavy weight which this method of valuing capital puts upon the assumption of equilibrium emphasizes the impossibility of valuing capital in an uncertain world. In a world where unexpected events occur which alter values, the points of view of the man of deeds, making investment decisions about the future, and of the man of words making observations about the past, are irreconcilable, and all we can do is botch up some conventional method of measuring capital that will satisfy neither of them' (Robinson 1953–54, p. 96). Notice how in these lines no emphasis is laid on the fact that even when the value of capital is equal to its supply price, it still depends on distribution and therefore cannot be a datum of the determination of equilibrium.

29. Cf., for example, 'When an unexpected event occurs, the three ways of evaluating the stock of goods part company and no amount of juggling with units will bring them together again' (1953–54, p. 84); 'To discuss accumulation we must look through the eyes of the man of deeds, taking decisions about the future, while to account for what has been accumulated we must look back over the accidents of past history. The two points of view meet only in the who's who of goods in existence to-day, which is never in an equilibrium relationship with the situation that obtains to-day' (p. 100). Thus the main problem with the measurement of capital is found, not in the vicious circle of its value depending on what the equilibrium should determine, but rather in the difficulty of the measurement of the value of a capital stock of not 'fully adapted' composition. A quantity of capital independent of distribution,

denial that accumulation is determined by decisions to save, a denial based above all on the role of uncertainty; but on the *effects* of accumulation there is little in the analysis with which a Pigou or a Solow might have disagreed:

> The production function, it seems, has a very limited relevance to actual problems, and after all these labours we can add little to the platitudes with which we began: in country Gamma, where the road builders use wooden shovels, if more capital had been accumulated in the past, relatively to labour available for employment, the level of real wages would probably have been higher and the technique of production more mechanised, and, given the amount of capital accumulated, the more mechanised the technique of production, the smaller the amount of employment would have been (Robinson, 1953–54, p. 100).[30]

A neoclassical economist might have been excused for concluding that Joan Robinson was not questioning the existence of the neoclassical factor substitution mechanisms, and was only questioning their simplified representation through an aggregate production function. As for Robinson's questioning – on the basis of Keynesian arguments, above all the pervasive presence of uncertainty – the ability of those substitution mechanisms to bring about a full-employment equilibrium, it could be argued that the issue was a separate one, concerning the solidity of the 'neoclassical synthesis' argument against Keynes.

In subsequent years Joan Robinson was increasingly able to abandon neoclassical factor-substitution notions, but she developed a very defective view of the logic of the theory she had absorbed when young, a view which perpetuated the misleading concentration on aggregate production functions as the target of criticism. In her article 'Capital theory up to date' (1970) the object of the criticism, called neo-neoclassical theory, is explicitly identified with the single-good, aggregate-production-function versions, furthermore caricatured as assuming that capital is a physically homogeneous substance and as assuming instantaneous costless adjustments. This article is replete

and determining a decreasing demand curve for labour and a single real wage compatible with the full employment of labour, appears on pp. 96–98; on p. 99 a fall of the rate of interest 'encourage[s] the use of more mechanised techniques' and 'accumulation may be conceived to push down the rate of profit, and raise the factor ratio'. Thus the production function is criticized, essentially, because by hiding the imperfect adaptation of the composition of capital to changes, it induces people to forget that 'the comparison between equilibrium positions with different factor ratios cannot be used to analyse changes in the factor ratios taking place through time, and it is impossible to discuss changes (as opposed to differences) in neo-classical terms' (p. 100).

30. Notice in particular the last three lines of this quotation, where the given 'amount of capital accumulated' is admitted to be compatible with more or less 'mechanised' production techniques, that is to say, the conception of capital as a single quantity of variable 'form' is fully accepted.

with misunderstandings of the differences between the various versions of the marginalist approach: the aggregate-production-function approach, instead of being described as a simplified application of the conception of capital as a single factor of variable 'form', is seen as 'derived from Walras' (p. 311). No recognition is given to the existence of a distinct marginalist approach to distribution, because the sole approaches to distribution that are recognized to have existed are the classical one (given real wages), the Marxian one (class struggle), and the Marshallian one, in which 'there is a normal rate of profit and the real wage emerges as a residual' but this normal rate of profit remains unexplained until 'an extension of Keynes's *General Theory* into the long period finds a clue to the level of profits in the rate of accumulation and the excess of consumption out of profits over saving out of wages' (p. 315). Walras is liquidated with the apodictic statement that he 'does not have a theory of profits at all' (ibid.). Later even Wicksell is accused of having no theory of distribution: 'Marshall's normal profits and Wicksell's natural rate of interest were supposed to apply to a capitalist economy but their level was never explained' (Robinson, 1974, p. 209). So, as her comment (Robinson, 1971) to F.M. Fisher (1969) also makes clear, the aggregate-production-function versions *were* the neoclassical theory of distribution, according to Joan Robinson.[31]

6.4.3. Thus, in Joan Robinson's contributions to the Cambridge controversy one would search in vain for a clarification of the true analytical roles of the

31. For a more detailed criticism of Joan Robinson's views on the deficiencies of the neoclassical approach, including the question (cf. the last quotation in footnote 29) whether this approach can analyse changes by means of comparisons, cf. Garegnani (1976, pp. 42–4; 1979b; 1979c, pp. 121–43; 1989). Here we limit ourselves to noting that for many years Joan Robinson was unable completely to abandon the belief in the existence of the marginalist factor substitution forces whose action, if given sufficient time and unimpeded by wage rigidities, were argued by the 'neoclassical synthesis' to be able to push the economy toward full employment. This made her identify long-period positions with the *marginalist* characterization of those positions, so that the denial of a tendency toward full employment became for her synonymous with a denial of a tendency toward long-period positions. In order to reach such a denial and salvage Keynes's conclusions (that appeared to her to be clearly confirmed by the empirical evidence), she was then brought to stress uncertainty, expectations, 'animal spirits' and continuous change, and finally to reject comparative statics and the method of long-period positions in general, without distinguishing between neoclassical and non-neoclassical applications of that method. On that basis she even argued 'The unimportance of reswitching' (1975). Similar views are found in other Post-Keynesian economists, for example Shackle, cf. Mongiovi (2000). The argument of this book implies, on the contrary, that acceptance of the method of long-period positions (that is, essentially, of the tendency of the market prices of produced goods to gravitate toward long-period prices) does not in the least imply acceptance of the marginalist forces supposedly pushing the economy toward full employment.

conception of capital as ultimately a single factor in the marginalist approach. (As the reader might recall from Chapter 1, these roles were, first, to make it possible to treat the total capital endowment as a datum of the equilibrium while leaving the endowments of the several capital goods to be determined endogenously, thus permitting the formulation of a notion of equilibrium compatible with time-consuming disequilibrium adjustments; second, to allow for a sufficient elasticity of the demand for labour by allowing capital to adapt its 'form' to the amount of labour to be employed; and third, to permit one to speak of capital–labour substitution in the same terms as for physically measurable factors, thus supplying a basis for Say's Law by making it possible to consider the interest rate as the price bringing investment into equality with savings.) Unfortunately this deficiency was not made good in the other writings of the critics published in English up to the mid-seventies.[32] Garegnani had clarified the first role in his 1958 Cambridge Ph.D. thesis, which was then published in Italian in 1960, but the results of that thesis were only published in English, in a condensed version, in 1990. Garegnani had also clarified the third role, but again in Italian, in a 1964–65 article which was translated into English only in 1978–79. (The earlier availability of Garegnani's analyses in Italian contributes to explaining the greater impact of the Cambridge criticism in Italy.) But even Garegnani started clarifying the differences between long-period and neo-Walrasian versions only in 1976. His 1970 article 'Heterogeneous capital, the production function and the theory of distribution' was followed by a comment by Christopher Bliss where equilibrium was identified with the Arrow–Debreu notion: Garegnani only replied very briefly that his analysis was aimed at the long-period versions – a reply which could not but fall on deaf ears, given what was by then a general inability among neoclassical economists to appreciate what a long-period marginalist analysis meant.

Indeed, by then the dominant position among neoclassical theorists had become the view that neo-Walrasian equilibria were the only true representatives of 'rigorous' marginalist/neoclassical capital theory.[33] The

32. The distinction between the long-period and the neo-Walrasian treatment of the composition of capital in disaggregated general equilibrium analyses is for example absent in Harcourt's widely cited surveys of the Cambridge controversy (Harcourt, 1972), and it is still absent in the more recent book on capital theory (favourable to the critical side) by Ahmad (1991) and in the very recent survey by Cohen and Harcourt (2003).
33. Section 4 of Chapter 5 and the Appendices to that chapter have documented the growing inability of neoclassical economists to appreciate the shift undergone by the theory of general equilibrium. The diffusion of the position expressed by Bliss outside the circle of the general equilibrium specialists is shown by Harry G. Johnson, essentially a macroeconomist, whose contributions were generally based on the treatment of capital as a single good homogeneous with output: 'The value of capital is not necessarily a relevant concept for analysis, and resort to it can be avoided by constructing appropriately disaggregated models'

discovery of reswitching and reverse capital deepening no doubt had an important stimulating role in this development, as admitted, for example, by Christopher Dougherty: 'Since then [the mid-1960s] the general equilibrium model has been the undisputed core of neoclassical capital theory' (Dougherty, 1980, p. 3).[34] But an important permissive role must also be attributed to the absence for many years of interventions re-establishing an understanding of long-period equilibria and of the central importance, for the marginalist approach, of the long-period substitution mechanisms based on capital the homogeneous factor. The road was thus open for F.M. Fisher, Hahn, Stiglitz or Bliss to recognize only two types of equilibrium notions, the neo-Walrasian ones, and steady states (mistaken for long-period equilibria).[35] Now, both are notions in which (differently from traditional long-period equilibria) a 'quantity of capital' does not explicitly appear in the specification of the equilibrium; on this basis, they could argue that 'aggregate capital' was only used by neoclassical theorists in the 'unrigorous' analyses based on aggregate production functions, and accordingly – and with the support of Joan Robinson's writings – these economists interpreted the Cambridge criticism as directed solely at the legitimacy of aggregate production functions, and could thus conclude that the criticisms left 'rigorous' GE theory unscathed: a thesis accepted also by some of the critics, for example Nuti (1976). So Fisher (1971) was able to reply to Joan Robinson that neoclassical equilibrium theory did not need the existence of aggregate production functions.[36]

6.4.4. The exclusive identification of disaggregated equilibria with neo-Walrasian equilibria is indeed one of the main current obstacles to communication. It is worth-while to illustrate how it engendered grave misunderstandings on the issue of capital aggregation.

Let us consider for example the views on capital aggregation expressed by Hahn (1982a). Hahn writes:

(Johnson, 1973, p. 123). Numerous other examples might be quoted. Appendix 6A2 is dedicated to a detailed discussion of one representative paper, Stiglitz (1974).

34. Thus the Cambridge controversies have had, if nothing else, the role of forcing neoclassical value theory to adopt the neo-Walrasian versions as its sole rigorous foundation, favouring a more general consciousness of the implausibility of these versions.

35. The confusion of long-period positions with steady states also frequently appeared in critical writings, for example in Robinson (1953–54, p. 88), Harris (1973, p. 100). Garegnani (1989) discusses at length this confusion in Joan Robinson.

36. In spite of Garegnani's clear dismissal of the versions of neoclassical theory based on aggregate production functions as being of only secondary importance (Garegnani, 1970), Hahn too (1982a, p. 370) identified Joan Robinson's views with 'The Sraffian picture of neoclassical theory'.

In general, there does not exist a function from the vector of endowments to the scalars such that knowledge of the scalar (and of preferences and of technology) is sufficient to allow one to determine a neoclassical equilibrium. If you put it the other way round, it is even more obvious. In general, the neoclassical equilibrium can be found given the vector of endowment[s] which may have, say, 10^8 components. It would be surprising if there were a single number which gives the same information as the 10^8 dimensional vector. In fact, sometimes and in very special cases, this surprising property holds. But neoclassical economists have shown these special cases to be without interest (p. 369).

Hahn here clearly means by 'neoclassical equilibrium' an equilibrium with *given* endowments of the several capital goods ('the neoclassical equilibrium can be found given the vector of endowment[s]'), so the aggregation he is looking for can only exist if a single scalar can *replace*[37] the full vector of *given* capital goods endowments in the equilibrium's data, and yet determine the *same* equilibrium.

It is important to note that the equilibrium Hahn has in mind is defined independently of whether such an aggregation is possible; which also makes it legitimate to be content, for certain purposes, with approximate aggregation only.[38]

This is a very different problem from the one arising in the formulation of long-period equilibria. In these, the endowments of the several capital goods are not *replaced* by the given quantity of 'capital', but co-exist with the latter, being variables to be determined endogenously on the basis of the latter and of the URRSP condition.[39] The theoretical determinability of the

37. Cf. also Bliss (1975a, p. 147), who makes it clear that his study of the problem of aggregation tries to elucidate 'what is involved in replacing a heterogeneous collection of inputs by an aggregate'.

38. Thus Hahn can write: 'we use simple models (e.g. macroeconomics) to gain insights of a certain kind. Simplification is never without cost and the cost is sometimes loss of rigour. It remains to be shown that the cost is too high in this instance, i.e. that in actual problem application the chance of large mistakes is great' (p. 370). If what is at issue is on the contrary the basic theory itself, then the problem changes radically. The question is further discussed in Appendix 9A.

39. Hahn (1982a) appears to overlook the fact that, in his own model of a wheat-and-barley economy, if the endowments of wheat and barley are both treated as variables and the model is 'closed' by the uniform-profit-rate assumption plus a given amount of value capital C, the scalar C does not *replace* the vector of endowments of wheat and barley, it only makes it possible to determine them endogenously. Some misunderstanding of traditional marginalist capital theory also appears to surface when Hahn adds: 'After all, there have been many attempts to find a scalar representation of the endowment vector, for example the period of production' (Hahn, 1982a, p. 369). But as explained in Appendix 3A, the period of production was not a scalar representation of the capital *endowment*, it was a scalar representation of the average capital *intensity* of production processes, necessary to determine the *demand* for 'capital'; the given supply (the endowment) of 'capital' was measured by Böhm-Bawerk and Wicksell as an amount of value.

'quantity of capital' is not simply a convenient simplifying device, it is *essential* to the theory of long-period equilibria: without it, one would find it impossible to determine the equilibrium and the whole theory would crumble away. Which is, of course, exactly what it does do.

The inability to get out of neo-Walrasian equilibrium conceptions also explains the frequent view that there is nothing special about the problem of capital aggregation. The problem of capital aggregation is seen as just one instance of the general problem of aggregating some inputs into an 'aggregate input index' in the formulation of the *production function* of a product. The basic result here is that Leontief's so-called weak separability condition (the rates of substitution between the factors one wishes to aggregate must be independent of the quantities employed of the other factors) is necessary and sufficient for the representability of a production function

$$y = f(x_1, ..., x_n, x_{n+1}, ..., x_{n+m})$$

in the form:

$$y = F(\psi(x_1, ..., x_n), x_{n+1}, ..., x_{n+m})$$

that is to be able technically to aggregate a number of production factors into a single 'factor' in a production function. In this case it is as if an intermediate good $k = \psi(x_1, ..., x_n)$ were produced by the factors $x_1, ..., x_n$ and then it were used together with the remaining factors to produce the final product. Solow, who first introduced this Leontief aggregation condition into the Cambridge controversy, used it to answer the question: 'When if ever can the various capital inputs be summed up in a single index-figure, so that the production function can be "collapsed" to give output as a function of inputs of labor and "capital-in-general"?' (Solow, 1955–56, p. 102). But it is clear from the formal statement of the problem that there is no reason why $x_1, ..., x_n$ should be (services of) capital goods; they might stand for amounts of services of any factors measured in physical (technical) units. The problem might as well be posed, for example, in relation to heterogeneous labour, or heterogeneous land. This is why Bliss (1975a), having accepted Solow's framework, concludes that there is:

> no support whatsoever for the idea that the aggregation of capital is relatively difficult. The conditions for general capital aggregation are identical to the conditions for the aggregation of labour, or of output. We may thus conclude that the widespread belief that there is a notable, particular and distinct problem posed

by capital aggregation is at best an ill-formulated idea, and at worst is based simply on ignorance (Bliss, 1975a, p. 162).[40]

What Bliss does not understand here is that 'capital aggregation' poses a 'particular and distinct problem' to the marginalist approach because of this theory's need to determine (i) a sufficiently persistent equilibrium, (ii) sufficiently elastic demand curves for factors, and (iii) a decreasing demand curve for the flow of savings. The endowments of each type of labour (or of land) pose no theoretical need for aggregation, because each one of them can be taken as given, since they can be assumed with some plausibility to change only very slowly relative to the presumable speed of the processes tending to establish equilibrium on their respective markets. The same cannot be assumed for the endowments of the several capital goods, which change with a speed comparable with the speed of change of the flows of products. Hence, the moment one admits, as of course one must, that adjustments are far from instantaneous, it is inconsistent to treat as endogenously determined by the equilibrium only the flows of goods produced, and not also the endowments of capital goods. But if one treats the endowments of each capital good as variables then without an endowment of 'aggregate capital' the equilibrium is indeterminable. Coming to point (ii), it has been illustrated in Chapter 2 that the treatment of capital as a factor of variable 'form' is necessary in order to obtain a sufficient elasticity of the demands for factors.[41] Finally, the conception of capital/labour substitution as functioning as though capital were a physically homogeneous factor in spite of its being a quantity of value is indispensable for the downward-sloping aggregate investment function and for the downward-sloping labour demand curve (this will be confirmed in Chapters 7 and 8). Therefore the 'particular and distinct

40. The 'conditions for general capital aggregation', which Bliss is here referring to, include the Leontief separability conditions for each industry, and furthermore the condition that the function $\psi(x_1, ..., x_n)$ be exactly the same in all industries. So it must be as if the same intermediate good k were produced in all firms by factors $1, ..., n$ (and according to the same production function), to be then employed together with factors $n + 1, ..., n + m$ to produce the several goods. It is then easy to realize that the economy is formally equivalent to an economy where there is only a single marketed capital good, k, which is produced by itself and by factors $n + 1, ..., n + m$ while the factors $1, ..., n$ are only temporary (and non-marketed) intermediate stages in the production process of k. Then reswitching is impossible (it requires heterogeneous capital); and a given scalar endowment of capital is implicit in any given vector of endowments of capital goods, because the latter vector corresponds (if one assumes the full and efficient utilization of these endowments) to a certain endowment of k. But, as Bliss and Hahn admit, the case is so utterly special as to be 'without interest'.
41. Necessary no doubt, but not always sufficient. Certain types of specialized labour are strictly tied to an industry and even to a production method. That the wages of these types of labour generally do not wildly oscillate confirms the role of forces other than the tendency toward equilibrium between supply and demand in the determination of wages.

problem posed by capital aggregation' is not that such aggregation is 'relatively difficult' but simply that it is *indispensable* to the logical consistency and plausibility of the theory.

6.4.5. Another aspect, on which for many years the criticism was gravely deficient, was the explanation of the importance of 'capital', the value factor, for the plausibility of the tendency toward full employment. For example, no one criticized at the time an important misreading of the implications of reverse capital deepening in Samuelson's widely read 'Summing-Up' which concluded the 1966 *Quarterly Journal of Economics'* Symposium on reswitching. In that article Samuelson conceded that reswitching and reverse capital deepening were perfectly possible, yet the only negative consequence he admitted was a danger of 'dynamic instability', by which he meant a danger that sequences of full-employment short-period equilibria may not converge to a unique steady state. He did not admit that the neoclassical foundations of Say's Law were undermined and that as a consequence the full-employment assumption itself became indefensible. Thus he wrote that, due to the possibility of reverse capital deepening, 'after sacrificing present consumption and accumulating capital goods, the new steady-state equilibrium can represent a rise in interest rate!' (Samuelson, 1966, p. 246). Here Samuelson clearly takes for granted that the only way to accumulate capital goods is by 'sacrificing present consumption', that is the full employment of resources is taken for granted.[42] He also leaves it unclear how, in the presence of reverse capital deepening, the accumulation of capital goods corresponding to a decision to sacrifice present consumption would come into being, since in this case an excess of savings over investment would require an *increase* of the interest rate in order to stimulate an increase in investment, while the market's tendency according to supply-and-demand analysis would rather be to *depress* the rate of interest.

On this issue too, the misunderstandings have crystallized. Thus in a recent paper Edwin Burmeister argues that neoclassical theory is not endangered by reswitching, because 'the *fundamental* neoclassical proposition' is 'that there exists a negatively sloped, concave trade-off between consumption today and consumption tomorrow' (Burmeister, 2000, p. 310, author's italics). An immediate objection is that this trade-off only exists under an assumption of full employment of all resources, hence perhaps the arguments supporting the full employment assumption are more fundamental still for neoclassical economics? But, strikingly, Burmeister finds it unnecessary to mention the need for the full-employment assumption,

---

42. This assumption is again implicitly taken for granted in Samuelson (1976, cf. in particular pp. 20–21 and fn. 7) and in Burmeister (1991; 2000, p. 310).

238   *General equilibrium, capital and macroeconomics*

as if it could be taken for granted and were not on the contrary one of the targets of the Cambridge criticism.

6.4.6. The arguments necessary to surmount these confusions started becoming available in English only with Garegnani (1976). This article was quickly followed by a number of other papers and books among which there were Petri (1978, 1991, 1998a, 1999), Garegnani (1978, 1979a, 1989, 1990a, 2000), Eatwell (1979, 1982), Milgate (1979, 1982), Eatwell and Milgate (1983), Schefold (1985, 1997, 2000), Kurz (1987). This wave of contributions finally started to clarify the difference between long-period and neo-Walrasian versions of the marginalist/neoclassical approach, as well as the different roles of the conception of capital as a single factor.

The neoclassical reaction was a poignant silence: no reply at all. Some of the neoclassical assessments of the Cambridge controversies (for example Blaug, 1974, Stiglitz, 1974, Bliss, 1975b) came out before this second critical wave, but others did not (for example Dougherty, 1980; Burmeister, 1980, 1991, Hahn, 1982a), and yet these contributions contain *no* reference to any of the post-1975 critical writings just mentioned. Whatever the reasons for this surprising refusal to confront the new arguments of the critics, the fact is that up to now (end 2002) none of the post-1975 critical writings listed above is mentioned in any of the writings of Hahn, Solow, Samuelson, F.M. Fisher or Burmeister, even when they return to the themes of the Cambridge controversy. No wonder that considerable misunderstandings persist – and it is these misunderstandings that have prompted me to write this book.

APPENDIX 6A1. RESWITCHING AND THE AVERAGE PERIOD OF PRODUCTION

6A1.1. What is the relevance of reswitching for the 'demand side' role of the average-period-of-production approach?

In the hypotheses necessary to determine the average period of production (only one primary factor; only circulating capital; simple interest), we can be certain that the 'roundaboutness' of techniques is a decreasing function of the rate of interest (cf. §3A.1.5). The decreasing shape of the demand for 'capital' in this case derives from the fact that there is no ambiguity in the ordering of different production techniques according to capital intensity (the latter being measured by *T*), and one can be certain that, as *r* increases, the goods produced by techniques with a lower *T* become relatively cheaper. The inversion of the movement of relative prices, whose possibility was shown by Sraffa and which lies behind reswitching and reverse capital deepening, cannot happen under these hypotheses. But we know that reswitching and reverse capital deepening *can* happen: that they cannot happen in the present case is a consequence of the restrictive hypotheses made; thus the results, reached with this approach under the listed assumptions, do not generalize and therefore do not give a correct insight into the nature of capital.

Here only some illustration will be given of the consequences of abandoning the hypothesis of simple interest. If we still want the average period of production to indicate the average wage 'advancement' which, if applied to all direct and indirect wages, would result in the same cost of production, then with compound interest the price *p* of a good must be representable through the average period of production as (still assuming yearly production cycles)

$$p = wh(1 + r)^T.$$

Then it is no longer possible (except in extremely special cases) to determine *T* – assuming the technical coefficients are given – independently of *r*; by replacing *p* with its expression in terms of dated quantities of labour, one obtains

$$wh(1 + r)^T = \Sigma_k[(1 + r)^k wL_{-k}]$$

a complex equation from which generally it is not possible to eliminate *r*.

The same impossibility of determining *T* independently of *r* would hold if one continued to write $p = wh + rwhT = wh(1 + rT)$ while admitting compound interest: this would yield $wh(1 + rT) = \Sigma_k[(1 + r)^k wL_{-k}]$ which also does not allow one to eliminate *r*.

It follows that, as r varies, T varies even when technical coefficients do not, and as a consequence one can no longer be certain that the ratio between the costs of production associated with two different products (or production techniques) is a monotonic function of r. This is why reswitching can happen.

APPENDIX 6A2. STIGLITZ ON THE CAMBRIDGE CONTROVERSIES

6A2.1. In 1974 Joseph Stiglitz published in the *Journal of Political Economy* a review article on Harcourt's (1972) survey of the Cambridge controversy, which is representative of the nature and extent of the misunderstandings on the neoclassical side.

The article's first section deals with what has been called the 'Cambridge theory of distribution' of Kaldor, Pasinetti and Joan Robinson. In its simplest version, this distribution theory holds that in the long run, if net savings only come from capitalists and are a given fraction s_c of profits P while wages are entirely consumed, and if capacity is utilized at the normal rate, then the rate of interest (or of profits, if the risk difference between the two is neglected) r must satisfy the condition (where I is net investment and P is profits or interest):

$$g = \frac{I}{K} = \frac{S}{K} = \frac{s_c P}{K} = s_c r.$$

The approach of Kaldor and Joan Robinson was to interpret this equation as signifying that the growth rate determines r, that is that income distribution is determined by the need for just the S/K ratio required by the growth rate; the latter being determined by animal spirits according to Joan Robinson (we shall not enter here into a discussion of the vaguer and shifting explanations of the primacy accorded to the growth rate by Kaldor). Pasinetti (1962) showed that the result also holds if workers save, as long as their savings propensity is smaller than the saving propensity of capitalists and one concentrates on steady growth. If workers save a portion s_w out of their income which consists both of total wages W and of the rate of interest on the part K_w they own out of the total capital stock, and if $s_w \neq s_c$, then in steady growth, in order for savings to grow at a constant rate, the share of capital owned by each class must be constant. Thus the savings of capitalists $S_c = s_c P_c$ must grow at the same rate as total savings and therefore at rate g, hence

$$g = \frac{S_c}{K_c} = \frac{s_c P_c}{K_c} = s_c r.$$

Stiglitz interprets the Cambridge theory as applying to an economy in 'long-run equilibrium' (p. 894)[43] with the rate of growth equal to the rate of

---

43. In this Appendix, unless otherwise indicated, the page references refer to Stiglitz (1974).

growth of the labour supply. (He does not say so explicitly but he uses for the rate of growth the symbol n, universally used in growth theory in those years to refer to the rate of growth of labour supply; furthermore, as will be pointed out below, he takes it for granted that growth is determined by the investment of full-employment savings, and this implies that the steady-state growth rate can only be equal to the growth rate of the labour supply.) Thus he identifies 'long-run equilibrium' with steady or, as he prefers to call it, balanced growth. The true notion of long-period equilibrium does not appear in the article. We see here one example of the widespread inability to distinguish the notion of long-period equilibrium from that of steady or balanced growth, mentioned in §5.4.6.

What is striking in this part of the article is Stiglitz's inability to admit that other authors may not be accepting the neoclassical approach to distribution and growth. By incorrectly imputing to the Cambridge (UK) theorists the marginalist pre-Keynesian views they were intent on rejecting, Stiglitz can argue that their claim, that the rate of profit (in balanced growth) is *determined* by the rate of growth, rests on a purely formal meaning of 'determined'. This is because, according to Stiglitz $g = n$ (the growth rate of the labour supply) which is given, and s_c is also given, then in the Cambridge equation the sole unknown is r; hence Stiglitz makes the following claim about the Cambridge (UK) position:

> there is a confusion between 'causation' in a temporal sense and 'causation' in the formal analysis of the structure of a set of equilibrium conditions. It is only in the temporal sense that causation has any economic significance. At any moment, there is a given vector of capital goods and of labor. Under the extremely simplified models conventionally used, these endowments determine the marginal productivity of the different capital goods and the rate of interest. Given the savings behavior, this determines the change in the stocks of capital goods; eventually the economy converges to a state where the rate of interest is equal to the rate of growth divided by the savings propensity; still, at each moment, it is the 'capital goods–labor ratios' which determine the rates of return on the different capital goods (Stiglitz, 1974, pp. 894–5).

Stiglitz here takes it for granted that growth is determined by the investment of full-employment savings, and that distribution is determined even in the very short period by relative factor scarcities, as if Joan Robinson had not been explicit that her version denied the full employment of labour even in the long run, and Kaldor had not denied it at least for the short run.[44] Be that

---

44. Stiglitz should have limited himself to arguing that the Cambridge equation is by itself no *refutation* of the marginalist theory of distribution because the latter, under the Cambridge savings hypotheses, also implies the Cambridge equation in balanced growth. At least Pasinetti (cf. 1974, p. 144) interpreted the Cambridge equation in a way open to this kind of objection.

as it may, we find here the same unquestioned acceptance as in Samuelson (1966) and Burmeister (2000) of Say's Law and of the full-employment assumption (cf. §6.4.5).

6A2.2. In the second section Stiglitz discusses reswitching. He interprets it as applying to comparisons among economies in balanced growth. 'All that this implies', he writes, is that:

> the weak qualitative assumptions we conventionally make in economics – that is, convexity of the technology, with its implications of diminishing returns – do not have any strong implications for comparisons of economies in steady states ... The conventional economic assumptions do enable us to make qualitative statements like 'a decrease of a unit in the level of consumption today, c^0, will allow an increase in consumption tomorrow, c^1, of $\partial c^1 / \partial c^0$, keeping consumption at all other dates constant; the one-period consumption rate of interest is equal to $\partial c^1 / \partial c^0$ and decreases (more accurately, does not increase) with successive increases in consumption today (Stiglitz, 1974, p. 896).

The second part of this quotation shows Stiglitz taking it for granted that the economy is at full employment, with prices determined by an intertemporal equilibrium. Since according to him the theory yields fully determinate results already in the very short period, he can argue:

> Steady states are of limited interest in themselves; even the best of well-run economies never have a choice of steady states. They have a choice of consumption paths beginning with present initial conditions; conventional assumptions do allow us to make qualitative statements about such paths (p. 896).

> ... reswitching has no implications for the validity of neoclassical distribution theory or for qualitative statements concerning the consequences of a given economy's increasing its level of consumption (p. 897).

But he has *not* demonstrated the correctness of these assertions; he has simply assumed their correctness as his starting point, because he has taken for granted 'the validity of neoclassical distribution theory' even in the very short run.

6A2.3. But why does Stiglitz not feel that 'the validity of neoclassical distribution theory' is endangered by reswitching? Because, as he argues in the third section of his article, where he discusses the criticism aimed at 'the existence of an aggregate capital stock':

... like the reswitching phenomena, this is now recognized to be a red herring – and for very much the same reasons. Neoclassical distribution theory nowhere requires the use of aggregates ... (Stiglitz, 1974, p. 898).

... the basic qualitative properties of economies out of steady state do not in any way depend on the ability to form aggregates (p. 899).

Stiglitz's wording suggests that he interprets the need for aggregation in the same way as Hahn (1982a). But the main points that it is now important to note are:

i.   the accord between Stiglitz, and Bliss or Hahn, as to the fact that 'neoclassical distribution theory' actually means the neo-Walrasian versions of that theory;

ii.   Stiglitz's bold certainty that 'neoclassical distribution theory' describes correctly the behaviour of actual economies,[45] without apparently feeling any need to confront the doubts expressed from inside the neoclassical camp itself,[46] or the insistence of the Keynesians on the empirical relevance of involuntary unemployment;

iii.   the absence of any recognition of the analytical roles of the conception of capital as a homogeneous factor in the marginalist approach. No mention appears of a possible relevance of reverse capital deepening for the processes supposedly bringing investment into equality with savings. Stiglitz (p. 899) mentions Wicksell but does not discuss why Wicksell, in spite of his rigour, is unable to abandon the treatment of capital as a single factor, an amount of value. Clearly Stiglitz is not conscious of the long-period character of Wicksell's general equilibrium.

What one may concede to Stiglitz is that Harcourt's book was not clear on these issues. Stiglitz is correct when noting that Harcourt's book contains no reference at all to the neo-Walrasian intertemporal versions of general equilibrium theory. But at the same time Stiglitz shows his ignorance of the

---

45. Thus Stiglitz also anticipates Hahn (1982a) (cf. §6.4.4, fn. 37) on the issue of the legitimacy of aggregative models: 'I believe that, under most circumstances and for most problems, the errors introduced as a consequence of aggregation of the kind involved in standard macroanalysis are not too important' (p. 899).

46. Hicks, Kuenne, B. Hansen and Koopmans have been mentioned earlier in this connection as either indicating problems with the neo-Walrasian versions (Hicks even rejected the temporary equilibrium method he had earlier advocated, cf. §2.2.1, fn. 19, and Petri, 1991), or refusing to adopt the neo-Walrasian versions. Stiglitz himself has subsequently become the main representative of the so-called New Keynesian school which opposes many standard neoclassical tenets.

history of economic analysis and of the logic of his own approach, by, without discussion, identifying those neo-Walrasian versions with 'neoclassical capital theory' *tout court.*[47]

This article confirms therefore that around the mid-1970s the neoclassical reply to the Cambridge criticism was based on the identification of neoclassical theory with the intertemporal neo-Walrasian versions. It was blind to the analytical roles of the notion of capital as a single factor in the development of the suppy-and-demand approach; it was unable to distinguish long-period equilibria from steady states; and it was characterized by a scientifically unwarranted presentation of the neo-Walrasian approach as the sole conceivable and no doubt correct theory of the working of market economies.

47. The absence in Harcourt's book, and in all critical contributions up to that book, of any discussion of intertemporal neo-Walrasian equilibria is used by Stiglitz to argue that 'This book, as well as the writings of the other Cambridge economists, makes perfectly clear that they do not understand neoclassical capital theory' (p. 901). The history of neoclassical capital theory is cancelled in favour of the illegitimate identification of 'neoclassical capital theory' with the by then still fairly new proposal to treat capital via an intertemporal re-interpretation of the atemporal model, a proposal whose general acceptance was no doubt greatly aided precisely by the Cambridge criticisms (cf. §6.4.1). It is possible that a majority of the Cambridge, UK, critics were at the time underestimating the spread of those recent neo-Walrasian developments; but their economic intuition was on the right track in acknowledging in those developments little scientific value, as we can better see now that the impossibility of deriving support for the neoclassical approach from the neo-Walrasian versions (an impossibility that will be confirmed in Chapters 7 and 8) is clearer.

APPENDIX 6A3. THE NON-SUBSTITUTION THEOREM

6A3.1. On the basis of what we have seen about long-period technical choice, it is possible to dispel some confusions surrounding an often-quoted result that has been named the non-substitution theorem.

This result was first reached in the course of an examination of the properties of the so-called open Leontief model with choice of techniques (Samuelson, 1951; Koopmans, 1951a; Arrow, 1951). The latter model is not always fully understood, so a brief reminder may be opportune. Suppose that in a certain economy in a given time interval n different goods are produced by single-product industries which utilize as inputs (some of) those same goods (as *circulating* capital goods – that is inputs which disappear in a single utilization) and homogeneous labour. Suppose that in each industry a single method of production is utilized, characterized by technical coefficients which can be represented, for the whole economy, by an $(n + 1) \times n$ matrix

$$\left\{ \begin{matrix} A \\ \ell \end{matrix} \right\}$$

or a couple (A, ℓ) where the $n \times n$ matrix $A = \{a_{ij}\}$ is the matrix of technical coefficients of good i in the production of product j, and the row vector ℓ is the vector of labour input coefficients. Each column represents the inputs per unit of output of the corresponding industry. It follows that if in a year quantities x (a column n-vector) are produced, then the inputs of goods which have been used up for those productions are given by Ax; so $y = x - Ax$ is the definition of the physical net product vector in that time interval according to the usual accounting conventions.

Note that it is not generally the case that the quantities Ax of inputs have to be all there at the beginning of the year in order for the production of x to be possible; a year may be longer than the length required by the production processes, so the production of x may be achieved through a number of production cycles within the year. For example, if all production processes take one month, it is possible that x is produced by 12 identical production cycles, in each one of which only $1/12$ of x is produced. In this case, if $Ax < x$, at the beginning of the year the economy needs only $1/12$ of Ax as stocks of goods inherited from the previous year in order to produce x over the year. If the production processes take a very short time, the stocks of goods needed at the beginning of the year in order to produce x during the year may be very small relative to x. But since production takes time, unless one assumes that no good is directly or indirectly necessary to produce itself, there *must* be not only labour but also some goods available as inputs at the beginning of the year in order for production to start. (The only case in which this would not be true is when unassisted labour produces some goods, which then together with labour produce the other goods, and real economies are not like that; nor did Leontief – nor the economists who developed the non-substitution theorem – assume such an unreal case.)

Note further that $x-Ax$ cannot be interpreted as what the economy finds itself with, after producing x. For example, suppose that all production processes take one year and are all started at the same time, at the beginning of the year, so x has been produced in a single production cycle which could only be started because at least stocks Ax of the several goods were available at the beginning of the year; then, at the end of the year the economy has at its disposal the entire x, plus whatever excess of the initial stocks over Ax survived the passing of time.

Note finally that the above analysis implies nothing as to the degree of resource utilization. The fact that the production of x requires the utilization of amounts Ax of circulating capital goods presupposes neither the full employment of labour, nor the full utilization of inventories.

Suppose now that you want to understand why the production processes adopted are (A, ℓ) when other processes might be utilized. If you believe that prices in the economy are sufficiently close to long-period prices, then you will analyse the choice of techniques in the way sketched in §6.2.3, and you will conclude that, at the given rate of profits or of interest, or at the given real wage, the processes (A, ℓ) are the ones on the outer envelope of the $w(r)$ curves corresponding to the alternative techniques available to the economy. Since, owing to the assumptions of constant returns to scale and only one primary factor, the $w(r)$ curves only depend on the technical coefficients and not on the quantities produced, you will conclude that – if sufficient time is allowed for the quantities of intermediate goods to be adapted to changed demands – as long as income distribution does not change, the technical coefficients will remain (A, ℓ) even if x changes.

The conclusion just reached is the non-substitution theorem. More precisely, assume an economy where[48]

i.   there exists only one primary factor, labour; all other inputs are produced goods, that is capital goods, and their amounts adapt to the demand for them;
ii.   all processes of production are perfectly divisible with constant returns to scale and have the same production period (which is taken as the time unit);

---

48. I essentially follow Salvadori (1987) in the presentation of the result.

iii. each process produces one perfectly divisible commodity (no joint production), with fixed coefficients of capital goods and of labour, at least some of which are positive;
iv. for each commodity there exists at least one process producing it;
v. each commodity requires labour for its production, either directly or indirectly;
vi. the price of capital goods is the same at the beginning and at the end of each production cycle;
vii. the price of each produced commodity equals the costs of the inputs plus a uniform and given rate of interest on that part of that cost which is paid in advance (that is at the beginning of the production cycle);
viii. either the rate of interest (or of profits) is less than the maximum one associated with a zero wage, or there exists a commodity that is basic in all alternative techniques that are equally profitable at the maximum rate of interest;[49]

then for each admissible value of the rate of interest, cost minimization implies a unique vector of relative prices of products and a unique wage rate (once a numeraire is chosen), independent of the composition of final demand. (At those prices and wage rate, either the process chosen in each industry is unique, or the industry can indifferently use alternative processes which yield the same unit cost.)

6A3.2. This result therefore concerns the nature of long-period choice of techniques when there is no joint production and no scarce natural resources.[50] But nowadays the result is presented in advanced microeconomics textbooks in a deeply misleading way that entirely obscures its true field of application (and also contains a logical slip).

For example Varian (1992, p. 350) presents it as follows: 'if there is only one nonproduced input to production and the technology exhibits constant returns to scale, then the equilibrium prices are independent of tastes – they are determined entirely by technology'.

The first thing to be noticed is that in this way the theorem is presented as though it referred to *equilibrium* prices (and, remember, the sole notions of equilibrium presented in this textbook, as in all other modern neoclassical textbooks, are the neo-Walrasian ones). The second is that these equilibrium

49. The need for condition (viii) is demonstrated in Kurz and Salvadori (1994).
50. Actually the non-substitution theorem still holds with 'pure' durable capital goods (that is without transferability of machines), and as long as the changes in the composition or level of production do not alter the no-rent land, but these extensions are unnecessary for the argument of this Appendix.

prices are seen as uniquely determined, that is, implicitly, income distribution is considered to be uniquely determined.[51]

Two misinterpretations of Leontief's analysis are at the basis of such a presentation.

The first misinterpretation is that Leontief's analysis was concerned with neoclassical equilibria. One consequence is that labour is assumed to be fully employed.

The second misinterpretation consists of a true logical slip. It derives from the use of 'netputs' as the way to represent production processes,[52] combined with the adoption of a 'static' perspective which is taken to imply no need to date commodities and therefore no need to distinguish between a good when used as input, and the same good as output. To make the point clear, consider a simple economy where two goods, corn and iron, are produced via fixed-coefficient processes which take one period and employ labour, corn and iron as inputs. Let the technical coefficients be (corn is good 1, iron is good 2, '$\oplus$' stands for 'together with', '$\rightarrow$' stands for 'produce'):

$$a_{11} \oplus a_{21} \oplus \ell_1 \rightarrow 1 \text{ unit of corn}$$

$$a_{12} \oplus a_{22} \oplus \ell_2 \rightarrow 1 \text{ unit of iron}$$

Since input and output of a good are treated as the same good, the netput representation of the processes of these two industries, if corn is good 1, iron is good 2, and labour is good 3, is the following (when the unitary activity level is taken to be the one which produces one unit of gross output):

$$1 - a_{11}, a_{21}, -\ell_1$$

$$1 - a_{21}, a_{22}, -\ell_2.$$

At this point a result of the analysis of production is implicitly invoked: that, with constant returns to scale, firms or industries can be aggregated into a single megaindustry producing the total output vector with the total inputs. The application of this result entails that it is possible, with opportune

51. Condition (viii) listed earlier can be neglected because, as explained below in the text, the equilibrium rate of interest is argued to be zero (wages absorb the entire net product).
52. The netput of good i at time t by a certain firm is the difference between the quantity produced (output) of good i and the quantity utilized (input) of the same good by the firm at time t. It is used in most modern formulations of general equilibrium theory in order to use the same symbol to represent both inputs (negative numbers), outputs (positive numbers), and also, in intertemporal equilibria, the amounts the firm can sell to other agents when the firm re-utilizes as input some part of its output of a certain date. Cf. for example Varian (1992, p. 2), Mas-Colell et al. (1995, p. 128).

activity levels of the two industries, to obtain an economy-wide netput vector where the sole negative element is the labour input, while the positive netputs of corn and iron equal the net products $x - Ax$.

A numerical example may help. Assume all a_{ij}'s are 1/4 while both ℓ_j's are 1. Assume that $x_1 = 4$ and $x_2 = 8$. Then the netputs for the two industries are

$$(3, -1, -4)$$

$$(-2, 6, -8)$$

and the aggregate netput vector is

$$(1, 5, -12)$$

formally identical to the netput vector of an economy where corn and iron are produced by unassisted labour.

This is somehow taken to imply that production in such an economy can be visualized as labour entering a black box out of which only the net products emerge. Labour is then conceived, not only as the sole primary factor, but also as the sole *scarce* factor, and thus as the factor appropriating the entire net income. Prices then are proportional to labours embodied and the rate of interest is zero; this explains the uniqueness of equilibrium prices.

Thus Arrow (1951, p. 155) interprets Samuelson's (1951) analysis of Leontief's model as including the following 'ASSUMPTION IV: *There is a given supply of labor from outside the system, but none of any product*'.

And Mas-Colell et al. (1995, p. 156) state that, with α the vector of activity levels and b the vector of labour technical coefficients,

> we can write the set of technologically feasible production vectors (assuming free disposal) as
>
> $$Y = \left\{ y : y \le \begin{bmatrix} I - A \\ -b \end{bmatrix} \alpha, \quad \text{for some} \quad \alpha \in R_+^L \right\}'.$$

There is here an evident logical slip, the moment the model is interpreted as determining a neo-Walrasian equilibrium. In the economy producing corn and iron with, as inputs, corn, iron and labour, there is only one *non-produced* input, labour; but any production cycle also requires that there be corn and iron available at the beginning of the cycle. The need for other initial inputs besides labour cannot be made to disappear via the incorrect trick of treating corn needed as input as being the same good as corn that is going to be produced only later. The latter cannot be an input to the initial production of corn, or of iron. Arrow's Assumption IV actually entails that no production process can be started except for those whose only input is unassisted labour. Hence in any neo-Walrasian equilibrium of economies with capital goods (except where production can be started with unassisted labour) there necessarily is more than one 'original' factor (*in the sense of factor available in given endowment at the beginning of the equilibrium*), because there must be given initial endowments of capital goods; and their given endowments entail that the non-substitution theorem is *inapplicable*.

6A3.3. So the non-substitution theorem does not apply to neo-Walrasian equilibria. This confirms that its domain of application is the different one indicated above: long-period technical choices, where the amounts of the several capital goods are treated as *variables* that adapt to the demand for them, and where a capital good is treated as having the same price as input and as output, the typical long-period approach to pricing.

It will come then as little surprise that the non-substitution theorem was already implicit in our analysis of the long-period neoclassical equilibrium with capital goods in Chapter 3. Indeed, take equations [3.7] and [3.10] or equations [3.7*], discussed in §3.3.2. Those equations uniquely determine, for each level of the interest rate r, the price vectors p, v and the wage rate w in terms of the chosen numeraire; and simultaneously they determine the cost-minimizing technical coefficients, unique unless two or more production methods are equally convenient at that rate of interest. Since those equations only depend on the technical coefficients and not on the quantities produced, then relative prices, the real wage and the optimal production methods do not change as long as income distribution does not change.

Thus the modern neoclassical presentations of the non-substitution theorem betray a loss of familiarity with long-period analyses, which causes even an inability to be clear about the logical requirements of neo-Walrasian equilibria. (From this point of view this Appendix should have been located at the end of Chapter 5; but its argument was easier to follow after a discussion of long-period technical choice.)

APPENDIX 6A4. ON SOME ATTEMPTS TO MINIMIZE THE RELEVANCE OF REVERSE CAPITAL DEEPENING

As shown in §6.3.3, the result, that the behaviour of the long-period capital–labour ratio as a function of the rate of interest provides no foundation for the belief in a negative elasticity of aggregate investment vis-à-vis the rate of interest, does not depend only on reswitching. This allows me to be very brief on the attempts (D'Ippolito, 1987; Mainwaring and Steedman, 2000) to argue that *reswitching* is, in some sense, a priori a very improbable occurrence. D'Ippolito (1987) explicitly says that he views reverse capital deepening as the really dangerous result for the neoclassical approach to distribution, but then it is unclear why he neglects the fact that reverse capital deepening does not need reswitching for its occurrence. Mainwaring and Steedman (2000) too concentrate on reswitching and only discuss reverse capital deepening caused by reswitching, without clarifying the reasons for their choice.

It may be useful, then, to add a few words on the relevance of reswitching on its own, independently of its entailing reverse capital deepening in value terms. This relevance can be likened to that of a counterexample to a physical theory. In physics, the counterexample will usually consist of an experiment, showing that some experimental results are incompatible with a theory; the implication is that the structure of reality was incorrectly grasped by that theory, and that one must look for a different theory, capable of explaining those experimental results as well. Reswitching is the result of what may also be called an experiment, which consists of building an ideal situation to study the choice of techniques, and checking whether the results are compatible with the theory that capital is a single factor of production. The results are incompatible with that theory. This suffices to show that the structure of reality is not like the one that that theory assumes. We need therefore a different theory.

This conclusion is totally independent of the probability of empirical occurrence of the phenomena incompatible with the theory; the simple *possibility* of the phenomenon suffices to show the need for a different theory. The probability of a spontaneous empirical occurrence of the phenomena produced in the so-called crucial experiments in physics is often zero, because of the very special circumstances associated with the experiment, and sometimes it is extremely low even in the special circumstances of the experiment; and yet the entire edifice of physics is built on these phenomena.

It may nonetheless be useful to point out some specific shortcomings of these articles, for the readers interested in further study of the issue. D'Ippolito (1987) argues that the a priori probability of reswitching is low, between 2 per cent and 8 per cent for plausible values of the rate of profits, but his calculations contain a logical slip (cf. Petri, 2000) and, when the slip is corrected, the probability that reswitching will occur comes out to be very high, easily above 30 per cent if one follows D'Ippolito's own approach to measuring it, and still easily above 12 per cent with other ways of measuring it. (The different assessments of the a priori probability of reswitching, depending on the method adopted, point to a general problem of all these studies, highlighted by Salvadori (2000): the probability of reswitching depends on necessarily arbitrary assumptions on the probability of different values of the technical coefficients, so the meaningfulness of these exercises is doubtful, because one may obtain nearly any result with the opportune assumptions.) Mainwaring and Steedman too argue that the probability of reswitching is very low, about 1 per cent. Reserving for a later article a detailed analysis of the (doubtful) legitimacy of some steps in their procedure, it may be pointed out here that their approach underestimates the likelihood of the occurrence of reswitching because (Ciccone, 1996, p. 45, fn. 8) in their two-sector model they compare techniques differing in only one process, that is employing the same capital goods, while in real economies different productive methods, more often than not, use different capital goods. The extent of the resulting underestimation of the probability of reswitching has not been the object of specific enquiries so far, but is in all likelihood considerable. In the analysis of Mainwaring and Steedman, where both goods are capital goods, and both are used in positive amounts in both techniques, it is necessary, for reswitching to occur, that the $w(r)$ curves of the two alternative techniques be both convex or both concave, thus considerably restricting the range of $w(r)$ curves which reswitch with a given $w(r)$ curve, relative to the case when the capital goods may differ. The much higher probabilities obtained by Petri (2000) for the Samuelson–Hicks–Garegnani–D'Ippolito model (where the capital goods differ as between techniques, so convex and concave $w(r)$ curves can reswitch) would appear to confirm this conjecture.

Let us now return to the criticism that these articles forget that reverse capital deepening can occur independently of reswitching. Zambelli (2004), who concentrates on the likelihood of reverse capital deepening whether caused by reswitching or by 'price Wicksell effects', concludes, on the basis of the random generation of hypothetical economies with several alternative techniques, that reverse capital deepening is not present in only about 40 per cent of the economies thus generated. In other words, the probability that the capital–labour ratio be an everywhere decreasing function of the rate of profits is less than one half.

Even much higher probabilities of absence of reverse capital deepening than Zambelli obtains would in no way salvage the neoclassical approach.

We have now had two centuries of capitalism, with all its technical changes and national peculiarities, so we have had very many 'random' extractions of sets of alternative techniques. Thus even very low probabilities of reverse capital deepening would not make it unlikely that, at least in some countries and some historical periods, the capital–labour ratio schedule had upward-sloping sections, which should have resulted in at least some cases in phenomena that, to the contrary, have not been observed. As noted by Garegnani (1970, pp. 427–8):

> Thus, after following in the footsteps of traditional theory and attempting an analysis of distribution in terms of 'demand' and 'supply', we are forced to the conclusion that a change, however small, in the 'supply' or 'demand' conditions of labour or capital (saving) may result in drastic changes of r and w. That analysis would even force us to admit that r may fall to zero or rise to its maximum, and hence w rise to its maximum or to fall to zero, without bringing to equality the quantities supplied and demanded of the two factors. Now, no such instability of an economy's wage and interest rates has ever been observed. The natural conclusion is that, in order to explain distribution, we must rely on forces other than 'supply' and 'demand'.

Or, as Ciccone (1996, p. 42, my translation) puts it:

> However small the evaluated probability of the instances in which the principle of substitution does not operate, obviously prices and incomes would take shape, and would therefore have an explanation, also in those circumstances. One would thus be implicitly admitting the existence of a theory of distribution, alternative to the neoclassical one, and without any basis for excluding that this alternative theory, differently from the neoclassical one, may apply to the generality of cases.

Another group of articles, motivated by a desire to defend the usefulness of Marx's labour values (Ochoa, 1989, Petrović, 1991, Bienenfeld, 1988), has tried to argue that relative prices change little with distribution and are therefore well approximated by labour values. There are reasons, which I cannot discuss here in any detail, to doubt the validity of this thesis (but cf. Garegnani, 1979b, p. 78); but if it were correct, the implication would be that there would be no change of any significance in the value of capital per unit of labour along the outer envelope of the $w(r)$ curves, because this outer envelope would be itself a straight line (or very close to one). Since the $w(r)$ curves are (very close to) linear, their outer envelope will not be so only if there are switches on it; but at a switch point between two techniques, all relative prices of goods produced in both techniques must be the same, so if relative prices in each technique are constant (as implied by linear $w(r)$ curves), a switch requires either that relative prices are the same for both techniques for all income distributions, or that there is only one good common to both techniques.[53] Both cases can be excluded as totally unrealistic for economies producing many goods; so apart from extreme flukes, the same technique would be the dominant one for all values of the rate of interest (Baldone, 1984, Salvadori and Steedman, 1988). So the capital–labour ratio would be totally inelastic to changes in distribution; substitution in consumer choice would be analogously unable to operate since relative prices would be unaffected by changes in distribution; hence, no decreasing demand curves for factors would be derivable, and a supply-and-demand approach to distribution would be indefensible. Thus even if Petrović (1991) were right to argue that, for *this* reason, 'capital reversal and double switching turn out to be highly improbable events in any actual economy' (p. 166), still, for the same reason, the plausibility of the marginalist approach would be anyway destroyed.

In other words, the sole way to exclude a high probability of reverse capital deepening, namely, $w(r)$ curves of alternative techniques that are close to being linear, results in an extremely high likelihood that there be nearly no variation of the desired average capital–labour ratio as distribution varies, with again an impossibility to assume the existence of the neoclassical capital–labour substitution mechanisms.

---

53. Samuelson's surrogate production function of 1962 satisfies the latter condition, and this is why he is able to have both linear $w(r)$ curves and switches of techniques.

7. Capital Theory and Macroeconomics. I: The Theory of Aggregate Investment

7.1. INTRODUCTION: EMPIRICAL EVIDENCE AND THEORETICAL DIFFICULTIES

7.1.1. This chapter argues that without recourse to the notion of a significant negative elasticity of the capital–labour ratio vis-à-vis the rate of interest – the notion refuted by reverse capital deepening – it is impossible to defend the thesis that investment is a decreasing function of the rate of interest, and therefore it is also impossible to argue that the rate of interest is capable of bringing investment into equality with full-employment savings; the thesis of a spontaneous tendency of market economies toward the full employment of resources – a thesis that many economists already find doubtful even when that view of investment is accepted – becomes clearly implausible.[1]

This thesis has been advanced by Garegnani (1978, pp. 36–7), but it is here proven with reference also to more recent derivations of the decreasing investment schedule, such as the adjustment-costs approach, or Tobin's q.

---

1. Keynes's rejection of the tendency toward full employment has lost its initial predominance essentially owing to the 'neoclassical synthesis', which argued that lower money wages are capable of stimulating employment by lowering the price level and thus the demand for money and the rate of interest (the so-called 'Keynes effect'), with a resulting increase in investment; therefore, it was argued, lower money wages are capable of increasing employment even within Keynes's own theory, and it is their rigidity that impedes the tendency toward full employment. This argument neglects possible multiplier–accelerator perverse interactions, vagaries of expectations, endogeneity of the money supply, possible rigidities of the interest rate due to liquidity traps or asymmetric information, and so on (and this contributes to explaining the survival of Keynesian positions, albeit minoritarian). But it crucially relies on a significant elasticity of aggregate investment with respect to the rate of interest, and it loses credibility if that theory of investment is rejected. Another possible defence of a spontaneous tendency toward full employment if money wages are flexible in the presence of labour unemployment is based on the 'Pigou effect' or 'real balance effect'. It is discussed and criticized in Appendix 7A2; its weaknesses explain why it draws considerably less support than the one based on the thesis that investment adapts to savings.

This will show that macroeconomic theory, when deprived of the possibility to rely on the traditional notion of 'capital' the value factor, does not provide reasons to believe that the path traced by sequences of neo-Walrasian equilibria describes with reasonable approximation the behaviour of market economies.

7.1.2. It is a well-known fact that *empirical* support for the negative influence of the rate of interest on aggregate investment is very weak. The empirical studies of the 1950s and 1960s on the determinants of aggregate investment concluded that it was difficult to ascertain a significant negative elasticity of aggregate investment with respect to the rate of interest, and that the influence of demand and of its variations was anyway much more important (cf. Junankar, 1972, for a survey). These results have not been disproved by later empirical research. The latest *Journal of Economic Literature* survey of investment theory concludes: 'While there is clearly no uniformity in the results and the role of shocks remains to be assessed, it appears to this author that, on balance, the response of investment to price variables tends to be small and unimportant relative to quantity variables' (Chirinko, 1993, p. 1906; also see ibid., pp. 1881, 1883, 1897, 1899). Thus empirical evidence would appear to suggest that the negative influence of the rate of interest on aggregate investment, if it exists at all, is too weak to justify the belief that investment adjusts to savings faster than savings adjust to investment via the Keynesian mechanism of variations of aggregate income.[2] It thus appears highly doubtful that economies tend toward the full employment of resources, and that long-run growth is determined with sufficient approximation by the investment of full-employment savings. This is a conclusion certainly not contradicted prima facie by the behaviour of the industrialized economies in the 1930s or since the mid-1970s.

A very similar conclusion is reached, in another recent assessment of the evidence on aggregate investment, by Edmond Malinvaud:

> In summarizing the implications of the results one ought to distinguish between the determinants of short-term fluctuations in investment and the determinants of comparative levels, as between industries, countries or periods separated by more than a few years. We have by now a fairly good qualitative knowledge of the first

2. It is a very negative aspect of the present situation of economics that students are again becoming unable – like economists before Keynes – to formulate and study situations of persistent unemployment, because macroeconomics textbooks often only introduce them to full-employment macroeconomics and no longer supply the analytical instruments necessary for the analysis of the influence of aggregate demand on output and employment. The so-called Keynesian cross or 45° diagram, and the multiplier, no longer appear in many contemporary textbooks. Empirical evidence should suffice to show the continued relevance of these concepts.

258 *General equilibrium, capital and macroeconomics*

group of determinants, but in many respects we are more interested in the second group, where the situation seems to me to be much less satisfactory.

The short-term determinants reflect first and foremost the strength of the need to expand productive capacity in order to meet demand. This is the so-called accelerator principle (...)

As for the longer-term determinants ... the main question is: how does investment respond to changes in relative prices and factor costs? These may give stronger or weaker incentives to risk-taking and to the substitution of capital for labour. Econometric studies have identified the expected effects, but indicate that they act slowly and are difficult to estimate precisely.

Much attention was given to the cost of capital, which depends in particular on interest rates ... Even where the effect of the indicator was found to be significant, it was usually small and spread over longer lags than the accelerator phenomenon. Hence, the conclusion that in the short run the demand for fixed productive investment is inelastic with respect to changes in relative prices. For completeness one should, however, recognize that a rise in interest rates fairly quickly depresses investment in housing and probably also inventory piling (this may also be because of credit rationing with which it is often associated).

The profitability of investment is of course correlated with the profitability of capital in use, for which a measure may be the ratio between the market value of capital and its replacement cost. This ratio, commonly denominated q, was advocated by Tobin (1969) as a relevant indicator for investment theory and its role was tested in a number of econometric studies. Again the results were disappointing for their lack of strength and accuracy (Malinvaud, 1995, pp. 125–6).[3]

Thus it is not surprising that he should conclude: 'The most systematic, transparent and embracing models apply to the macroeconomic field the logical structure built for the theory of prices and resource allocation. They lead to the view that saving is the driving force of evolution in market economies ... .I find it difficult to accept this view' (Malinvaud, 1995, p. 127). An even more recent survey, by Caballero (1999), states yet again that, although there would appear to be some econometric evidence of an influence of the 'cost of capital' on aggregate investment, the correlation is quite low.[4]

3. Note the sentence 'Even where the effect of the indicator was found to be significant', which reveals that the cost of capital was frequently found *not* to be significant. Also to be noticed is Malinvaud's admission that the negative effect of a higher interest rate on some types of investment (he mentions inventories, but why not other types too?) might be due more to the credit rationing which monetary policy frequently associates with increases in interest rates, than to a direct influence of the interest rate.
4. Caballero admits that this evidence leaves most of aggregate investment unexplained, for example by stating: 'The movement from aggregate to microeconomic data, by itself, has not done much to improve affairs. Although microeconomic data has improved precision, coefficients on the cost of capital and q in investment equations have remained

7.1.3. It is only natural, then, to suspect that there might be something unconvincing in the *theoretical* arguments which support the expectation that investment *ought* to exhibit a negative elasticity vis-à-vis the interest rate. The remainder of this chapter argues that the suspicion is well founded.

All the main derivations of the decreasing investment schedule from Keynes onward will be discussed. The history of the interest-elastic investment schedule before Keynes will not be discussed,[5] because its connection with the demand-for-'capital' function seems at the same time to have been considered obvious, and yet not to have been explicitly analysed, by the older marginalist authors. Thus in 1936 Keynes found that he could not simply rely on what had been written previously, as shown by the following passage from the *General Theory*:

> The Marginal Productivity or Yield or Efficiency or Utility of Capital are familiar terms which we have all frequently used. But it is not easy by searching the literature of economics to find a clear statement of what economists have usually intended by these terms. [...] There is, as I have said above, a remarkable lack of any clear account of the matter (Keynes, 1936, pp. 137–9).

He nonetheless felt no hesitation to use the marginal efficiency *of capital* to build the *investment* schedule.

Thus the precise connection, implicit in traditional marginalist analyses, must be reconstructed from the logic of the approach; the most consistent reconstruction, due to Garegnani (1964 [1978]), was presented in Section 4.3.

That reconstruction clarified the fundamental role of the assumption of full employment. The traditional marginalist connection between demand for capital and investment was based on two premises: (i) the negative influence of the rate of interest on the desired K/L ratio in new plants (where K is 'free' capital), and (ii) a given flow of labour available for combination with 'free' capital in any proportion, to which that K/L ratio could be applied; this given flow of 'free' labour was derived from an assumption of full employment of labour, together with the argument that only a portion of the labour supply would be 'released' each period by the gradual closure of the oldest plants.

If labour employment is *not* given, the marginal product of 'capital' is not determinate; and if labour employment can increase together with the stock of 'capital', the marginal product of 'capital' need not be decreasing even on

embarrassingly small' (1999, p. 822). Also cf. Hall (1993, pp. 278–9): 'established models are unhelpful in understanding this [1990–91] recession, and probably most of its predecessors. ... In spite of low interest rates, firms cut all forms of investment. ... Little of this falls into the type of behavior predicted by neoclassical models'. These lines would appear applicable also to the more recent experience of Japan and of the USA.

5. Cf. Panico (1988, ch. 4, app. B), for a discussion of Marshall's views on investment.

marginalist terms. In other words: the marginalist approach argues that the rate of interest determines the optimal *capital–labour ratio*, but this does not suffice to determine the desired 'capital' *stock* unless labour employment is given. Analogously, a given K/L ratio to be adopted in new plants leaves the demand for the flow of 'free' capital, that is investment, indeterminate because the flow of labour to be employed in new plants can be greater or smaller than the flow of labour 'released' by the closure of the oldest plants, owing to the possibility of reducing or increasing labour unemployment.

Now, the legitimacy of *assuming* the full employment of labour was destroyed by Keynes; after Keynes, the tendency to the full employment of labour could only be, at most, a *conclusion* of an analysis based on, among other things, a theory of aggregate investment. For example, no full–employment assumption is made in the IS–LM model; therefore, the theory of aggregate investment in IS–LM analysis cannot *assume* the full employment of labour.[6]

The difficulty is already present in Keynes, since the *General Theory* does not assume the full employment of labour. But Keynes does not appear to have been conscious of it. What one finds in the *General Theory* is a derivation of the schedule of the marginal efficiency of capital which appears to attribute to the decrease of the marginal product of 'capital' the decreasing shape of the investment schedule once one leaves transitory elements aside. The well-known passage is:

> The relation between the prospective yield of a capital asset and its supply price or replacement cost, i.e. the relation between the prospective yield of one more unit of that type of cpaital and the cost of producing that unit, furnishes us with the marginal efficiency of capital of that type. More precisely, I define the marginal efficiency of capital as being equal to that rate of discount which would make the present value of the series of annuities given by the returns expected from the capital-asset during its life just equal to its supply price. This gives us the marginal efficiencies of particular types of capital-assets. The greatest of these marginal efficiencies can then be regarded as the marginal efficiency of capital in general.
> [...]
> If there is an increased investment in any given type of capital during any period of time, the marginal efficiency of that type of capital will diminish as the investment in it is increased, partly because the prospective yield will fall as the supply of that type of capital is increased, and partly because, as a rule, pressure on the facilities for producing that type of capital will cause its supply price to

---

6.　Some recent textbooks derive the investment schedule from a decreasing demand curve for capital which, explicitly or implicitly, assumes the full employment of labour, and then, with a clear inconsistency, they use the same investment schedule in order to derive the IS curve in the IS–LM model, where full employment is not assumed. A recent example is Farmer (1999).

increase; the second of these factors being usually the more important in producing equilibrium in the short run, but the longer the period in view the more does the first factor take its place. Thus for each type of capital we can build up a schedule, showing by how much investment in it will have to increase within the period, in order that its marginal efficiency should fall to any given figure. We can then aggregate these schedules for all the different types of capital, so as to provide a schedule relating the rate of aggregate investment to the corresponding marginal efficiency of capital in general which that rate of investment will establish. We shall call this the investment demand-schedule; or, alternatively, the schedule of the marginal efficiency of capital.

[...] the rate of investment will be pushed to the point on the investment demand-schedule where the marginal efficiency of capital in general is equal to the market rate of interest (Keynes, 1936, pp. 135–7).

Here Keynes attributes a role in the short-period equilibration not only to the rising supply price of capital goods but also to expectations; but one should not forget the passage from the letter to Kalecki dated 12 April 1937, already quoted in Appendix 2A1 but partly reproduced here for the reader's convenience:

I regard behaviour as arrived at by trial and error, and no theory can be regarded as sound which depends on the *initial* reaction being of a particular kind. One must assume that the initial reaction may be anything in the world, but that the process of trial and error will eventually arrive at the conclusion which one is predicting (*KCW*, XII, p. 797).

This argument can only become stronger when one considers longer time periods. As to the rising supply price, it is Keynes himself who argues that in the longer period this reason loses importance and the decrease in the marginal efficiency of a capital asset depends essentially on the increase in its endowment. But if the endowments of all types of capital goods increase together with the employment of labour and with aggregate demand, there is no reason why the returns from investment should decrease.

The Marshallian origins of Keynes's approach to investment[7] perhaps help one explain Keynes's inconsistency. Marshall had nowhere explicitly discussed an *aggregate* investment schedule; he had only explained investment by reference to the convenience of investing in each capital good, as in the following passage:

so long as the resources of an individual producer are in the form of general purchasing power, he will push every investment up to the margin at which he no longer expects from it a higher net return than he could get by investing in some

---

7. Panico (1988, ch. 4, app. B) shows that Keynes's analysis of investment follows Marshall's very closely.

other material, or machine, or advertisement, or in the hire of some additional labour: every investment will, as it were, be driven up to a valve which offers to it a resistance equal to its own expanding force (Marshall, 1920 [1970], V, viii, 6, pp. 340–41).

Keynes takes from Marshall this misleading empiricism, and again approaches the problem of investment in terms of individual capital goods: this made it perhaps easier for him to forget that his argument that 'the prospective yield will fall as the supply of that type of capital is increased' (which is valid for increases in the utilization of an individual capital good relative to the utilization of other factors) no longer holds if investment in all capital goods is expanded together with the employment of labour.[8]

This problem has induced some economists to argue that Keynes's approach to investment does not rely, or can be made not to rely, on the marginalist conception of capital–labour substitution. I discuss this approach next.

7.2.   THE 'ARRAY-OF-OPPORTUNITIES' APPROACH, AND THE DEPENDENCE OF YIELDS ON THE RATE OF INTEREST

7.2.1. A number of authors, including Marglin (1970), Pasinetti (1974, p. 37), Vickers (1992), Samuelson and Nordhaus (1985, ch. 7), propose what has been called an 'array-of-opportunities' approach,[9] which is claimed to be independent of the marginalist conception of 'capital'–labour substitution and to reflect Keynes's own approach to the issue. This justification is nowadays nearly absent from mainstream textbooks, but it has been important historically, it still has adherents, and above all it allows a clear discussion of a mistake that reappears in many other approaches: the mistake of treating the yields (gross of interest costs) of investment projects as independent of the rate of interest.

At any given point in time, it is argued, each firm or entrepreneur is 'aware of a considerable number of possible investment projects, for each of which it can calculate, given its best estimates of all the relevant variables, its

---

8.   According to Garegnani (1964 [1978], cf. especially pp. 59–60, fn. 44), this difficulty highlights the uneasy co-existence in Keynes of an innovatory nucleus (the principle of effective demand) and of traditional marginalist notions hardly reconcilable with it; and these difficulties 'can also explain how the desire to bring consistency back into economic theory might have encouraged the attempts to confine the implications of Keynes's theory strictly to short-period analysis' (ibid., p. 60).

9.   I borrow the term from Witte (1963, p. 445), and Junankar (1972, p. 23).

marginal efficiency' (Ackley, 1978, p. 622[10]). By 'marginal efficiency' what is meant here is the expected internal rate of return, derivable from the project's prospective net income stream; it is not really a marginal notion, it applies to the entire project. The idea is that the entrepreneur will find it convenient to implement all the projects whose 'marginal efficiency' is higher than the rate of interest. The aggregate investment function is, for each level of the interest rate, the sum of all the projects the entrepreneurs decide to implement. The lower the interest rate, the more projects have an internal rate of return greater than the interest rate, so the investment function is a decreasing step function; see Figure 7.1 where the amounts of investment associated with the different investment projects are ordered along the horizontal axis in decreasing order of internal rate of return, and where at the interest rate r' aggregate investment is OF. Arguably, the jumps are at different levels of the interest rate for different firms or industries, so the aggregate investment schedule is close to being a continuous downward-sloping curve.

In these presentations, no discussion is supplied of how the prices, on the basis of which the rates of return of the various investment projects are determined, should be assumed to change with the rate of interest: but the fact that the ranking of the projects and their internal rates of return are taken as given independently of the level of the interest rate obliges one to interpret the 'array-of-opportunities' approach as assuming that the prospective net yields (gross of interest payments) of the various investment projects are given independently of the level of the rate of interest, that is, that expected

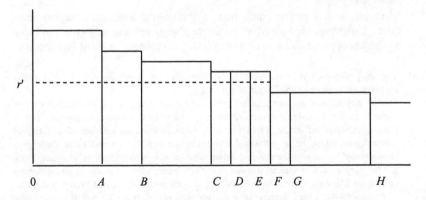

Figure 7.1 The 'array-of-opportunities' investment schedule

10. Ackley is not a supporter of this approach; he explains it only in order to criticize it. Not all his acute criticisms can be reported here.

relative prices are assumed to be independent of the level of the interest rate.[11]

For our purposes it is not important whether such an analysis correctly describes Keynes's own reasons why the schedule of what Keynes called the marginal efficiency of capital is decreasing. Be it what Keynes meant or not,[12] it has been argued to be a consistent motivation for a decreasing investment schedule, and this is the claim we must examine.

A decisive criticism has been enunciated in various forms by numerous authors, so it is somewhat surprising that it should not be discussed by the proponents of this approach. It was most succinctly put as follows: 'If one way of using capital is more profitable than others, why employ the other methods at all?' (Witte, 1963, p. 445).[13] Ackley explains the point in greater detail:

> ... what the firm's investment schedule, so derived, reflects – and thus so must the aggregate schedule – is the existence of temporary disequilibrium in the internal structure of the firm's and the economy's capital stock. In a competitive economy with perfect knowledge and foresight and no lags of adjustment, we know that, in the resulting instantaneous and continuous equilibrium, the yields of all investments that were in fact made would be identical and equal to the interest rate. For, if any type of investment yielded more than others, firms would instantaneously rush to invest in it, driving up costs of any factors especially adapted to this kind of production and/or driving down the price of the output of that type of investment, until the excess yield disappeared. All those investments that were made would have exactly the same yield and all those not made would have lower yields.
>
> Of course, such a perfect equilibrium in the internal structure of capital never exists. Exogenous changes of all kinds are always opening up newly profitable investment opportunities as well as depressing the relative yields of investment in

11. The array-of-opportunities approach is therefore not to be confused with the increasing-supply-price argument to be discussed in §7.4.2.

12. Keynes himself saw his marginal efficiency of capital schedule as just another way of formulating the standard, that is marginalist, analysis of the *demand for capital*: 'Nor is there any material difference, relevant in this context, between my schedule of the marginal efficiency of capital or investment demand-schedule and the demand curve for capital contemplated by some of the classical writers who have been quoted above' (Keynes, 1936, p. 178). Keynes uses 'classical' to mean essentially 'marginalist': the authors he is referring to here are Marshall, Cassel, Walras, Taussig, and elsewhere Pigou and Wicksell. Also cf. ibid., pp. 140–41, where Keynes states that his marginal efficiency of capital is essentially the same notion, and used for the same purpose, as Irving Fisher's rate of return over cost.

13. Also cf. Kaldor (1937, pp. 201–3): '... the rate of return should correspond in equilibrium to the current rate of interest not only on the marginal unit of investment, but on all units. It can be argued that 'inframarginal' investments will earn rents which, in terms of money costs, will equalise this difference; but then the question still arises, why should "rents", if they arose, not be eliminated by competition?'

other lines, and the adjustment to these changes in relative yields is not and cannot be instantaneous. This adjustment, through more investment where relative profitability has improved, requires an information and learning process and the production and installation of new capital goods and the recruiting of labor; thus, considerable time is necessary to eliminate the higher yields. Where profitability has been depressed, the adjustment requires information and learning, and, particularly, the wearing out of existing equipment.

It is true that an array of possible yields on alternative investments always presents itself to a firm and to all firms together, requiring investment choices. But the slope of the schedule so derived reflects essentially only the extent of the forces producing change in the economy and the speed and effectiveness of the adjustment process. If change is slow and investment responses quick, the schedule will at all times be quite flat; in the opposite case it will be much steeper. But we can say nothing systematic on the basis of such a schedule about the determinants of the rate of aggregate investment. For, under this derivation, we learn nothing about what determines the aggregate rate of investment which will be made at the prevailing interest rate, nor about why this rate would have been higher had the interest rate been lower. The existence and extent of internal disequilibrium in the structure of capital does not answer this question (Ackley, 1978, pp. 623–4).[14]

The main point stressed by Ackley is that, since the working of competition tends to make the rate of return net of risk (the 'yield') of all adopted investment projects *equal to* the rate of interest, then if competition is given time to achieve its workings, there cannot be investments which yield a rate of return (net of risk) higher than the interest rate. The construction of Figure 7.1 is therefore illegitimate the moment one wants to inquire into the persistent effects of changes in the interest rate. But Ackley goes on, in the final part of the quotation ('But we can say nothing systematic ...'), to stress a very important implication of the first point: namely, that the position of the entire schedule relative to the interest rate is left indeterminate by the 'array-of-opportunities' approach. Let us clarify the reason why.

The rate of interest is a cost, and if, for example, the rate of interest decreases, this means that costs decrease in all firms, and competition will then cause product prices to decrease (relative to those costs that have not changed, such as money wages, land rents, or imports), thus lowering the rates of return on all investment projects.[15] Thus, when the rate of interest

14. The chapter of Ackley's 1978 textbook, from which this quotation is taken, is as far as I know the best discussion of investment theory by an author accepting the neoclassical conception of 'capital', and it should be required reading in all macroeconomics courses. Also cf. Ackley (1961, pp. 472–3, n. 6) and Junankar (1972, p. 23).

15. On this basis, Sraffa (1960, p. 33) has suggested that the rate of profits might be determined by the rate of interest; also cf. Panico (1988), Pivetti (1985, 1991). It has been noticed by Garegnani (1979a, p. 60, n. 45) that Keynes allows for some effects of variations of the

decreases, there will be two processes going on. One process was already going on before the change in the rate of interest, because it is going on all the time: the tendency of investment to go in greater proportion toward the employments where the rate of return is higher. This is the process that tends to equalize the rates of return in all lines of investment, a process that never ends because novelties continually recreate differences in yields; and the change in the rate of interest is one of these novelties. But at the same time a second process will also be going on: price-cutting competition, made possible by the decrease in costs due to the lower interest rate, will cause the returns on all investments to decrease. So, even if for the sake of argument one were to leave out of consideration the first process, and one were to take the differences of yields among different alternative investments as given, the second process would cause the entire disequilibrium 'array of possible yields on alternative investments' to move with the rate of interest.

Therefore it is not legitimate to take the 'array of possible yields on alternative investments' as given when the rate of interest changes. But then this approach gives no clue as to the level of the 'array of possible yields on alternative investments' relative to the rate of interest. In order to understand how a given level of the rate of interest will affect investment, there appears to be little alternative to the traditional argument that investment will generally be close to the level which would be determined by all prices having already perfectly adapted to the new rate of interest (the greater convenience of some investments, due to disequilibrium, being compensated by the lesser convenience of other investments). So in order to determine aggregate investment there appears to be no alternative to a study of how investment changes with the rate of interest, under an assumption of prices equal to costs of production.

So, if a decrease in the rate of interest is to increase investment, it can only be, Ackley argues, 'by selectively favoring the production of more capital-intensive products as opposed to labor- or land-intensive products' and 'by favoring more capital intensive *methods of production* as opposed to less capital-intensive ones' (Ackley, 1978, p. 620): 'the original classical basis for the declining investment schedule ... clearly lies in consideration of aggregate 'factor proportions' for the entire economy' (ibid., p. 625, fn. 15).

interest rate on the prospective yields of investment: 'an expectation of a future fall in the rate of interest will have the effect of *lowering* the schedule of the marginal efficiency of capital; since it means that the output from equipment produced to-day will have to compete during part of its life with the output from equipment which is content with a lower return' (Keynes, 1936, p. 143): the implication is, clearly, that the 'output from equipment which is content with a lower return' will be sold at a lower price. Also see Pivetti (1985, p. 98).

However one then runs into the problems connected with reverse capital deepening, and with the absence of the right to assume the full employment of labour.

7.2.2. One implication of the above reasoning deserves repeating, because it will be important again and again in the remainder of the chapter. *The assumption that the returns to individual investment projects are given independently of the level of the interest rate, is not acceptable.*[16] If the investment schedule is to have any persistence, the expected relative prices implicit in each point of the aggregate investment schedule must be cost-of-production prices; and therefore they must vary with the interest rate.[17]

This consideration cannot be pushed aside by arguing that the analysis is intended to be a very short-period one, concerned with expectations and investment decisions at a point in time (then, it is sometimes argued, expected prices are given, because they reflect the agents' expectations at that point in time). Even if one tried to predict investment at a point in time, one would have no right to consider expected prices as not changing, in the face of variations of the interest rate which are expected to last. The returns relevant to an investment project are usually spread over a considerable length of time, and therefore investors must be presumed to take into account the predictable return of product prices to the normal levels associated with zero extra-profits. Anyway the fruitfulness of trying to explain and predict investment moment by moment is more than doubtful, because at each moment investment will be influenced by expectations that may depend on the whims and accidents of the moment and that are admittedly shortly to be revised, and by any other sort of accidental and transitory causes. These influences will make it impossible to predict the effects on investment of a change in the rate of interest or in other variables; also, investment decisions can be reversed or modified, and, if the expectations motivating the original decisions turn out to be incorrect, they *will* usually be reversed or modified, even if this incurs a cost; so the determination of investment decisions at a point in time is uninteresting. The analysis must therefore aim at determining the *persistent* forces acting on investment, and thus the average, or trend, of

16. Garegnani (1979a, p. 60, fn. 45); Pivetti (1985, p. 98).
17. This is not often admitted, but see for example Jorgenson (1967, p. 152), quoting Alchian (1955). One important implication is that a lower interest rate entails a higher real wage, without any need for increases in the demand for labour in order for this higher real wage to come about: with a given money wage, the higher real wage can be brought about simply by price-cutting competition by firms whose costs have been lowered by the decrease in the interest rate.

aggregate investment emerging from the multitude of temporary influences.[18] And if one wants to explore the persistent influence of the interest rate on investment, one must allow time for the changes in interest rate to affect relative prices and distribution.

A brief consideration may now be given to the argument, that the problem of infinite investment if prices are given might be avoided by assuming that entrepreneurs are conscious that they can only sell more at a lower price, that is, by assuming generalized imperfect competition. Such an assumption would make it possible to argue that the indefinite replication of an investment project encounters a limit in the decrease of the expected returns due to the decrease of the expected selling price. The decreasing shape of the investment schedule would then be derived from given demand curves for the single firms; a decrease in the interest rate would shift the cost curves downward and thus would make it convenient to sell more at a lower price, and therefore to increase productive capacity. But what may cause the demand for a product to increase if its price decreases is the fact that the product has become more convenient *relative to other products*. If, following a lowering of the interest rate, all products decrease in price, then relative convenience will not be altered at all if relative prices do not change (all demand curves shift downward in the same percentage as costs), and, to the extent to which they change, the rightward shift of the demand curve for some products will be compensated by the leftward shift of the demand curve for other products; thus, in the aggregate, demand does not change.[19] Besides, if all invest more, then aggregate demand increases, such that all demand curves shift to the right, so not only it is unclear why a decrease in the interest rate should be a *sufficient* condition for an increase in investment, it is also unclear why it should be a *necessary* condition for greater investment.

7.3. THE INCREASING-RISK APPROACH

7.3.1. Another derivation of a decreasing investment function, making no reference to the 'capital' intensity of production, relies on Kalecki's 'principle of increasing risk'. Kalecki (1937, 1971) argues that in competitive conditions the marginal efficiency of investment (the rate of return over additional investment) for a single firm should be taken to be constant, rather than decreasing: the competitive firm treats prices (of inputs as well as of outputs) as given. Also, he argues, decreasing returns to scale

---

18. This would appear to have been also Keynes's opinion, as expressed in the letter to Kalecki dated 12 April 1937, quoted earlier.
19. See Ackley (1978, p. 624).

are not plausible; and therefore economists should have concluded that, if even only one investment project has a MEC (Marginal Efficiency of Capital, that is, internal rate of return of the variation in prospective income stream due to the last unit of investment) greater than the rate of interest, the firm will plan to replicate it an indefinite number of times, that is the firm will plan an infinite amount of investment. He adds, however, that this does not happen, because risk is an increasing function of the rate of investment. In order to invest more, a firm must increase its debt–asset ratio (given that normally a part of investment comes from internal funds, such that not all assets are matched by a corresponding debt), thus increasing the firm's risk of default and bankruptcy. Given this situation, a greater differential between profit rate and rate of interest is required in order to induce the entrepreneur to invest; that is, a greater debt–asset ratio; and also, owing to increasing risk for the lender, a rising addition to the basic 'safe' rate of interest must be offered to lenders. The amount of investment is determined by the equality between the given rate of return (which for the single firm is independent of the amount of investment) and the rising 'cost curve' of borrowing, resulting from the addition to the basic rate of interest of the two rising risk differentials.

The conclusion (stressed very little by Kalecki, but implicit in the approach) is that a decrease in the basic rate of interest will shift the 'cost curve' of borrowing downward, and thus induce firms to adopt a higher debt/asset ratio, that is to borrow more and invest more.

The approach remains very much the same in Minsky (1975, pp. 109–16), and in the so-called liquidity approach (Fazzari and Mott, 1986–87; Fazzari, Hubbard and Petersen, 1988; Hubbard, 1998). Similar theories are reviewed in Ackley (1978, ch. 19) and Nickell (1978, who on p. 198 recognizes the seminal role of Kalecki's article).

For our purpose here,[20] which is to discuss the influence of changes in the rate of interest, it suffices to note one basic weakness of this approach to the determination of investment: the expected rate of return on investment (the expected rate of profits) is considered independent of the cost of borrowing.[21] If it is accepted that autonomous variations in the real interest rate will result

---

20. For a more detailed discussion of Kalecki's views on investment, and of the objections moved to them, cf. Petri (1993a).
21. Or what is treated as independent from the cost of borrowing is the entire *demand curve* for capital by a single firm, cf. Hubbard (1998, p. 197). This recent article shares with many other recent contributions to the analysis of investment its concentration on the single firm, without asking how far the conclusions generalize to economy-wide phenomena (we will meet other examples later). In this article, by the way, the reason why the demand curve for capital by the single firm is downward-sloping is not explained (Kalecki had treated it as horizontal, due to price-taking and to the possibility of varying the employment of labour together with the stock of capital).

in variations in the same direction of the rate of profits via variations of the price level relative to money wages, then a variation of the interest rate will *not* cause a persistent variation in the opposite direction of the difference between interest rate and profit rate, and therefore will not create any (non-transitory) incentive to investment.

Therefore the debt–asset ratio might well be an important determinant of the investment of some firms, and perhaps even of the entire economy; but it does not seem legitimate to derive from it an investment schedule of negative elasticity with respect to the interest rate.

7.4. THE SPEED-OF-ADJUSTMENT PROBLEM, AND LERNER

7.4.1. Let us now turn to the derivations of the decreasing investment schedule which admit as necessary a link with the notion of a decreasing demand curve for 'capital' the single, somehow homogeneous factor.

Strikingly, to the best of my knowledge the difficulty, that the marginal product of capital – and hence the decreasing demand-for-capital schedule – is not determined without a full-employment-of-labour assumption, is not mentioned in these analyses. One is thus prompted to interpret these analyses as assuming the full employment of labour; but this interpretation is often made difficult by the fact that the investment schedule derived from the decreasing demand-for-capital schedule is then used for Keynesian analyses that admit unemployment, for example to arrive at the IS–LM model. I have no clear explanation for what appears to me a patent inconsistency.

Another common characteristic is that there is no mention of the fact that capital and investment are *value* magnitudes reflecting heterogeneous aggregates, of a composition that changes with the rate of interest. More and more, the theory is based on one-good aggregate-production-function models, with no discussion of the legitimacy of this 'simplification'. The implicit thesis, clearly, is that the one-good assumption makes no difference to the analysis. Even in the more recent contributions, reverse capital deepening, which shows the falseness of this thesis, is not mentioned.[22]

---

22. Junankar (1972, pp. 12–13) at least mentions the problem, although only to put it aside: 'There are several problems involved in measuring aggregate capital stock {...} Cambridge economists have argued very strongly that it is impossible to measure capital in value terms in a way that is independent of the rate of interest and wages. For the purposes of this survey I shall sidestep this controversy and assume that we can measure capital in value terms'. Most other authors do not even bother to mention the Cambridge controversy. A notable exception is Nagatani (1981), who presents its main results (pp. 207–13), but does not seem to realize their implications.

A problem which was on the contrary openly recognized,[23] and which explains many aspects of the subsequent evolution of the theory of aggregate investment, was formulated, in an often-quoted passage, as follows:

> the demand for investment cannot simply be derived from the demand for capital. Demand for a finite addition to the stock of capital can lead to any rate of investment, from almost zero to infinity depending on the additional hypotheses we introduce regarding the speed of reaction of capital users (Haavelmo, 1960, p. 216).[24]

Therefore the analysis was typically formulated as a two-stage problem: '(a) what determines the *optimal* capital stock and (b) how does the firm or economy adjust from its *actual* capital stock to the *optimal* capital stock' (Junankar, 1972, p. 19). This speed-of-adjustment problem derives from the marginalist conception of the demand for capital as a function of the interest rate. If the demand for capital were derived from aggregate output with a given technology, then, since aggregate output only changes gradually, the optimal capital stock would change gradually too, and the sole problem in deriving from its rate of change the flow of net investment would be the possibility of lags in the adjustment of the actual to the optimal capital stock. The possibility of a 'demand for a *finite* addition to the stock of capital', that is of a discrete jump in the optimal capital stock, derives from the possibility of a jump in the rate of interest, causing (in the marginalist approach) a discontinuous change in the desired capital–labour ratio.

This connection with the traditional marginalist conception of capital is, for example, clear in the following presentation of the two-stage format, taken from the section on investment theory of a textbook on rational expectations of some years ago:

> First, we require a model determining K_t^*, the capital stock which firms currently believe they wish to hold in the long run. This will have the property that q^*, the marginal cost of purchasing an additional unit of capital in the steady state, just equals the Present Discounted Value (PDV) of Operating Profits (OP) on this marginal unit over its lifetime of T periods. Thus competitive profit maximisation implies

$$q^* = \Sigma_{i=1}^{T} \left\{ \frac{OP_i^*}{(1+\delta)^i} \right\}$$

23. It is, however, no longer mentioned in contemporary mainstream textbooks.
24. These lines by Haavelmo are quoted for example by Lund (1971, p. 27), Junankar (1972, p. 15), Nickell (1978, p. 12), D. Fisher (1983, p. 295). The same point had been made earlier by Lerner (1944, pp. 330–33, 338).

where δ is the relevant discount rate. Given diminishing marginal productivity of capital, it is assumed that a higher value of K^* will bid down the stream of returns *OP* on the marginal unit of capital. Secondly, we require an adjustment rule or function

$$I_t = f(K_t^* - K_{t-1})$$

which determines the rate at which I_t, investment at time t, eliminates the discrepancy between K_{t-1}, the capital stock carried over from the end of the previous period, and K_t^*, the capital stock to which firms currently wish to converge. Without some kind of sluggish adjustment, firms would continuously hold their desired long-run capital stocks and it would be hard to explain a continuous flow of investment without supposing perpetually changing views about the steady state itself (Begg, 1982, pp. 185–6).[25]

A surprising aspect of these discussions of the speed-of-adjustment problem is that it is not perceived that the solution was already implicit in the older literature (one more indication of a loss of familiarity with traditional marginalist analyses!). The problem only arises because a 'putty-putty'[26] conception of capital obscures the important element of reality which *was* taken into account by traditional marginalist authors (and was embodied in Garegnani's reconstruction of their approach presented in Section 4.3).[27] Old plants, in their view, could not be remoulded into new shapes; and variations in their quasi-rents could *and would* make it convenient to go on utilizing them for as long as the cost of other factors did not absorb the entire revenue from their use. Therefore even a jump of the interest rate would not generally make investment indeterminate and potentially infinite: there was no impulse *immediately* to reach the new optimal capital–labour ratio in the employment of the *entire* available labour force.

Since this traditional approach was lost sight of, the solution to the speed-of-adjustment problem was sought in other directions. The ones which have been influential in the development of investment theory are three: the short-period rising-supply-price approach of Lerner (1944), important because it re-surfaces in Tobin's q approach which is very popular nowadays; the adjustment-cost approach, also used as a way to arrive at Tobin's q approach;

25. It will be noticed that Begg does not clarify what is assumed about labour employment.
26. Capital is said to be 'putty-putty' if it is assumed that the capital–labour proportion can be changed in existing plants at any time; the 'putty-clay' conception on the contrary admits that, once capital has been given the 'form' adapted to a certain capital–labour ratio, it cannot change 'form' any more until it is scrapped.
27. Cf., for example, Wicksell's distinction between 'capital which is more or less fixed or tied up in production, such as buildings, ships, machinery, etc.' and 'mobile capital in its free and uninvested form' (Wicksell, 1935, p. 192); the distinction appears in nearly all traditional marginalist authors.

and Jorgenson's (1967) so-called neoclassical approach, which, being no longer popular, is discussed in Appendix 7A1.

7.4.2. Let us examine Lerner's approach. The argument's starting point is that, since investment, a flow, only changes the existing stock of capital very gradually, the *rental* of capital cannot rapidly change and therefore one cannot attribute the declining shape of the Marginal-Efficiency-of-Capital schedule (which Lerner renames Marginal Efficiency of Investment, MEI, reserving the term MEC for the long-period curve of the marginal product of capital *across stationary states*) to a decrease of the prospective yield on the flow of new capital goods. That yield must be assumed to remain essentially unchanged as the flow of investment changes, because it depends on the *stock* of capital, and a doubling of the investment flow will not relevantly change the marginal product of capital in the period one is considering, nor for some time in the future. Therefore one must find some way to prevent investment from becoming infinite the moment the rate of interest becomes lower than the marginal product of capital. The solution is Keynes's short-period rising supply price: the purchase price of capital goods increases with their rate of production owing to short-run increasing marginal costs, and this will put a limit on investment.[28] Ackley (1978, p. 629) puts it very clearly with the help of the triple diagram reproduced in Figure 7.2.

The upper left-hand diagram shows the Marginal-Product-of-Capital schedule, or MPK, that is the MEC as intended by Lerner, which is also the schedule of the long-period (stationary) demand for capital as a function of the interest rate. (Clearly one must assume the full employment of labour.) This curve describes the total stock of capital demanded at each level of the interest rate, all other markets being in equilibrium and prices being long-period prices and with a net investment equal to zero.[29] This curve therefore assumes that the capital stock itself has adapted to the rate of interest; the productive capacity of the capital goods industry is completely adapted to the demand for capital goods, the supply price of capital goods coincides therefore – when net investment is zero – with their long-period price. The

---

28. Asimakopulos (1971, p. 383) attributes this argument to Keynes himself, perhaps on the basis of Keynes's statement that the short-period rising supply price of investment goods is 'usually the more important in producing equilibrium in the short run': but, as remembered in the text, Keynes admits that this is a short-period reason only, which tends to disappear in the longer run, so the persistent reason for the decreasing shape of the MEC schedule is the decreasing returns to an increasing *supply* of capital goods.

29. The demand for capital also depends on the composition of output and therefore it also depends on the share of gross investment in output, as was remembered when discussing the issue of whether a long-period marginalist equilibrium must be stationary in Chapter 4. This is why some assumption as to the level of net investment is necessary.

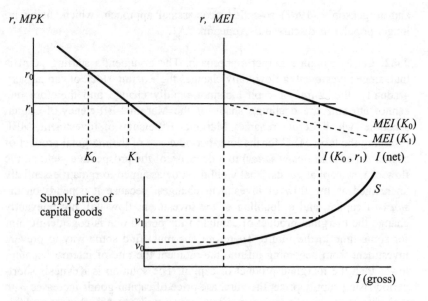

Source: Ackley (1978, p. 629).

Note: The supply price v_1 makes the rate of return on net investment $I(K_0, r_1)$ equal to r_1.

Figure 7.2   Lerner's approach to investment based on the short-period rising supply price of capital goods

given supply of capital then determines the level of the interest rate r_0 such that the economy is content with its stock of capital and net investment is equal to zero: that is equal to the marginal product of the existing stock of capital K_0.

If the interest rate were lower than this level, if the supply price of capital goods remained the same, since the marginal product of capital has not changed, a positive difference would arise between expected revenue and costs, and desired investment would be infinite. But as net investment increases, the supply price of capital goods rises (lower diagram), lowering the prospective net yields (upper right-hand diagram). The MEI curve thus obtained gives us the short-period function relating *net* investment to the interest rate; it is decreasing, and it crosses the vertical axis at a level equal to r_0. If net investment is positive because the interest rate is fixed at a level $r_1 < r_0$, the existing stock of capital gradually increases, its marginal product gradually decreases, and the entire MEI curve shifts downward, because its intersection with the vertical axis must indicate the rate of interest corresponding to the marginal product of capital. This shift downward of the

MEI schedule implies (if the interest rate stays at the new level r_1) a slowdown of net investment, so that net investment will asymptotically tend to zero as the marginal product of capital tends to become equal to r_1, that is as the existing stock of capital tends to become equal to the long-period (stationary) demand for it, K_1, at the interest rate r_1.

This description of the adjustment of the stock of capital to the new desired long-period stock of capital K_1 suffers from a deficiency that must be briefly mentioned but is not central for our purposes. The determination of the MEI schedule, and of its shift, assumes that the productive capacity of the capital goods industries is initially the one adapted to a zero level of net investment, and changes during the transition so as to remain adapted to a zero level of net investment. This is shown by the fact that the MEI schedule is assumed to intersect all the time the vertical axis (that is to correspond to zero net investment) at the rate of interest corresponding to the MPK of the changing stock of capital. This assumption is not generally justified. A higher rate of investment, if the supply of labour is fully employed, as one must assume in order to derive the MPK curve, means a different composition of aggregate demand, and therefore, a convenience also to alter the composition of productive capacity: that is investment should go in greater proportion to the capital goods industries. This means a shift to the right (and an increase in the elasticity) of the short-period supply curve of capital goods depicted in the lower diagram, and therefore a rate of return on investment higher than the MPK if net investment is zero: the MEI schedule tends to rise and become more elastic. This process will go in the opposite direction to, and might well overpower, the tendency of the MEI to shift downward owing to the decrease of MPK. Therefore there is no guarantee that as the stock of capital increases, net investment will gradually decrease at the constant rate of interest $r_1 < r_0$; net investment might well accelerate, stimulating a further expansion of the productive capacity of the capital goods industries. There is a distinct possibility, then, of an overshooting of the stock of capital, because if, when it has reached the level K_1, the productive capacity of the capital goods industry is greater than required by zero net investment, then net investment will remain positive for some time, with a consequent cycle. But it seems unnecessary to delve any further into the doubts which thus arise as to the dynamic stability of the adjustment process, because more fundamental criticisms of this theory are possible.

In spite of the short-period framework, the traditional conception of 'capital', a factor ultimately homogeneous with the product[30] and embodied

---

30. No price of capital p_k, such that the rate of interest is related to the value of capital $p_k K$, appears in the analysis: therefore K is either an amount of value independent of the rate of interest, or physically homogeneous with output – and actually this second assumption is the sole one that can justify the first one.

in the several capital goods, is clearly the basis of the analysis, as evidenced by the decreasing MPK or MEC schedule. Therefore this approach falls under the Cambridge criticism of 'capital' recalled in Chapter 6. But several additional criticisms are possible, that even a marginalist economist should find compelling.

First, as noticed by Ackley (1961, p. 485; 1978, p. 630) and Witte (1963, p. 449), empirical evidence suggests that the price of most capital goods shows a remarkable constancy over the trade cycle, so in real economies the short-run supply schedule of capital goods appears to be horizontal rather than upward-sloping. Perhaps for this reason, the rising-supply-price theory does not seem currently to enjoy much favour (except that it is somewhat reabsorbed in the adjustment-cost and q theories, as will be made clear later).

Second, there is a contradiction in the approach, between on the one hand the recognition (evident in the assumption of given productive capacity of the capital-goods industries) that capital cannot instantaneously change its 'form', and on the other hand the absence of recognition of the fact that existing plants, by adaptation of quasi-rents, will keep employing the greater part of the labour supply and will release 'free' labour only gradually, so that the adoption of the new optimal 'capital'–labour proportion in the new investments will *not* imply an infinite investment even if the supply price of capital goods is constant at the long-period level. Recognition of the latter fact also entails that it is wrong to conclude that the marginal product of capital, and therefore the rate of return on investment if supply prices are the long-period ones, are not affected (except very gradually, by the increase in the total stock of 'capital') by changes in the flow of investment. The relevant marginal product of 'capital' is the one on new plants, which can adapt to the new rate of interest by adaptation of the 'capital'–labour ratio on new plants, that is without requiring that the total stock of 'capital' reaches the new desired long-period level (§§4.3.1–4.3.5).

Lastly, the analysis needs the full employment of labour in order to justify the decreasing marginal product of 'capital' in the top left-hand portion of Figure 7.2.[31]

31. Nor can any greater solidity of this approach be attained by arguing that the essential elements of this explanation of a short-period decreasing MEI schedule need not depend on the marginalist approach to value and distribution. The argument (see, for example, Chick, 1983, pp. 127–9), which is not always clearly distinguished from the array-of-opportunities approach, is that, on the one hand, the givenness of expected yields might be explained simply by taking long-term price expectations as given (that is, as not influenced by price variations believed to be transitory); while, on the other hand, the derivation of the short-period rising supply price, from a short-period fixed capacity causing rising short-period marginal cost curves, is not necessarily dependent on the general marginalist approach to value and capital. But beside the low empirical plausibility of the assumption of rising short-period marginal cost curves, such an argument runs against the criticism that long-term

7.5. ADJUSTMENT COSTS

7.5.1. The second solution to the speed-of-adjustment problem is nowadays widely accepted: adjustment costs (Eisner and Strotz, 1963; Lucas, 1967; Gould, 1968; Treadway, 1969; Takayama, 1974, pp. 697–703; Sargent, 1979, ch. VI; see Söderstrom, 1976, Galeotti, 1984, and Abel, 1990, for surveys and bibliography, and Heijdra and Van der Ploeg, 2002, pp. 39, 80, 432, for a recent advanced textbook accepting the approach).

The basic idea is well known: if the optimal capital stock *of a firm* exceeds the actual capital stock, but there are increasing marginal costs to expansion (a more rapid adjustment is proportionately more costly than a slower adjustment) due, for example, to installation or break-in costs, then the firm will not find it convenient to adjust immediately to the new optimal capital stock, and will prefer to spread out its adjustment over time, choosing an optimal adjustment path.

Although I know of no empirical enquiry as to the actual relevance of adjustment costs, the idea of adjustment costs most probably contains some truth. When, for example, Eisner writes: 'costs of planning, ordering, supply, and construction may well be an increasing function of the speed with which they are accomplished' (Eisner, 1978, p. 5), he points to elements quite possibly relevant in reality and useful for the explanation of the lags in the adjustment of industry capacity to variations of aggregate demand.[32] The problem under discussion here is whether these elements can support the thesis that a decrease in the interest rate stimulates investment.

I do not reproduce the full analytics of the approach because they are well known, but I remember the relevant aspects. A single price-taking firm is considered, producing a single product in quantity $Q(t)$ which it sells at price $p(t)$ with a putty-putty technology $Q(t) = F(K(t), L(t))$. The capital stock

relative price expectations cannot be taken as given in the face of variations of the interest rate.

32. In a non-marginalist approach based on the method of long-period positions, the costs considered by Eisner will appear, it would seem, as those costs – higher than minimum long-period production costs – which it may nonetheless be convenient for a firm to incur in order to be the first to exploit higher-than-normal profit opportunities. Thus they may be relevant to explain the speed with which new plants are built in particularly profitable fields of productive investment: but further or potential entry of firms adopting the cost-minimizing construction speed will anyway cause prices to tend to the normal long-period levels defined by the cost-minimizing technology. (A cost-minimizing construction speed no doubt exists, because too slow a construction process implies a deterioration of the plant even before it starts producing; technological obsolescence will also play a part.) The extent and speed of entry will anyway prevent the analysis from reaching definite results on the speed of adjustment of the productive capacity of an industry to demand simply on the basis of Eisner's adjustment costs (cf. §7.6.2).

depreciates at a constant rate δ. The real interest rate, as well as the real wage rate w/p, are expected to remain constant over time. The given stock of capital at time 0, $K(0)$, can be varied by the acquisition of capital goods that is by investment I:

$$\dot{K}(t) = I(t) - \delta K(t)$$

but investment causes costs $C(I(t))$, non-negative and increasing *at an increasing rate* (that is more than proportionally) with the absolute magnitude of investment. The firm aims at maximizing the present value $V(0)$ of its net cash flow (net of adjustment costs too) $pQ - wL - C(I)$ over an infinite horizon. Labour employment can be freely adjusted.

Note that $C(I(t))$ is the sum of the purchase cost of investment goods, and of all other adjustment costs. If the purchase cost of investment goods is an increasing function of the investment rate, the approach also embodies a rising-supply-price hypothesis; accordingly the literature distinguishes the *external* adjustment costs due to rising supply price, from the other, *internal* adjustment costs which are the truly new contribution of the approach. But when one aggregates over all firms in order to arrive at aggregate investment, the presence of external adjustment costs would mean that at least for the firms producing investment goods the selling price of the product is *not* given, this would require a radical modification of the analysis; so the assumptions appear to imply that the adjustment costs are only internal.

The key to the result is the assumption that adjustment costs increase more than proportionally as investment increases. The intuition is as follows. Suppose to start with that, due to decreasing returns to scale, at time 0 the optimal capital stock K^* is well-determined and finite; and suppose that it is greater than the actual capital stock of the firm $K(0)$. Without adjustment costs, the firm would like to reach K^* instantaneously, that is the rate of investment would be infinite at $t = 0$. The faster K^* is reached, the smaller the loss of potential profits[33] from the less-than-optimal production, but the greater the adjustment costs; since adjustment costs increase at an ever faster rate with the increase in the speed with which K^* is reached, there will be an adjustment speed beyond which the increase in adjustment costs is greater than the extra profits, so a unique optimal $\dot{K}$ exists. And the optimal $\dot{K}$ is a decreasing function of the rate of interest because, since unit sales revenues are assumed not to change when the rate of interest changes and since the rate of interest is a cost, a higher rate of interest decreases profits and therefore also decreases the rate of expansion that maximizes profits net of adjustment costs. Now, the amount of labour employable by the firm is *not*

33. Here profits are in the marginalist sense, and gross of adjustment costs.

given; then, if expansion is convenient at all at the given prices and interest rate, an optimal finite K^* for the price-taking firm can only exist if one assumes decreasing returns to scale; but the assumption that adjustment costs increase at an increasing rate with $\dot{K}$ determines a finite optimal *investment* even with constant returns to scale;[34] and again this optimal investment will be a decreasing function of the rate of interest because a higher rate of interest decreases profits.

It is important to note that the adjustment-cost approach, so formulated, does not need the traditional conception of capital: even with fixed coefficients, the opening up of profit opportunities due to a decrease of the interest rate (while by assumption prices, including the real wage, do not change) would make expansion profitable, and the existence of increasing adjustment costs would render the rate of expansion finite, and a decreasing function of the interest rate. Thus the way the speed-of-adjustment problem is solved also solves the problem of the indeterminate marginal product of capital if labour employment is not fixed. In all likelihood this aspect has favoured the popularity of the approach.

7.5.2. However, decisive objections can be raised about this approach. To start with, doubts have been advanced as to the empirical relevance of the assumption that there are generalized positive adjustment costs which not only increase, but also increase at an increasing rate, with the level of investment.[35] But even leaving these doubts aside, there remain grave theoretical problems.

A fundamental shortcoming of the approach is the assumption that as the interest rate varies, the other prices can be assumed unchanged, so that returns (gross of interest payments and adjustment costs) are unaffected by the level of the interest rate. This assumption, legitimate for a single price-taking firm, is untenable when one passes from the individual firm to the aggregate economy, or even only to the industry, for the reasons discussed in Section 7.3. Surprisingly, many economists who, when they teach microeconomics, explain that prices tend toward average costs, tend to forget

---

34. Again, the intuitive reason is that a sufficiently great $\dot{K}$ would increase the adjustment cost per time unit so much as to make this cost overcompensate the gain in profits from expansion. It deserves notice that the adjustment-cost approach was originally proposed as a rationalization of the flexible accelerator, but this is only possible if decreasing returns to scale are assumed (see for example Galeotti, 1984, app.). With constant returns to scale K^* is infinite, hence 'In this case there is no long-run equilibrium capital stock and the flexible accelerator would be a mis-specification' (Junankar, 1972, p. 43). This conclusion depends on the fact, which will be stressed in the next paragraph, that the product price is kept fixed when costs decrease and create the opportunity for extra-profits.

35. For more on these doubts, see, for example, Nickell (1978, pp. 37–9); Hamermesh and Pfann (1996).

that the rate of interest is a cost and that therefore its changes alter average costs and hence prices.

A second grave shortcoming of the approach is the neglect of entry. The analysis attempts to determine the optimal adjustment path of *an individual firm;* the passage to the *aggregate* investment function is obtained by assuming 'that the macro function is simply a 'blown-up' version of the micro function' (Junankar, 1972, p. 61; see also ibid., p. 43). The implicit assumption appears to be that investment is only performed by the already existing firms, so that one can obtain aggregate investment by simple summation of the investment decisions of the several firms. The issue, of the effect of possible variations in the number of firms, is never explored. Now, the assumption that aggregate investment cannot comprise the setting up of new firms would clearly be absurd: if there is a field in economic theory where the birth of new firms must be admitted, this is aggregate investment. But then one must admit that the positive extra-profits that stimulate existing firms to grow will also stimulate the setting up of new firms. Then, even conceding all the other assumptions of the approach, the growth rate of the *aggregate* capital stock is still indeterminate because it also depends on the rate of creation of new firms. For example, with completely free entry and price-taking, a decrease in costs that creates positive profits would imply the entry of an infinite number of firms, that is an infinite rate of investment.

This is partially admitted by Söderstrom (1976, p. 386), who writes that in adjustment-cost theories of investment 'market equilibrium ... may be indeterminate under free entry': however, rigour would require replacing 'may be' with 'is' in this admission.[36] This confirms the mistake of generalizing from the partial-equilibrium analysis of a single firm to aggregate investment.

A limit to investment derived from 'external' adjustment costs, that is from a rising-supply-price schedule for capital goods, being derived from a general-equilibrium perspective, would not suffer from this fallacy of composition.[37] However, then, as noticed in the previous paragraph, other assumptions of the approach would become questionable; and anyway, once it were admitted that rates of return adapt to the rate of interest, decreases in the rate of interest would not create the extra profits which in this approach would cause infinite investment in the absence of adjustment costs. In the search for a negative influence of the rate of interest on investment, there

36. In spite of Söderstrom's admission, the problem is not mentioned at all by Romer (1996) or Heijdra and Van der Ploeg (2002).
37. Nickell (1978, p. 35), remaining at the level of the individual firm, states that the assumption of increasing supply price of capital will be legitimate if the firm is large relative to the industry supplying the specific capital goods it needs. Of course little can be deduced on aggregate investment from considerations of this type.

would appear to be little alternative to the 'consideration of aggregate "factor proportions" for the entire economy' lucidly recognized to be indispensable by Ackley (1978, p. 625 fn. 15: cf. the end of §7.3.1). However, one then meets the problems raised by reverse capital deepening and by the variability of labour employment.

7.6. TOBIN'S q

7.6.1. Tobin's approach (Tobin, 1969, 1980, 1982; Tobin and Brainard, 1977) argues that investment is a positive function of the ratio q between the market value of the capital assets of a firm and their replacement cost, and in particular that net investment will generally be positive or negative according to whether q is greater or less than 1. It is specified (Tobin and Brainard, 1977, p. 243) that one should calculate these magnitudes at the margin. The numerator will then be greater than the denominator if the internal rate of return on the stream of net returns expected from additional capital goods is higher than the interest rate, that is, in Keynesian terminology, if the marginal efficiency of capital is higher than the interest rate. This theory argues, therefore, that investment will be positive if the marginal efficiency of capital is greater than the interest rate, and more specifically, that investment will be an increasing function of the difference between the two. At first sight, the difference from Keynes is that Keynes argued that investment would be pushed to the point where the marginal efficiency of capital *equals* the interest rate; Tobin's theory would then be adding to Keynes's a sluggish adjustment of the investment level, which is justified in terms of adjustment costs and/or short-period rising supply price of investment goods. In fact, there are elements in what Tobin and Brainard write, that suggest that their theory is closer to Keynes's than one might at first imagine, and that the difference is made to look greater than it is by their different definition of the marginal efficiency of capital, which is connected with their measurement of the replacement cost at the denominator of q at *long-period* normal prices:

> Investment would not be related to q if instantaneous arbitrage could produce such floods of new capital goods as to keep market values and replacement costs continuously in line ... such arbitrage does not occur. Discrepancies between q and its normal value do arise. The speed with which investment eliminates such discrepancies depends on the costs of adjustment and growth for individual enterprises, and for the economy as a whole on the short-run marginal costs of producing investment goods (Tobin and Brainard, 1977, p. 244).

The last lines of this sentence show that Tobin and Brainard do not include the short-period divergence of the supply prices of investment goods from their normal levels in the determination of q. Tobin and Brainard argue that even Keynes really agreed with their theory:

> Since Keynes discusses at length independent variations in the marginal efficiency of capital and the rate of interest, he does not really imagine that investment adjusts the capital stock fast enough to keep them continuously equal. Indeed the true message is that investment is related to discrepancies between the marginal efficiency and the interest rate (ibid.).

This sentence shows that, differently from Keynes, Tobin and Brainard define the marginal efficiency of capital as *not* incorporating a short-period rising-supply-price-of-capital-goods hypothesis, that is in the same way as Lerner.[38] On this definition, Keynes's own theory yields the q approach.

7.6.2. It has been shown that the adjustment-cost approach too can yield a q approach (Hayashi, 1982). But Tobin's q-theory need not rest on the very debatable hypotheses of the adjustment-cost approach, because it can be justified through appeal to other reasons. For instance, entry of new firms does not undermine the theory because Tobin includes short-period rising supply price, or delivery lags, among the causes of the non-instantaneous tendency of q to 1.

Tobin's main contribution appears to consist in the suggestion that the stock market valuation of firms may, with caution, be used to infer the current evaluation of the present value of expected future returns. Now, if the stock market could be trusted to such an end, then Tobin's q would first of all reflect the degree of utilization of capacity. If, on average, capacity utilization is below normal and expected to remain below normal for some not inconsiderable time, at the given interest rate the capitalized flow of returns will be less than the replacement value of existing plants. It will approximately equal the value of the smaller plants (of similar age) sufficient to produce the current output at a normal rate of utilization (because empirical evidence strongly suggests that relative prices remain close to the long-period ones associated with a given rate of interest even when most firms operate below normal capacity). This fact may have contributed to the widespread acceptance of Tobin's q because the approach, besides being capable of incorporating Keynes's own approach or the adjustment-cost

---

38. They appear to think that Keynes's definition of the marginal efficiency of capital coincides with the marginal product of capital at long-period normal prices: 'Keynes's condition that the marginal efficiency of capital equal the rate of interest determines not the flow of investment but the stock of capital' (ibid.).

approach, is also capable of indicating the influence of capacity utilization (and therefore of aggregate demand) on investment, an influence that many economists find it impossible to deny.[39]

But on the explanation of a negative elasticity of investment vis-à-vis the rate of interest, Tobin appears to have added nothing new to the other explanations internal to the marginalist two-stage format, that is relying on an optimal capital stock determined by long-period capital–labour substitution, and then relying on short-period rising supply price or on delivery lags or construction lags or adjustment costs in order to explain the sluggish adjustment to the optimal capital stock. Nor should this conclusion be surprising, given Tobin's unproblematic acceptance of the marginalist theory of value and distribution and of the notion of 'capital' as a single factor, reflected in his use of aggregate production functions. But then the criticisms advanced against those other explanations also apply to any attempt to use Tobin's q in order to defend the traditional decreasing investment schedule.

7.6.3. None of the explanations of the decreasing investment schedule discussed so far is very recent; but the theory has not advanced beyond them, as one can confirm by examining the most recent advanced macro textbooks. In recent years theoretical enquiries into investment theory by mainstream economists have concentrated on the influence of uncertainty upon investment,[40] and afford no new insight into possible reasons for a negative influence of the rate of interest on aggregate investment.

One must conclude that the justifications obtainable from the recent and not-so-recent macroeconomic literature of the view of aggregate investment as a decreasing function of the interest rate are either unacceptable even apart from the criticisms of marginalist–neoclassical capital theory, or must ultimately rely on the indefensible notion of a significant negative elasticity of the demand for 'capital' with respect to the interest rate, or sometimes suffer from both kinds of deficiencies. In particular, the mistake recurs again and again in the analyses elaborated after Keynes, of treating the yields from investment projects as independent of the level of the interest rate, a mistake pointed out also by mainstream theorists, for example, Ackley (1978) or Alchian (1955).

---

39. An empirical finding of a positive correlation between Tobin's q and aggregate investment might therefore simply reflect the influence on investment of the average degree of utilization of capacity (in other words, of the accelerator).
40. For example, Dixit and Pindyck (1994).

7.7. INVESTMENT IN GENERAL EQUILIBRIUM NEO-WALRASIAN MODELS AND CONCLUSIONS

7.7.1. Does one obtain some support for a negative interest-elasticity of investment from modern general equilibrium analyses?

Two basic difficulties of any attempt to derive conclusions on aggregate investment from modern general equilibrium models are the impermanence problem (that is the lack of any guarantee that the model's equilibrium, even when unique, may be a reasonable approximation to the behaviour of an economy where adjustments are not instantaneous), and – the moment it is admitted that complete futures markets do not exist – the indefiniteness problem caused by the introduction of expectations (§2.1.3). In particular, when expectations are introduced in the analysis, the reaction of investment to changes in the interest rate comes to depend on how these changes will influence the investors' expectations (Garegnani, 1978, p. 36). It is not difficult to conceive of instances in which this influence may go, in the short period, in what a neoclassical economist would call a 'perverse' direction: it might for instance happen that *a decrease* in the interest rate causes expectations of further decreases, inducing a postponement, that is a *decrease,* of investment.

Against this background, the nature of the traditional marginalist conclusion that investment is a decreasing function of the rate of interest becomes clearer: this conclusion only aimed at describing the persistent force, capable of dominating over longer periods the accidents and temporary disturbances of the short or very short period, and of letting a clear trend emerge. To prove the existence of such a persistent force it was necessary to have recourse to long-period analysis, that is to the full working out of the effects of changes of the rate of interest on prices, quantities and technical choices, with sufficient time given for the correction of erroneous expectations.

This is confirmed by the theory of general temporary equilibrium. In this theory, the assumption that investment is adjusted to full-employment savings is only part of the *definition* of equilibrium: no argument is given for believing that there are forces tending to bring such a state about. Thus Bliss, after writing that 'Many of the issues that make the theory of investment a peculiarly interesting and challenging subject of study arise precisely because it is not in the context of a full intertemporal equilibrium that actual investment decisions are taken' (Bliss 1975b, p. 318), is only able to prove that, in the absence of complete futures markets, 'the firm will maximize a particular function of its choice variables' (p. 325), that is, that the objective of the firm under uncertainty is sufficiently definite as to allow a determination of the firms' decisions. The assumptions (for example on returns to scale) made by Bliss to reach this result are questionable, but for our purposes the important thing is that even so, no argument is provided suggesting that the firms' maximizations will yield a decreasing aggregate investment schedule. Subsequent work by Bliss on temporary equilibrium (Bliss 1976, 1983) has been exclusively concerned with the problem of *existence* of a temporary equilibrium, and says nothing on the stability of the savings-investment market. This latter problem is also absent from the surveys of temporary equilibrium theory by Grandmont (1977, 1987), which only discuss the problem whether a sequence of temporary equilibria converges to a steady state, *assuming* that in each period a full-employment temporary equilibrium is reached.

As to the savings-investment markets of intertemporal Arrow–Debreu equilibria with complete futures markets, a debate on their nature and stability has only very recently started (Schefold 1997, 2000; Garegnani 2000, 2003; Mandler, 2002). For the moment what has been made clear is that savings-investment markets are present in intertemporal equilibrium models too; and that so far the issue of their stability has been neglected because of the habit of representing production via 'vertically integrated' intertemporal production functions, where the sole inputs are 'original' factors, and intermediate goods do not appear. In this way one is induced to think that demand for consumption goods immediately implies a demand for 'original' factors, and one does not notice the implicit assumption that the supply of the intermediate goods needed for the production of the consumption goods adapts without difficulty to the demand for them. This adaptation should on the contrary be doubted, because factor substitution in the intermediate periods of intertemporal equilibria may encounter difficulties similar to those highlighted by reswitching and reverse capital deepening in long-period analysis: the relative prices of intermediate goods depend on distribution in intertemporal equilibria as much as in long-period analysis; it is this dependence that permits the 'anti-neoclassical' behaviour of factor substitution illustrated in Chapter 6; the analogous dependence in intertemporal equilibria can only cause analogous 'anti-neoclassical' phenomena. The exploration of how these phenomena present themselves in intertemporal equilibria has barely started. Anyway, it seems evident that what can emerge from the debate is only further weaknesses of a theory, the theory of intertemporal equilibria, which cannot by itself prove anything definite about aggregate investment. There are extremely few futures markets in real economies, foresight is far from perfect (who, in the 1980s, expected the growth rate of Japan to fall nearly to zero in the 1990s?), adjustments are slow, and there is no finite horizon. In order to be credible, the demonstration of a tendency of investment to adjust to savings must be based on realistic, time-consuming mechanisms that permit mistakes, disequilibria and expectation correction: in other words, long-period mechanisms. Now, no other long-period mechanism attempting such a demonstration is in sight, capable of replacing the traditional marginalist argument, illustrated in §4.3.2, based on the conception of capital as a single factor.

7.7.2. To conclude, neoclassical macroeconomists keep assuming the stability of the savings-investment market, on the basis of a decreasing relationship between investment and the interest rate. Those (not many nowadays) who have studied the problem, admit that the notion of 'capital' as a single factor is indefensible, but they appear not to realize that without it, that relationship cannot be postulated, and that general equilibrium theory can give them no help.

A consequence of this is that the full employment of labour, which is assumed in general equilibrium models and in mainstream analyses of growth, should also be abandoned, and not as a result of rigid prices as in fixprice models, or due to other 'imperfections' such as incomplete or implicit contracts or asymmetric information, but simply because the marginalist approach provides no plausible market mechanism ensuring that investment will rise to the level required to absorb the full-employment volume of savings.

Clearly, it is then impossible to argue that a sequence of neo-Walrasian equilibrium positions represents, however approximately, the path followed by a market economy.

The forces determining the level of aggregate output must be admitted to be different from those postulated by the marginalist approach; a different theory of employment and growth is required.

APPENDIX 7A1. JORGENSON AND PRECIOUS

7A1.1. The discussion of the adjustment-cost approach in Section 7.6 will make it possible to be brief in the examination of an approach that, according to one survey (D. Fisher, 1983), enjoyed at least until the 1970s (together with Tobin's *q*) the greatest popularity among applied economists: Jorgenson's so-called 'neoclassical' analysis. This analysis is no longer popular, but it is worth while to examine it in order fully to appreciate the little theoretical clarity that for some decades now has characterized aggregate investment theory.

Jorgenson's econometric studies will not be discussed here; attention is paid only to his more theoretical analyses (Jorgenson, 1963, 1967). Nor will a detailed exposition of Jorgenson's theory be attempted here. The interested reader can consult Precious (1987) for a clear introduction, Bliss (1975b, pp. 306–9) and Ackley (1978, pp. 625 fn., 634–8, 640–41) for critical commentaries.

Jorgenson's 1963 article is very different from his 1967 contribution. In the former article Jorgenson argues that the rate of interest will determine the desired K/L ratio and hence will determine the desired K, *given the output to be produced*. The desired K is then reached with a (distributed) lag (which is left unexplained theoretically, and simply estimated econometrically). The analysis is formulated for a single firm with constant returns to scale, but, because of its dependence on a given output level, it can easily be re-interpreted as applying to industries, or to the entire economy: the latter version was adopted in the textbook by Dornbusch and Fischer (1987). It is openly based on the notion of 'capital'–labour substitution and therefore, when applied to the entire economy, it is subject to the Cambridge criticisms. (Some further considerations on this approach appear at the end of §8.2.2.)

The 1967 contribution is something else. Output is no longer taken as given; only prices are. The analysis concerns the investment decision of a single perfectly competitive firm, which, as in the adjustment-cost approach, takes as given the current and expected output price $p(t)$, the labour wage $w(t)$, the supply price $z(t)$ of the single investment good, and the discount (interest) rate $r(t)$. But no adjustment costs are introduced (it is also assumed that there is a perfect market for second-hand capital goods), nor is the employment of labour taken as given; in order to determine a finite optimal capital stock K^* (a finite dimension of the firm), Jorgenson must assume (which he does, see 1967, p. 141, without spending one word to justify the assumption) decreasing technological returns to scale. The firm's maximand is:

$$\max V(0) = \int_0^\infty \left\{ p(t)Q(t) - w(t)L(t) - z(t)I(t) \right\} e^{-r(t)t} dt$$

s.t. $Q(t) = F\big(K(t), L(t)\big)$ (with decreasing returns to scale),

$I = \dot{K} + \delta K.$

where Q is output, p its price, L labour, w its wage, I is physical investment, z the price of capital goods, r the rate of interest, K the capital stock, $\dot{K}$ its derivative with respect to time, and δ the radioactive deterioration rate of the capital stock. (In fact Jorgenson simplifies the analysis by assuming p, w, r to be constant in time.)

The assumption that the amounts of capital and labour employed can be changed without cost, together with the assumption of instantaneous flow production, implies that, much as in static analysis, the firm will want to adjust its labour force until the marginal product of labour at each instant equals the real wage at that instant:

$$\frac{\partial Q}{\partial L} = F_L = \frac{w}{p}$$ (where the magnitudes refer to the same instant t),

and that the firm will desire the capital stock which makes the marginal product of capital equal to the marginal cost of capital. The only complication is the definition of the marginal cost, which must now include not only depreciation but also the possible capital gain or loss on the capital good during the period, due to changes in the selling price of capital goods. This new notion of marginal cost, often called 'user' or 'rental' cost of capital, or opportunity cost of the services of capital, is given by $c = z(r+\delta) - \dot{z}$:

$$\frac{\partial Q}{\partial K} = F_K = \frac{c}{p} = \frac{z(r+\delta) - \dot{z}}{p},$$

where, again, all magnitudes refer to the same instant t. Unless the production function exhibits (sufficiently) decreasing returns to scale,[41] these two marginal conditions do not determine a finite profit-maximizing size of the firm and input proportions, and hence do not determine a finite K^*; this is why Jorgenson assumes decreasing returns to scale.

41. Jorgenson needs more than simply decreasing returns to scale: if for example returns to scale were decreasing but less and less so (tending asymptotically to constant), then a finite optimum might not exist. This is not usually noticed.

With these assumptions, Jorgenson proves that $K^*(t)$ depends only on the values at the same moment of $p(t)$, $w(t)$, and $c = z(r + \delta) - \dot{z}$ (the thing is evident from the two marginal conditions listed). In order to obtain that $K^*(t)$ will change continuously, and thus obtain a finite net investment $\dot{K}^*$, Jorgenson *assumes* that p, w, c are continuous functions of time (in fact he assumes that p, w, r remain constant). As a consequence, K^* changes continuously from $K^*(0)$ onward, thus determining desired investment along the optimal path. But, with an arbitrarily given initial capital stock $K(0)$, there is no guarantee that $K^*(0) = K(0)$, and the desired investment at $t = 0$ might be infinite. In order to avoid this problem, Jorgenson restricts his analysis to the case $K^*(0) = K(0)$, that is he assumes that the firm is *already*, at time 0, on an optimal path (no justification is given for this assumption either). In order to study the influence of changes in the interest rate upon investment at time 0, one is therefore restricted to comparing optimal paths for all of which $K^*(0) = K(0)$, in spite of $r(0)$ being different; the difference in the evolution of K^* from $t = 0$ onward will cause a difference in $\dot{K}^*$ at time 0. Having assumed that $p(0)$, $w(0)$ and $z(0)$ are given, and having further assumed that p, w, r remain the same from moment 0 onward, Jorgenson finds that the only paths satisfying $K^*(0) = K(0)$ are those for which the differences in $r(0)$ are tied to differences in $\dot{z}$ as follows: 'all changes in the rate of interest are precisely compensated by changes in the rate of change of the price of current and future investment goods so as to leave the own-rate of interest on investment goods unchanged' (Jorgenson, 1967, p. 148). The reason is that, since $K^*(0)$ depends only on $p(0)$, $w(0)$ and $c(0)$, and since $p(0)$, $w(0)$ and $z(0)$ are given and hence common to all paths, two paths differing as to $r(0)$ and both satisfying $K^*(0) = K(0)$ must have the same $p(0)$, $w(0)$, $z(0)$ and $c(0)$; the fact that $c(0)$ must not change as $r(0)$ is made to change to generate alternative paths implies, since $c = z(r + \delta) - \dot{z}$ and $z(0)$ and δ are given, that $z - (\dot{z}/z)$, the own-rate of interest on investment goods, must not change at time 0 as $r(0)$ is changed. Jorgenson then proceeds to *assume* (again, without a word of justification) that this is just the case. He is then able to prove that, for the case $\dot{r} = \dot{w} = \dot{p} = 0$, and given $w(0)$ and $p(0)$, as $r(0)$ is made to vary the paths change in such a way that $dK^*(0)/dr < 0$, that is, since gross investment at time 0 is simply $I(0) = \dot{K}^*(0) + \delta K(0)$, that investment at time 0 is a decreasing function of the interest rate.[42]

---

42. The reason is that, as r rises at time 0, then $\dot{z}$ rises to compensate so as to leave $c(0)$ constant, but all future $c(t)$'s are higher, so $K^*(0)$ remains the same but all future $K^*(t)$ will be lower (because $dK^*(t)/dc(t)$ is negative) and hence $\dot{K}^*(0)$ will be lower. That future $c(t)$'s must be higher can be shown as follows. The price at time s, $z(s)$, of a new investment good purchased at that time must be equal to the value of all future capital services of that investment good, discounted to time s. Or equivalently, discounting to time 0, one obtains:

7A1.2. Even a neoclassical theoretician should agree that this way of deriving a decreasing investment schedule runs against at least the following grave objections:

1. the criticism advanced in §7.6.2 against the adjustment-cost approach, that aggregate investment remains indeterminate because the number of firms cannot be taken as given, applies to Jorgenson's analysis too;
2. the assumption implicit in the analysis that z may go on increasing forever in the face of given p, w and r, is incompatible with the accepted view that prices in the long run must equal costs of production;
3. more generally, again as for the adjustment cost school, the assumption that the price of the investment good and the real wage are given independently of the level of the interest rate is indefensible; it implies, among other things, that it may happen that firms earn extra profits for ever;
4. the assumption of decreasing returns to scale is highly debatable;
5. there is no discussion of the mechanism which should ensure that z varies in such a way as to leave $r - (\dot{z}/z)$ unchanged, nor more generally of whether and when this assumption is plausible, or even only logically possible, what it will generally *not* be: for example, in a one-good world such as the one of the Solow neoclassical one-sector growth model, $p = z = 1$ necessarily, so $\dot{z}(0) = 0$ whatever $r(0)$, and Jorgenson's analysis is logically impossible.

Thus, even from the perspective of the marginalist approach to value, Jorgenson's 1967 theory appears totally indefensible (and, for instance, is so judged by Tobin (1967) in his Commentary on Jorgenson's article in the same volume – in sharp contrast with the enthusiastic comment of another econometrician, Griliches, 1967).

Only the last of the above-mentioned five shortcomings is overcome, at the price of the introduction of a rational expectations assumption, in a subsequent integration of Jorgenson's analysis with the approach based on short-run rising supply price for capital goods due to Precious (1987, ch. 3). Precious maintains anyway the unacceptable assumptions of decreasing returns to scale, given number of firms, and given returns to capital in the face of variations of the interest rate.

$$e^{-rs}z(s) = \int e^{-rt}c(t)dt.$$

Now, by assumption, as r varies, $\dot{z}$ varies in such a way that the own-rate of interest on investment goods does not vary, that is the discounted value of future investment goods remains unchanged as r varies, $d(e^{-rs}z(t))/dr = 0$, so the value of the integral on the right-hand side must not change as r varies. If r increases, e^{-rs} decreases so the $c(t)$'s must increase.

APPENDIX 7A2. THE PIGOU OR REAL BALANCE EFFECT

This Appendix discusses the other possible defence, based on the 'Pigou effect' or 'real balance effect' (Patinkin, 1987), of a spontaneous tendency toward full employment (although not of a tendency of investment to adjust to savings) if money wages are flexible in the presence of labour unemployment. The well-known argument is that, if the supply of 'outside' money (money holdings not offset by debts) is given, then a decrease of the price level induced by the decrease of money wages increases the wealth of the consumers who hold 'outside' money, and this increase in wealth raises the average propensity to consume. Thus a decrease of money wages causes an increase of expenditure even if investment remains fixed.

The presence of a wealth effect on expenditure is not universally accepted;[43] some observers have, for example, denied its relevance, especially in the short run, on the basis of the little influence on consumption in the USA of the stock market collapse of recent years. For the long run, there is a majority agreement that the wealth effect on consumption exists; but it also appears to be universally agreed that the Pigou or real balance effect is very weak, because of the very small proportion of wealth represented by 'outside' money, and because of the way through which the increase in wealth is reached, namely, through a price deflation that can have negative side effects. Even the economist who owes most of his fame to his contributions on the analytics of the real balance effect has concluded that it is highly doubtful 'whether it is strong enough to offset the adverse expectations generated by a price decline – including those generated by the wave of bankruptcies that might well be caused by a severe decline' (Patinkin, 1987, p. 100).

It is not easy to find dissenting opinions. A recent advanced textbook states for example:

> In a modern economy, the monetary base is a small proportion of M1 and an even smaller proportion of broader money aggregates. It is an almost insignificant proportion of total wealth in the economy. Therefore, increases in its real value are likely to be of minimal importance in terms of increasing total expenditures in the economy. Therefore, in practical terms, if the real balance effect was the only mechanism for taking an economy in recession with deficient demand to its full employment demand level, one could not put much faith in its efficacy in restoring full employment within a reasonable period (Handa, 2000, p. 493).

A simple calculation, based on recent econometric estimates of the wealth effect, strongly supports Handa's conclusion. Davis and Palumbo (2001)

43. Cf. for example Lerner (1973).

estimate that the wealth effect in the USA is of the order of 3–6 per cent, that is an increase in wealth of 100 million dollars increases yearly expenditure by an amount between 3 and 6 million dollars.[44] The USA monetary base (outside money) in 1995 was roughly 380 billion dollars (Handa, 2000, p. 11) while nominal GDP was around 7500 billon dollars, that is approximately 20 times bigger. A doubling of the real value of outside money in that year (that is a halving of all prices) would therefore have meant, according to the Davis–Palumbo estimate, an increase in consumption expenditure roughly between 12 and 18 billion dollars. This amounts to between 0.15 per cent and 0.25 per cent of GDP, or roughly one-fifth of 1 per cent. This means that for any plausible level of price decreases, the real balance effect is unnoticeable.[45]

A calculation by Malcolm Sawyer (1997, sect. 6) based on the NAIRU model of Layard, Jackman and Nickell similarly concludes that a decrease of the fiscal stance causing a 1 per cent decrease of aggregate demand would require a 67 per cent decrease of money prices in order for the real balance effect to counterbalance it (assuming no perverse effects of the price decrease on investment).

The conclusion that one cannot rely on the Pigou effect to establish a tendency toward full employment can only be strengthened if one admits that the foregoing calculations are based on the most favourable comparative-statics assumptions, while in reality one has to take into account the effects of the dynamic transition, effects which are generally recognized to be negative, and the more so, the faster the reduction in money wages. An (incomplete) list of these negative effects must include the following:

i.   the increased difficulties of repayment of debts by firms not only causes a danger of bankruptcies and a discouragement of investment, but can also entail a worsening of the position of creditors because of the increased risk of default by debtors, so that the assumption of a compensation of the effects as between debtors and creditors is unwarranted;

44. The estimates of other authors on the long-run wealth effect are in the same range, with only some admission of a possibility (of very low probability) that the effect may be greater, up to 15 per cent (Dynan and Maki, 2001). It is generally admitted that the effect takes time to show up, so the short-run effect is lower.
45. A yearly rate of deflation of 10 per cent (that is a real interest rate not less than 10 per cent, since the nominal interest rate can hardly become negative) would certainly have disruptive effects, and yet, after seven years, it would achieve, through a halving of the price level, only the extremely weak real balance effect indicated; even the highest estimate of the wealth effect in the recent literature, 15 per cent, would only mean an increase in expenditure a little above one half of one percentage point in the seventh year. Clearly the negative effects would greatly dominate this almost unnoticeable positive effect.

ii. the fall in prices will probably entail a greater fall in the value of real estate and of stock markets, whose nominal values are known to fluctuate widely, with a negative wealth effect;

iii. money price reductions generally follow money wage reductions only with a lag (which may be of months), and therefore the first effect of money wage reductions is a redistribution away from lower- to higher-income groups, that is plausibly towards higher-saving groups. This causes a smaller multiplier, hence a decrease of aggregate demand, with possible adverse effects on investment (if the latter depends on aggregate demand and on its variations) and further adverse effects on aggregate demand along well-known multiplier–accelerator vicious circles. If money wage reductions continue for a long time (as requested by the very big falls of the price level necessary to make the Pigou effect significant), the lag is not eliminated for a long time, so real wages remain lower for a long time.

Besides these possibilities of dynamic instability, static instability may result from the existence of interest-bearing government debt. It is frequently acknowledged that the increase in the real value of government bonds in the hands of the public will most probably not contribute to the Pigou effect because the decrease of nominal government revenue from taxation will most probably cause an increase in taxation.[46] But it is seldom noticed that the result may go counter to the Pigou effect: if interest payments go prevalently to higher-income groups, and if, to finance the increased real value of these payments, the government increases real taxation on all groups, then the resulting redistribution of income toward higher-income groups will increase the average propensity to save, possibly overpowering the real balance effect (Garegnani, 1978, p. 57, fn. 39).

Finally, the assumption that the monetary base would remain unchanged is highly questionable. It is more and more widely admitted that central banks aim at a reasonable stability of the interest rate and therefore largely adapt the supply of the monetary base to the demand for it. The thesis advocated most famously by Kaldor, that the supply of monetary base is largely endogenous, has been recently accepted by David Romer (2000), who has proposed to give up the LM curve of the IS–LM model owing to the observation that central banks increasingly target the interest rate rather than the money supply. Pivetti (1991, ch. 2) summarizes evidence suggesting that

---

46. If there is no compensatory increase in taxation, the government either runs a deficit, that is it operates an expansionary fiscal policy (and then it is not the Pigou effect that raises aggregate demand), or cuts public spending, that is decreases aggregate demand owing to Haavelmo's theorem, which aggravates the situation.

this is not only a recent tendency as Romer suggests, but a nearly universal aspect of capitalism in industrialized countries.

In any case, the mechanism based on the Pigou effect, even if it could be shown to cause neither static nor dynamic instability, would in no way rehabilitate the marginalist approach to value and distribution. By itself – that is, if the marginalist approach is rejected – it would constitute an extremely weak argument in favour of laissez-faire. For instance, it would offer no defence against the argument that, if what is wanted is a decrease of the average propensity to save, a faster and safer way to obtain it is by redistributing income or wealth from the rich to the poor or, if one wants to avoid redistributions, by printing and distributing money with Friedman's helicopter, or by letting the government use this newly printed money for deficit spending. The recourse to the Pigou effect rather than to these other interventions, even conceding its efficacy, would only mean a preference for aiding the groups with relevant holdings of cash, that is, the wealthier groups, and for a decrease of real wages (due to the lag with which product prices adjust to decreases of money wages) during the long transition period.

8. Capital Theory and Macroeconomics. II: The Labour Demand Curve

8.1. THE LABOUR DEMAND CURVE: NEO-WALRASIAN OR LONG-PERIOD?

8.1.1. Let us now discuss how the other pillar of the applications of the neoclassical approach to reality, the decreasing labour demand curve, is affected by the arguments of the earlier chapters. (The simplifying assumption will be made that labour is homogeneous.)

The aggregate labour demand curve aims to exhibit the relationship between real wage and aggregate employment. The direction of causation depends on whether one accepts Say's Law, or the principle of effective demand. If Say's Law is believed to hold such that investment adapts to the level of savings generated by each level of employment, then the labour demand curve aims to show, for each given level of the real wage, the labour employment toward which one may expect actual employment to gravitate. If Say's Law is not accepted, and if one follows Keynes in taking the money wage as given and in assuming that an excess of aggregate demand over aggregate output causes the price level to rise, then the aggregate labour demand curve indicates the real wage that must and will come to rule (through variations of the price level relative to the money wage) if a certain level of employment is imposed by a Keynesian determination of aggregate output.

In either case, that is both when the direction of causality is from the real wage to aggregate output, and when it is from the aggregate output level to the real wage, the labour demand curve is the curve implied by the solutions of a general equilibrium model where the equation 'demand for labour = supply of labour' has been eliminated, and in its place the real wage (or the rate of interest, in the more Keynesian version) is treated as a parameter; and where, furthermore, the labour income, which goes to demand final goods, is the income of the employed amount of labour only.[1] For example, in a one-

---

1. Thus unemployed workers do not demand final goods (except with income from sources other than their labour); for each level of the real wage, the economy is in equilibrium on all markets except the labour market: Walras' law as normally intended does not hold (there is

good economy such as the one of the Solow growth model, it is the curve connecting L_D to w, derived from the following model, where capital is made of the same stuff as consumption, w is the parametric real wage, Y is gross output, L_D and K_D are labour employed and capital employed, $F_L^{-1}(w, K_D)$ is the function yielding the labour employment which makes the marginal product of labour equal to w when the capital employed is K_D, F_K^{-1} does the same for capital and the rate of interest, K and L are the given supplies of capital and of labour, and δ is the rate of radioactive depreciation:

$$Y = F(K_D, L_D)$$

$$L_D = F_L^{-1}(w, K_D)$$

$$K_D = F_K^{-1}(r + \delta, L_D)$$

$$K_D = K$$

Labour unemployment is determined by $L - L_D$. The real wage is treated as a parameter, so the endogenously determined variables are three: Y, K_D, L_D. The absence of the condition of full employment of labour implies that one can derive L_D as a function of w. This function is the labour demand schedule.

The problem which I intend to discuss now is: the moment one admits a multiplicity of capital goods, how precisely is the capital endowment specified, which is kept fixed while varying the real wage and the employment of labour?

disequilibrium in only one market), because the demand for final goods is not based on the income consumers *count on* obtaining from their desired supplies of factors (as in the tâtonnement with 'tickets'), it derives only from the factor supplies which do find purchasers (cf. §1.2.4). (The spread of neo-Walrasian notions of equilibrium and of the habit of conceiving the equilibrium as reached by a tâtonnement evidently obscured this assumption implicit in the derivation of the traditional labour demand curve, to the point that Clower's rediscovery of it under the name of 'dual-decision hypothesis' – cf. Clower, 1967, 1969 – was hailed as a great analytical advance. This is further confirmation of the loss of contact with traditional modes of analysis.) Clearly, if one cannot assume that all workers are identical in tastes and endowments, this traditional labour demand curve is somewhat indeterminate outside the full-employment equilibrium point. When labour supply is greater than demand, the composition of demand, and hence the demand for labour, are affected by precisely *which* workers remain unemployed; when there is excess demand for labour, then the demand for labour is affected by which hypotheses one makes as to the tastes of the imaginary workers employed in excess of the supply of labour. But the resulting indeterminacy could be argued to be of negligible importance, because it certainly did not affect the sign of the slope of the curve and hence the qualitative conclusions derivable from the analysis.

A moment's reflection will show that what is kept fixed cannot be the vector of endowments of the several capital goods: endowments for example of nails, screws, component parts of final goods only waiting to be assembled. These endowments would have *no persistence*, being susceptible to drastic changes in the span of even only a few hours, so the labour demand curve based on them would have no validity for assessing the effects of changes in the real wage on labour demand, effects that necessarily take some time to become manifest. Also, the labour demand curve would be *extremely inelastic*, suffering from the nearly total absence of substitutability between labour and capital goods once the 'form' of capital was completely specified. Small changes in the endowments of the several capital goods might then cause very large changes in the demand for labour associated with a given real wage, which, given the impermanence of those endowments, would in practice mean an *indeterminacy* of the influence of the real wage on labour demand. It is thus clear that the aggregate labour demand curve cannot have a neo-Walrasian specification of the given capital endowment behind it.

In fact, the origin of the notion of the labour demand curve is found in long-period marginalist analysis: Hicks and Robertson (cf. the discussion of their contributions on this topic in §§1.3.2, 2.1.4) admitted that the determination of a useful marginal-product-of-labour schedule requires that the 'form' of 'capital' be adapted to the changing level of labour employment. The labour demand curve is a long-period notion, indicating the labour employment associated with a given real wage when sufficient time is allowed for the given quantity of 'capital' (treated as a single factor of variable 'form') to take the most appropriate 'form'.

Indeed, if this traditional conception of capital were not in the background – if the several capital goods were not seen as elements of a single factor 'capital' employed in a given quantity, and whose optimal ratio to labour increases with the real wage – it would be unclear why the disappearance of some kinds of capital goods and the appearance of different ones, normally associated with the changes in the 'form' of capital brought about by a change in real wage, should always entail a change in the demand for labour of opposite sign to the change in real wage.

But such a long-period labour demand curve needs a given endowment of 'capital', conceived as a single factor and therefore as a quantity of value, and we know that this given endowment is theoretically undefinable independently of distribution. Thus one cannot even *start* to discuss the shape of the long-period labour demand curve because one does not possess sufficient data for its determination.[2]

2. This point has not been adequately stressed in the discussions of the implications of the capital theory debates for the demand for labour.

8.1.2. For an evaluation of the notion of a long-period neoclassical demand for labour, what reverse capital deepening adds to the above considerations is this: *even if* one were to concede the legitimacy of the assumption of a given 'capital' endowment of variable 'form', still one would be unable to derive a decreasing shape of the long-period labour demand curve even assuming no 'troublesome' income effects. The possibility that the demand for 'capital' increases with the rate of interest, when labour employment is given, would imply – since rate of interest and real wage are inversely related – that the demand for labour might increase with the real wage when the amount of 'capital' employed is given. Instabilities, or indeterminacies, or implausible equilibrium levels of the real wage might result. This would again oblige one to conclude that the real wage is determined by forces other than the tendency toward an equilibrium between supply and demand.

8.2. SHORT-PERIOD ANALYSES OF KEYNESIAN TYPE

8.2.1. Let us then ask whether some basis can be found for a downward-sloping demand curve for labour, which need not rely on the indefensible conception of capital as a single factor, an amount of value, but which does not go to the sterile opposite of taking as given the entire vector of capital goods. It seems to be a widespread opinion that there is indeed a half-way house, which corresponds to the Marshallian–Keynesian short period, where a decreasing short-period labour demand schedule can be derived, without any reference to a well-behaved 'capital'–labour substitution, by taking as given the 'productive capacity' of the economy, that is its more durable capital goods and fixed plants in physical terms. I will now try to argue that, if the traditional notion of 'capital'–labour substitution is rejected, this derivation of a decreasing labour demand schedule is no more feasible than the other two.

A first supply-side obstacle is the question of how to separate capital goods into two groups, those whose stocks might be treated as given, and the others. There appears to be no single clear-cut divide between kinds of capital goods, in terms of the speed with which their endowments can change; rather, there is a continuum, so that any separation of capital goods into two categories – one with given endowments and one with endogenously determined endowments – appears arbitrary. It is not without reason, then, that this separation has never been proposed by general equilibrium theorists, who, when attempting to formalize a Keynesian general equilibrium, have felt compelled to interpret the latter as a temporary equilibrium (cf. Appendix 2A1).

8.2.2. Even if this difficulty were somehow considered surmountable, other supply-side difficulties would arise when one seeks to determine the endowments of the capital goods of the second group. There appear to be two possibilities, both encountering severe problems.

One possibility is to assume that what varies with labour employment is only the *composition* of the second group of capital goods (let us describe them, for simplicity, as intermediate goods or, in Keynes's terminology, 'work-in-progress'): they would be seen as constituting a given 'quantity of capital' that can change 'form' without changing in amount, with this 'form' determined endogenously by the short-period equilibrium. It is highly doubtful that in this way one might obtain a sufficiently elastic labour demand schedule: the proportions between labour and intermediate goods, once the technology is constrained by the available fixed plants and durable capital goods, would in most cases appear to be very rigid. Moreover, one would be back to the illegitimacy of a given value endowment of 'capital', although this endowment would now represent only one part of the total 'capital' of the economy.

The other possibility is to admit that what varies with labour employment is the *total quantities* of intermediate goods (work-in-progress), which adapt to the quantities to be produced; the decreasing 'marginal product' of labour[3] derives then, if at all, solely from the constraints imposed by the given fixed plants. This, as argued in Appendix 2A1, would appear to have been Keynes's own conception. But most fixed plants are made in such a way that, for the usual variations in production around the normal utilization level, increases in production require proportional (or even less than proportional) increases in the amounts of production-process labour and of intermediate goods utilized. In this interval, average labour productivity is usually an *increasing* function of the level of output, due to the presence of overhead labour (for example accountants, managers) whose amount does not vary with output. So within this interval the 'marginal product' of labour-cum-intermediate-goods is in most cases not regularly decreasing, but rather constant, or even increasing. Apart perhaps from a few agricultural productions, the need for more-than-proportional increases in labour employment only arises when production approaches the *technical* maximum-utilization level. At that point (as Hicks admitted) the marginal product falls abruptly, with a risk of a very inelastic demand for labour; but at least as importantly, this production level is very seldom approached,

. 3. That is, in this case, the increase in production due to increase by one unit of the employment of labour together with an appropriate increase in the utilization of intermediate goods.

because firms decide on their fixed plants so as to maintain ample margins of spare capacity.

This is a point with very important implications. Firms want to be able to increase production, at the peak moments when production varies cyclically, or in order not to lose market shares in case of an unexpected increase in demand; they want to avoid the extra labour costs of overtime or night shifts; or they may want bigger plants than necessary in a certain period, because of the expectation of future increases of average demand.[4] The resulting spare capacity explains the adaptability of production to demand that is typical of market economies, and whose implications will be further discussed in Chapter 9. A result of the existence of ample planned spare capacity is that, within the usual range of production variations, marginal cost is below average cost. This motivates the full-cost or average-cost theories of pricing, which argue, with considerable empirical support, that firms do not equate price and current marginal cost, but rather fix prices by adding a mark-up to prime cost so as to cover fixed costs and to obtain at least the normal rate of return when plants are normally utilized; this price is usually not altered in the short period as production is adapted to demand.[5] Then in the short period the employment of labour depends on demand, not on the real wage; an economy-wide decrease of the real wage does not imply an increased demand for labour with the given fixed plants, it only implies an increase of the mark-up.[6] Also there is no reason why a short-period increase in

4. Steindl (1952, pp. 11–13), Marris (1964), Betancourt and Clague (1981), Kurz (1986). The US Census Bureau collects firms' responses as to their capacity utilization; these data indicate a persistent underutilization of what the firms define as 'normal' capacity utilization, for example for the fourth quarters of 1997 to 1999 (http://www.census.gov/prod/2001pubs/mqc1-99.pdf) the data show an average utilization rate for all manufacturing of respectively 76 per cent, 73 per cent and 74 per cent, which can be compared with an average utilization rate over the period 1967–99 of about 82 per cent. These are measures of the utilization rate relative to what the firms consider 'normal' full-capacity production, but firms also indicate a 'national emergency' potential production from 40 per cent to 80 per cent higher than 'normal' full-capacity production. In the longer run, productive capacity adapts to demand, so production levels must be expected to be almost always inside the interval to which the considerations in the text apply.
5. These theories originate in the famous *Oxford Studies in the Price Mechanism* (Wilson and Andrews, 1955); for some discussion cf. for example Koutsoyiannis (1975, ch. 12), Lee (1998, especially pp. 208–14).
6. If the decrease in wages happens in a single firm or industry, the mark-up may remain constant and the lower real wage may simply imply a lower product price. Since plausibly the lower product price will cause an increased demand for the product, and hence a higher demand for labour in that industry, one will observe a negative association between real wage and employment at the industry level, but due to the change in demand, not to factor substitution. This would have no implication for the effect of changes in the general level of real wages on aggregate labour demand. Thus for our problem, the studies which attempt to prove the existence of a decreasing labour demand curve at the level of a single firm or a

aggregate output and employment should go together with a lower real wage (to the contrary, the higher utilization of fixed plants tends to leave room for increases in real wages without a fall in profits).

Then, in order to obtain a decreasing short-period labour demand schedule, the neoclassical economist can only rely on changes in technology associated with changes in fixed plants induced by the changed real wage. He must refer to a not-so-short short period, and must argue that long-period technical choices (changes of fixed plants) are sufficiently present as to make their character felt even in the short period: but then the short-period demand curve for labour is downward-sloping not *because* of the short-period nature of the analysis, but rather *in spite of* it; and it is again based on long-period analysis, that is on the notion of 'capital'–labour substitution, applied to new plants.

(As a digression, it deserves notice that if the neoclassical economist admits that capital–labour substitution can only operate in new plants, while in existing plants labour employment essentially depends on demand, then the thesis that a lower real wage entails an increase in the demand for labour in the short run cannot dispense with considering what happens to aggregate demand. Then considerable complications arise for the neoclassical theorist, the moment the assumption of continuous full labour employment is dropped and some role for aggregate demand in the determination of short-run output is admitted. This is because when the real wage goes down, according to neoclassical theory the K/L ratio in new plants[7] decreases; if the output that the new plants aim at producing is given – for example because new plants only aim at replacing the production lost by the gradual closure of the oldest plants – this will entail a *decrease* of investment, and thus of aggregate demand and therefore of the demand for labour.[8])

single industry have little significance. And even if in such studies one were able to prove the existence of some factor substitution, this would be at given prices of the non-labour inputs, and therefore not generalizable to the effects of a general change in real wages, which alters all prices and the rate of return on capital. At the economy-wide level, which is the relevant one for the purposes of our discussion, a lower real wage necessarily implies a higher average mark-up, reflecting a higher average rate of return on capital.

7. Cf. Section 4.3 on why the K/L ratio can only be modified in new plants.
8. These complications arise for example in the Dornbusch–Fischer approach to investment (Dornbusch and Fischer, 1987), which accepts the neoclassical conception of capital–labour substitution but does not assume the full employment of labour; firms are assumed to determine their desired capital stock on the basis of the expected levels of demand. At the aggregate level, the negative influence of the rate of interest on investment is then obtained as follows: the rate of interest selects the capital–labour proportion on the aggregate isoquant corresponding to the planned level and composition of aggregate output; the desired capital stock will change if either the rate of interest, or planned output (that is expected demand), or both, change. Thus the desired capital stock is determined by the neoclassically determined capital–labour average ratio, and by the level of aggregate output.

8.2.3. Furthermore, any result reached on the basis of the assumption of given endowments of some capital goods is bound to have at most temporary validity, and to be modified to a greater and greater extent, as time passes, by the increasing influence of long-period choices.

Indeed, since in any given time period, however short, there will always be long-period choices being made together with short-period choices, and since it is generally accepted that in the short period the possibilities to alter labour employment per unit of product are more limited than in the long period,[9] then if short-period and long-period choices do not act in the same direction it seems highly doubtful that one may find a period length short enough for the short-period choices clearly to dominate over the long-period ones, and yet long enough for the short-period choices to be implemented (they too require some time to be implemented!) and to dominate over the accidents and vagaries of day-by-day disequilibria.

In neoclassical macro analyses this problem does not arise, because short-period and long-period choices as to capital–labour ratios are thought to be in the same direction; the demand for labour from a given capital stock is simply seen as more elastic in the long run than in the short. But the long-period demand for labour, in these analyses, is based on the traditional conception of 'capital'. If this traditional conception is rejected, then even if it were possible to demonstrate that the demand for labour is decreasing if based on given fixed plants, the possibility that long-period choices might lead in the opposite direction to that of short-period choices would make the short-period analysis of doubtful relevance, because the short-period choices, being of more limited elasticity, might be counterbalanced by the – less numerous but more elastic – long-period choices implemented in the same time span. Indeed the long-period choices, even if not immediately dominant, would come to dominate as time passed, with the result that the danger of instabilities avoided in the short run would re-emerge in the longer run, depriving the theory of plausibility.

Thus, unless 'capital' remains the ultimate foundation of the analysis,[10] the recourse to a Marshallian–Keynesian short-but-not-so-short period does not

A lower interest rate increases the desired K/L ratio and K/Y ratio; with expected Y initially unchanged, the desired capital stock increases, although by less than if L, rather than Y, were kept fixed; the increase of the desired capital stock causes an increase of investment; through the multiplier, this raises Y, and thus the desired capital stock too. This approach, relative to the other neoclassical approaches to investment discussed in Chapter 7, has at least the advantage of not being undermined by the absence of full employment; but it enjoys no popularity nowadays, perhaps because of the complications mentioned in the text, to which one can add the possibility of nasty multiplier–accelerator interactions.

9. On this cf. §1.3.2.
10. And problems arise even in that case, as pointed out at the end of §8.2.2, and in the next footnote.

save the decreasing labour demand curve. There appears to be no way to justify the standard decreasing labour demand curve except by appealing to the long-period traditional marginalist analysis of 'capital'–labour substitution, undermined by reverse capital deepening.[11]

8.3. CONCLUSION

8.3.1. The analysis of this chapter and of the preceding one shows that, as a theory of real-world economies, marginalist/neoclassical theory is, at present, in a blind alley. The two basic pillars of neoclassical analyses of real-world market economies, the decreasing labour demand schedule and the decreasing investment schedule, need the traditional notion of 'capital'–labour substitution which has been shown to be without logical foundations.

Let us then remember what was argued in §1.4.4: an analysis of the tendencies of economies that are *not* at all times in equilibrium is

11. Nor can the neoclassical labour demand curve find support in the empirical evidence, which is inconclusive and, if anything, would appear to go against neoclassical predictions. The empirical studies which more convincingly support a negative correlation between labour employment and real wages are studies of single-firm or single-industry behaviour, where the correlation can be explained as due to the higher sales made possible by the lower costs – a partial-equilibrium effect not generalizable to the entire economy. The studies of the economy-wide relationship between real wages and employment are inconclusive both because they reach no unanimity of results (Zenezini, 1992; Brandolini, 1995), and because of the problem that employment may negatively depend on real wages because the latter influence international competitiveness, or government policy: for example if an increase in real wages causes inflation that induces the government to adopt recessionary policies, the negative association between real wages and employment does not derive from a decreasing labour demand schedule. The one fact on which there appears to be wide agreement, the non-countercyclical behaviour of real wages (Hamermesh, 1993, p. 337; Brandolini, 1995), would rather appear – and was so considered by Keynes (1939) – to raise serious doubts on the short-period decreasing labour demand schedule. Subsequent theoretical elaborations have argued that it is possible to reconcile this empirical finding with a decreasing marginal-product-of-labour schedule, by assuming technological shocks that shift the latter schedule, or by complicating the model through the introduction of imperfect competition, or of inventories, or of bargaining (for a succinct survey cf. Brandolini, 1995, pp. 107–11). But the attempts based on technological shocks (as in real business cycle theory) have notoriously encountered much scepticism (cf. Summers, 1986, and the recent assessments in Romer, 1996, pp. 186–8 and in Heijdra and Van der Ploeg, 2002, pp. 523–4), a scepticism which can only be reinforced by a better understanding of how the technological shocks are measured (cf. the discussion of what the Solow residual might pick up in §9A.3). As to the other arguments, I limit myself to noting that with friends like these, the neoclassicals need no enemies, because these arguments attempt to save the notion of a decreasing marginal product of labour by giving reasons to deny that this decreasing marginal product implies a decreasing aggregate labour demand schedule – neoclassical theory and policy conclusions are undermined anyway.

indispensable, in order to ascertain whether the extent, to which the results of an assumption of instantaneous equilibration are misleading relative to a reality where disequilibrium transactions and productions do happen, is considerable or negligible. It was seen in Chapter 2 that Franklin Fisher's analysis reaches no definite result; we have now seen that neoclassical macroeconomic analyses are analogously of no help the moment one admits the inconsistency of the conception of 'capital' as a single factor. The implication is that the neoclassical approach has no basis on which to argue the existence of the traditional neoclassical tendencies. The theory of value, distribution, employment and growth must look for a different foundation.

9. Summary of the Critical Argument, and Sketch of an Alternative Approach

9.1. SUMMARY OF THE ARGUMENT SO FAR

9.1.1. The first section of this chapter summarizes the argument of the previous chapters. I will remember that the argument implies that one must reject:

1. the distinguishing element of the contemporary versions of the marginalist/neoclassical approach to value and distribution: namely, the abandonment of the long-period method, that is the rejection of an explanation of market prices as gravitating around long-period normal values, in favour of adopting very-short-period notions of equilibrium based on data deprived of sufficient persistence;
2. the distinguishing element of the marginalist/neoclassical approach as such: the determination of income distribution on the basis of the tendency to a supply-and-demand equilibrium, a tendency resting on decreasing demand curves for factors.

In the second section, an attempt is made to illustrate the implications of these rejections by sketching one possible alternative, based on a resumption of the classical approach to income distribution, combined with the Keynesian principle of effective demand. It is not one of the objectives of this chapter to survey the alternatives to the neoclassical approach, nor even to present one or another of them in any detail. The task attempted in this concluding chapter is a minimal one: to show that the basic elements for a promising alternative to neoclassical economics are already implicitly or explicitly accepted by a large proportion of economists (including many of neoclassical formation). In other words, the limited aim of that section is to reject an opinion, frequent among general equilibrium specialists: that the abandonment of the neoclassical approach would leave us in the dark as to what determines distribution, employment and growth, obliging the economic profession to re-start more or less from scratch.

Appendix 9A tries to clarify the reasons why economists should stop using aggregate production functions.

9.1.2. There can be no doubt as to the existence of widespread dissatisfaction with what is accepted to be the rigorous formalization of the supply-and-demand approach to value and distribution: general equilibrium theory, even before one gets to problems of uniqueness, or of stability of tâtonnement-like adjustments.[1] This dissatisfaction is notable also among the specialists of general equilibrium theory, as illustrated in Chapter 1. The preceding chapters of this book may be viewed as an extended diagnosis of the reasons for this dissatisfaction. The argument was that one can distinguish a proximate reason, and, behind it, a deeper and less-understood reason, for this dissatisfaction.

The *proximate reason* has arisen in recent decades with the adoption of neo-Walrasian notions of (temporary or intertemporal) equilibrium. These equilibria are based on data lacking sufficient persistence: the vector of endowments of the several capital goods, and, in temporary equilibria, also the shape of expectation functions. These data may be drastically altered by the processes of adjustment toward equilibrium, if these processes are admitted to take time and to involve the actual carrying through of production and consumption decisions. Thus, the moment one admits – as one must – that in real economies adjustments are time-consuming, one cannot determine what equilibrium the economy may be tending towards: the only certain thing is that the economy will *not* tend toward the equilibrium determined by the initial data. The very little substitutability among factors that obtains when each capital good is treated as a different factor, by entailing that even small changes in the data may cause very big changes in equilibrium prices, confirms the relevance of this problem. As a result, the usefulness of this type of equilibria is, to say the least, problematic. Comparative statics exercises, for example, become useless because the economy cannot be assumed to tend to the new equilibrium. These problems have not gone unnoticed, and are a frequent reason for complaint. It would seem, though, that the dissatisfaction has stopped short of a full appreciation of how serious the problem is. As argued in Chapter 2, neo-Walrasian analyses cannot by themselves tell us *anything at all* about the behaviour of actual economies, because the connection between the equilibria or

---

1. A recent example outside the field of GE specialists: Mark Blaug writes that 'theories like those of Walras or Kenneth Arrow and Gerard Debreu ... consistently fail to throw light on how markets adjust in disequilibrium to attain final end-state equilibrium' and speaks of 'sterile formalism that has characterized general equilibrium theory in its modern Arrow–Debreu form' (Blaug 1999, p. 229). Also cf. Shubik (1993). Similar opinions appear in earlier writings such as those by Leontief (1971), Phelps Brown (1972), Worswick (1972), Ward (1972); this shows that the dissatisfaction grew strong as soon as it became clear that the neoclassical theory of value and distribution was becoming identified with the neo-Walrasian versions.

sequences of equilibria, and the actual behaviour of real economies, remains totally unspecified: nothing can be known on the extent of the divergence between the behaviour predicted by the equilibrium and the actual behaviour of the economy.

Why has neoclassical value theory allowed itself to march into such a blind alley? Here we are able to approach the *deeper and less understood reason* behind the present dissatisfaction: namely, the inability of the supply-and-demand approach to insert capital goods into its supply-and-demand explanation of distribution in such a way as to arrive at a consistent determination of sufficiently persistent, that is long-period, positions. The original aim of all founders of the approach was to determine long-period equilibria; the shift to neo-Walrasian notions of equilibrium was due to the difficulty that these attempts encountered. The conception of equilibrium as a sufficiently persistent state, plus the need for sufficient substitutability, required an endogenously determined composition of capital; but then the capital goods had to be seen as embodying different amounts of a *single* factor of production 'capital', capable of changing 'form' (that is composition) while not changing in 'quantity'. This was in fact the conception of capital adopted by all founders of marginalist theory, with the sole exception of Walras (who was simply contradictory because he too originally aimed to determine a long-period equilibrium); and this remained the overwhelmingly dominant conception for decades. The difficulties with Wicksell's and with Walras' determination of long-period equilibria remained unnoticed for a long time. As noted in §5.1.1, the supply-and-demand approach to the determination of value and distribution was able to become entrenched at the end of the nineteenth century, on the basis of the mistaken belief that that approach was capable of determining a *long-period* equilibrium. The shift to neo-Walrasian notions of equilibrium was a subsequent defensive move, an expedient for trying to salvage the supply-and-demand approach to distribution when the impossibility of treating capital goods as embodying a single factor 'capital' started being recognized. The shift was made possible by the fact that by that point the supply-and-demand approach had become so exclusively dominant that the forces it assumed were thought to be obviously present in reality. It is doubtful that the neoclassical approach would have been able to impose itself so completely, if it had been clear from the beginning that at most it could determine equilibria that could be reached – if at all – only by instantaneous adjustments. Indeed, for decades after the birth of the approach, it was taken for granted that the equilibrium was to be conceived as the centre of gravitation of time-consuming disequilibrium processes. It was also clear to many of the best theorists that the arguments for the tendency to equilibrium rested on the possibility of treating the 'form' of capital as variable. This emerges clearly in the admissions by Hicks and by Robertson that it is impossible to determine an economically meaningful marginal product of labour without changes in the 'form' of capital (cf. §§1.3.2, 2.1.4).

9.1.3. But in the shift to neo-Walrasian equilibria the abandonment of the conception of 'capital' as somehow a single factor has been no more than apparent. Only an implicit reliance on that conception of 'capital' can justify the belief in a decreasing and sufficiently elastic demand curve for labour, as well as the belief in investment as a decreasing function of the rate of interest; and these two beliefs, by providing a foundation for the argument that market economies tend to the full utilization of resources, are indispensable to the thesis that neo-Walrasian equilibria (which are full-employment equilibria) describe with sufficient approximation the tendencies of market economies.

Let us briefly remember the essential terms of the issue. Neo-Walrasian equilibrium theory is silent on the behaviour of economies not continuously in equilibrium, so the tendency toward the full employment of resources cannot be argued on its basis. If then we look for disequilibrium foundations for that tendency, these must be found in the existence of persistent forces or tendencies; nowadays these are only found in neoclassical macroeconomic theory, and their pillars are precisely the decreasing demand curve for labour and the decreasing investment schedule. But in Chapter 8 the following question was posed: when, from a general equilibrium system, we derive the 'demand curve' for labour which indicates how labour employment varies as an exogenously imposed real wage rate is varied, what are we to take as given in terms of the endowment of capital goods? If we take as given the several endowments of each type of capital good, then the 'demand curve' for labour cannot be presumed to have an elasticity sufficient to prevent implausible equilibrium values of the real wage. Furthermore, we are determining equilibria based on data of no persistence, with the implication that, before the real wage has had sufficient time to tend toward its equilibrium level, this equilibrium level itself may have significantly changed. In addition, the absence of aggregate demand problems (pre-supposed when one argues that a decrease of wages raises the demand for labour) requires that investment be determined by savings, but, as argued in Chapter 7, without the traditional conception of capital–labour substitution there is no way to justify such an assumption. If one does not take as given the several endowments of each type of capital good, then how can one fix the capital endowment? Traditionally, the value of capital would be taken as given: but this is clearly illegitimate (for example it means different things, as the real wage varies, depending on the choice of numeraire). Furthermore, owing to the possibility of reverse capital deepening, there would be no guarantee that the 'demand curve' for labour derived on the basis of a given value of the capital stock would be decreasing and sufficiently elastic. Either way, one runs into a blind alley.

Nor can neoclassical theory appeal to empirical evidence for support. To the contrary, the empirical evidence has always created difficulties for neoclassical economists, given such factors as the frequently pro-cyclical behaviour of real wages, the great difficulty with proving a significant negative elasticity of aggregate investment to the interest rate, the persistence of unemployment.

The assumption of full resource utilization central to neo-Walrasian models is therefore devoid of legitimacy, unless one implicitly accepts precisely that traditional conception of 'capital'–labour substitution (with 'capital' a single factor of variable 'form'), the avoidance of which was the aim of the neo-Walrasian versions.

Thus the defensive *détour* attempted by neoclassical theorists, who have abandoned the long-period method in order to try and dispense with homogeneous 'capital' while retaining their supply-and-demand explanation of prices and distribution, comes out to have no foundation, unless one *presupposes* the validity of the long-period tendencies originally derived by marginalist authors on the basis of the conception of 'capital' as a single factor.

In conclusion, neoclassical economics cannot do without a conception of factor substitution in which 'capital' is conceived as somehow a single factor; and yet such a conception is logically indefensible.

This internal critique not only *reinforces* but also to a large extent *explains* the doubts that, in numerous fields of applied economics, are frequently voiced vis-à-vis marginalist/neoclassical analyses. The internal critique gives strong, indeed decisive, support to the thesis that the fundamental forces at work to determine value, distribution and outputs in a market economy cannot be those envisaged by the marginalist tradition; it is then no longer surprising that grave difficulties should often arise when trying to reconcile the marginalist/neoclassical approach with what reality shows.

9.2. TOWARD AN ALTERNATIVE APPROACH

9.2.1. We have seen in Chapters 1 and 2 that several general equilibrium theorists admit that, in the words of a very recent contribution, 'the present state of general equilibrium theory must therefore be regarded as unsatisfactory or incomplete when it comes to the provision of a positive theory of value' (Fisher, 2003, p. 91). But the usual indication of how to surmount this situation is some variation on the theme that 'serious modeling of disequilibrium is required. If we are ever to understand how resources are allocated, how consumption and production are organized, how prices come to be what they are and the role that they play, we must examine disequilibrium behavior' (Fisher, 2003, p. 91). In the same volume containing these lines by Franklin Fisher, Alan Kirman rejects general equilibrium theory as a positive theory of market economies, but supplies no indication of what might replace it, except for vague statements such as 'We need statistical descriptions of the states of an economy, the evolution of which will be generated by, but not similar to, the evolution of the individuals' states' (Kirman, 2003, p. 482).

On the basis of these statements and of similar ones by other authors, it seems possible to say that nowadays a majority of those general equilibrium theorists, who admit that their theory is not a satisfactory positive theory of the working of market economies, are not aware of existing alternatives to the supply-and-demand approach to value and distribution. If this approach is rejected, they appear to see little alternative to re-starting more or less from scratch, from a re-examination of how disequilibrium concretely works, in the hope of deriving some (possibly statistical) generalizations from this re-examination.

Such a nihilistic opinion is unwarranted, and appears due to an insufficient acquaintance with the alternatives to the supply-and-demand approach that have existed in the past, and that exist and are actively being developed today by a rapidly growing literature. Actually, as I will now try to show, when one considers the broader economic profession and not just the mathematical specialists in general equilibrium theory, then the elements for a promising alternative are already widely accepted in one form or other, even among otherwise neoclassical economists.

9.2.2. The first widely accepted element on which the reconstruction of the theory of value can be based is the existence in the real world of a strong tendency toward a uniformity of rates of return on supply price. This thesis is very generally accepted, usually couched in terms of a tendency of prices toward 'normal costs of production', or in terms of a tendency of (pure) 'profits' to disappear in the longer run.[2] While doubts have sometimes been

---

2. Thus all introductory textbooks describe a long-period tendency of product prices toward minimum average costs. This tendency is described in introductory textbooks in the context of partial-equilibrium analysis, that is with input costs taken as given. But for the input costs due to the utilization of produced inputs (capital goods), logical consistency requires that those costs must themselves be the long-period ones (that is the ones associated with prices of capital goods equal to *their* minimum average costs), because the same tendency of price toward minimum average cost must be admitted to be operating for the produced inputs, and

raised about many assumptions of economic theory, for example about the assumption of rationality, or about the empirical existence of relevant technological or psychological substitutability, I am not aware of any serious challenge ever having arisen to the thesis that abnormal profits – in the absence of barriers to entry – tend to disappear. This thesis is for example confirmed by Dennis Mueller (1986) in a book where he writes:

> In an economy subject to uncertainty, profits and losses signal the existence of excess demand or excess supply at long-run competitive price. If resources are free to respond to market signals, they should move into areas where profits are being earned and out of areas suffering losses. This movement of resources continues until returns are equalized across all markets (with appropriate adjustment for risk). Of course, each new period brings new uncertainties and new positions of profits and loss, so that a point in time when all firm or industry profit levels are equal never obtains. But if the market is capable of responding to the signals of profits and losses, the long-run movement of individual firm and industry profit rates should be toward a common competitive level. All observed profits and losses should be short-run deviations around this trend ... Although most studies of profit rate determinants have focused on industry profit levels, the competitive environment hypothesis of convergence on a single competitive level should be equally valid for firm-level profits and for industry profits. For a homogeneous product, all firms in an industry should charge the same price under competitive conditions. Free entry and exit should ensure that only the most efficient firms survive, that all firms have the same average costs as well as price (Mueller, 1986, pp. 8–9).

These lines describe the traditional conception of normal competitive prices as long-period prices, yielding a uniform rate of return on (the supply price of) capital,[3] and as centres of gravitation of market prices; the book, whose findings support such a conception, shows that in industrial economics this conception is still alive and well. Nor is this surprising. Obviously, barriers to entry, or, sometimes, cumulative advantages for even lengthy periods, due to learning-by-doing by innovating firms, may slow down the process of convergence of rates of return or may prevent it from completely eliminating the differences in rates of return. But without the tendency of rates of return towards uniformity, there would be no reason why differences in rates of

the time scale of the two tendencies is generally the same. This means that for all produced goods which are directly or indirectly inputs into their own production, the determination of their long-period prices can only be simultaneous; and the thesis that for all produced goods there is a long-period tendency of the price toward the long-period minimum average cost implies that one is admitting the tendency of relative prices toward the prices determined by equations such as [3.7*] of §3.3.3.

3.   Notice however how Mueller oscillates between the marginalist definition of profit ('profits and losses') and its classical definition ('profit rates').

return as big as 1 per cent versus 1000 per cent could not go on forever. The tendency of rates of return toward uniformity is an undeniable fact of life in competitive economies.[4]

Therefore, there would appear to be little obstacle to a return to viewing long-period prices (and the associated normal quantities) as the central object of value theory. What is perhaps useful to repeat is that long-period relative prices and normal quantities are not what the economy will approach in some hopefully not-too-distant future, but are, more concretely, what the economy continually gravitates toward and is therefore never far from, and are therefore the appropriate object of study for all analyses concerned with the economy-wide effects of, say, changes in distribution, or technical progress, or extension of cultivation to inferior lands.

In this way one does no more than return to the traditional method of long-period positions.[5] The earlier chapters, in particular Chapter 5, have shown that the abandonment of the method of long-period positions in the pure theory of value, and the adoption of neo-Walrasian notions of equilibrium, were not motivated by intrinsic difficulties of the traditional long-period method, but rather, by the difficulties that the *marginalist approach to distribution* encountered in introducing capital goods into models aiming at determining long-period positions. That the reasons for the abandonment were not connected with difficulties of the method of long-period positions per se is shown by the fact that no qualms were raised about that traditional method by marginalist economists as long as they believed that their theory was able to determine long-period positions.

Nowadays the main obstacles to a full return to the method of long-period positions appear to be two: first, the confusion of those positions with steady states; second, the identification of long-period positions with their neoclassical or marginalist characterization.

4.   Anyway the long-period method does not need that rates of return (when risk is appropriately taken into account) be uniform; it only needs that differences (or ratios) between rates of return be sufficiently persistent so that one can take them as given, at least in a first approximation, when one enquires into, for example, the effects of technical progress or of changes in real wages.

5.   It might indeed be suggested that the long-period method has never been abandoned except in the neoclassical pure theory of value; most applied neoclassical economists are Marshallian, not neo-Walrasian, that is they accept that the tendency to equilibrium takes time and is never perfectly realized, and accordingly try to determine *persistent* equilibria susceptible of being seen as representing the average, or the tendency, of actual events. This is the case as well in many contemporary neoclassical macroeconomic analyses that claim to be based on general equilibrium theory, but in fact use one-good models (that is 'capital') and, because of that, can be interpreted as describing the *persistent* forces affecting the trend of economic variables, without any strict assumption of instantaneous or continuous equilibration (cf. Appendix 9A).

It is often argued that long-period relative prices, being *defined* as constant through time, for their validity presuppose a stationary or steady-growth economy, and therefore are inapplicable to real economies. As explained in Chapter 4, this is a double misconception. First, the assumption of constancy through time is not *essential* to the definition of long-period relative prices; it is only a first step, from which one may go on to more complex analyses if the case so requires. The defining characteristic of long-period prices is only the uniform rate of return on supply price (Petri, 1999, pp. 36–7; Garegnani, 2003, app. 2A). Second, the neglect of the changes of relative prices over time can be considered a very good *approximation* in most situations, because the slowness with which the data determining long-period relative prices change endogenously (for example because of population growth or capital accumulation) relative to the speed of adaptation of the composition of capital, makes it generally legitimate to neglect their changes. Thus neither Ricardo or Marx, nor Marshall or Wicksell or Knight or Walras, thought that the long-period prices they were determining were only relevant for stationary or steady-growth economies. The effects of *exogenous* changes of normal economic conditions (for example the effects of technical progress, or of changes in the non-competitively determined price of oil), or the very-long-period effects for example of the extension of cultivation to inferior lands, are obviously to be studied via comparative statics.

Another mistake, frequent also among Keynesian economists, is the belief that to accept the existence of a tendency toward long-period positions means to accept the tendency toward a *marginalist* long-period position, characterized for example by the full employment of resources. This mistake derives from a belief in the existence of the marginalist factor substitution mechanisms (a belief shared by many Post-Keynesian economists,[6] who must then rely on radical uncertainty or 'animal spirits' or asymmetric information in order to prevent those mechanisms from reaching an equilibrium). But since those mechanisms must be rejected, to accept the long-period method does not in the least imply an acceptance of the long-period tendencies postulated by the marginalist approach. The classical authors are there to show the independence of that method from the marginalist approach to distribution and employment.

Which problems are left in need of a theory by a return to the long-period method? As Ricardo and Marx had already perceived, and Sraffa has shown for very general hypotheses, the tendency toward the uniformity of rates of

6. Cf. Chapter 6, fn. 31.

314   *General equilibrium, capital and macroeconomics*

profit[7] will suffice to determine technical choices and long-period normal competitive prices, once the available technologies, the quantities produced, and either the real wage or the rate of profits, are determined.[8] What is needed for a reconstruction of economic theory is therefore, essentially (i) a theory of outputs and employment and (ii) a theory of distribution, neither of them based on the marginalist conception of 'capital'–labour substitution: and theories satisfying this requirement are not lacking.

9.2.3. For the determination of the *level* of output and of employment, a solid starting point is Keynes's (and Kalecki's) principle of effective demand, that is the tendency of savings to adjust to investment via variations of the level of output. This principle is independent of the neoclassical approach to distribution. Indeed, the 'Keynesian cross' or 45°-line diagram used to be explained in textbooks before any assumption was made about the marginal product of labour, and with investment taken simply as given. True, in Keynes the application of the principle of effective demand is based on a marginalist element, the decreasing labour demand curve or decreasing marginal product of labour: according to the analysis of *The General Theory*, if aggregate demand is greater than production, money prices increase relative to money wages, the real wage decreases, and it is this that induces firms to employ more labour and thus to produce more. But it is widely accepted that the tendency to adjust production to demand need not be based on that mechanism; it can (and more plausibly so) be based on the desire of firms to avoid undesired inventory accumulation when demand is slack, and better to exploit their fixed plants and not to lose market shares when demand is buoyant.

As for the determination of the *composition* of output, nothing important would appear to be lost if one abandons the neoclassical approach. The composition of gross investment is explained in *all* approaches as motivated by (i) the need to replace the worn-out capital goods, (ii) technical progress, (iii) the observed gradual changes in the composition of consumer demand due to changes in consumption habits (due to changes in income, in the

7. Or toward given differences (or given ratios) among rates of profit, cf. fn. 4. Here profit means what classical authors meant by it, that is gross of interest.
8. Research continues into the problems raised by joint production; it must be kept in mind, in this connection, that the non-uniqueness of the technique to which the economy may converge in the long run, which appears to be a possibility in these cases (Bidard, 1997), does not endanger the approach because the determination of the real wage (or of the rate of return on capital or rate of profits, if one follows Sraffa's suggestion that the rate of profits might be the variable on which the social forces affecting distribution more directly act, cf. Garegnani, 1979b) is not simultaneous with the determination of relative prices, as, to the contrary, is the case with the marginalist approach. The only thing that need be admitted is some dependence of relative product prices on historical accidents.

products available, in family structures, in fashions and so on). In so far as consumer choices are concerned, the neoclassical need to inquire into the uniqueness and stability of equilibrium motivates an intense study of abstract general properties of consumer choices (income versus substitution effects and so on), while their concrete contents are left unanalysed; in the latter respect, little is derived from the approach beyond the truism that consumers purchase what they prefer among what they can afford. (The analysis is anyway not internally inconsistent, only rather narrow and indeterminate in its results.) The abandonment of the neoclassical approach will hopefully mean a greater research into the determinants of the contents of consumer choices: for example into the influence of advertising on preferences; or into the explanation of the reversal in recent years of the secular decrease of the length of the working week; or into the importance of social inequalities and demonstration effects for consumerism; or into the historical evolution of what is considered indispensable to a decent living. (What no doubt will need profound rethinking is welfare economics.)

The rejection of the neoclassical theories of investment does not create a void either. Here the problem is rather the opposite one, of many theories that are in contention in the field. Therefore the task facing investment theory nowadays appears to be the discrimination between the several competing alternative non-neoclassical explanations of investment. It is not the purpose of this chapter to embark upon this task. The main need appears to be for a series of careful historical studies of investment, attempting to sort out the relative validity, in different historical periods and for different nations, of the accelerator principle, and of the theories that make investment depend on profits, on technical progress, on state intervention, on the availability of finance, and so on. There can be little doubt anyway that desired productive capacity will be confirmed to be a main determinant of investment. Innovations also cannot but be another fundamental influence. The role of profits (which are seen, by many economists influenced by Kalecki, as supplying investible funds that slacken the financial constraint on firms) appears to be an open question: Kalecki's argument, in so far as it is not the accelerator under a different garb, is not solid theoretically, and the empirical evidence is ambiguous.[9] Kaldor's argument, that a redistribution against

9. Petri (1993a). Indeed, the moment one admits – as one must – that, in the long run, in competitive conditions the rate of interest and the normal rate of profits must adapt to each other so that normal extraprofits (net of the appropriate risk allowance, which will depend on the industry) are zero, there appears to be little reason why entrepreneurs should be more prone to invest when the rate of interest is 5 per cent than when it is 3 per cent. As to the empirical evidence, Bowles, Gordon and Weisskopf (1989) and Gordon, Weisskopf and Bowles (1994) find a strong positive association between rate of profits and investment but their measure of the rate of profits mostly reflects capacity utilization. Glyn (1997) finds

wages decreases aggregate demand, suggests that a higher rate of profit may end up by damaging, rather than aiding, investment (an argument also in Marx). Probably no simple theory that makes aggregate investment depend on a few variables only can be correct. For instance, the influence of governments' direct intervention and/or (overt or covert) supportive stance vis-à-vis private investments is certainly of great importance, and I am inclined to think that it can explain a considerable part of the observed differences in the growth rates of nations. Historical research and attention to the specificities of each nation and period will therefore have to integrate theoretical and econometric research. (The dependence of investment on the interest rate as specified by neoclassical theory will have to be rejected, but it is not excluded that, according to circumstances, a variation of the interest rate may temporarily affect investment.[10] The problem will have to be explored taking into account, for example, how rapidly the rate of profits is

that, in a comparison between nations, there is a positive association between rate of profits and rate of growth, which is taken to indicate a positive association between rate of profits and investment; but the association only emerges on average, there being several nations that constitute counter-examples. Also, the result, even if empirically stronger, might reflect the tendency of the total world investment to go in greater proportion where the rate of return is higher, without implying that a higher worldwide average rate of return would stimulate worldwide investment. Finally, the causation might go in the opposite direction: a higher rate of growth may imply a higher rate of utilization of capacity and hence higher profits. Seguino (1999–2000) finds evidence, for South Korea, of a decrease in the share of profits associated with an increase of investment.

10. That some negative influence of the interest rate on investment may be sometimes detected by empirical studies does not appear surprising to the non-neoclassical theorist. There are several non-neoclassical indirect routes through which such an influence might operate, but their working is not guaranteed. There are also routes through which the influence might be of opposite sign, such that no general and unambiguous conclusion independent of the specificities of the situation appears derivable. For example, a lower interest rate in a single nation may cause outflows of financial capitals; this in turn may cause a devaluation which stimulates exports and thus, through the accelerator, stimulates investment. Or, with a fixed exchange rate, the lower interest rate, by decreasing production costs in that nation relative to other nations (just like a decrease in real wages), may lower the price level or slow down its rate of increase and thus increase the nation's competitiveness and again stimulate exports and thus investment. On the other side, the lower-than-abroad rate of return on investment, associated with the lower product prices, or higher import prices, may well for some time discourage, rather than encourage, investment. Or the lower interest rate, by being associated with a redistribution of income away from property incomes toward labour incomes, may induce an increase in the average propensity to consume, and thus in the multiplier, and thus again stimulate investment through the accelerator. On the other side, the increase in consumption may induce the business community to expect restrictive government policies because of balance-of-payment constraints or fears of inflation, and thus it may discourage investment. Also, a higher rate of interest which is believed to be temporary may cause a temporary postponement of investment.

affected by the variation in interest rate, and whether the latter variation is felt to be temporary or permanent.)

9.2.4.[11] The principle of effective demand is generally accepted for the short period even among neoclassical economists. Now, acceptance of this principle implies the admission of a flexibility of production in response to variations of aggregate demand, and ample evidence shows that this flexibility is indeed considerable, not only downward, but also upward: plants are normally utilized for much less than 24 hours a day, so there seldom are technological limits to even very considerable increases in production. These observations also apply to the industries producing capital goods; therefore the production of capital goods too, and therefore the rate of growth of productive capacity, must be admitted to depend on the level and growth rate of the demand for increases in productive capacity. Up to limits rarely reached, the speed of accumulation of capital depends therefore on the growth of desired productive capacity, induced above all by the growth of aggregate demand. In the long run, demand creates the productive capacity it needs.

Much the same would appear to be true for the supply of labour. In the short run, the supply of labour is obviously no constraint to decreases of aggregate production; as to increases, there is nearly universal agreement on the fact that official unemployment rates, besides being always positive, hide the presence of hidden unemployment, and that the rate of participation increases if labour demand increases. This is indeed part of the accepted explanation of Okun's Law; furthermore, employed workers generally do not object to temporary periods of overtime work and wages. Thus only exceptionally will the supply of labour be a constraint to accelerations of growth (up to limits from which economies usually remain quite far). If one turns to the ample time intervals relevant for the theory of long-run economic growth, historically one observes clear signs of a (spontaneous or engineered) tendency of the supply of labour to adapt to the demand for labour, so that capitalist economies seem to have always been able to avoid a labour supply constraint. Pre-capitalist sectors, agricultural underemployment and domestic labour have historically supplied the labour reserves necessary for the industrial revolution and for subsequent growth when population growth was not enough. When that was insufficient (as in post-war Germany, or in the USA), there were huge and carefully regulated immigration flows, or sometimes policies promoting fertility (or, in the opposite case of excessive population, combating fertility, as now in China). Retirement age is another element which can be, and has been, altered to

11. This paragraph is based on Petri (2003c).

regulate the supply of labour. It would seem therefore that historically for labour supply too, in the long run demand has created – spontaneously or through policy interventions – its own supply. The present pressure for immigration from poorer countries toward the industrialized ones suggests that there is little obstacle to the same being true now and in the foreseeable future.

The road is thereby open to admitting a significant influence of the evolution of aggregate demand on the growth rate of output and of productive capacity. These two widely accepted principles: the principle of effective demand, and the productive capacity adjustment principle, imply the possibility of looking at the determinants of long-run growth from a perspective radically different from the supply-side perspective of the neoclassical approach.

This demand-side perspective has been and is being developed by numerous economists.[12] Therefore, in the theory of growth as well, the abandonment of the neoclassical approach does not in the least imply a need to re-start from scratch.

9.2.5. When we turn to income distribution, again we find a wide acceptance of ideas that can be the basis for a totally non-marginalist approach. The notion of a customary wage, crystallized in conventional ideas of a 'fair wage', is accepted, for example, by Robert Solow (1990) and has been recently supported by Bewley (1998). The idea that this customary wage is imposed by the relative bargaining power of informal class coalitions, and changes slowly as a result of changes in the balance of power between social groups, is also widely accepted. The admission is widespread that *money* wages are generally rigid downward, and that reductions in *real* wages will usually be strongly resisted too (except in special situations, for example very high unemployment, a dictatorial government, war). If asked why the money, and often the real, wage is rigid downward, most economists will point to trade unions, or to informal mechanisms of group or class solidarity, to lobbies, to the influence of political parties, and so on.

Thus, large numbers of people in the economics profession admit that income distribution is determined – or is capable of being determined – by forces different from the equilibrium between supply and demand envisaged by the marginalist approach. The main additional step required by the argument of this chapter is to cease viewing those forces as superimposed upon, and *impeding* the smooth functioning of, the marginalist mechanisms, and instead, to look at these forces as *necessary* constituents of a capitalist

12. Some recent references are Thirlwall (2002), Ciccone (1990), Vianello (1985), Garegnani (1992), Garegnani and Palumbo (1998), Trezzini (1995, 1998), Petri (2003c).

economy: without them, the capacity of a market economy to function, as well as the income distribution reigning in it, would not be explainable.

Indeed, an indefinite wage flexibility in the face of unemployment could only be assumed by marginalist economists because of their belief in a decreasing and sufficiently elastic demand curve for labour. That belief implied that unreasonable variations in real wages would not be required in order to reach an equilibrium; without that belief, the assumption of indefinite wage flexibility would have produced absurd consequences: a lack of response of employment to changes in real wages would have implied, whenever unemployment arose, a process of indefinite wage reduction, not only clearly contradicting historical evidence, but also incompatible with the need for a sufficient predictability of economic conditions, required for the functioning of a market economy.

The argument of this chapter implies that the belief in a decreasing and sufficiently elastic demand curve for labour must be rejected; a lack of positive response of employment to decreases of real wages must be admitted to be a quite plausible occurrence; then the non-existence of the indefinite wage flexibility postulated by the neoclassical conception of competitive markets will appear, not only indispensable to an explanation of the historical evidence, but also natural. If the level of employment is not significantly affected by the real wage, then it is only to be expected that historical experience should have taught workers that wage competition must be avoided. Let us try to visualize what would happen if the unemployed workers offered to work for less than the employed workers: the latter – in the absence of collusive behaviour – would themselves accept the lower wage in order not to be replaced, and then even very small hiring and firing costs would imply that firms would not find it convenient to fire them. So since the resulting lower wage would not increase employment, the unemployed workers would have gained nothing: they would still be unemployed, and would only have made the employed workers worse off, and themselves too, in so far as they receive support from the income of their employed relatives. So there is no incentive for unemployed workers to offer themselves at lower wages, once they realize the consequences.[13] No wonder,

13. An analogous damage to the employed workers with next to no advantage for the unemployed would derive from the birth of new firms hiring unemployed workers at a lower wage, and competing with the already existing firms by asking for lower prices for their products. The already existing firms, enjoying greater organizational experience, established custom, and so on, would most probably win in the competitive struggle with the new firms if wages were uniform; the competitive struggle would tend to bring such a wage uniformity about, so the new firms would go bankrupt, their workers would join the unemployed again, and in the meanwhile average wages would have decreased. I would suggest that entrepreneurs are not unaware of these considerations, and that this contributes to explaining why the creation of new firms solely in order to compete with existing firms by employing

then, that popular culture should have developed a variety of ways ('fair wage' notions, social ostracism against strike-breakers, and so on) to spare new entrants into the labour market the need to learn through experience – a learning process which would greatly damage their fellow workers in the meanwhile – that wage competition brings no advantage even from a strictly selfish viewpoint (Petri, 1994). The road is thus open for a return to the different conception of competition in the labour market of the classical authors, who saw it as embodying in its operation the social forces that determine the prevalent level of the real wage, and acting therefore within the limits set by those forces.

One implication of the above considerations deserves to be stressed. The zero-excess-demand assumption, relative to the labour market, has become part of the standard conception of equilibrium only because it was taken for granted that a lower wage would bring about a significant increase in employment, so that the unemployed would succeed in finding employment by a not implausible lowering of wages. Therefore the marginalist *definition* itself of equilibrium is influenced by the forces that marginalism sees at work in market economies.

Another common conception must be discarded: that there is a necessary association between level of the real wages, and level of labour employment; for example, that there is a level of the real wage, necessary for full employment. This conception rests on the notion of a demand curve for labour, and it has been argued that this curve cannot be determined. Let us now go beyond criticism, to illustrate how the flexibility of production in response to changes in aggregate demand, mentioned in §9.2.4, allows one to clarify the independence of the level of wages from the level of employment. For example, let us suppose that the government wants to raise both the level of real wages, and employment. An increase in aggregate demand will be generally capable of attaining both objectives: the adaptability of production to demand in the capital goods industries will mean that there will be little problem with adopting the new optimal technologies in the new plants, while at the same time increasing the overall level of production and employment.[14]

unemployed workers at a lower wage is a very infrequent occurrence (except when the new firms can be located in other nations, that is when the forces tending to equalize wages can be supposed absent).

14. Given this adaptability of production to demand, even the marginalist conception of 'capital'–labour substitution would not prevent the technology in new plants from adapting to the given real wage rather than determining it. A higher real wage would imply a higher K/L ratio in new plants, but the resulting increase in investment would be accommodated by a higher capacity utilization in the capital goods industry, in the same way as an increase in investment resulting simply from a higher aggregate demand. The flexibility of capacity utilization, joined with the general absence of stringent limits to variations in labour employment, is a further reason to reject the thesis that investment is determined by savings.

Over longer periods, the flexibility of capacity utilization will mean that it will be productive capacity (of the new composition) that will adapt to the desired level of employment. The obstacles will come, if at all, from political opposition to such a policy (Kalecki, 1943).

9.2.6. The alternative approach to value, distribution and growth briefly sketched can be characterized as a combination of a classical approach to distribution, with a Keynesian approach (purged of the neoclassical elements surviving in Keynes) to employment and growth.

The adoption of a classical perspective – which sees distribution as determined by a complex process of class bargaining in which the rate of unemployment is only one of the elements affecting the relative bargaining power of the parties (other crucial elements worth mentioning here being government policies, such as monetary policy,[15] government attitudes to the labour movement, and the degree of unity and ideological motivation of workers) – also suggests that government intervention may sometimes be aimed at *increasing* unemployment, as a way to weaken the workers. More generally this appears to be a fruitful starting point for historically specific analyses of how the conflictual nature of a capitalistic economy may show up in the government's recourse to inflation, to incomes policies, to 'social contracts', to the threat of dictatorships, or conversely to controls over investment, redistributions from property income to wages, creation of the welfare state, and so on.

This may seem overly vague to economic theorists, who nowadays usually want economic theory to produce definite predictions about the outcomes of economic interactions (at least, definite qualitative predictions on the direction of change) on the basis of a very parsimonious number of universal principles. This ambition, the result of the long dominance of the marginalist approach, appears excessive when it comes to issues so influenced by political elements as income distribution (and growth[16]). It will be readily admitted that political processes can seldom be completely explained by general regularities or laws: the emergence of Fascism, the

15. An interesting recent development is the attempt to explore the possibility that income distribution be determined, not by a given real wage, but rather by a given real rate of interest, imposed by the monetary authorities (Pivetti, 1985, 1991). The study of the working of monetary institutions often points to an institutional determination of the rate of interest (Nagatani, 1989, p. 227; Romer, 2000). Schefold (2003) advances interesting considerations on this issue, as well as on the possibility that the rate of growth of the economy may in certain circumstances affect distribution.
16. Economic historians know that state intervention played a very important role in the industrialization of, for example, Germany, Japan, Italy and Taiwan. Another example of political influences on growth is the role of military support to technological research in the USA, with spillovers for the international competitiveness of many industries.

322   *General equilibrium, capital and macroeconomics*

abandonment of communism in the USSR, and so on, are events where, it would seem, the social scientist can do little more than what historians and social analysts have always attempted; namely, the weaving of complex explanations, no doubt relying to an extent on general principles, but also attentive to the peculiarities of the place and period, and making room for the unique in history. The classical perspective argues that the political element in income distribution makes the explanation of the observed income distribution the result of a similarly complex interaction of historically changing forces. Consequently, one should not expect to be able to discover a simple way of explaining income distribution, based on few relevant regularities, valid for all nations and decades since the birth of capitalism: history is constantly throwing up novelties, for example colonialism, the welfare state, world wars, neo-corporatism, student protest. From such a perspective, asking the question why in certain places and periods – for example in Italy in the so-called 'hot autumn' of 1969 – real wages shoot up by great proportions, and why in other places and periods they stagnate for years in spite of increases in labour productivity, is not very different from certain other questions, such as why did the French Revolution happen, and why not earlier or later; or from questions such as why the welfare state developed, why it developed differently in different nations, and why now it is being partly torn down. This does not in the least mean giving up the attempt to explain real wages. It simply means that the explanations will have to combine economic, sociological and historical elements.[17]

Economists will probably have to renounce the dream of explaining nearly everything on the basis of very few universal principles, and accept the necessity of dirtying their hands with history, institutions and conflict to a much greater degree than is generally the case now. Such an approach, while perhaps less aesthetically appealing (and, for some, less morally appeasing?)

17. Thus I completely agree with the methodology propounded by Frank Wilkinson when he writes: 'A central purpose of this paper is to argue for a more active role for historical analysis in filling out and extending classical theory. Firstly, what is required is a more modern vision of capitalist growth which would not only include such classical variables as the rate of profit and accumulation but also take into account the changing level and composition of the standard of living and how this interrelates with the compositional evolution of the industrial structure, including the effect of new technology and changes in industrial organisation (such as the development of new industries, new products and new systems of marketing). The second important need is for a more differentiated class analysis with which to study the growth process. This would require a detailed consideration of the historical stratification and re-stratification of the working class, and would incorporate an analysis of the impact of, and the interaction between, the evolving industrial and political organisation of labour, state policy, collective bargaining, the restructuring of labour resulting from changing power relations in the market and in the labour process, changing technology and industrial organisation' (Wilkinson, 1988).

than the marginalist simultaneous explanation of everything in one single theoretical edifice, promises to be much more fruitful, both because it is free of logical inconsistencies, and because of its adaptability to a diverse and historically changing world.

APPENDIX 9A. WHAT IS WRONG WITH USING AGGREGATE PRODUCTION FUNCTIONS

9A.1. The argument of the previous chapters, and in particular the illustrations, however brief, of possible non-neoclassical analyses of distribution, employment and growth in Chapter 9 should allow greater clarity on the issue, of where the fundamental error lies in the use of aggregate production functions $Y = F(K, L)$ in theoretical and in empirical enquiries.

The point that this Appendix intends to stress is that the use of aggregate production functions – APFs for brevity – is the modern way to express the acceptance of the marginalist (or neoclassical, or supply-and-demand) approach to value and distribution, in its version (internal to the long-period method) yielding applicable explanations and predictions; in other words, it expresses the acceptance of the *traditional* marginalist approach, which, as explained in earlier chapters, did *not* assume that the economy functioned as if a single good were produced by itself and labour, but *did* rely on – and could not do without – the conception of capital as ultimately a single factor, an amount of value. APFs essentially add, to the acceptance of that traditional approach and of the connected conception of capital, the further assumption that one can treat the economy as if producing a single good.[18] This further assumption can be, and has been, criticised, and in many cases the criticism stops at this, that is, one does not question the fundamental qualitative conclusions of the traditional marginalist approach; then, since similar qualitative conclusions are derived from the use of APFs, the issue becomes whether the *quantitative* estimates based on APFs can be considered reasonable *approximations* to the behaviour of economies where output is not homogeneous. This Appendix argues that the criticism must go deeper. The fundamental error in the use of APFs lies in the acceptance of the marginalist approach to the determinants of distribution and growth with its associated indefensible conception of capital; for this reason, models based on APFs cannot reflect, not even approximately, the actual working of market economies.

9A.2. The use of APFs for theoretical purposes (that is the use of models, which include an APF, for the exploration of theoretical questions and qualitative comparative statics for example in growth theory) is generally justified by recourse to the description of one-good neoclassical models as

---

18. The assumption that labour is homogeneous is less important and will not be further discussed (cf. §6.4.4 on the absence of any need to aggregate labour in neoclassical theory, differently from the case with capital).

'parables' (Samuelson, 1962). A parable is an illustration of a general *truth* through the narrative of a concrete example. Models based on APFs are considered 'parables' in that they are assumed to bring out the essence of the rigorous, disaggregated versions of neoclassical theory by reaching in a simple way results qualitatively similar to the ones that – it is argued – one might derive from the rigorous versions. The fundamental problem with such a view is easy to point out: as this book has shown, there is no such thing as a defensible 'more rigorous', disaggregated version of neoclassical theory from which one may derive those results. To repeat, long-period disaggregated general equilibria are an inconsistent notion because of the impossibility to specify their capital endowment; as to the neo-Walrasian versions, it is rather the faith in the existence of the tendencies described by one-good neoclassical models that allows one to believe that neo-Walrasian analyses may have any connection with reality,[19] but these tendencies require the legitimacy of the traditional conception of capital–labour substitution undermined by reverse capital deepening.

Those who use the term 'parable', by revealing their acceptance of the traditional marginalist approach, reveal that they are not conscious of this

---

19. As I have written elsewhere: '... neither the initial-period neo-Walrasian equilibrium nor the equilibrium path (if it can be determined) based on the initial data can tell us *anything at all* on the actual evolution of an actual economy, because no force exists in the theory, capable of limiting the initial deviation from equilibrium, or of preventing a cumulation of deviations over a number of periods, in real economies ... Given the earlier conclusion that, by themselves, neo-Walrasian equilibria and their sequences tell us *nothing at all* about the actual path a market economy will follow, it would seem that only a more or less conscious belief that things work out *as if* capital could be treated in the traditional marginalist way ... can justify to some extent the belief that (sequences of) neo-Walrasian equilibria describe with acceptable approximation the behaviour of market economies. In fact then the choice between the traditional marginalist treatment of capital, and the neo-Walrasian one, would be of little consequence. The path traced by a sequence of neo-Walrasian equilibria would exhibit the same general characteristics, as to distribution and growth, as predicted by traditional analyses based on "capital" the value factor. The assumption of instantaneous adjustment to equilibrium would not be crucial to the results, since the actual economy would anyway gravitate toward a situation of full employment growth, and with distribution determined essentially in the way indicated by traditional analyses. But then – the reasoning might continue – for many purposes one might as well derive the qualitative correct results from models as simple as possible: one-good neoclassical models. Such a line of reasoning can however only rest on an implicit faith in the traditional notion of "capital". It would seem therefore that those neoclassical macroeconomists, who claim that their one-good models are only simplifications and refer to neo-Walrasian analyses as the rigorous microfoundation of their macro theories, have got it the wrong way round ... Neoclassical analyses based on one-good models are *not* "simplifications" of neo-Walrasian disaggregated analyses, on the contrary, they embody a "vision" which is prior to, and the only possible foundation of, the belief that neo-Walrasian analyses may have any connection with reality' (Petri, 1999, pp. 50, 53–4).

problem. Indeed, one may explain the favour currently enjoyed by one-good models as due to their being the sole avenue remaining nowadays to a neoclassical economist – given the sterility of the modern, very-short-period versions of general equilibrium theory and the abandonment of the long-period disaggregated versions – to reach the traditional distinguishing conclusions of the marginalist approach, those conclusions applicable to explanation and prediction that are only derivable (in disaggregated analyses) from the long-period versions of marginalist theory, where capital was conceived as a single factor of variable 'form'. In spite of the insistence of Solow that he is truly assuming a single good, the applications of his model show that capital is taken to be a summary index of the heterogeneous capital endowment of the economy, that remains unchanged (if net savings are zero) when the composition of the capital endowment in the real economy changes due to changes in relative factor prices. In other words, capital in Solow's model has exactly the same role as the single 'capital' of traditional long-period equilibria. Importantly, its quantity, being only altered by accumulation, has the persistence that allows one to dispense with the assumption that the economy is *continually* perfectly in equilibrium. The model's 'momentary' equilibrium is endowed with the persistence of traditional long-period equilibria (its data have the same persistence as the data of long-period equilibria, they are indeed a subset of the data of a disaggregated long-period equilibrium), therefore it *is* a long-period equilibrium, where the typical long-period element (the endogenous determination of the composition of capital) is obscured because of the one-good assumption but is in fact implicitly taken for granted whenever the model is considered applicable to real economies. The model can therefore aim at describing the average trend of the economy's growth path, allowing for oscillations or temporary deviations from it owing to the time required for the adjustment mechanisms to work; it does not need the auctioneer. It is therefore internal to the traditional and fruitful method of long-period positions, no doubt an important reason for its popularity. And it embodies the theses, and produces the comparative-statics results, that traditional marginalist authors obtained (or believed they could obtain) from their long-period disaggregated analyses: investment is determined by savings; there is the full employment of resources; factor rentals reflect marginal products; *ceteris paribus* increases in the supply of a factor decrease its rental. One-good APF models are the modern form of traditional marginalist theory.

True, many of the comparative statics results derivable from neoclassical aggregate-production-function models do not extend to more general neoclassical models, but this only confirms that behind the acceptance of Solow's model there is a prior decision to accept at all costs the validity of the traditional marginalist approach to distribution and growth. For example, in a marginalist labour–land model with two consumption goods produced with different factor intensities, if the demand for the more labour-intensive good comes mainly from wages, and the demand for the more land-intensive good comes mainly from land rents, then a decrease of real wages may well imply a shift in the composition of demand against the labour-intensive good in spite of its decrease in relative price, because now less income goes to the consumers who have a greater preference for that good; the result will be a lower labour–land ratio in the demand for factors in the economy as a whole. In such an economy an increase in the employment of labour may be associated with a higher, not a lower real wage. But the really important implication of such an observation is not that therefore one-good models are insufficient and one should use more complex neoclassical models; it is that, even leaving aside the problems connected with capital, the demand curves for factors cannot be assumed to be always downward-sloping; this result questions the plausibility of the supply-and-demand approach to income distribution, thus raising doubts not only on one-good neoclassical models but on the entire neoclassical approach. If in spite of this result one keeps believing in the neoclassical approach, one must have decided that this result, and more generally the Sonnenschein–Mantel–Debreu results that radically question the presumption of uniqueness and stability of equilibria, can be neglected. Then why not adopt a one-good model where these problems cannot arise?

Thus, I would argue that behind the use of one-good models with their APF there is a prior decision to have the analysis reproduce the traditional marginalist views. Little wonder, then, that capital be assumed homogeneous, homogeneous with output, and smoothly substitutable with labour: that is the simplest way to let the traditional marginalist conclusions emerge.

9A.3. Of course, there is some unease with the drastic 'simplifications' (this is how they are perceived) implied in the adoption of one-good models. At least the more attentive economists are aware, for example, that the assumption of a single product means that the model cannot correctly grasp the effects of changes in tastes or in the composition of output.[20] But the

20. Suppose labour and corn-capital, supplied in given amounts, produce cloth and corn (which is also demanded as a consumption good) in fixed-coefficient industries without technical choice, and distribution is determined according to marginalist theory, by the indirect substitution mechanism based on consumer choices. Suppose the equilibrium is unique, stable (the instability whose possibility was pointed out in the text with reference to the labour–land economy does not arise), with both factors fully employed, and stationary because consumers do not wish to perform net savings. A change in tastes (for example it is discovered that one of the two consumption goods is particularly good for health) will alter income distribution without any change in technology (by assumption there is no technical choice) nor – if there still is full employment of both factors – in the quantities produced: the

difficulties are seen as difficulties of *approximation*, due to the necessity to simplify. At least as far as the *direction* of the effects, it is felt that APFs cannot produce wrong predictions.

To the contrary, the moment the marginalist or neoclassical or supply-and-demand approach is rejected, one must look for alternative theories; and these will produce explanations and predictions different from those derivable from neoclassical theory and therefore also from aggregate-production-function neoclassical models.

For example, in the models of the recent so-called New Growth Theory the use of APFs reflects the acceptance of the neoclassical theory of distribution, with the associated tendency toward the full employment of resources, and investment determined on average, with sufficient approximation, by full-employment savings. This theory is used to argue that the rate of output growth of an economy fundamentally depends on its propensity to save; and that in order to increase investment (in real or in human capital or in R&D) an economy must decrease its propensity to consume. On the contrary, the usual existence of not-maximally-utilized fixed plants and of unemployed labour (including potential immigrants) means that an increase of aggregate demand will stimulate increases of production and will generally make it possible to have both more investment and more consumption; conversely, deficiencies of aggregate demand will cause a lower growth rate independently of changes in the average propensity to save. The forces influencing the growth rate of aggregate demand, and hence of output, will also influence the growth rate of labour productivity, if the latter is admitted, as in the New Growth models, to depend on the former (Petri, 2003c).

Or let us consider the use of APFs to explain changes in income distribution at the economy-wide level. If the share of wages or of property income in Y changes, in the absence of technical progress this change is explained as due to changes in factor supplies, and to the elasticity of substitution of the APF. The latter is supposedly revealed by the observed changes in income distribution and in the K/L ratio. Let us separate here the thesis that income distribution is determined by the tendency toward equality between supply and demand for labour and capital, from the thesis that the

given technical coefficients plus the given factor supplies plus the assumption of full employment of both factors uniquely fix the quantities produced. This change in distribution without any change in technology nor output cannot be reflected in a model based on an APF where it is assumed that factors earn their marginal products. Now suppose the same economy and the same change in tastes but assume factor substitutability in each industry: both income distribution and the composition of net output change, and again, since neither technical knowledge nor factor supplies have changed, there is no way to reflect this fact in a one-good model where as long as factor supplies and technical knowledge do not change, income distribution should not change.

demand functions for labour and capital, and hence the equilibrium income distribution, can be derived from an APF. The first thesis is the more fundamental one. Now, this book has argued that the supply of capital conceived as a single factor cannot be determined independently of distribution; therefore the equilibrium between supply and demand for capital cannot be determined. For the same reason the demand curve for labour cannot be determined, because the quantity of capital, that should be given and kept fixed when the real wage is changed, cannot be determined. Thus, even before getting to the issue whether an APF exists, we can conclude that the forces determining income distribution cannot but be other. Therefore any explanation of changes (or of the absence of changes) in income distribution, derived from marginalist postulates (whether expresses through APFs or otherwise), is simply groundless. The explanation will have to be looked for in other directions. For example, I would think that an explanation for the decrease in the share of wages in the USA in the last decades must be sought in whatever has changed the bargaining power of labour vis-à-vis employers. The increase in unemployment brought about by the first oil crisis of 1973, and the electoral victories of Ronald Reagan, are clearly going to be essential elements of this explanation.

Thus neither the growth of output nor the evolution of income distribution can be explained by the forces that motivate the equations of the one-good neoclassical model. This undermines the legitimacy of these models,[21] even before one gets to the legitimacy of APFs.

9A.4. A last-ditch defence of the use of APFs might be based on an attempt to separate the issue, of what determines growth and income distribution, from the issue of the usefulness of APFs.

This attempted separation might be based on accepting a more restricted role for APFs, along an argument more or less as follows. Let us concede – it might be argued – that growth is determined, not by the investment of full-employment savings, but by other forces. Let us for example accept Joan Robinson's animal spirits or an important role of state intervention and let us take the rate of growth of output as given. Let us furthermore accept that income distribution is determined, not by the equilibrium between supply and demand for factors, but by 'class struggle'. Then Solow's growth theory is of course not valid, but production techniques depend anyway on income distribution; at least under a hypothesis of given net output composition, labour productivity too (net output per unit of labour) as well as the capital–labour ratio will depend on income distribution. These functional

---

21. And of the theory of growth associated with them, and thus also of its predictions about secular convergence.

relationships must exist, and some way should be found to estimate them. APFs are one way to go about this task; if they give a good statistical fit, it must mean that the world, in spite of the possibility of being otherwise, in fact looks like as if there were APFs, and then the APF can be used as a way to represent the world and to formulate explanations and predictions. For example, one can estimate technical progress through Solow's notion of Total Factor Productivity.

A fundamental stumbling block for such an 'instrumentalist' argument is the 'Shaikh critique', reiterated and extended in numerous recent articles by J. Felipe and J.S.L. McCombie (Shaikh 1974, 1980, 2002; McCombie and Thirlwall, 1994, pp. 93–103; the very numerous articles by McCombie and Felipe can be reconstructed from the references in McCombie, 1998, 2000–2001, and Felipe and McCombie, 2003). This critique points out that the goodness of fit of APFs proves nothing, because a *perfect* replication of the data is *always* achievable, owing to the degrees of freedom of the problem that derive from the existence of technical progress. The essence of this critique can be put in extremely simple terms.[22] Let us consider the simplest case, corresponding to Solow's original formulation in 1957. Output is produced by labour and capital, and it goes either to wages, or to interest (profits, in classical terminology). When one tries to estimate an APF for such an economy, one has time series for aggregate output Y_t, for labour employment L_t, for capital K_t, for the share of wages $w_t L_t / Y_t = \alpha_t$, and for the share of profits or interest, $r_t K_t / Y_t = 1 - \alpha_t$. For each period t, since $0 < \alpha_t < 1$, it is possible to find a positive number A_t such that

$$Y_t = A_t L_t^{\alpha_t} K_t^{1-\alpha_t},$$

an equality where the sole unknown is A_t, which is therefore residually determined so as to satisfy the equality. This Cobb–Douglas production function, which we may call 'ex-post', allows one to view income shares as resulting from each factor receiving its marginal product. Since output, employment, capital and income shares change gradually, also A_t and α_t will change gradually. It is then possible to attribute these changes to technical progress; in this way the evolution of the data can be 'explained' through the changes in the two parameters of a Cobb–Douglas APF plus the assumption that factors receive their marginal products, *whatever* was in fact the cause of the evolution of output and of income distribution.

When so constructed, the time evolution of the ex-post Cobb–Douglas APF and of income distribution according to marginal products of course

---

22. I do not reproduce here the details of the arguments of Shaikh, McCombie or Felipe but only my interpretation of their basic message.

perfectly replicates the data. For example, the economy may be producing corn with corn and labour with fixed coefficients altered through time by technical progress and with income distribution determined by Goodwin's Lotka–Volterra 'class struggle' mechanism: the evolution of output and of income distribution will be anyway describable as due to changes in A and α in an ex-post Cobb–Douglas APF with income distribution determined by marginal products.[23]

From the perspective of the applied neoclassical economist, the trouble with such an ex-post Cobb–Douglas APF is that, if one does not postulate that the time paths of A or α are predictable, then one is reduced to ex-post accounting with no right to make predictions. For example, if the shape of the production function and the speed of technical progress are all the time unpredictably changing, one cannot predict the steady state to which an economy represented by Solow's growth model tends. This explains why the question is posed, whether a Cobb–Douglas APF can explain the data when α is assumed constant and A is assumed to follow a well-defined time path (usually, that it grows at a constant rate). Then one no longer uses factor shares to measure α but one simultaneously estimates α and A directly from the data series for output and inputs, with the help of the logarithmic expression of the Cobb–Douglas APF, that turns it into a linear relation. The resulting α can then be compared with the observed shares of wages. If α is assumed constant, but (as in Solow, 1957) no restriction is imposed on the time path of A, then if relative shares are approximately constant, the fit will obviously be very good, with the estimated α coinciding with the observed average share of wages.[24] If in addition to a constant α one imposes a predetermined time path of A, for example a constant growth rate, then the

---

23. This example shows that an ex-post Cobb–Douglas APF correctly determining income distribution according to marginal products can be derived even when capital is physically homogeneous with output (no dependence of the value of capital on distribution enters the problem) but no APF exists. The reason why this is always possible (and therefore it proves nothing as to what is actually happening in the economy) is the degree of freedom deriving from the absence of independent evidence as to the effects of technical progress on the production possibility set of the economy. Solow (1987) in his rebuttal of Shaikh's criticism conveniently omits to mention this problem and only discusses the case of no technical change (under the assumption, again conveniently left implicit, that the observer *knows* that there is no technical change).

24. Thus the reason why Cobb–Douglas APFs with a constant α so often yielded nearly perfect fits must be found in the near constancy of relative shares in the data utilized. The inevitability of a very good fit in this case – the point on which Shaikh has insisted most – was almost immediately noticed, in a comment on Solow (1957), by Hogan (1958, pp. 410–11), so the 'Shaikh critique' should perhaps be called the 'Hogan critique'.

resulting fit will often be poor;[25] but by juggling around with the form of the APF (for example CES or translog instead of Cobb–Douglas) or with the form of the time path of A_t (for example by assuming some sufficiently complex oscillatory path) one can always obtain an excellent fit (McCombie and Dixon, 1991; Shaikh, 2002). However the need to have recourse to more complicated time paths for A_t or more flexible forms for the APF is only due to the arbitrary assumption that α is constant through time (why should it be? if it reflects a technological characteristic of the economy, why should technical progress leave it unaltered?) while still assuming that it must reflect the share of wages, and/or to the arbitrary assumption that A_t follows some regular time path (again, why should it? Not even Solow assumed it in 1957).

Thus, criticisms of APFs based on poor statistical fits can always be overcome by invoking shifts and modifications of the shape of isoquants due to technical progress, that are either unpredictable or obeying sufficiently complex paths. But precisely because it can always be done, this proves nothing on what is actually happening in the economy.[26]

9A.5. So one must turn to what theory can show. The question is whether one can have any faith that, given the alternative techniques available to the economy, the relationship between income distribution and output per unit of labour or capital per unit of labour behaves as if deriving from an APF yielding the real wage as the marginal product of labour and the rate of interest as the marginal product of capital.

This is not the same issue as the legitimacy of the treatment of capital as a single factor in long-period equilibria, nor the same issue as the existence of a 'technical' capital aggregate in production functions discussed by Leontief, Solow (1955–56), or Bliss (1975b) (cf. above, §6.4.4). A detailed formal clarification of these differences is left for a future paper; a good discussion does not exist yet in the literature; even the recent praiseworthy effort by Felipe and Fisher (2003) to remind the profession of the illegitimacy of APFs, while it recognizes that there is a difference between these problems,

25. McCombie (2000–2001) shows that this is for example the case with Solow's 1957 data. Indeed Solow (1957) had found a markedly saw-like behaviour of the growth rate of A_t, including frequent episodes of hard-to-believe negative growth rates.
26. In his first reply to Shaikh, Solow wrote: 'The factor-share device of my 1957 article is in no sense a test of aggregate production functions or marginal productivity theory or of anything else. It merely shows how one goes about interpreting given time series if one starts by assuming that they were generated from a production function and that competitive marginal-product relations apply' (Solow, 1974, p. 121). But later he admitted: 'I suspect, however, that the workability of aggregate production functions, and their ability – if they have it – to reproduce the broad distributional facts does reinforce the marginal productivity theory – or, better, the supply-and-demand theory – of distribution' (Solow, 1987, p. 17). The 'Shaikh critique' shows that such a 'suspicion' has no foundation.

is unable clearly to pinpoint it. I attempt now briefly to indicate the main differences in intuitive terms. Relative to the problem of capital in long-period equilibria, the existence of an APF differs because an economy-wide aggregate production function as usually specified, with only one type of labour, also requires for its technical existence that heterogeneous labour be aggregable (for example, that relative wages of different types of labour are fixed): as pointed out in chapters 3 and 6, there is no need to aggregate labour for the determinability and stability of a long-period general equilibrium – which is the condition for the acceptability of the marginalist approach to value and distribution, and the real issue at stake in the Cambridge debates. Output aggregability too is required for the existence of an APF (as already pointed out in footnote 20), but not for the determinability of a long-period equilibrium. Relative to the problems discussed in the 'technical' aggregation literature, the existence of an APF differs because of the *necessarily long-period* nature of the comparisons for whose interpretation an APF is used in macroeconomic models (many of the aggregation problems studied by F.M. Fisher and summarized in Felipe and Fisher (2003) concern short-period situations where capital goods are tied to firms), and because in these comparisons the data about capital are in value terms.

Let me clarify the meaning and implications of this last statement. When one discusses the possibility to explain the growth path of an economy over, say, 40 years in terms of an APF, the data relative to the capital stock of different years are value data that must be assumed to reflect different compositions of the physical capital stock (determined by the adaptation to demand and to technical choices), as well as relative prices of the year to which the data refer; now, prices cannot but reflect the tendency of prices to equal normal costs of production; the differences of market prices from long-period normal prices can be presumed more or less to compensate one another; therefore there is little reason to presume that the prices behind the value of capital of a certain year will yield a total value of capital considerably different from the one which would have been obtained, had prices coincided with long-period prices; hence these data must be treated as approximately reflecting the *normal* (i.e. long-period) value of capital.[27] Therefore for issues, such as whether the changes in the normal value of capital associated with changes in distribution can be seen as deriving from an APF, the relevant results are the ones produced in models, such as those used in the Cambridge debates (or in Brown and Chang, 1976), where prices

---

27. Of course there are many statistical difficulties and arbitrarinesses in the actual computation of the aggregate value capital stock of an economy, but these can only be a source of additional problems for any attempt to estimate the actual technology of an economy and therefore, for the sake of argument, I assume these difficulties to be negligible.

are assumed to be long-period prices. For our purposes here, the central result is Garegnani's demonstration (1970) that income distribution can be seen as reflecting the 'marginal products' of an APF *only if* the economy produces, to all relevant effects, a single good (that is if capital goods are produced with exactly the same physical input proportions as output), or at least if relative prices are unaffected by changes in distribution along the entire outward envelope of the $w(r)$ curves.[28]

The relevance, for this result, of the fact that capital is a value magnitude can be highlighted as follows. Suppose the data about output, labour, capital and income distribution derive from a two-sector economy identical with the two-sector neoclassical growth model: capital (physically homogeneous) and labour produce capital and a consumption good in sectors with different production functions. Suppose that the economy is stationary, so net output is physically homogeneous (consisting only of the consumption good); that income distribution is determined in the neoclassical way; that there is no technical progress; and that the data refer to different income distributions (so the collinearity problem does not arise). What the capital data will show is the *value* of capital in terms of the consumption good, and owing to the so-called price Wicksell effects the value of capital will change with distribution in such a way as to render the rate of interest different from the derivative of net output with respect to (the value of) capital. Thus income distribution will not be interpretable in terms of the marginal products of an APF in spite

28. This of course means that the labour theory of value holds. For given technical coefficients, when two or more capital goods are utilized the validity of the labour theory of value does not require that input proportions be the same in all industries; it only requires that Marx's 'organic composition of capital', or equivalently the share of wages in value added, be the same in all industries (Petri, 1998b, pp. 14–15). Brown and Chang (1976) note that, in exceptional cases, this (already exceptional) equality of the organic composition of capital in spite of different input proportions can survive changes in income distribution even when these changes induce changes in input proportions because there is technical choice (cf. their example with two capital goods and CES production functions on p. 1184). For example, this will be the case if, starting from a situation of equal organic composition of capital but proportions between capital goods that are different in different industries, a rise in the real wage does not alter the proportions in which capital goods are combined in each industry, but causes everywhere the same percentage decrease in the labour technical coefficient (input per unit of output) and the same percentage increase in all capital technical coefficients. (Different percentage increases of different capital goods can be allowed if – with circulating capital – they leave the labour embodied in the 'constant capital' unchanged.) The possibility of such an exceptional fluke escapes Garegnani who writes that 'a "surrogate production function" exists only for an economy where a single commodity is produced by itself and labour' (1970, p. 268); however this minor oversight in no way affects his results as to the possible shapes of the relationships between income distribution, and capital per unit of labour or per unit of output.

of the physical homogeneity of capital[29] and of the neoclassical determination of income distribution: for the existence of an APF, capital must also be physically homogeneous with output, or at least relative prices must be independent of distribution.[30]

Garegnani's article should be attentively studied by all serious economists and therefore I do not explain here how he reaches his results. But it is worth while to report here that Garegnani also proves that capital's share can be *very* different from the elasticity of output per unit of labour with respect to the amount (that is the value) of capital per unit of labour; the latter elasticity may easily be negative,[31] or it may even not exist, since – as shown by Figure 6.8 in §6.3.3 – the value of capital may not change at all as optimal techniques and output per unit of labour change with the rate of interest. Thus there is also no ground for any hope that income shares may reflect *at least approximately* the elasticity of output with respect to capital or to labour.[32]

9A.6. These results deprive of credibility the estimates of technical progress based on the notion of total factor productivity, TFP. Changes in total factor productivity are generally estimated by postulating that[33]

$$Y(t) = A(t)F\,[L(t), K(t)],$$

29. If the Leontief-type capital aggregation conditions looked for by Solow (1955–56) or Bliss (1975b) or Franklin Fisher and discussed in §6.4.4 were satisfied, the economy would only be formally equivalent to the two-sector neoclassical growth model; the determinability of the endowment of capital in 'technical' terms, and therefore the determinability of a long-period equilibrium (which is what the so-called 'momentary equilibrium' of the two-sector model would actually be, for the same reasons as for the Solow growth model), would not imply the existence of an APF where K measures the value of capital. This further highlights the difference between the aggregation problem explored by Fisher, and the problem of the existence of an APF.

30. This result in no way contradicts what was pointed out in connection with the 'Shaikh critique', because the possibility always to interpret the data in terms of a Cobb–Douglas was due there to the existence of technical progress, that implies that the data of different years do *not* arise from the same set of alternative techniques.

31. Cf. for example figure 10 in Garegnani (1970, p. 289), which shows the relationships between output per unit of labour and capital per unit of labour corresponding to the three examples of possible relationships between r and k represented here in Figure 6.8 (§6.3.3). In the second and third case the relationship is entirely or partly negative, indicating a negative 'marginal product' of capital and hence a negative elasticity of output with respect to capital.

32. These implications of Garegnani's results for the relationship between income shares and output elasticities appear to have escaped Felipe and Fisher (2003).

33. Note that F, the shape of the production function when one leaves the term A aside, is assumed to be unaffected by the passage of time. If F is Cobb–Douglas, this means that α is assumed constant.

where TFP is represented by A, and that therefore, with g_i the growth rate of $i = Y, A, L, K$, and with $Y_j = \partial Y/\partial j$ for $j = L, K$, it must be

$$g_Y = g_A + Y_L(L/Y)g_L + Y_K(K/Y)g_K.$$

By further postulating that $w = Y_L$ and $r = Y_K$, one obtains that $Y_L L/Y$ is the share of wages in national income and $Y_K K/Y$ is the share of profits or interest, so from data on the growth rates of Y, L, K and on the income shares one can determine g_A, the growth rate of A. (I leave aside here the issue of the comparison of technology levels of different nations.)

It should be intuitive that the arbitrary positing of the existence of an APF when in fact there is none must deprive the estimate of TFP of any significant relationship with what is actually happening in the economy. If income shares do not correspond to the marginal products of an APF, then they cannot be interpreted as output elasticities[34], and therefore they cannot be used to infer what would happen to output in the absence of technical progress when labour and/or capital increase, and then residually to derive the contribution of technical progress by comparing the variation of output thus obtained with the actual variation of output.

The following two examples can perhaps give some concreteness to this statement.

First example. It has been seen in Chapter 6 that it is possible that, with no change in technical knowledge, as the real wage increases and the rate of return on capital decreases, the net product per unit of labour increases while the value of capital per unit of labour remains constant, cf. Figure 6.8 in §6.3.3. Suppose that this is what happens in a certain economy when there is an increase in real wages due for example to political mobilization. To help intuition, let us assume a constant labour employment: one will observe an increase in output occurring together with an increase in the real wage, a decrease of the rate of interest, and a constancy of (the value of) capital. Neither labour nor capital have changed, but output has increased, and income shares have changed (the share of capital has decreased, hence the share of labour has increased). The neoclassical economist must necessarily explain these observations by postulating that there has been non-neutral technical progress that, while raising total factor productivity, has raised the marginal product of labour while lowering the marginal product of capital. Nothing of the sort would actually have been happening. The absence of any technical progress, in particular, would become evident if income

34. The elasticity of output with respect for example to labour is $(dY/Y)/(dL/L) = (\partial Y/\partial L)\cdot L/Y$ which is the share of wages if $w = \partial Y/\partial L$.

distribution were to become again the old one: then output would go back to the old level.

Second example. Suppose that at each moment there is a single dominant technique that gives rise to a linear (or approximately linear) $w(r)$ curve; the value of capital is unaffected by changes in distribution. This linear $w(r)$ curve may result from the fact that the economy produces a single good (corn produced by corn and labour), and there always is one technique that dominates all others: the example to be given applies also to this case in which the value of capital does not change with distribution, if one can assume that the neoclassical economist does not know what the economy's technology looks like. But one can also assume that the linear $w(r)$ curve refers to a complex economy and results from the fact that relative prices change very little with changes in distribution (Ochoa, 1989; Petrović, 1991; Bienenfeld, 1988; Shaikh 1984 would argue that this is very close to what can be empirically observed, cf. Appendix 6A4[35]). Labour employment is constant. Technical progress changes the dominant technique in such a way that the $w(r)$ curve shifts to the right without changing its slope; thus, again, labour and (the value of) capital do not change while Y (the vertical intercept of the $w(r)$ curve) increases, see Figure 9A.1. A neoclassical economist who wants to use a Cobb–Douglas production function can assume that α does not change only if income shares do not change. But we assume that income distribution is determined by forces other than the neoclassical ones, and we assume that income shares do in fact change, and that the share of wages increases, but the rate of interest also increases somewhat. The neoclassical economist who insists in interpreting income shares as determined by marginal products is obliged to admit that α is not constant.

Then expressing the Cobb–Douglas function in logarithms, one has

$$\ln Y_t = \ln A_t + \alpha_t \ln L_t + (1 - \alpha_t) \ln K_t.$$

Differentiating this with respect to time, and indicating with g_i, for $i = Y, A, \alpha, L, K$, the growth rates of the variables, one obtains

$$g_Y = g_A + \frac{d\alpha}{dt} \ln L + \alpha g_L - \frac{d\alpha}{dt} \ln K + (1 - \alpha) g_K. \qquad (*)$$

This would in fact yield the well-known formula

---

35. As observed in that same Appendix, if relative prices do not change with distribution then, except for a totally improbable fluke (the fluke pointed out by Brown and Chang, 1976), the dominant technique will be independent of income distribution.

$$g_Y = g_A + \alpha\, g_L + (1-\alpha)\, g_K \qquad\qquad (**)$$

if it were $d\alpha/dt = 0$. But here it cannot be assumed to be zero. However $g_L = g_K = 0$ so one obtains

$$g_Y = g_A + \left(\ln L - \ln K\right)\frac{d\alpha}{dt}.$$

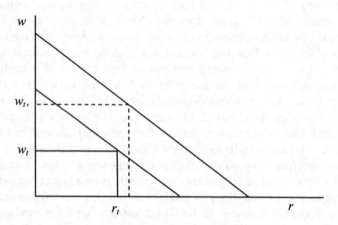

Figure 9A.1   The second example

This shows that g_A, the growth rate of TFP, depends on how income shares change.

These examples show that the measurement of TFP gives technological significance to changes in income distribution even when there is no justification for such an interpretation.[36] The reason can be grasped in general terms by considering the identity

$$Y = wL + rK.$$

Differentiating it with respect to time and dividing by Y, one obtains – where α is again the share of wages, and g_i is the growth rate of the variable i = Y, w, L, r, K:

$$g_Y = \alpha(g_w + g_L) + (1 - \alpha)(g_r + g_K).$$

---

36. Another example of misinterpretation of technical progress when measured through TFP is in Michl (1999).

Comparison of this expression with equation (**) shows that

$$g_A = \alpha g_w + (1-\alpha)g_r.$$

The growth rate of TFP is simply a weighted average of the growth rates of w and r (with the income shares as weights), whatever the determinants of those growth rates.

9A.7. We have, in a sense, come back full circle. The impossibility to believe in the TFP estimates of technical progress derives from the impossibility to believe that APFs may reflect, even only approximately, the dependence of labour productivity on income distribution. This in turn derives from the fact that capital cannot be expected even approximately to behave in the way traditional marginalist theory envisioned it. But this is precisely the reason adduced in this book why the marginalist approach to distribution and growth must be rejected (not the sole reason, but certainly a sufficient reason). Thus we clearly see that the real issue in the discussions on the legitimacy of the use of APFs is the legitimacy of the entire marginalist, or neoclassical, approach to value, distribution and growth.

This book has argued that the continuing faith in this approach largely derives from confusions. It is illegitimately believed that general equilibrium theory in its modern versions can support the approach because it (apparently) does not need the conception of capital as ultimately a single factor, but then it is contradictorily believed that this gives one the right to reason as if capital could in fact be treated like a single factor. I hope this book has dispelled some of these misunderstandings.

However, a puzzle remains: if they rely on modern general equilibrium theory for support for the validity of their approach, then why do so few neoclassical economists pay serious attention to the problems due to the Sonnenschein–Mantel–Debreu results on non-uniqueness, or to the Scarf results on the instability of general equilibrium? These problems are not discussed in this book, but they are admitted by many general equilibrium theorists to be a cause for deep concern about the acceptability of the supply-and-demand approach, and therefore a reason strongly to doubt the results of simple neoclassical models. The obstinate acceptance of the neoclassical approach in spite of all its problems appears to be often due to an inability to conceive of possible alternatives, due in turn to an insufficient acquaintance with the non-neoclassical approaches. Thus Burmeister has recently argued that it is an open question whether one can rely on one-capital-good models (he clearly meant, aggregate-production-function neoclassical models) for empirical work and policy recommendations, but he has gone on to add that 'those interested in doing empirical work have few alternatives available to them ... the approximate answers provided by one-capital-good models are likely to prevail, lacking both clear evidence why they should not and any viable alternative' (Burmeister, 2000, p. 313). Not surprisingly, *no* evidence is adduced by Burmeister in support of his opinions concerning the absence of 'clear evidence why they should not', or the absence of 'any viable alternative'. The examples and the literature quoted in this Appendix rebut the first of these opinions; as to the second, it is flatly contradicted by a vast non-neoclassical applied and econometric literature, and it appears rather to testify to modest efforts by Burmeister to keep informed on what non-neoclassical economists produce. Unfortunately, as pointed out in §6.4.6, his is not an isolated case.

References

Abel, A.B. (1990), 'Consumption and investment', in B.M. Friedman and F.H. Hahn (eds), *Handbook of Monetary Economics*, vol. II, New York: Elsevier Science Publishers BV, pp. 725–78.

Ackley, G. (1961), *Macroeconomic Theory*, New York: Macmillan.

Ackley, G. (1978), *Macroeconomics: Theory and Policy*, New York: Macmillan.

Ahmad, S. (1991), *Capital in Economic Theory: Neo-Classical, Cambridge and chaos*, Aldershot, UK and Brookfield, US: Edward Elgar.

Alchian, A. (1955), 'The rate of interest, Fisher's rate of return over costs and Keynes's internal rate of return', *American Economic Review*, December, 938–42.

Archibald, G.C. and R. Lipsey (1958), 'Monetary and value theory: a critique of Lange and Patinkin', *Review of Economic Studies*, **26**, 1–22.

Archibald, G.C. and R. Lipsey (1960), 'Monetary and value theory: a further comment', *Review of Economic Studies*, **28**, 50–56.

Arrow, K.J. (1951), 'Alternative proof of the substitution theorem for Leontief models in the general case', in Koopmans (1951b), pp. 155–64.

Arrow, K.J. (1953), 'Le rôle des valeurs boursières pour la repartition la meilleure des risques', *Econometrie. Colloques internationaux Centre National de la Recherche Scientifique*, Paris, 1952, **40**, pp. 41–7; discussion, pp. 47–8. CNRS, Paris, 1953. English translation: *Review of Economic Studies*, April 1964, **31**, pp. 91–6.

Arrow, K.J. (1959), 'Toward a theory of price adjustment', in M. Abramovitz (ed.), *The Allocation of Economic Resources*, Stanford: Stanford University Press, pp. 41–51.

Arrow, K.J. (1964), 'The role of securities in the optimal allocation of risk-bearing', *Quarterly Journal of Economics*, **31**, 91–6.

Arrow, K.J. (1989), 'Joan Robinson and modern economic theory: an interview', in G. Feiwel (ed.), *Joan Robinson and Modern Economic Theory*, London: Macmillan, 1989, pp. 147–85.

Arrow, K.J. and F.H. Hahn (1971), *General Competitive Analysis*, Edinburgh: Oliver and Boyd.

Asimakopulos, A. (1971), 'The determination of investment in Keynes's model', *Canadian Journal of Economics*, **21**(3), 382–88.

Asimakopulos, T. (1982), 'Keynes' theory of effective demand revisited', *Australian Economic Papers*, **21**, June, 18–36.

Baldone, S. (1984), 'From surrogate to pseudo production functions', *Cambridge Journal of Economics*, **8**(3), 271–88.

Ball, R.J. and R. Bodkin (1960), 'The real balance effect and orthodox demand theory: a critique of Archibald and Lipsey', *Review of Economic Studies*, **28**, 44–9.

Baumol, W.J. (1960), 'Monetary and value theory: comments', *Review of Economic Studies*, **28**, 29–31.

Becker, G.S. and W.J. Baumol (1952), 'The classical monetary theory: the outcome of the discussion', *Economica*, new series, **19** (76), 355–76.

Begg, D.K.H. (1982), *The Rational Expectations Revolution in Macroeconomics*, Oxford: Philip Allan.

Betancourt, R.R. and C.K. Clague (1981), *Capital Utilization: a Theoretical and Empirical Analysis*, Cambridge: Cambridge University Press.

Bewley, T. (1982), 'An integration of equilibrium theory and turnpike theory', *Journal of Mathematical Economics*, **10**, September, 233–68.

Bewley, T. (1998), 'Why not cut pay?', *European Economic Review*, **42**(3–5), 459–90.

Bewley, T. (1999), *Why Wages don't Fall During a Recession*, Cambridge, MA, USA: Harvard University Press.

Bharadwaj, K. and B. Schefold (eds) (1990), *Essays on Piero Sraffa*, London: Unwin and Hyman (reprinted 1992 by Routledge, London).

Bidard, C. (1997), 'Pure joint production', *Cambridge Journal of Economics*, **21**(6), 685–701.

Bienenfeld, M. (1988), 'Regularity in price changes as an effect of changes in distribution', *Cambridge Journal of Economics*, **12**, 247–55.

Blaug, M. (1974), *The Cambridge Revolution: Success or Failure?*, London: The Institute for Economic Affairs.

Blaug, M. (1999), 'Misunderstanding classical economics: the Sraffian interpretation of the surplus approach', *History of Political Economy*, **31**(2), 213–36.

Bliss, C.J. (1970), 'Comment on Garegnani', *Review of Economic Studies*, **37**(3), 437–8.

Bliss, C.J. (1975a), 'The reappraisal of Keynesian economics. An appraisal', in M. Parkin and A.R. Nobay (eds), *Current Economic Problems*, Cambridge: Cambridge University Press, pp. 203–213

Bliss, C.J. (1975b), *Capital Theory and the Distribution of Income*, Amsterdam: North-Holland.

Bliss, C.J. (1976), 'Capital theory in the short run', in Brown et. al. (1976), pp. 187–202.

Bliss, C.J. (1983), 'Consistent temporary equilibrium', in Fitoussi (1983a), pp. 141–152.

Böhm-Bawerk, E. von (1891), *The Positive Theory of Capital*, London: Macmillan.

Bowles, S., D.M. Gordon and T.E. Weisskopf (1989), 'Business ascendancy and economic impasse: a structural retrospective on conservative economics, 1979–87', *Journal of Economic Perspectives*, **3**(1), 107–34 (reprinted in Gordon, 1998, pp. 283–310).

Brandolini, A. (1995), 'In search of a stylised fact: do real wages exhibit a consistent pattern of cyclical variability?', *Journal of Economic Surveys*, **9**(2), 103–63.

Bray, M.M. (1982), 'Learning, estimation, and the stability of rational expectations', *Journal of Economic Theory*, **26**, 318–39.

Brown, M. and W.W. Chang (1976), 'Capital aggregation in a general equilibrium model of production', *Econometrica*, **44**(6), November, 1179–200.

Brown, M., K. Sato and P. Zarembka (eds) (1976), *Essays in Modern Capital Theory*, Amsterdam: North-Holland.

Brunner, K. (1951), 'Inconsistency and indeterminacy in classical economics', *Econometrica*, **19**(2), 152–173.

Burda, M. and C. Wyplosz (1993), *Macroeconomics: a European Text*, Oxford: Oxford University Press.

Burmeister, E. (1980), *Capital Theory and Dynamics*, Cambridge: Cambridge University Press.

Burmeister, E. (1991), 'Comment on Steedman', in N. deMarchi and M. Blaug (eds), *Appraising Economic Theories*, Aldershot, UK and Brookfield, US: Edward Elgar, pp. 456–69.

Burmeister, E. (2000), 'The capital theory controversy', in Kurz (2000), pp. 305–14.

Burmeister, E. and R. Dobell (1970), *Mathematical Theories of Economic Growth*, New York: Macmillan.

Caballero, R.J. (1999), 'Aggregate investment', in J.B. Taylor and M. Woodford (eds), *Handbook of Macroeconomics*, vol. 1B, Elsevier Science BV, pp. 814–62.

Caminati, M. (1981), 'The rate of interest in the classical economists', *Metroeconomica*, **33**(1–2–3), February–October, 79–104.

Casarosa, C. (1981), 'The microfoundations of Keynes's aggregate supply and expected demand analysis', *Economic Journal*, **91**(361), March, 188–94.

Chick, V. (1983), *Macroeconomics after Keynes*, Oxford: Philip Allan.

Chirinko, R.S. (1993), 'Business fixed investment spending: modeling strategies, empirical results, and policy implications', *Journal of Economic Literature*, **31**, December, 1875–911.

Ciccone, R. (1990), 'Accumulation and capacity utilization: some critical notes on Joan Robinson's theory of distribution', in Bharadwaj and Schefold (1990), pp. 417–29.

Ciccone, R. (1996), 'Possibilità e probabilità di comportamento "perverso" del capitale', *Studi Economici*, **58**(1), 41–73.

Ciccone, R. (1999), 'Classical and neoclassical short-run prices: a comparative analysis of their intended empirical content', in Mongiovi and Petri (1999), pp. 69–92.

Clark, J.B. (1899), *The Distribution of Wealth*, New York: Macmillan.

Clark, J.B. (1925), *The Distribution of Wealth*, New York: Macmillan.

Clower, R.W. (1963), 'Classical monetary theory revisited', *Economica*, **30**(118), 165–70.

Clower, R.W. (1967), 'A reconsideration of the microfoundations of monetary theory', *Western Economic Journal*, **6**, 1–9 (reprinted in Clower, 1969, pp. 202–11).

Clower, R.W. (ed.) (1969), *Monetary Theory*, Harmondsworth: Penguin.

Cohen, A.J. and G.C. Harcourt (2003), 'Whatever happened to the Cambridge capital theory controversies?', *Journal of Economic Perspectives*, **17**(1), 199–214.

Currie, M. and I. Steedman (1989), 'Agonising over equilibrium: Hayek and Lindahl', *Quaderni di Storia dell'Economia Politica*, **7**, 75–99.

Currie, M. and I. Steedman (1990), *Wrestling with Time*, Ann Arbor: Michigan University Press.

Davis, M.A. and M.G. Palumbo (2001), 'A primer on the economics and time series econometrics of wealth effects', Working Paper 2001-09, Finance and Economics Discussion Series, Washington, DC: Federal Reserve Board.

Debreu, G. (1959), *Theory of Value*, New York: Wiley.

D'Ippolito G. (1987), 'Probabilità di perverso comportamento del capitale al variare del saggio di profitto: il modello embrionale a due settori', *Note Economiche*, 2, 5–37.

D'Ippolito G. (1989), 'Delimitazione dell'area dei casi di comportamento perverso del capitale in un punto di mutamento della tecnica', in L.L. Pasinetti (ed.), *Aspetti controversi della teoria del valore*, Bologna: Il Mulino, pp. 191–8.

Dixit, A.K. and R.S. Pindyck (1994), *Investment under Uncertainty*, Princeton, NJ: Princeton University Press.

Donzelli, F. (1986), *Il concetto di equilibrio nella teoria economica neoclassica*, Roma: La Nuova Italia Scientifica.

Dornbusch, R. and S. Fischer (1987), *Macroeconomics*, 4th edn., New York: McGraw-Hill.

Dougherty, C. (1980), *Interest and Profit*, London: Methuen and Co.

Duménil, G. and D. Lévy (1985), 'The classicals and the neoclassicals: a rejoinder to Frank Hahn', *Cambridge Journal of Economics*, December, 327–45.

Dynan, K.E. and D.M. Maki (2001), 'Does stock market wealth matter for consumption?', Board of Governors of the Federal Reserve Board, Finance and Economics Discussion Series, 2001-23, http://www.federalreserve.gov/pubs/feds/2001/200123/200123pap.pdf.

Eatwell, J.L. (1979), *Theories of Value, Output and Employment*, London: Thames Polytechnic (reprinted in Eatwell and Milgate, 1983, pp. 93–128).

Eatwell, J.L. (1982), 'Competition', in I. Bradley and M. Howard (eds), *Classical and Marxian Political Economy*, London: Macmillan, pp. 203–28.

Eatwell, J.L. (1987), 'Walras's theory of capital' (reprinted in Eatwell et al., 1990, pp. 247–56).

Eatwell, J.L. and M. Milgate (eds), (1983), *Keynes's Economics and the Theory of Value and Distribution*, London and New York: Duckworth and Oxford University Press.

Eatwell, J.L., M. Milgate and P. Newman (eds) (1987), *The New Palgrave Dictionary of Economics*, 4 vols, London: Macmillan.

Eatwell, J.L., M. Milgate and P. Newman (eds) (1990), *Capital Theory*, London: Macmillan.

Eisner, R. (1978), *Factors in Business Investment*, Cambridge, MA, USA: Ballinger.

Eisner, R. and R. Strotz (1963), 'Determinants of business investment', Research Study Two in CMC, *Impacts of Monetary Policy*, Englewood Cliffs: Prentice-Hall.

Ellis, H. S. (1937–38), 'Some fundamentals in the theory of velocity', *Quarterly Journal of Economics*, **52**, 431–72.

Encarnaciòn, J. (1958), 'Consistency between Say's identity and the Cambridge equation', *Economic Journal*, **68**, 827–30.

Epstein, L.G. (1987), 'The global stability of efficient intertemporal allocations', *Econometrica*, **55**(2), 329–55.

Farmer, R.E.A. (1999), *Macroeconomics*, Mason, OH: South-Western College Publishing.

Fazzari, S.M. and T. Mott (1986–87), 'The investment theories of Kalecki and Keynes: an empirical study of firm data, 1970–82', *Journal of Post-Keynesian Economics*, **9**(2), Winter, 171–87.

Fazzari, S.M., R.G. Hubbard and B.C. Petersen (1988), 'Financing constraints and corporate investment', *Brookings Papers on Economic Activity*, 1, 141–95.

Feiwel, G.R. (ed.) (1989), *Joan Robinson and Modern Economic Theory*, London: Macmillan.

Felipe, J. and F.M. Fisher (2003), 'Aggregation in production functions: what applied economists should know', *Metroeconomica* **54**(2 and 3), 208–62.

Felipe, J. and J.S.L. McCombie (2003), 'Some methodological problems with the neoclassical analysis of the East Asian miracle', *Cambridge Journal of Economics*, **27**(5), 695–721.

Ferber, R. (ed.), (1967), *Determinants of Investment Behaviour*, New York: NBER.

Fisher, D. (1983), *Macroeconomic Theory: a Survey*, London: Macmillan.

Fisher, F.M. (1969), 'The existence of aggregate production functions', *Econometrica.*, **37**(4), 553–77.

Fisher, F.M. (1971), 'Reply to Joan Robinson', *Econometrica*, **39**(2), 405.

Fisher, F.M. (1983), *Disequilibrium Foundations of Equilibrium Economics*, Cambridge: Cambridge University Press.

Fisher, F.M. (1987), entry 'aggregation problems', in Eatwell at. al. 1987.

Fisher, F.M. (2003), 'Disequilibrium and stability', in Petri and Hahn (2003), pp. 74–94.

Fisher, I. (1892), *Mathematical Investigations in the Theory of Value and Prices* (reprinted 1961 by Augustus M. Kelley, New York).

Fisher, I. (1907), *The Rate of Interest*, New York: Macmillan.

Fisher, I. (1922), *The Purchasing Power of Money* (reprint of 2nd edn., 1963, by Augustus M.Kelley, New York).

Fisher, I. (1930), *The Theory of Interest*, New York: Macmillan.

Fitoussi, J.P. (1983a), *Modern Macroeconomic Theory*, Oxford: Basil Blackwell.

Fitoussi, J.P. (1983b), 'Modern macroeconomic theory: an overview', in Fitoussi (1983a).

Friedman, M. (1968), 'The role of monetary policy', *American Economic Review*, **58**(1), 1–17.

Galeotti, M. (1984), 'Recent developments in investment theory', *Giornale degli economisti e annali di economia*, **43**(5–6), 393–415.

Garegnani, P. (1960), *Il capitale nelle teorie della distribuzione*, Milan: Giuffrè.

Garegnani, P. (1962), 'On Walras's theory of capital', unpublished manuscript, distributed at the 1986 CISEP International Summer School, Trieste.

Garegnani, P. (1964), 'Note su consumi, investimenti e domanda effettiva. Parte I', *Economia Internazionale*; reprinted in *Valore e domanda effettiva*, Turin: Einaudi, 1979; English translation in Garegnani (1978).

Garegnani, P. (1970), 'Heterogeneous capital, the production function and the theory of distribution', *Review of Economic Studies*, 407–36 (reprinted in E.K. Hunt and J.G. Schwartz (eds), *A Critique of Economic Theory*, Harmondsworth: Penguin,

1972, pp. 245–91). (The Mathematical Appendix referred to in this article is available, in Italian, in the Italian translation published in P. Sylos Labini (ed.), *Prezzi relativi e distribuzione*, Turin: Boringhieri, 1973.)

Garegnani, P. (1976), 'On a change in the notion of equilibrium in recent work on value and distribution', in Brown et al. (1976), pp. 25–45 (reprinted in Eatwell and Milgate, 1983, pp. 129–45).

Garegnani, P. (1978), 'Notes on consumption, investment and effective demand. Part I', *Cambridge Journal of Economics*, **2**(4), 335–53 (reprinted in Eatwell and Milgate, 1983, pp. 21–41).

Garegnani, P. (1979a), 'Notes on consumption, investment and effective demand. Part II', *Cambridge Journal of Economics*, **3**(1), 63–82 (reprinted in Eatwell and Milgate, 1983, pp. 41–69).

Garegnani, P. (1979b), 'Notes on consumption, investment and effective demand: a reply to Joan Robinson', *Cambridge Journal of Economics*, June, **3**(2), 181–7 (reprinted in Eatwell and Milgate, 1983, pp. 72–78).

Garegnani, P. (1979c), *Valore e Domanda Effettiva*, Turin: Einaudi.

Garegnani, P. (1984a), 'Value and distribution in the classical economists and Marx', *Oxford Economic Papers*, **36**(2), 291–325.

Garegnani, P. (1984b), 'On some illusory instances of marginal products', *Metroeconomica*, July–October, 143–60.

Garegnani, P. (1987), entry 'surplus approach' in Eatwell et al. (1987).

Garegnani, P. (1989), 'Some notes on capital, expectations and the analysis of changes', in Feiwel (1989), pp. 344–67.

Garegnani, P. (1990a), 'Quantity of capital', in Eatwell et al. (1990).

Garegnani, P. (1990b), 'Sraffa: classical versus marginalist analysis', in Bharadwaj and Schefold (1990), pp. 112–40.

Garegnani, P. (1990c), 'Comment on Samuelson', in Bharadwaj and Schefold (1990), pp. 283–301; reproduced in Kurz (2000), pp. 48–68.

Garegnani, P. (1992), 'Some notes for an analysis of accumulation', in J. Halevi, D. Laibman and E. Nell (eds), *Beyond the Steady State: a Revival of Growth Theory*, London: Macmillan, pp. 47–72.

Garegnani, P. (1994), 'Capital and general equilibrium', unpublished manuscript (revised text of the Sraffa Lecture, Cambridge, 1993).

Garegnani, P. (2000), 'Savings, investment and capital in a system of general intertemporal equilibrium', in Kurz (2000), pp. 392–445.

Garegnani, P. (2003), 'Savings, investment and capital in a system of general intertemporal equilibrium', in Petri and Hahn (2003), pp. 117–72.

Garegnani, P. and A. Palumbo (1998), entry 'accumulation of capital', in H.D. Kurz and N. Salvadori (eds.), *The Elgar Companion to Classical Economics*, Cheltenham, UK and Lyme, USA: Edward Elgar.

Gehrke, C. (2003), 'On the transition from long-period to short-period equilibria', *Review of Political Economy*, **15**(1), 85–106.

Glyn, A. (1997), 'Does aggregate profitability really matter?', *Cambridge Journal of Economics*, **21**(5), 593–619.

Gordon, D.M. (1998), *Economics and Social Justice*, ed. by S. Bowles and T.E. Weisskopf, Cheltenham, UK and Lyme, USA: Edward Elgar.

Gordon, D.M., T.E. Weisskopf and S. Bowles (1994), 'Power, profits and investment: an institutionalist explanation of the stagnation of US net investment after the mid-1960s', New School for Social Research Working Paper no. 12 (reprinted in Gordon, 1998, pp. 236–66).

Gould, J.P. (1968), 'Adjustment costs in the theory of investment of the firm', *Review of Economic Studies*, **35**(1), 47–55.

Grandmont, J.-M. (1977), 'Temporary general equilibrium theory', *Econometrica*, 45(3), 535–72.

Grandmont, J.-M. (1987), *Temporary Equilibrium: Selected Readings*, San Diego: Academic Press.

Griliches, Z. (1967), 'On Crockett-Friend and Jorgenson', in Ferber (1967), pp. 160–62.

GT, see Keynes (1973–79).

Haavelmo, T. (1960), *A Study in the Theory of Investment*, Chicago: Chicago University Press.

Hagemann, H. (1987), entry 'internal rate of return' in Eatwell et al. (1987).

Hahn, F. H. (1960), 'The Patinkin controversy', *Review of Economic Studies*, **28**(1), 37–43.

Hahn, F.H. (1966), 'Equilibrium dynamics with heterogeneous capital goods', *Quarterly Journal of Economics*, **80**(4), 633–46.

Hahn, F. H. (1981a), 'General equilibrium theory', in D. Bell and I. Kristol (eds), *The Crisis in Economic Theory*, New York: Basic Books, pp. 123–38.

Hahn, F.H. (1981b), review of M. Beenstock, *A Neoclassical Analysis of Macroeconomic Policy* (Cambridge University Press, 1980), *Economic Journal*, December 1981, 1036–9.

Hahn, F. H. (1982a), 'The neo-Ricardians', *Cambridge Journal of Economics*, **6**(4), 353–74.

Hahn, F. H. (1982b), *Money and Inflation*, Oxford: Basil Blackwell.

Hahn, F. H. (1984), 'Introduction', in *Equilibrium and Macroeconomics*, Oxford: Basil Blackwell.

Hahn, F.H. (1987), entry 'auctioneer', in Eatwell et al. (1987).

Hahn, F.H. (1999), 'Labour market flexibility and "welfare"', in M.M.G. Fase, W. Kanning and D.A. Walker (eds), *Economics, Welfare Policy and the History of Economic Thought: Essays in Honour of Arnold Heertje*, Cheltenham, UK and Northampton, MA, USA: Edward Elgar, pp. 183–98.

Hahn, F.H. and T. Negishi (1962), 'A theorem on non-tâtonnement stability', *Econometrica*, **30**, 463–9.

Hall, R.E. (1993), 'Macro theory and the recession of 1990–91', *American Economic Review*, May, 275–9.

Hamermesh, D.S. (1993), *Labor Demand*, Princeton: Princeton University Press.

Hamermesh, D.S., and G.A. Pfann (1996), 'Adjustment costs in factor demand', *Journal of Economic Literature*, **34**(3), 1264–92.

Handa, J. (2000), *Monetary Economics*, London and New York: Routledge.

Hansen, B. (1970), *A Survey of General Equilibrium Systems*, New York: McGraw-Hill.

Harcourt, G.C. (1972), *Some Cambridge Controversies in the Theory of Capital*, Cambridge: Cambridge University Press.

Harris, D.J. (1973), 'Capital, distribution and the aggregate production function', *American Economic Review*, 63, 100–13.

Hayashi, F. (1982), 'Tobin's marginal *q* and average *q*: a neoclassical interpretation', *Econometrica*, 50(1), 213–27.

Hayek, F.A. von (1928), 'Das intertemporale Gleichgewichtssystem der Preise und die Bewegungen des "Geldwertes"', *Weltwirtschaftliches Archiv*, 28, 33–76 (English translation: 'The system of intertemporal price equilibrium and movements in the "value of money"', in I.M. Kirzner (ed.), *Classics in Austrian Economics, vol. III: The Age of Mises and Hayek*, London: William Pickering, 1984, pp. 161–200).

Hayek, F.A. von (1932), 'A note on the development of the doctrine of "forced saving"', *Quarterly Journal of Economics*, 47(1), 123–33.

Hayek, F.A. (1936), 'The mythology of capital', *Quarterly Journal of Economics*, 1, February, 199–228; as reprinted in *Readings in the Theory of Income Distribution*, ed. by the American Economic Association, Toronto, 1946, pp. 355–83.

Heijdra, B.J. and F. Van Der Ploeg (2002), *Foundations of Modern Macroeconomics*, Oxford: Oxford University Press.

Hennings, K.H. (1987a), entry 'Böhm-Bawerk, Eugen von', in Eatwell et al. (1987); also reprinted in Eatwell et al. (1990).

Hennings, K.H. (1987b), entry 'roundabout methods of production', in Eatwell et al. (1987); also reprinted in Eatwell et al. (1990).

Hickman, W.B. (1950), 'The determinacy of absolute prices in classical economic theory', *Econometrica*, 18, 9–20.

Hicks, J.R. (1932 [1963]), *The Theory of Wages*, London: Macmillan; as reprinted with additions, 2nd edn., 1963.

Hicks, J.R. (1934), 'Léon Walras', *Econometrica*, 2(4), 338–48; as reprinted in J.R. Hicks, *Classics and Moderns, vol. III Collected Essays on Economic Theory*, Oxford: Basil Blackwell, 1983, pp. 86–95.

Hicks, J.R. (1935a), 'A suggestion for simplifying the theory of money', *Economica*; as reprinted in J.R. Hicks, *Critical Essays in Monetary Theory*, Oxford: Oxford University Press, 1967, pp. 61–82.

Hicks, J.R. (1935b [1963]), 'Wages and interest: The dynamic problem', *Economic Journal*, 45(4), 456–68; as reprinted in Hicks (1932 [1963]), pp. 268–85.

Hicks, J.R. (1936), 'Mr. Keynes's theory of employment', *Economic Journal*, 46(2), June, 238–53.

Hicks, J.R. (1946), *Value and Capital*, 2nd edn., Oxford: Clarendon Press.

Hicks, J.R. (1965), *Capital and Growth*, Oxford: Oxford University Press.

Hicks, J.R. (1973), *Capital and Time*, Oxford: Oxford University Press.

Hicks, J.R. (1980–81), 'IS–LM: an explanation', *Journal of Post-Keynesian Economics*, Winter; as reprinted in Fitoussi (1983a), pp. 49–63.

Hirshleifer, J. (1970), *Investment, Interest and Capital*, Englewood Cliffs, NJ: Prentice-Hall.

Hogan, W.P. (1958), 'Technical progress and production functions', *Review of Economics and Statistics*, 40, 407–11.

Hubbard, R.G. (1998), 'Capital–market imperfections and investment', *Journal of Economic Literature*, **36**(1), 193–225.

Ingrao, B. and G. Israel (1990), *The Invisible Hand: Economic Equilibrium in the History of Science,* Cambridge, MA: The MIT Press.

Jevons, W.S. (1871 [1970]), *The Theory of Political Economy*, Harmondsworth: Penguin Books.

Johnson, H.G. (1962), 'Monetary theory and policy', *American Economic Review*, **52**(3), 335–384.

Johnson, H.G. (1973), *The Theory of Income Distribution*, London: Gray-Mills.

Jorgenson, D.W. (1963), 'Capital theory and investment behavior', *American Economic Review*, **53**(2), 247–59.

Jorgenson, D.W. (1967), 'The theory of investment behavior', in R. Ferber (ed.), *Determinants of Investment Behaviour*, New York: NBER, Columbia University Press, pp. 129–55.

Jossa, B. (1963a), 'La dicotomia nei sistemi monetari', *Moneta e Credito*, **16**(1), 109–127.

Jossa, B. (1963b), 'Della pretesa invalidità dei modelli neoclassici di teoria monetaria', *Economia Internazionale*, **16**(3), 437–59.

Junankar, P.N. (1972), *Investment: Theories and Evidence*, London: Macmillan.

Kaldor, N. (1934), 'The equilibrium of the firm', *Economic Journal*, **44**(1), 60–76.

Kaldor, N. (1937), 'Annual survey of economic theory: the recent controversy on the theory of capital', *Econometrica*, **53**(3), 201–33.

Kalecki, M. (1937), 'The principle of increasing risk', *Economica*, **4**(4), 440–7.

Kalecki, M. (1938), 'A reply', *Economica*, **5**(4), 459–60.

Kalecki, M. (1943), 'Political aspects of full employment', *Political Quarterly*, reprinted in M. Kalecki, *Selected Essays on the Dynamics of the Capitalist Economy, 1933–1970*, Cambridge: Cambridge University Press, 1971, pp. 138–145.

Kalecki, M. (1971), 'Entrepreneurial capital and investment', in M. Kalecki, *Selected Essays on the Dynamics of the Capitalist Economy*, Cambridge: Cambridge University Press, pp. 105–109.

KCW, see Keynes (1973–79).

Keynes, J.M. (1936), *The General Theory of Employment, Interest and Money*, London: Macmillan.

Keynes, J.M. (1939), 'Relative movements of real wages and output', *Economic Journal*, **49**, 34–51.

Keynes, J.M. (1973–79), *Collected Writings*, ed. by D. Moggridge, vols. I–XXIX, Cambridge: Cambridge University Press. Referred to in the text as *KCW* followed by the volume number in Roman numerals, except for *The General Theory*, vol. VII, referred to as *GT*.

Kirman, A. (1999), 'The future of economic theory', in A. Kirman and L.-A. Gérard-Varet, *Economics beyond the Millennium*, Oxford: Oxford University Press, pp. 8–22.

Kirman, A. (2003), 'General equilibrium: problems, prospects and alternatives: an attempt at synthesis', in Petri and Hahn (2003), pp. 468–85.

350   *General equilibrium, capital and macroeconomics*

Kirzner, I. (1981), 'The "Austrian" perspective on the crisis', in D. Bell and I. Kristol (eds), *The Crisis in Economic Theory*, New York: Basic Books, pp. 111–38.

Knight, F.H. (1917–18), 'The concept of normal price in value and distribution', *Quarterly Journal of Economics*, **32**, 66–100.

Knight, F.H. (1946), 'Capital and interest', *Encyclopaedia Britannica*, vol. IV, 779–801 (reprinted in *Readings in the Theory of Income Distribution*, ed. by the American Economic Association, Toronto, 1946).

Kompas, T. (1992), *Studies in the History of Long-Run Equilibrium Theory*, Manchester: Manchester University Press.

Koopmans, T.C. (1951a), 'Alternative proof of the substitution theorem for Leontief models in the case of three industries', in Koopmans (1951b), pp. 147–54.

Koopmans, T.C. (1951b), *Activity Analysis of Production and Allocation*, New York: John Wiley and Sons.

Koopmans, T. (1957), *Three Essays on the State of Economic Science*, New York: McGraw-Hill.

Koutsoyiannis, A. (1975), *Modern Microeconomics*, London: Macmillan.

Kregel, J.A. (1976), 'Economic methodology in the face of uncertainty: the modelling methods of Keynes and the Post-Keynesians', *Economic Journal*, **86**(2), June, 209–25.

Krueger, A.B. (2003), 'An interview with Edmond Malinvaud', *Journal of Economic Perspectives*, **17**(1), 181–98.

Kuenne, R.E. (1963), *The Theory of General Economic Equilibrium*, Princeton, NJ: Princeton University Press.

Kurz, H.D. (1985), 'Sraffa's contribution to the debate in capital theory', *Contributions to Political Economy*, **4**, March, 3–24.

Kurz, H.D. (1986), ' "Normal" positions and capital utilization', *Political Economy: Studies in the Surplus Approach*, **2**, 37–54.

Kurz, H.D. (1987), entry 'capital theory: debates', in Eatwell et al. (1987).

Kurz, H.D. (ed.), (2000), *Critical Essays on Piero Sraffa's Legacy in Economics*, Cambridge: Cambridge University Press.

Kurz, H.D. and N. Salvadori (1994), 'The non-substitution theorem: making good a lacuna', *Journal of Economics*, **59**(1), 97–103.

Kurz, H.D. and N. Salvadori (1995), *Theory of Production*, Cambridge: Cambridge University Press.

Lange, O. (1942), 'Say's law: a restatement and criticism', in O. Lange et al. (eds), *Studies in Mathematical Economics and Econometrics*, Chicago, pp. 49–68 (reprinted in O. Lange, *Papers in Economics and Sociology*, Oxford and Warsaw: Pergamon Press, 1970, pp. 149–70).

Lee, F.S. (1998), *Post-Keynesian Price Theory*, Cambridge: Cambridge University Press.

Leontief, W.W. (1950), 'The consistency of the classical theory of money and prices', *Econometrica*, **18**, 21–4.

Leontief, W.W. (1971), 'Theoretical assumptions and nonobserved facts', *American Economic Review*, **61**(1), March, 1–7.

Lerner, A.P. (1944), *The Economics of Control*, New York: Macmillan.

Lerner, A.P. (1973), 'Money, debt and wealth', in W. Sellekaerts (ed.), *Econometrics and Economic Theory*, New York: Macmillan, pp. 245–59.

Levhari, D. (1965), 'A nonsubstitution theorem and switching of techniques', *Quarterly Journal of Economics*, **79**(1), 98–105.

Lindahl, E. (1929), 'The place of capital in the theory of price', originally published in Swedish in 1929, as translation as Part III of Lindahl (1939), pp. 271–350.

Lindahl, E. (1939), *Studies in the Theory of Money and Capital*, London: George Allen & Unwin (reprinted 1970 by Augustus Kelley, New York).

Lloyd, C. (1970), 'Classical monetary theory and the velocity of circulation', *Canadian Journal of Economics*, **3**(1), 87–94.

Lucas, R.E. Jr. (1967), 'Adjustment costs and the theory of supply', *Journal of Political Economy*, **75**(3), August, 321–34.

Lund, P.J. (1971), *Investment: the study of an economic aggregate*, London: Oliver and Boyd.

Lutz, F.A. (1967), *The Theory of Interest*, Dordrecht: Reidel (translation of *Zinstheorie*, Tubingen: Mohr, 1956).

Madden, P. (1984), 'Review of Fisher, 1983', *Economic Journal*, **94**(4), 986–8.

Mainwaring, L. and I. Steedman (2000), 'On the probability of re-switching and capital reversing in a two-sector Sraffian model', in Kurz (2000), pp. 323–53.

Malinvaud, E. (1995), 'About investment in macroeconomics', in J.-P. Fitoussi (ed.), *Economics in a Changing World, vol. 5: Economic Growth and Capital and Labour Markets*, New York: St. Martin's Press, pp. 123–41.

Mandler, M. (2002), 'Classical and neoclassical indeterminacy in one-shot versus ongoing equilibrium', *Metroeconomica*, **53**(3), 203–222.

Marglin, S.A. (1970), 'Investment and interest: a reformulation and extension of Keynesian theory', *Economic Journal*, **80**(4), 910–31.

Marglin, S.A. (1984), *Growth, Distribution and Prices*, Cambridge, MA: Harvard University Press.

Marris, R. (1964), *The Economics of Capital Utilization*, Cambridge: Cambridge University Press.

Marshall, A. (1920 [1970]), *Principles of Economics*, 8th edn., London: Macmillan.

Marshall, A. (1923), *Money, Credit and Commerce* (reprint 1965 by Augustus M. Kelley, New York).

Marshall, A. (1961), *Principles of Economics*, 9th (Variorum) edn., vol. 1, ed. by C.W. Guilleband, London: MacMillan, 1961.

Mas-Colell, A. (1989), 'Capital theory paradoxes: anything goes', in G. Feiwel (ed.), *Joan Robinson and Modern Economic Theory*, London: Macmillan, pp. 505–20.

Mas-Colell, A., M.D. Whinston and J.R. Green (1995), *Microeconomic Theory*, New York and Oxford: Oxford University Press.

Mauer, L. J. (1966), 'The Patinkin controversy: a review', *Kyklos*, **19**(2), 299–313.

McCombie, J.S.L. (1998), 'Paradigms, rhetoric, and the relevance of the aggregate production function', in P. Arestis (ed.), *Method, Theory and Policy in Keynes. Essays in Honour of Paul Davidson*, vol. III, Cheltenham, UK and Lyme, USA: Edward Elgar, pp. 44–68.

McCombie, J.S.L. (2000–2001), 'The Solow residual, technical change and aggregate production functions', *Journal of Post Keynesian Economics*, **23**(2), Winter, 267–97 (Errata, **23**(3), 544).

McCombie, J.S.L. and R. Dixon (1991), 'Estimating technical change in aggregate production functions: a critique', *International Review of Applied Economics*, **5**(1), 24–46.

McCombie, J.S.L. and A.P. Thirlwall (1994), *Economic Growth and the Balance-of-Payments Constraint*, London: Macmillan at St. Martin's Press.

McKenzie, L.W. (1987), entry 'general equilibrium' in Eatwell et al. (1987).

Meade, J. (1936–37), 'A simplified model of Mr. Keynes' system', *Review of Economic Studies*, **4**, 98–107.

Metzler, L.A. (1950), 'The rate of interest and the marginal product of capital', *Journal of Political Economy*, **58**(3), August, 289–306.

Michl, T.R. (1999), 'Biased technical change and the aggregate production function', *International Review of Applied Economics*, **13**(2), 193–206.

Milgate, M. (1979), 'On the origin of the notion of "Intertemporal Equilibrium"', *Economica*, **46**(1), 1–10.

Milgate, M. (1982), *Capital and Employment*, London and New York: Academic Press.

Mill, J.S. (1904), *Principles of Political Economy*, reprinted from the 6th edn., London: Longmans, Green and Co.

Minsky, H.P. (1975), *John Maynard Keynes*, London: Macmillan.

Mongiovi, G. (2000), 'Shackle on equilibrium: a critique', *Review of Social Economy*, **63**(1), 108–24.

Mongiovi, G. and F. Petri (eds) (1999), *Value, Distribution and Capital: Essays in honour of Pierangelo Garegnani*, London and New York: Routledge.

Morishima, M. (1964), *Equilibrium, Stability and Growth*, Oxford: Clarendon Press.

Morishima, M. (1969), *Theory of Economic Growth*, Oxford: Clarendon Press.

Morishima, M. (1977), *Walras's Economics*, Cambridge: Cambridge University Press.

Mueller, D.C. (1986), *Profits in the Long Run*, Cambridge: Cambridge University Press.

Nagatani, K. (1978), *Monetary Theory*, Amsterdam: North-Holland.

Nagatani, K. (1981), *Macroeconomic Dynamics*, Cambridge: Cambridge University Press.

Nagatani, K. (1989), *Political Macroeconomics*, Oxford: Clarendon Press.

Nickell, S.J. (1978), *The Investment Decisions of Firms*, Cambridge: Cambridge University Press.

Niehans, J. (1978), *The Theory of Money*, Baltimore and London: The Johns Hopkins University Press.

Nikaido, H. (1983), 'Marx on competition', *Zeitschrift fur Nationalokonomie*, **43**(4), 337–62.

Nikaido, H. (1985), 'Dynamics of growth and capital mobility in Marx's scheme of reproduction', *Zeitschrift fur Nationalokonomie*, **45**(3), 197–218.

Nuti, D.M. (1976), 'On the rates of return on investment', in Brown et al. (1976), pp. 47–69.

Nuti, D.M. (1977), 'Price and composition effects and the pseudo-production function', *Revue d'Economie Politique*, **87**(2), 232–43.

Ochoa, E. (1989), 'Values, prices, and wage–profit curves in the US economy', *Cambridge Journal of Economics*, **13**, 413–29.

Okun, A.M. (1981), *Prices and Quantities: a Macroeconomic Analysis*, Washington, DC: The Brookings Institution.

Orosel, G.O. (1987), entry 'period of production', in Eatwell et al. (1987) (also reprinted in Eatwell et al., 1990).

Panico, C. (1981), 'L'analisi dell'investimento nei lavori di Marshall e Keynes', in A. Graziani, C. Imbriani and B. Jossa (eds), *Studi di economia keynesiana*, Napoli: Liguori, pp. 301–330.

Panico, C. (1988), *Interest and Profit in the Theories of Value and Distribution*, London: Macmillan.

Panico, C. and Petri, F. (1987), entry 'long-run and short-run', in Eatwell et al. (1987).

Pareto, V. (1909), *Manuel d'Economie Politique*, 2nd edn. (reprinted, 1963 by R. Picon et R. Durand Auzias, Paris).

Parrinello, S. (1980), 'The price level implicit in Keynes' effective demand', *Journal of Post Keynesian Economics*, **3**(1), 63–78.

Pasinetti, L.L. (1962), 'Rate of profit and income distribution in relation to the rate of economic growth', *Review of Economic Studies*, **29**, 267–79.

Pasinetti, L.L. (1974), *Growth and Income Distribution*, Cambridge: Cambridge University Press.

Patinkin, D. (1948), 'Relative prices, Say's law and the demand for money', *Econometrica*, **14**, 135–54.

Patinkin, D. (1949), 'The indeterminacy of absolute prices in classical economic theory', *Econometrica*, **17**, 1–27.

Patinkin, D. (1950–51), 'A reconsideration of the general equilibrium theory of money', *Review of Economic Studies*, **18**, 42–61.

Patinkin, D. (1951), 'The invalidity of classical monetary theory', *Econometrica*, **19**, 42–61.

Patinkin, D. (1954), 'Dichotomies of the pricing process in economic theory', *Economica*, **21**, 113–28.

Patinkin, D. (1965), *Money, Interest and Prices*, 2nd edn., New York: Harper and Row.

Patinkin, D. (1972), 'Samuelson on the neoclassical dichotomy: a comment', *Canadian Journal of Economics*, **5**(2), 279–83.

Patinkin, D. (1987), entry 'real balances', in Eatwell et al. (1987).

Petri, F. (1978), 'The difference between long-period and short-period general equilibrium and the capital theory controversy', *Australian Economic Papers*, **17**, December, 246–60.

Petri, F. (1982), *The Patinkin Controversy Revisited*, Quaderni dell'Istituto di Economia, no. 15, University of Siena.

Petri, F. (1983), *The Connection between Say's Law and the Theory of the Rate of Interest in Ricardo*, Quaderni dell'Istituto di Economia, University of Siena, no. 17.

Petri, F. (1988), *The Long Period and the Short in Economic Theory: an Essay in Clarification*, Siena: University of Siena.

Petri, F. (1989), *Teorie del valore e della distribuzione*, Florence: La Nuova Italia Scientifica.

Petri, F. (1991), 'Hicks's recantation of the temporary equilibrium method', *Review of Political Economy*, 3(3), 268–88.

Petri, F. (1993a), 'Critical notes on Kalecki's theory of investment', in G. Mongiovi and C. Rühl (eds.), *Macroeconomic Theory: Diversity and Convergence*, Aldershot, UK and Brookfield, US: Edward Elgar, pp. 189–207.

Petri, F. (1993b), *The Impermanence Problem in General Equilibrium Analyses*, Quaderni del Dipartimento di Economia, no. 156, University of Siena.

Petri, F. (1994), 'The golden age of capitalism, investment, efficiency wages: a review article', *Economic Notes* (by Monte dei Paschi di Siena), 23(1), 142–59.

Petri, F. (1997), *On the Theory of Aggregate Investment as a Function of the Rate of Interest*, Quaderni del Dipartimento di Economia Politica, no. 215, University of Siena.

Petri, F. (1998a), 'The "Sraffian" critique of neoclassical economics: some recent developments', *Revista da Sociedade Brasileira de Economia Política*, no. 3, December, 5–44.

Petri, F. (1998b), entry 'labour theory of value', in H.D. Kurz and N. Salvadori (eds), *The Elgar Companion to Classical Economics*, Cheltenham, UK, and Lyme, USA: Edward Elgar, vol. II, pp. 12–22.

Petri, F. (1999), 'Professor Hahn on the Neo-Ricardian criticism of neoclassical economics', in Mongiovi and Petri (1999), pp. 19–68.

Petri, F. (2000), *On the Likelihood and Relevance of Reverse Capital Deepening*, Quaderni del Dipartimento di Economia Politica, no. 279, University of Siena (http://www.econ-pol.unisi.it/quad2000.html).

Petri, F. (2002), review of Kurz (2000), *European Journal of the History of Economic Thought*, 9(1), 130–41.

Petri, F. (2003a), 'Introduction', in Petri and Hahn (2003), pp. 1–26.

Petri, F. (2003b), 'A "Sraffian" critique of general equilibrium theory, and the classical-Keynesian alternative', in Petri and Hahn (2003), pp. 387–421.

Petri, F. (2003c), 'Should the theory of endogenous growth be based on Say's Law and the full employment of resources?', in N. Salvadori (ed.), *The Theory of Economic Growth: a 'Classical' Perspective*, Cheltenham, UK and Northampton, MA, USA: Edward Elgar, pp. 139–60.

Petri, F. and F. Hahn (eds) (2003), *General Equilibrium: Problems and Prospects*, London: Routledge.

Petrović, P. (1991), 'Shape of a wage-profit curve, some methodology and empirical evidence', *Metroeconomica*, 42, 93–112.

Phelps Brown, E.H. (1972), 'The underdevelopment of economics', *Economic Journal*, 82(1), March, 1–10.

Pigou, A.C. (1917–18), 'The value of money', *Quarterly Journal of Economics*, 32(1), 38–65.

Pigou, A.C. (1943), 'The classical stationary state', *Economic Journal*, 53, December, 343–51.

Pivetti, M. (1985), 'On the monetary explanation of distribution', *Political Economy–Studies in the Surplus Approach*, **1**(2), 73–103.

Pivetti, M. (1991), *An Essay on Money and Distribution*, London: Macmillan.

Precious, M. (1987), *Rational Expectations, Non-market Clearing, and Investment Theory*, Oxford: Clarendon Press.

Radner, R. (1972), 'Existence of equilibrium of plans, prices and price expectations in a sequence of markets', *Econometrica*, **40**, 289–303.

Ricardo, D. (1951–73), *The Works and Correspondence of David Ricardo*, ed. by Piero Sraffa, Cambridge, UK: Cambridge University Press; 1st edn. 1951 for both vol.1, *On the Principles of Political Economy and Taxation*, and vol. 2, *Notes on Malthus's Principles of Political Economy*.

Robbins, L. (1930), 'On a certain ambiguity in the conception of stationary equilibrium', *Economic Journal*, **40**(2), June, 194–214.

Robertson, D.H. (1931), 'Wage-Grumbles', in *Economic Fragments*, London: P.S. King & Son Ltd., pp. 42–57, as reprinted in American Economic Association, *Readings in the Theory of Income Distribution*, London: George Allen & Unwin, 1950, pp. 221–236.

Robertson, D.H. (1936), 'Some notes on Mr. Keynes' General Theory of Employment', *Quarterly Journal of Economic*, **51**(1), November, 168–91.

Robertson, D.H. (1957–59), *Lectures on Economic Principles* (vol. 1: 1957; vol. 2: 1958; vol. 3: 1959), London: Staples Press.

Robinson, J. (1953–54), 'The production function and the theory of capital', *Review of Economic Studies*, **21**(1), 81–106.

Robinson, J. (1969), 'The theory of value reconsidered', *Australian Economic Papers*, **8**, June, 13–19.

Robinson, J. (1970), 'Capital theory up to date', *Canadian Journal of Economics*, new series, **3**, May, 309–17.

Robinson, J. (1971), 'The existence of aggregate production functions: comment', *Econometrica*, **39**(2), 405.

Robinson, J. (1974), 'History versus equilibrium', *Indian Economic Journal*, **21**, March, 202–13.

Robinson, J. (1975), 'The unimportance of reswitching', *The Quarterly Journal of Economics*, **89**(1), 32–9.

Romer, D. (1996), *Advanced Macroeconomics*, New York: McGraw-Hill.

Romer, D. (2000), 'Keynesian macroeconomics without the LM curve', *Journal of Economic Perspectives*, **14**(2), 149–69.

Salvadori, N. (1987), entry 'non-substitution theorem', in Eatwell et al. (1987).

Salvadori, N. (2000), 'Comment' (to Mainwaring and Steedman, 2000), in Kurz (2000), pp. 354–7.

Salvadori, N. and I. Steedman (1988), 'No reswitching? No switching!', *Cambridge Journal of Economics*, **12**, 483–6.

Samuelson, P.A. (1951), 'Abstract of a theorem concerning substitutability in open Leontief models', in Koopmans (1951b), pp. 142–6.

Samuelson, P.A. (1962), 'Parable and realism in capital theory: the Surrogate Production Function', *Review of Economic Studies*, **29**(3), June, 193–206.

Samuelson, P.A. (1966), 'A summing-up', *Quarterly Journal of Economics*, **80**, 568–83; as reprinted in G.C. Harcourt and N.F. Laing (eds), *Capital and Growth*, Harmondsworth: Penguin, 1971, pp. 233–50.

Samuelson, P.A. (1968), 'What classical and neo-classical monetary theory really was', *Canadian Journal of Economics*, **1**(1), 1–15 (reprinted in Clower, 1969, pp. 170–90).

Samuelson, P.A. (1976), 'Interest rate determination and oversimplifying parables: a summing up', in Brown et. al. (1976), pp. 3–24.

Samuelson, P.A. and W.D. Nordhaus (1985), *Economics*, 12th edn., New York: McGraw-Hill.

Sargent, T.J. (1979), *Macroeconomic Theory*, New York: Academic Press.

Saulnier, R.J. (1938), *Contemporary Monetary Theory*; as reprinted in AMS Reprint of Columbia University Studies in the Social Sciences, no. 443, New York, 1970.

Sawyer, M. (1997), *The NAIRU: a Critical Appraisal*, The Jerome Levy Economics Institute Working Paper No. 201.

Schefold, B. (1985), 'Cambridge price theory: special model or general theory of value?', *American Economic Review*, **75**(2), 140–45.

Schefold, B. (1989), *Mr. Sraffa on Joint Production and Other Essays*, London: Unwin Hyman.

Schefold, B. (1997), *Normal Prices, Technical Change and Accumulation*, New York: Macmillan.

Schefold, B. (2000), 'Paradoxes of capital and counterintuitive changes of distribution in an intertemporal equilibrium model', in Kurz (2000), pp. 363–91.

Schefold, B. (2003), 'Applications of the classical approach', in Petri and Hahn (2003), pp. 439–67.

Seguino, S. (1999–2000), 'The investment function revisited: disciplining capital in South Korea', *Journal of Post Keynesian Economics*, **22**(2), 313–38.

Shaikh, A. (1974), 'Laws of production and laws of algebra: the humbug production function', *Review of Economics and Statistics*, **56**(1), 115–20.

Shaikh, A. (1980), 'Laws of production and laws of algebra: Humbug II', in E. Nell (ed.), *Growth, Profits and Property*, Cambridge: Cambridge University Press, pp. 80–95.

Shaikh, A. (1984), 'The transformation from Marx to Sraffa', in E. Mandel and A. Freeman (eds), *Ricardo, Marx, Sraffa*, London: Verso, pp. 43–84.

Shaikh, A. (2002), 'Nonlinear dynamics and pseudo-production functions', Unpublished Working Paper, available at http://homepage.newschool.edu/ ~AShaikh /papers.html

Shove, G.F. (1933 [1963]), 'Review of "The Theory of Wages"', *Economic Journal*, **43** (reprinted in Hicks, 1932[1963], pp. 249–67).

Shubik, M. (1993), 'Accounting and its relationship to general equilibrium theory', *Economic Notes by Monte dei Paschi di Siena*, **22**(2), 226–34.

Smith, A. (1776 [1975]), *The Wealth of Nations*, 2 vols., London: Dent Dutton, Everyman's Library.

Söderstrom, H. (1976), 'Production and investment under costs of adjustment: a survey', *Zeitschrift für Nationalökonomie*, **36**, September, 369–88.

Solow, R.M. (1955–56), 'The production function and the theory of capital', *Review of Economic Studies*, **23**, 101–108.

Solow, R.M. (1956), 'A contribution to the theory of economic growth', *Quarterly Journal of Economics*, **70**(1), February, 101–108.

Solow, R.M. (1957 [1970]), 'Technical change and the aggregate production function', *Review of Economics and Statistics*, **39**, 312–20; as reprinted in A. Sen (ed.), *Growth Economics*, Penguin, 1970, pp. 401–19.

Solow, R.M. (1962), 'Substitution and fixed proportions in the theory of capital', *Review of Economic Studies*, **29**, 207–18.

Solow, R.M. (1974), 'Laws of production and laws of algebra: the humbug production function: a comment', *Review of Economics and Statistics*, **56**(1), 121.

Solow, R.M. (1980), 'On the theories of unemployment', *American Economic Review*, **70**(1), 1–11.

Solow, R.M. (1987), 'Second thoughts on growth theory', in A. Steinherr and D. Weiserbs (eds), *Employment and Ggrowth: Issues for the 1980s*, Dordrecht: Martinus Nijhoff, pp. 13–28.

Solow, R.M. (1990), *The Labor Market as a Social Institution*, Oxford: Basil Blackwell.

Sraffa, P. (1925), 'Sulle relazioni tra prezzo e quantità prodotta', *Annali di Economia*, **2**(1), 277–328.

Sraffa, P. (1926), 'The laws of returns under competitive conditions', *Economic Journal*, **36**, December, 535–50.

Sraffa, P. (1930), 'A critique' and 'A rejoinder' in 'Increasing returns and the representative firm: a symposium', *Economic Journal*, **40**(1), 89–92, 93.

Sraffa, P. (1932), 'Dr. Hayek on money and capital', *Economic Journal*, **42**(1), 42–53.

Sraffa, P. (1951), 'Introduction', in *The Collected Works of David Ricardo*, vol. 1, Cambridge: Cambridge University Press, pp. 13–62.

Sraffa, P. (1960), *Production of Commodities by Means of Commodities*, Cambridge: Cambridge University Press.

Steedman, I. (1972), 'Jevons's theory of capital and interest', *The Manchester School*, **40**, 31–52.

Steindl, J. (1952), *Maturity and Stagnation in American Capitalism*, Oxford: Basil Blackwell.

Stiglitz, J.E. (1974), 'The Cambridge–Cambridge controversy in the theory of capital: a view from New Haven: a review article', *Journal of Political Economy*, **82**(4), 893–903.

Stigum, B. (1969), 'Competitive equilibria under uncertainty', *Quarterly Journal of Economics*, **83**, 533–61.

Summers, L.H. (1986), 'Some skeptical observations on real business cycle theory', *Federal Reserve Bank of Minneapolis Quarterly Review*, Autumn, 23–27.

Sundrum, R.M. (1990), *Economic Growth in Theory and Practice*, Houndmills: Macmillan.

Takayama, A. (1974), *Mathematical Economics*, Hinsdale, Ill.: The Dryden Press.

Thirlwall, A.P. (2002), *The Nature of Economic Growth: an Alternative Framework for Understanding the Performance of Nations*, Cheltenham, UK and Northampton, MA, USA: Edward Elgar.

Tobin, J. (1967), 'Comment on Crockett-Friend and Jorgenson', in Ferber (1967), pp. 156–60.

Tobin, J. (1969), 'A general equilibrium approach to monetary theory', *Journal of Money, Credit and Banking*, **1**(1), February, 15–29.

Tobin, J. (1980), *Asset Accumulation and Economic Activity*, Oxford: Basil Blackwell.

Tobin, J. (1982), 'Money and finance in the macroeconomic process', Nobel Lecture, *Journal of Money, Credit and Banking*, **14**(2), May, 171–204.

Tobin, J. (1987), entry 'Irving Fisher', in Eatwell et al. (1987).

Tobin, J. and W. Brainard (1977), 'Asset markets and the cost of capital', in B. Balassa and R. Nelson (eds), *Economic Progress, Private Values and Public Policy: Essays in Honour of William Fellner*, Amsterdam: North-Holland, pp. 235–62.

Trezzini, A. (1995), 'Capacity utilisation in the long run and the autonomous components of aggregate demand', *Contributions to Political Economy*, **14**, 33–66.

Trezzini, A. (1998), 'Capacity utilisation in the long run: some further considerations', *Contributions to Political Economy*, **17**, 53–67.

Valavanis, S. (1955), 'A denial of Patinkin's contradiction', *Kyklos*, **7**, 351–66.

Varian, H. (1992), *Microeconomic Analysis*, 3rd edn., New York and London: W.W. Norton & Company.

Vianello, F. (1985), 'The pace of accumulation', *Political Economy – Studies in the Surplus Approach*, **1**(1), 69–87.

Vickers, D. (1992), 'The investment function: five propositions in response to Professor Gordon', *Journal of Post Keynesian Economics*, **14**(4), 445–64.

Walker, D.A. (1987), *Classical and Neoclassical Economic Thought*, Aldershot, UK and Brookfield, US: Edward Elgar.

Walker, D.A. (1996), *Walras's Market Models*, Cambridge: Cambridge University Press.

Walker, Donald A. (1997, *Advances in General Equilibrium Theory*, Cheltenham, UK and Lyme, USA: Edward Elgar.

Walras, L. (1954), *Elements of Political Economy*, Jaffé translation, Homewood, Ill.: Richard D. Irwin (reprinted 1977 by Augustus M. Kelley, New York).

Walras, L. (1988), *Eléments d'économie politique pure: ou théorie de la richesse sociale*, ed. Pierre Dockès et al., Paris: Economica.

Ward, B. (1972), *What's Wrong with Economics?*, New York: Basic Books

Weintraub, E.R. (1983), 'On the existence of a competitive equilibrium: 1930–1954', *Journal of Economic Literature*, **21**(1), March, 1–39.

Wicksell, K. (1893 [1954]), *Über Wert, Kapital und Rente*, Jena: G. Fischer. Translated by S. H. Frowen as *Value, Capital and Rent*, London: Allen & Unwin, 1954.

Wicksell, K. (1923 [1934]), 'Real capital and interest', English translation of an article first appeared in the *Ekonomisk Tidskrift* (1923), nos. 5–6, 145–89, in Wicksell (1934), pp. 258–99.

Wicksell, K. (1934), *Lectures on Political Economy*, vol. I, London: Allen & Unwin (1st edn. originally published in Swedish in 1901; the translation is from the 3rd edn., 1928).

Wicksell, K. (1935), *Lectures on Political Economy*, vol. II, London, Allen & Unwin (1st edn. originally published in Swedish in 1906; the translation is from the 3rd edn., 1929).

Wicksell, K. (1936), *Interest and Prices*, London: Macmillan (originally *Geldzins und Güterpreise bestimmenden Ursachen*, Jena: G. Fischer, 1898).

Wilkinson, F. (1988), 'Where do we go from here? 2. Real wages, effective demand and economic development', *Cambridge Journal of Economics*, **12**(1), 179–91.

Wilson, T. and P.W.S. Andrews (eds) (1955), *Oxford Studies in the Price Mechanism*, Oxford: Clarendon Press.

Witte, J.G., jr. (1963), 'The microfoundations of the social investment function', *Journal of Political Economy*, **71**(5), October, 441–56.

Worswick, G.D.N. (1972), 'Is progress in economics possible?', *Economic Journal*, **82**, no. 325, 73–86.

Yano, M. (1984a), 'Competitive equilibria on turnpikes in a McKenzie economy, I: a neighborhood turnpike theorem', *International Economic Review*, **25**(3), October, 695–717.

Yano, M. (1984b), 'The turnpike of dynamic general equilibrium paths and its insensitivity to initial conditions', *Journal of Mathematical Economics*, **13**, 235–54.

Zaghini, E. (1986), 'Market prices and natural prices: a reinterpretation of Walras's model of capital accumulation', *Economic Notes by Monte dei Paschi di Siena*, **15**(1), 10–59.

Zaghini, E. (1990), 'Quale equilibrio?', *Economia Politica*, **7**(1), April, 3–12.

Zaghini, E. (1993), 'Equilibrio istantaneo ed equilibrio dinamico nella teoria walrasiana', in E. Zaghini (ed.), *Economia matematica: equilibri e dinamica*, Turin: UTET, pp. 285–342.

Zambelli, S. (2004), 'The 40% neoclassical aggregate theory of production', *Cambridge Journal of Economics*, **28**(1), 99–120.

Zenezini, M. (1992), 'Esistono veramente le funzioni neoclassiche di domanda di lavoro?', *Politica Economica*, **8**, Aprile, 19–59.

Index

Abel, A. B. 277
abstinence 104–6
accelerator 256, 258, 279, 283, 293, 302, 315
accumulation 27, 36, 42, 46, 62, 66, 80, 91, 120–1, 124, 34, 146, 159–60, 183–7, 203, 229–31, 237, 313–4, 317, 322
Ackley, G. 263–6, 268–9, 273–4, 276, 281, 284, 287
adding-up theorem 12, 76
adjustment costs *see* investment
adjustment, instantaneous, not needed if data are persistent 49, 52, 174, 230, 307, 325
adjustment, of expectations to realized events 44
adjustment principle, of productive capacity to desired capacity 38
adjustment procedures in real time 2, 48, 50, 195–6 *also see* Fisher, F.M.; non-tâtonnement
alter the data of neo-Walrasian equilibria 3, 39–43, 306
adjustment processes, time-consuming and involving mistakes 22–3, 36, 49, 62, 65, 70, 163, 232
adjustments, non-tâtonnement 35
adjustments, tâtonnement-like 5, 20, 50, 194
adjustments to equilibrium take time 21, 162, 188, 201, 237, 306
advances 11, 41, 114
aggregate demand curve and aggregate supply curve in Keynes 56–9
aggregate demand price 58–9
aggregate production function or APF 5–6, 228, 233, 270, 283, 305, 324, 326, 332, 339
and Joan Robinson 230–1

mistakenly identified with conception of capital as a single factor 32, 72
ex-post Cobb–Douglas 330–1
aggregation problem *see* capital
Ahmad, S. 100, 232
Alchian, A. 150, 267, 284
alternatives to the neoclassical approach 5, 305, 309–23
Andrews, P. W. S. 300
animal spirits 231, 241, 313, 329
APF (aggregate production function) 324–39
appliances 64
Archibald, G. C. 166, 173, 181–6
array-of-opportunities *see* investment
Arrow, K. J. 37, 45–6, 49–50, 54, 70, 93, 123–4, 161–4, 187–93, 197–201, 232, 246, 250, 285, 306
Asimakopulos, Athanasios or Tom 57, 273
atemporal 45, 161–2, 245
auctioneer 1, 6, 11, 13–4, 35, 40–3, 49, 67, 160, 163, 167, 175, 184, 187, 196, 204–5
must be a central planner when there are constant returns to scale 163, 190–201
not needed if data of equilibrium have sufficient persistence 11, 326
Austrian 28–9, 99, 113, 115, 122, 157–60
representation of technology 83, 116
structure of production 110, 117, 208
also see dated labour
average period of investment 153
average period of production or degree of roundaboutness 28–9, 92,

NEW DIRECTIONS IN MODERN ECONOMICS

The Economics of the Profit Rate
Competition, Crises and Historical Tendencies in Capitalism
Gérard Duménil and Dominique Lévy

Corporatism and Economic Performance
A Comparative Analysis of Market Economies
Andrew Henley and Euclid Tsakalotos

Competition, Technology and Money
Classical and Post-Keynesian Perspectives
Edited by Mark A. Glick

Investment Cycles in Capitalist Economies
A Kaleckian Behavioural Contribution
Jerry Courvisanos

Does Financial Deregulation Work?
A Critique of Free Market Approaches
Bruce Coggins

Pricing Theory in Post Keynesian Economics
A Realist Approach
Paul Downward

The Economics of Intangible Investment
Elizabeth Webster

Globalization and the Erosion of National Financial Systems
Is Declining Autonomy Inevitable?
Marc Schaberg

Explaining Prices in the Global Economy
A Post-Keynesian Model
Henk-Jan Brinkman

Capitalism, Socialism, and Radical Political Economy
Essays in Honor of Howard J. Sherman
Edited by Robert Pollin

Financial Liberalisation and Intervention
A New Analysis of Credit Rationing
Santonu Basu

Why the Bubble Burst
US Stock Market Performance since 1982
Lawrance Lee Evans, Jr.

Sustainable Fiscal Policy and Economic Stability
Theory and Practice
Philippe Burger